HARRIS COUNTY PUBLIC LIBRARY

3 4028 04480 7676

DISCARD

D1349115

First Ladies of Texas

First Ladies of Texas

A HISTORY

Mary D. Farrell

and

Elizabeth Silverthorne

Stillhouse Hollow Publishers, Inc.
Belton, Texas

SKETCHES OF FIRST LADIES BY MARTY STEPHENS

PHOTO CREDITS:
Mrs. James V. Allred, by Jimmie Collier's Studio, Wichita Falls, Texas
Mrs. W. Lee O'Daniel and Mrs. Mabel Buchanan Jester Morriss, courtesy Austin-Travis County Collection, Austin Public Library, Austin, Texas
Mrs. Coke Stevenson, Sr., Mrs. Coke Stevenson, Jr., and Mrs. Allan Shivers, by Christianson Leberman, Austin, Texas
Mrs. Price Daniel, by Gittings, Dallas-Fort Worth-Houston, Texas
Mrs. John Connally, by Bill Malone, Austin, Texas
Mrs. Preston Smith, by Avalon Studio, Lubbock, Texas
Mrs. Dolph Briscoe portrait painted by Peter Stevens and reproduced photographically
(All First Lady photos taken in the Executive Mansion at time of residence or date from that time.)

All rights reserved
including the right of reproduction
in whole or in part in any form
Copyright © 1976 by Mary D. Farrell
and Elizabeth Silverthorne
Published by Stillhouse Hollow Publishers, Inc.
106 W. Central Avenue
Belton, Texas 76513

First Printing 1976
Second Printing 1978

Library of Congress Catalog Card Number: 76-14700

Manufactured in the United States of America
Printed by Stillhouse Hollow Publishers, Inc., Belton, Texas
Bound by Universal Bookbindery, Inc., San Antonio, Texas

FOR H. C. FARRELL, JR.

and

FOR IVY

THE FIRST LADY OF TEXAS
1976
Betty Jane Slaughter Briscoe

Portrait painted by Peter Stevens
Commissioned by Fine Arts Society
of Texas and presented to
the State of Texas October, 1975

Foreword

Each woman in this book has contributed in a silent, supportive role to the dramatic pattern of the history of Texas. Each, curiously has been a reflection of the emotional mood, the cultural, intellectual and moral climate of her historic moment.

As a group, these ladies have little in common. Yet they join in a sisterhood of devoted service to Texas and to the Governor's Mansion which was their realm. Each has been a proud Texan, each has possessed a sincere love for this state, and each has given the very best of herself to loving public service as first chatelaine of Texas.

JANEY (MRS. DOLPH) BRISCOE

Austin, Texas
June, 1976

Contents

ix

x

Preface

The authors of this book have tried to show something of the growth of Texas by describing the lives of the women whom we call the First Ladies. An effort has been made to recapture the personality and life story of each of the thirty-one women who filled that role from the beginning of the Republic in 1836 through the centennial year of 1936. A final chapter sketches briefly the lives and contributions of the eight women who have been mistresses of the Governor's Mansion since that time. Included are references to the happy occasions and the sad ones, the successes and the failures, the small incidents as well as the momentous ones that made up the fabric of these women's lives.

There is no stereotype for the First Ladies of the Republic and State, for while there are some similarities, there are more differences in family backgrounds, formal education, personality, appearance, and physical strength of these women. In addition to being chief aid and assistant to her husband, each woman left her own unique contribution in art, music, education, religious leadership, or civic activities.

Of the thirty-one who actually served as First Ladies during the one hundred years between 1836 and 1936, five were from the North, one from the Midwest, and twenty-five from the South. Thus, many of the customs and cultural patterns of other regions of the United States were introduced to the developing area of Texas.

All of the women were well-educated for their time. Twenty-one of the thirty-one had more formal education than their husbands at the time of their marriages. Although many of them met or exceeded the fondest modern dreams of individual expression, accomplishment, and identity, each expressed her personality and made her contributions within the framework of the accepted role of women in her time.

In almost every case the women seem to have had remarkably close and affectionate relationships with their husbands. With only one exception, every husband greatly respected and appreciated his First Lady. Even that exception, Pendleton

Murrah, in time of crisis expressed his concern for his wife in his own way.

There is evidence of a strong religious faith on the part of each woman. Though expressed in different ways, this quality undoubtedly gave to each life strength, optimism, and appreciation for her fellowman. Without this kind of woman beside the men leading the struggling Republic and growing State, there could not have been the spiritual climate that developed.

Although most of the women enjoyed good health, three of them were partial invalids, and even they fulfilled their responsibilities as well as their health permitted. The sheer physical demands made upon a woman living a public life can only be appreciated by those who have experienced it.

The women who have enjoyed the title and privileges of First Lady of Texas have, without exception, made great sacrifices. The largest single one has been in the time and attention of their husbands. Many lonely nights, weeks, and months were spent keeping farm, office, and home in order by wives whose husbands were attending to affairs of state. Therefore, it seems fitting that we appreciate their part in the growth and development of the state.

In addition to the Governors mentioned in the text, Texas had a bachelor Governor who made important contributions to the Republic and the State. Peter Hansborough Bell, who served as Governor from 1849 to 1853, was a veteran of the Battle of San Jacinto and of the War with Mexico. Just before his second term expired, Bell resigned to fill a vacancy in Congress, and while living in Washington, D.C., met and married Ella Reeves Eaton Dickens in a wedding attended by President Franklin Pierce and members of his Cabinet. Bell County was named after Governor Bell.

When Bell resigned as Governor, Lieutenant Governor J. W. Henderson took over the duties of the office for the remaining few weeks of the term. Another Lieutenant Governor who served as Governor briefly was A. C. Horton, who assumed J. Pinckney Henderson's position while Governor Henderson was fighting in the War with Mexico.

Fletcher S. Stockdale also performed some acts as Governor when Governor Pendleton Murrah left for Mexico after the fall of the Confederacy.

Many words have been written about the men who were the Presidents and Governors of Texas during its first one hundred years of existence as an independent nation and state. And much has been said about the influences of heredity, environment, temperament, and world events on these leaders. However, with the exception of Sam Houston's wife, most biographers have almost completely overlooked the most significant influence of all — the women who shared the lives of the men who shaped the growing territory. This book is an attempt to help remedy that oversight.

MARY D. FARRELL
ELIZABETH SILVERTHORNE

Temple, Texas
June, 1976

1.

The Peripatetic Wife

Hannah Este Burnet

The newlyweds stood on the deck of the vessel *Call,* straining to see through the heavy fog that hid their destination. Beneath her outward calm, Hannah Burnet felt her pulse quicken as she caught the first glimpse of her new home — the Mexican state of Coahuila and Texas. The time was early summer of 1831.

The long trip from New York had been smooth and uneventful; and if Hannah thought with sadness of the family she had left in Morristown, New Jersey, she was comforted by the presence of her strong husband, whose enthusiasm for Texas was contagious. It was also reassuring to know that the hold of the ship contained not only materials for a sawmill her husband planned to build, but also the fine furniture and other household furnishings they had bought on their honeymoon in New York. At least she would be able to set up housekeeping in a civilized manner — no matter how rough the country.

Suddenly the couple were forced to take shelter as huge raindrops pelted them, and strong gusts of wind made it dangerous to stand on the open deck. Without warning, a storm had sprung up as they were entering Galveston Bay.

Before the sailors could get the ship under control, it was grounded on Bolivar Point. All efforts to float the vessel failed, and it became clear that some of the cargo would have to be jettisoned in order for the ship to clear the sand bar.

Sadly, Hannah watched the steam boiler and bricks for the sawmill as well as most of the Burnets' carefully selected household furnishings thrown over the side of the ship into the rough waters of the Gulf of Mexico. Then she made her first landing in Texas by wading through the wild surf onto a sandy beach.

There the Burnets shared their first home in a makeshift camp set up by the crew of the *Call*. About all the newlyweds had to be thankful for was that their lives had been spared. Fortunately, they could not know that five years later, they would again be camped in crude quarters on Galveston Island — fearfully awaiting the outcome of the Battle of San Jacinto.

Not surprisingly, Hannah became ill following this experience, and Burnet was forced to leave her with a friend while he searched for a promising site and purchased land to set up the sawmill along the heavily wooded San Jacinto River. During this period Hannah had time to marvel at the changes that a few months had brought in her life.

Six months earlier, when she married David Gouverneur Burnet, Hannah Este was thirty, somewhat older than the usual bride of the nineteenth century; but the bridegroom was forty-two himself. Both were from New Jersey, and it was in Morristown at the home of her brother-in-law that they were married on December 8, 1830, by the minister of the Presbyterian church.

As a young man, David Burnet had spent two years in Texas among the Comanche Indians, recovering from a lung ailment — the rather unusual treatment prescribed for him by his doctor being to "live with the Indians like an Indian." Vigorous exercise, fresh air, and a diet of buffalo meat and other wild game did seem to cure him. But during his stay with the Indians, he contracted "Texas fever," the chief symptom of which was the burning desire to live in Texas and to influence others to do so, too. He became a close friend of a fellow lawyer and frontier colonizer, Stephen F. Austin, and made an unsuccessful attempt as a colonizer himself.

His failure did not change his mind about settling in the Texas territory, and he returned to New Jersey to ask Hannah to marry him and come with him to set up a home in the frontier country. He chose well, for Hannah Este was a sturdy descendant of pioneer stock, well-educated by the standards of that time.

Her father, Moses Este (sometimes spelled Estey), was a maker of fine furniture and owned a chair factory in Morristown. He was a strong supporter of the Presbyterian church and one of the original trustees of the Morris Academy in Morristown. With her parents and six brothers and sisters Hannah lived in a large, comfortable house. Her closest companion and the friend with whom she shared all of her feelings was her younger sister, Mary, who later married Joseph Clopper and moved to Cincinnati, Ohio.

The Burnets' second home in Texas was a considerable improvement over the first. It was located on a rise overlooking a splendid view near the body of water now called Burnet's Bay. They called it Oakland, and when Hannah's sister, Mary, visited there, she wrote to a relative back in Ohio:

> Hannah has a very convenient house — 4 nice rooms, the dining room & kitchen separate from the main building; the blacks have 2 nicely furnished small houses near & it makes quite a settlement . . . . Hannah has very excellent servants . . . .

Although the sawmill did not do as well as the Burnets had hoped, it continued in operation for several years; and in spite of being a losing proposition financially, it did furnish a center around which the town of Lynchburg grew up. To provide food for themselves and to add to their income, the Burnets operated Oakland as a farm. In addition, Burnet practiced law.

He kept an uneasy watch on the increasing discontent of the Texans with their Mexican rulers, corresponding with friends like William Barret Travis about current events. His honesty and fair-mindedness impressed his fellow Texans so much that in April, 1833, Burnet was elected as a delegate to the San Felipe Convention, which among other things, requested from the Mexican government authority to establish a government for Texas, separate from that of Coahuila and Texas.

After his active participation in this convention, Burnet was elected a judge with a large jurisdiction in the area near Oakland. Hannah was proud that her husband was so well-respected, and she readily assumed more of the responsibility of running the farm even though she now had two small sons, William and Jacob George, to look after.

A deep religious faith was one of the Burnets' strong ties, and Hannah supported her husband's inflexible honesty and iron-willed determination to do what he thought was right. He was, as their friend and neighbor Dr. Ashbel Smith said, "a man John Knox would have hugged with grim delight." Recognizing their need for such a leader, the convention that met at Washington-on-the-Brazos to declare Texas' independence in March, 1836, chose Burnet to be the *ad interim* President of the newly created Republic. He was inaugurated by candlelight at four in the morning on March 17, 1836.

The next few weeks were traumatic ones for the new government. Waiting for news at Oakland, Hannah suffered from the uncertainty of not knowing where her peripatetic husband and his cabinet were as they moved from farmhouse to farmhouse enroute to Harrisburg, with Santa Anna breathing down their necks. When the Mexican forces got uncomfortably close to Harrisburg, Burnet ordered the seat of government moved once again, to the eastern end of Galveston Island. Then he hurried back to Oakland to gather up his wife and two small sons — William, not quite three, and Jacob George, about four months.

Burnet and Hannah collected their most valuable household goods to put on a boat for Galveston and spent the night at New Washington while they waited for transportation. They escaped by only a hair's-breadth the next morning. Burnet and Hannah, having started their horses for Lynchburg in charge of two Negro servants, busied themselves at the dockside

warehouse getting their things ready to be put aboard a
steamer. Suddenly the Negroes came galloping back shouting,
"The Mexicans are coming!" A skiff was hastily manned by the
servants; Burnet and a friend, Dr. George Patrick, lifted the
two children down into the boat. Because of the height of the
warehouse flooring, Hannah could not jump into the boat. She
had to run the full length of the warehouse and onto the beach
to get into the boat.

They had scarcely shoved off when the Mexicans appeared
on the beach. Although unarmed and fully expecting to be
fired at, Burnet insisted on standing up and manning an oar.
Perhaps the Mexican General Juan Almonte did not suspect it
was the President of Texas who was within range of his
musket, or perhaps, as some historians think, it was the
presence of a lady that stirred his chivalry and made him
order his dragoons not to fire. At any rate, no sooner had the
refugees gotten safely out of range of the armed Mexicans
than they saw a boat bearing down on them. At first they
thought it was more of the enemy; Burnet and Hannah
thought capture was sure. The President said, "I will not be
taken alive."

His wife replied, "Neither will I. I will take a child in each
arm and jump overboard." Fortunately, the boat did not
contain a hostile force.

Living conditions on Galveston Island were primitive,
uncomfortable, and unsanitary. Tents and flimsy driftwood
huts served as shelter. The drinking water was brackish, and
food was scarce. Having lost nearly all of their belongings in
the escape at New Washington, the Burnets lived in a tattered
tent with two borrowed blankets for beds and bedding. Boxes
and barrels served as furniture. Hannah cooked over a
shell-lined hole in the sand. To add to her worries, the children
were sick much of the time.

Through everything, Hannah stayed calm and was a source
of strength and comfort to her harassed husband. Edward
Este, Hannah's brother, who was on the island with them,
wrote to a brother-in-law in Ohio describing their sufferings:

Mr. Burnet has lost nearly everything he had . . . . . . the Country is in such an uproar at this time all we look for at present is our health and enough to eat.

Edward went on to speak of the horrors of the Runaway Scrape, when thousands of Texans fled from their homes in advance of the Mexican troops, ". . . such distress as our families have suffered by moving I never before heard, seen or read of." He referred to the Battle of San Jacinto casually as the battle that took place on "Old Peggy McCormick's land." The good news of the victory took almost a week to reach the exiled government on Galveston Island, and Edward was undoubtedly right when he said, "The people could hardly believe it for some time. I assure you it was the most grateful news that was every told."

But Hannah's rejoicing was short-lived, as her husband's problems soon multiplied. Determined to treat the defeated Santa Anna in a humane and honorable way, Burnet brought upon himself not only threats of impeachment, but also threats of physical violence. The boisterous citizens of Texas demanded that the Napoleon of the West "be done unto" as he had done unto so many Texans and refused to try to understand Burnet's farsighted diplomacy and unwillingness to break the spirit or the letter of the agreement made with the dictator.

An unruly mob surrounded the capitol building in Velasco, where the floating seat of government was removed after the Battle of San Jacinto. They shouted hysterically, threatening to lynch Burnet because he would not release Santa Anna to them, but the President stood his ground, and Hannah stood beside him. While his life was in danger, she kept nightly watch with loaded pistols beside an open window so he could get a few hours sleep.

Living conditions in Velasco were hardly better than they had been on Galveston Island. Food was still scarce, and the President's home was more of a shack than a house. A visitor to the Chief Executive described Hannah's existence:

His amiable and accomplished lady, without servants or hired help, superintended and managed in person her domestic arrangements, and their household and table comforts were sufficiently sparse and limited to have called forth the admiration of the Spartan lawgiver.

Even if comforts had been available, the Burnets would not have been able to afford them. The President could draw no salary from the deflated treasury and was forced to sell a Negro woman and a boy to pay their bills. While Hannah was struggling to keep her family clothed and fed, members of the army were writing bitterly to Burnet accusing him of living in "abundance" while they suffered shortages!

Threats of renewed invasions by the Mexican army and of Indian intrigue against the weak new country hung over their heads. When the children became ill again because of the wretched conditions, Burnet began planning to send his family to stay with his relatives in the United States for their safety and their health. But Hannah refused to go, saying that no one "should leave Texas at such a juncture."

When the wandering capital again was moved, this time to Columbia, there were no accommodations for the family, and Hannah stayed alone in the ramshackle quarters in Velasco with the children. Soon a terrible personal tragedy was added to their other griefs; ten-month-old Jacob George died. His father recorded the baby's death in the family Bible:

Jacob George died at Velasco September 23/1836 aged 10 months and eight days of whooping cough and cholera infantum combined — a victim to the War of Revolution.

Hannah needed all of her pioneer strength and endurance to get through the fall and winter of 1836. After the election of Sam Houston as President and Mirabeau Lamar as Vice President of the new Republic, Burnet felt so harassed by his enemies and exhausted from his efforts to guide the rowdy country that he resigned before his term ended.

Lamar, a lifelong friend of Burnet and an enemy of President-elect Houston, wrote in his diary:

> Houston was so anxious to enter upon the duties of office that Burnet was forced by the threats of Members of Congress that if he did not retire for the new President, he would be pushed out. Burnet was forced to retire . . . . This was the first Act of the Government, a palpable violation of the Constitution.

Before they could move back into their Oakland home, Hannah and Burnet had to refurnish and repair it, as they discovered that during their absence it had been completely stripped and badly damaged. The mercantile company of Toby and Brother of New Orleans had served the emerging nation as a supplier of goods during the war, and Burnet continued to do business with them afterwards. He wrote to tell them that he had lost everything he owned in the war, saying, "I do not own a blanket in the world and am equally destitute of other dispensables." He placed an order for Hannah:

> It is with unfeigned regret that I trouble you with any little matters of my own, but really I am dependent upon your kindness, and must crave your indulgence. My family are much in want of household articles for we are entirely stripped by the wrecks of war. Please send me, one cast iron or soap stone furnace for cooking, of good size: the same thing in small size. The soap stone, well put up, is preferable to cast iron on account of rust.

When Oakland had been made livable, they moved back, planning to rely on farming and Burnet's law practice to make their living.

At the end of that fateful year they were saddened when their good friend Stephen F. Austin died on December 27. Burnet served as chairman of the committee formed to pay honor to the Texas statesman.

After Houston's term expired in 1838, Burnet was urged to run for President. He refused in favor of his friend Lamar, but he did run for Vice President and was elected. He also served as Secretary of State and Indian Commissioner for Lamar and acted temporarily as President during Lamar's illness. While her husband carried out his multiple duties in Houston (the current seat of government), Hannah stayed at Oakland to manage the farm as best she could. Her heart was heavy when a daughter, Gertrude Gouverneur, was born on January

16, 1838, and buried the same day at Oakland in a tiny grave.

When Lamar and his cabinet decided to expel the Cherokee Indians from East Texas in 1839, Burnet took an active part in the fighting and was slightly wounded. The engagement was bloody but successful for the white men, and the Cherokees were driven into Arkansas. Many Texans were pleased with the outcome, and in 1839, for a few months anyway, Hannah could take pride in the acclaim given her husband. The capital was moved again — this time to Austin, and the move was marked by celebrations that included a big dinner where eulogies were made to Burnet for his statesmanship and predictions were made that he would be the next President.

The unnatural period of sweetness and light soon passed, and the next year found the House of Representatives accusing Burnet of misusing money paid out to the unhappy Santa Fe Expedition. For a time both Lamar and Burnet were under threat of impeachment. They escaped arraignment by only twelve votes.

Hannah must have felt great relief with the passing of this threat, but the calm did not last long. The Presidential campaign of 1841 found Houston and Burnet opposing each other as candidates for the highest office. Both felt they had earned it. The result was a rough-and-tumble battle fought with tongue and quill by the two famous builders of the Republic. Accusations of misconduct in connection with the war for Texas' independence were met with counter accusations. Name-calling was met with name-calling — Houston called Burnet "Wetumpka" (hog thief); Burnet called Houston "Big Drunk." At one point, legend says that Burnet challenged Houston to a duel, but Burnet's friends denied it.

Burnet, so upright and resolute in his actions and convictions, could never tolerate criticism, and the Burnet household was turned into battle headquarters as words of slander flew like arrows between the two warriors. It must have been a disappointment after all the sound and the fury for Hannah to see her husband lose the race by a vote of 7,915 to 3,616.

The Burnets were still desperately poor, and the bitterness of the campaign and of the defeat hung like a dark cloud over Oakland. The chief happiness of the couple centered in their only remaining child, William. They realized that he could get a better education by going to Ohio and staying with their relatives than he could by remaining with them in Texas. Therefore, they borrowed the necessary money to send him on the long journey — and endured their loneliness. When William decided to make the army his career, Hannah and Burnet sold personal property to send him to Kentucky Military Institute near Frankfort. After he graduated, he was assigned to several outlying Texas frontier stations, far from Oakland. Hannah's greatest joy and consolation were the long descriptive letters he wrote home.

It was difficult to eke out a living on the farm, and both Burnet and Hannah worked hard. In a letter to Lamar, Burnet said that he and Hannah depended heavily on their garden for food. In their retired life, Hannah was delighted when her sister Mary could come for a long visit. The sisters were still very close, and Mary shared Hannah's duties of sewing for the slaves, candlemaking, and preparing medicines as they visited.

In a small leather notebook Hannah copied her home remedies for various ailments and several methods for making candles out of tallow or lard. These dim pencil entries reveal the practical and optimistic nature of this woman who stoically shared poverty and danger with her husband.

She promised a "Sure cure for a Felon" (infection at end of a finger) by applying a paste of soap and slacked lime in a leather thimble, and she recommended simmering yellow dock in vinegar to make a cure for ringworm. Her "Infallible Remedy for Sore Throat" was to "make a poultice of wormwood boiled in sweet milk and apply to throat. It will give relief in the worse case in eight hours."

Toothache "proceeding from whatever cause" could be cured by applying a balsam made from "oil of origanum, oil of cloves, tincture of henbane, sweet spirits of nitric, tincture of opium and white wax." She also knew how to compound an "efficacious and agreeable toothpowder for whitening the teeth and reddening the gums" out of chalk, cuttle fish powder, orris root powder, and rose pink.

In a letter written from Oakland, Mary revealed Hannah's deep concern for others in spite of her own hardships:

> . . . a Mrs. Walker who come here for her health from Galveston died in our room 4 weeks since with yellow fever — Hannah nursed her during the whole of her illness, then shrouded her for her coffin — she is buried near the house — her family now have all left . . . Oh, her [Hannah's] fatigue in nursing Mrs. Walker & her own sickness has caused a great change in her looks since we parted last.

Hannah's illness is not explained, but she seems to have gradually weakened from this time on. In another letter dated April, 1854, Mary remarked that her sister was ill and "says she knows she never will be well anymore." Mary also mentioned that although Mr. Burnet would like some company, "Hannah prefers being alone, says they have entertained company enough, now she wants retirement . . . ."

The Burnets' last years together were spent in work and solitude. On January 31, 1858, Hannah wrote to Mary saying the weather had been so bad, they had been to the landing only once that winter; they were having trouble finding anyone to help with the plowing; the servants, Sal and Em and Puss wanted her to say "howde" for them; and one of their children named Julius Sezar was a fine child "not a year old and running all over." She asked Mary to send her some flower seeds and some "Lilly of the Valley" and some bulbous roots.

She added prophetically, "The old year has passed away, one month of the new one gone, and we are still the spared monuments of mercy. May we set our house in order, for the Lord may have said, 'this year thou shalt die and not live.' "

In October of 1858 she became seriously ill again, and on October 30 she died. The next day, a Sunday, Burnet buried her beside their infant daughter.

Hannah's obituary was written by her friend and physician,

Ashbel Smith, who along with Burnet had served the Republic as an outstanding statesman. Dr. Smith praised Hannah for the courage and loyalty she had displayed through the years of suffering and hardship that she shared with her husband as the Republic took shape. Many newspapers wrote eulogies about her, and Mary's husband, Joseph Clopper, wrote a poem to comfort his wife. In it he suggested Mary make a pilgrimage to Hannah's grave:

> *The grave of one of loftiest sentiments,*
> *Of dauntless courage, and of rare good sense;*
> *One formed to fill with dignity and grace,*
> *With him she loved, her country's proudest place;*
> *Fitted as wife, as mother, sister, friend,*
> *To act her part consistent to the end;*
> *Her brightest ornament — the counterpart*
> *of Christ — a sympathizing, faithful heart.*

But the tribute Hannah would probably have liked best was the one her broken-hearted husband entered in the family Bible:

Hannah E. Burnet died at Oakland, Harris Co. on Saturday, October 30, 1858 at 6 o'clock a.m. and was buried at the family cemetery on Sunday following. She died the death of the righteous and is forever blessed.

D.G.B.

Without Hannah, the last years of Burnet's life were forlorn. He opposed secession but lost their only remaining child in the Civil War. When news of William's death at Spanish Fort near Mobile on March 31, 1865, reached Burnet, he took down the old family Bible once more and in an uneven, shaky hand recorded the time and place of death and added:

A victim to an unhappy war and I only am left — poor and desolate — Oh! God! Thy will be done and give me grace to submit cheerfully to it.

D.G.B.

When he became too feeble to manage the farm, Burnet wandered about, living with various relatives and friends. He wrote to his old friend, Lamar:

I hope you will never experience the desolation which I constantly feel of having no home. The world is to me a mere blank, a solid sheet without an intelligent or an interesting trace upon it. May such never be your destiny.

On December 5, 1870, he died at the home of friends in Galveston.

Over the years, since Burnet's death, his contributions to Texas have been recognized in various ways, including the naming of Burnet County and the town of Burnet in his memory.

2.

"The Conqueress of the Conqueror"

Margaret Lea Houston

"Oh! it is woman that makes the hero. It is she that instills the fire of patriotism — it is she who inspires every generous and noble purpose that animates the bosom of man."

When Sam Houston was inaugurated as President of the Republic of Texas for the second time on December 31, 1841, he expressed the sentiment above. Although he was well-known for his eloquence and ability to please the ladies, there is every reason to believe these words were heartfelt, because the old warrior had married the year before a woman who truly changed his life style. Margaret Lea Houston provided a dramatic contradiction to the truism that a woman should never marry a man with the expectation of reforming him.

Why was this so? The answer lies partly in the characters of Sam Houston and Margaret Lea, and in the timing of their marriage. At forty-seven Houston was ready for the emotional security of knowing he had a peaceful home to escape to when the affairs of state grated on his nerves. But the real reason for Margaret's success in making a Christian and a tee-totaller (and perhaps a statesman instead of merely a politician) out of Sam Houston was simply that theirs was a deep and lasting love affair. He worshipped her, and therefore wanted to please her more than he wanted to indulge in his old habits.

The record of their devotion is preserved in his letters to her and in her letters and poems to him. Margaret's verses may not equal in poetic skill the *Sonnets From the Portuguese* (written during the same time period), in which Elizabeth Barrett recorded her love for Robert Browning, but they convey the same intensity of feeling.

Margaret Moffette Lea was born on her family's farm in Perry County, Alabama, on April 11, 1819. From her father, who was a Baptist minister, she inherited her gentleness and her dreamy, introspective qualities and from her mother, who was a clever business woman, her strong-willed practicality. She was devoted to her father, who guided her early education and encouraged her love of reading. He died when she was fifteen, and for months she was inconsolable.

At Pleasant Valley Seminary and Judson Female Institute (in Marion) she developed two interests that dominated the rest of her life — religion and writing. From the time she was baptized at the age of nineteen, religion was a controlling force in her daily life. The urge to write, especially poetry, was also a compelling force. She had a poet's need to capture events and emotional experiences by putting them into verse. Several of her early poems were published in Alabama newspapers and in *Mother's Monthly Journal* in Philadelphia.

Strong tradition has it that Margaret Lea first saw Sam Houston when he was brought to New Orleans after the Battle of San Jacinto for medical treatment of his wounded knee. She was a visitor in New Orleans at the time and was in the crowd that gathered at the dock to see the famous hero. When he fainted from pain, the seventeen-year-old girl burst into tears. From that time on the romantic Margaret had a dream that she would meet Sam Houston again.

Her dream came true in the spring of 1839 when Houston came to Mobile after his first term as President of the

Republic had ended. He had come looking for good horses for the plantation he was creating at Cedar Point in Texas, and to find buyers for some real estate he was promoting. It happened just at that time that Margaret's mother, Nancy Lea, had some money to invest, so Houston's business was really with her. However, after he was introduced to Margaret at a garden party in her sister's home, his chief interest was in promoting his suit with the attractive young woman.

Descriptions of Margaret at that time say she was tall, with "arresting violet eyes" and an oval face framed in dark brown wavy hair. A daguerreotype, made when she was about twenty-one, shows a serious, intelligent face with a sweet, sensitive mouth. In addition to her talent for writing poetry, she had a good singing voice and played the piano, harp, and guitar.

Strong-minded Nancy Lea objected to Margaret's growing friendship with Houston for a number of reasons: there was the twenty-six-year age gap; there was his reputation as a heavy drinker; there was his lack of religion (nominally he was Catholic to satisfy Mexican requirements for land ownership in Texas); and certainly not least, there was the scandal connected with his first two marriages.

In the first marriage, a decade earlier, Sam Houston, then Governor of Tennessee, had wed Eliza Allen, a young belle of Gallatin, Tennessee, in a socially brilliant ceremony. Andrew Jackson, Houston's mentor and lifelong idol, was also a friend of the bride's family. Jackson was so pleased by the union that for a wedding gift he sent a silver service that had belonged to his beloved wife Rachel.

Three months after the impressive ceremony, the bride had returned home, and Sam Houston had resigned his position as governor and his future in Tennessee and had gone to live with the Cherokee Indians in Arkansas. The cause of the break-up of the seemingly "ideal" marriage was (and still is among biographers and historians) a matter of speculation. To the distress of their friends and the public, Houston and the

Allens refused to explain the reason for the abrupt ending to the marriage. For years newspapers continued to print widely varying versions of "the facts about Houston's first marriage." In a somewhat disjointed letter to Mr. Allen and in his non-committal resignation, Houston defended Eliza from slander, but offered no explanation of the mystery. In 1833, when he was pursuing another romance, he filed a petition for a divorce decree from Eliza Allen. Descendants of Margaret and Houston believe that he told her the truth of the matter or enough of it to satisfy her.

The circumstances of his second marriage were probably even more shocking to the strait-laced Nancy Lea. According to Indian custom, he married Tiana Rogers Gentry (who was part Cherokee) by setting up housekeeping with her. He was deeply depressed and drinking heavily at this time, and Tiana patiently provided the care and attention he needed. When he decided to go to Texas, he tried to get her to go with him, but she refused to leave her people. In the views of the Cherokees this constituted a divorce.

Nancy Lea had the help of Margaret's brothers, sisters, and other relatives in trying to talk her daughter out of becoming serious about Sam Houston. But to no avail; in spite of her gentleness, Margaret knew her own mind. Firmly she resisted all pressures to reject her unsuitable suitor. However, out of deference to her mother's wishes she did agree to wait to marry Houston until he had paid a proper visit to their home in Marion.

Before he left Mobile, Houston had Margaret's promise to marry him. In keeping with her poetic nature, she treasured symbols of their love. One night Sam pointed out the evening star (possibly he knew it was named Venus!) and called it "their star of destiny." She looked for the star each evening and mentioned it in letters to him. It also inspired one of her poems.

As they were saying good-bye in her sister's garden, Houston picked some garden pinks and put them in her hand. She wore them in her hair until they faded and then pressed them and wrote a poem called "Lines to a Withered Pink" which said in part:

> 'Tis true, no beauty now doth dwell
> Within thy leaflets sere
> But — ah — for me a holy spell
> Doth ever linger there.
>
> He placed thee in my hand, that friend
> Who now doth distant roam,
> I took thee, little thinking then
> How dear thou wouldst become.
>
> Time onward flies and swift advance
> The years when friends are few
> The years when I shall live perchance
> Like thee, to wither too.
>
> Thou sweet memento! Gentle flower!
> Say will he cherish me
> And love me in that dark hour
> As now I cherish thee?

Her most tangible symbol was the cameo likeness of himself that Houston gave to her before they parted. It was a memento that she could wear daily.

A long year was to pass before Houston could return to Alabama to marry Margaret. He had hoped that Margaret would accompany Nancy Lea when she came to Texas to look over possible land to invest in. But he had underestimated his future mother-in-law. Ignoring the salute that was booming from the guns of a group of Houston's friends who had come to meet the future Mrs. Houston, Mrs. Lea told him tartly, "My daughter is in Alabama. She goes forth in the world to marry no man."

At home, Margaret and her personal slave, Eliza, prepared a trousseau which included "a purple silk and a blue muslin" as well as the white satin gown for the wedding. Letters and poems bridged the gap of space and time until Houston could return to Marion, pay his formal visit to Margaret's relatives and obtain a marriage license. Finally, on May 9, 1840, as violins played in the parlor of the home of Margaret's brother, Henry, the ceremony was read before Margaret's still doubtful friends and relations. How could a union with so much against it succeed?

The first week of their marriage was spent at the Lafayette Hotel in Marion. At a dinner given in their honor just before they left for Texas, a Major Townes proposed a toast to Margaret. He remarked that Sam Houston "in spite of San Jacinto and other victories" had been compelled to "bow a suppliant knee at the feet of our fair townswoman." And he ended the toast by naming Margaret "the conqueress of the conqueror." Although the toast was made in a joking spirit, it was to prove prophetic.

Margaret began her efforts at reformation on the long boat trip to Texas. Wisely she did not expect or ask for an overnight change but was pleased when Houston agreed to moderate his drinking habits. This he faithfully did, to the astonishment of his friends and enemies. Dr. Ashbel Smith, Houston's physician, friend, and neighbor, at Galveston, recorded his surprise in a letter to a friend:

> His health is excellent, as good or *better* than I have ever seen it. He indulges in no conviviality with his friends — but strange to say is a model of conjugal propriety. I had dreadful misgivings as to the propriety of his taking this step — thus far I have been most agreeably disappointed. His health and ways are infinitely mended. Will it last . . . ?

It did last, but Houston's enemies never ceased to rake up old stories of his drinking escapades in efforts to discredit him. Houston tapered off by drinking "bitters," for which he asked his friends to save him orange peels. He progressed to complete abstinence and finally to making temperance speeches.

Margaret was to live in various homes in Texas. The more permanent ones were at Cedar Point on Galveston Bay, in

Houston, at Huntsville (in three different locations), and at
Independence. She loved the seclusion and privacy of their
first home at Cedar Point, which she christened Ben Lomond
from a name she remembered in one of Scott's romances. She
either didn't know or ignored the fact that "Ben" means
mountain or high peak, for the land at Cedar Point was
anything but mountainous. Houston thought it a "fairy land"
and considered it the most healthful spot in Texas. Margaret
asked for and got an orchard of oak trees planted there; these
were to prove a financial blessing during the Civil War.

When Houston began to campaign for the presidency in
1841 against Burnet, Margaret was appalled by the bitter
name-calling and denunciations that were a part of the
contest. At first she read the newspaper reports of Houston's
speeches and essays, but was so distressed by the language
and ideas that she quit reading them and occupied herself with
music, books, long walks on the beach, tending her flower
garden, and writing poetry. She comforted herself in her
husband's absence by looking at his picture and wrote a poem
called "My Husbands Picture". The first verse says:

> Dear gentle shade of him I love
> I've gazed upon thee till thine eye,
> In liquid light doth seem to move,
> and look on me in sympathy!

In the middle of the summer of 1841, Houston came home
for several idyllic weeks. Margaret recorded their quiet
pleasures in a poem titled "Cedar Point — Ben Lomond":

> Yes dearest, we are happy here
> In this sweet solitude
> Of ours, no heartless ones come near
> Or tiresome scenes intrude.
>
> The mock-bird on our green yard tree
> Sings through the live-long night,

And greets the moon, his heart less free
Than ours, his hopes less bright!

At eve beside our cottage door
We watch the sky's last hue,
And listening to the ocean's roar
Our thoughts the day review.

Would that we thus might ever be
Far from the world's dark snares!
'Mid nature's wildwood purity,
Untrammeled by earth's cares!

After Houston won the presidency by an overwhelming 7,915 votes to Burnet's 3,616, he and Margaret attended a big barbecue victory celebration given by citizens of Washington County. According to one participant, there were "2 thundering big beeves, 13 hogs, honey, taters, chickens and goodies in general," but it was only a "cold water doins." To the amazement of Houston's old friends, he refused to touch a "drop of the ardent." Margaret had won her campaign, too.

Houston disliked having the capital located at Austin for a number of reasons, and he certainly didn't want Margaret there. He believed the climate of the Gulf Coast was better for her health, which was never strong. She suffered from recurrent asthma and malarial attacks. Also, Austin was on the edge of the frontier, and was plagued by Indian raids and threats of Mexican invasions. There was no decent home for her and no money in the treasury for anyone including the President; in fact, there was not even enough firewood to keep the President warm.

Again Margaret and Houston bridged their separation with long love letters. When Congress adjourned February 5, 1842, Houston mounted his trusty mule, Bruin, and rode back to Margaret, now in the city of Houston, as fast as the animal could go — making the trip in a record time of just "two hours under four days."

For a time Houston operated the government out of the city of Houston, much to the dismay of Austin citizens and newspapers. Then the little town of Washington-on-the-Brazos made a bid to be the capital. The city of Houston could not or would not match Washington's offer of free office space and facilities, so Houston decided to move the government once again.

This time Margaret packed up her household to move by wagon with him. At first they stayed in the home of Judge John Lockhart in Washington-on-the-Brazos. The President must have been something of a trial to Mrs. Lockhart. To give Margaret more privacy, he moved a large wardrobe over the inside door to their room and had another door cut in the outside wall. He shared the common pioneer habit of chewing tobacco, and at one time Mrs. Lockhart complained of his messing up her nice clean porch railing when "by exerting no undue energy and exercising a bit of consideration he could have expectorated *over* the rail." Worse yet, while Margaret was on a visit to relatives, he got lonesome for her and slipped back into his old habits, consumed a bottle of wine (that he had bought as a peace offering for Mrs. Lockhart) and had a servant chop off one of the posts of her fine old bed.

Mrs. Lockhart was probably not sorry to see the Houstons move into their own home on the outskirts of Washington. It was plain and cheaply built, but Margaret put fringe on the furniture, used her good silver and dishes for entertaining, and made it as attractive as she could.

Early in the year Houston sent in an order for household supplies; it included a bolt of linen diaper cloth. Nancy Lea came to help out in May, and on the 25th of that month Sam Houston, Jr. was born. A friend wrote to Ashbel Smith, ". . . you would suppose the General is proud of his boy — and you would not be mistaken!"

Margaret and Houston were doting parents. A little later in a letter to friends, Houston reported, "Mrs. H. bids me say to Madam, 'Sam has no less than four teeth' and I say, 'Sam's mother has recovered from her ecstasy at the discovery of his first tooth.' "

In 1844 when Houston's second term as President ended, he drew plans for a plantation home to be located fourteen miles outside of Huntsville. He had his slave Joshua build the house out of axe-squared logs. He called the home by his Indian name, "Raven" Hill. Oddly, there actually were ravens there. He wrote to wish the new President, Anson Jones, well and said of himself that he was "only intent upon domestic happiness and prosperity." Margaret was delighted to have her husband to herself again. She wrote a poem called "To My Husband." The first two verses said:

> Dearest, the cloud has left thy brow,
> The shade of thoughtfulness, of care
> And deep anxiety; and now
> The sunshine of content is there.

> Its sweet return with joy I hail;
> And never may thy country's woes
> Again that hallowed light dispel.
> And mar thy bosom's calm repose.

She had her new home, her adored son, and her devoted husband, who to please her had completely given up drinking. But she anxiously worried about the next step in her reformation program, which was to bring Houston into the church as a true Christian. The last verse of the poem referred to this dream:

> Far from the busy haunts of men
> Oh may thy soul each fleeting hour
> Upon the breath of prayer ascend
> To Him who rules with love and power!

However, Houston was not to be pushed into professing religious feeling until he was ready, and Margaret accepted the fact that the time was not yet.

Her peace and contentment lasted until Houston was stirred into action over the annexation issue. For a time he dashed about Texas making speeches denying specific attitudes attributed to him regarding the issue.

When he learned that Andrew Jackson was dying, he bundled up Margaret and Sam and rushed them off to Nashville; they arrived at the Hermitage three hours after the old warrior had died. After the funeral services, Margaret and Houston stayed in Nashville for a time while Houston was honored with dinners and barbecues. Finally they made their way slowly to Marion, Alabama, where Margaret remained to let Sam, Jr. become acquainted with his relatives, while Houston returned to Texas to attend to the farm — and to politics.

Margaret returned to Raven Hill in January to find her husband a likely candidate for Senator from the new state of Texas. When he was elected in February, she planned to go to Washington, D.C., with him but delayed leaving when she found she was pregnant. As her pregnancy advanced, she gradually abandoned the idea of following him to Washington. But the days were long and lonely at Raven Hill. Never had they been separated for so long a time or by so many miles.

Again letters bridged the miles between them — and they were still love letters, although his contained news of the excitement over the war with Mexico that followed the annexation of Texas. Hers contained news of the farm and a great deal of religious theology, and, of course, reported Sam, Jr.'s every antic.

Margaret wrote, "Oh my love if you could look into my heart at this moment, I know you would never leave me again!" He was lonely, too, and urged her to join him, but her health was not good. Even so, she was tempted until her sister-in-law, Eliza Moore, came to visit and talked her out of attempting the 3,000-mile trip. Margaret told Houston, "I felt willing at first to risk my life in the attempt rather than be longer without you."

She yearned for him physically as well as "spiritually." She wished that she could bestow her kisses on the writer instead of his letters, and she dreamed of the time when "I shall be sitting as in bygone days, on your lap, with my arms around your neck, the happiest, the most blest of wives."

As the fever of war mounted in Texas, she helped make a flag for a company of Texas volunteers, but when Houston wrote asking if he should "go out with the army" she replied:

> Alas, what has always been my decision when my own happiness or the good of the country was to be sacrificed? Have I not invariably ascertained your views and then coincided with them, let my own sacrifices be what they might? . . . I wish you to be governed entirely by your own judgment, and though the decision may bring misery upon me beyond description, I will try to bear it without a murmur.

Obviously she did not want him to go, and in spite of the great temptation of meeting his old enemy Santa Anna again and the possibility of winning the glory of planting the United States flag in Mexico City, Sam Houston bowed to his wife's feelings.

Margaret felt that her prayers were beginning to be answered when Houston started dropping in on Sunday services in the fashionable E Street Baptist Church in Washington, D.C. With his poncho and gold-headed cane and his habit of whittling toys for the children in the congregation during the sermon, he was a conspicuous figure. But he listened attentively to the minister's message and usually spent Sunday afternoon writing Margaret his impression of it.

The Twenty-ninth Congress finally closed its first session on August 10, 1846. Houston was as anxious to be home as Margaret was to have him there. He wrote to a friend, "I am most painfully anxious to see my dear Wife, and my young Pioneer. I was always fond of home but I now place something like a true estimate, upon the source of true happiness — Home."

He arrived at Raven Hill a few days before the birth of his first daughter, Nancy Elizabeth (Nannie), who was named after her two grandmothers. The time passed too quickly now for Margaret, and Houston did not have as many hours to spend at home as she had hoped for. There were speeches to make, political dinners and endless barbecues to attend, constituents to talk with about the war and other national and state issues.

The end of November came too soon, and she saw him off on the long trip back to Washington, D.C. Having two children to watch over did not distract her from continued anxiety over the possibility of Houston's being talked into joining the war and over the "unsaved" state of his soul. Nor did she omit to look for signs of his devotion to her; she scolded him mildly for omitting from one letter "that very important expression 'I love you.' "

Then a personal problem overtook her other fears. She began to suffer sharp pains in her right breast and discovered a lump there. Her mother was living with Margaret's brother Vernal at nearby Grand Cane on the Trinity River. There Margaret fled with the children. When the lump broke and began to bleed, Dr. Ashbel Smith was hurriedly sent for. He operated on Margaret and removed the tumor — without an anesthetic because the only one available was whiskey and she refused to touch it. Houston left the Senate early to be with Margaret and wrote Smith a letter expressing a "deep and abiding sense of obligation" to the doctor.

Houston's short term as a Senator was at a close, but his re-election was pending in the Legislature. Margaret hated the thought of spending more lonely months on Raven Hill if he were elected to a full six-year term, so in June of 1847 Houston traded the plantation home for a one-room house only a couple of miles out of Huntsville. He described it as "a bang up place" to a friend. The slaves were set to work to expand the cabin according to plans drawn up by Houston.

It had the traditional "dog run" or center breezeway to catch the prevailing wind. A porch was added — it would be a pleasant place to eat in warm weather. A loft was constructed for the children to play in between the two upstairs bedrooms, and a room was added to accommodate "Mother Dear," as Houston called Nancy Lea. In the yard were two one-room cabins; one would serve as Houston's office and the other would be the kitchen. And, of course, there was a garden area for Margaret's flowers. Of all the Houstons' homes, this would be Sam Houston's favorite. They named it Woodland. Over the years, four of their children would be born there.

Margaret was more contented in being closer to town and especially in being nearer to church friends. She began a letter to Houston on April 12, 1848, but was interrupted by labor pains. On the next day their second daughter was born. A few days later Margaret finished the letter, telling him, "There is no doubt about it, my dearest Love, she is one of the loveliest little creatures you ever beheld." She enclosed a lock of the baby's hair and a little white rose the infant had held in her hands. Margaret told Houston he must name the child, and he chose to name her Margaret Lea (Maggie). She was well-named, for she grew to resemble her mother closely in temperament, becoming very serious and pious at an early age.

Two more years passed with Houston alternating between his senatorial duties at Washington, D.C., and his leaves spent with his growing family at Woodland. He bought Margaret a big yellow coach to travel in, so she could spend time at Cedar Point when she wanted a change.

When he was at home she entertained graciously for him — with Eliza preparing delicious meals. Their guests ranged from Houston's Indian friends in scanty dress to some of the most important political figures in the country, including E. M. Pease, the candidate for Governor.

On April 9, 1850, Houston was in Washington when their third daughter, Mary William (Molly), was born. She was the prettiest of the Houston daughters, with her mother's delicate features and her father's auburn hair.

Late in 1850, Margaret underwent a disturbing experience. She was charged with assault and battery upon a ward, an impudent girl named Virginia Thorne, whom she had thrashed for her insolence after Virginia angered Margaret by treating Nannie roughly. Houston, unable to leave Washington at the time, hired a friend, the attorney and historian Henderson

Yoakum, to defend Margaret. He wrote to Yoakum to put off
Mrs. Houston's trial until he could get to Huntsville, saying, "I
would not fail to be present for millions . . . her alarm and
feelings would subject her to pain if I were not present." But
the hearings began without him and resulted in a mistrial.
Later the Baptist church investigated the charges and
vindicated Margaret. Yoakum believed that the case had been
brought to court by Houston's enemies to embarrass him.
Houston arrived a week after the trial to comfort Margaret.

The summer of 1851 was again a time for a happy reunion,
and Houston had serious thoughts of retiring. He wrote to a
friend, "When I am at home in my woodland residence with
my wife and brats, I feel no disposition to return again to
scenes of official conflict and disputation." But he did return.

On January 20, 1852, another daughter was added to the
family, Antoinette Power (Nettie), named after Margaret's
favorite sister. In Washington, Houston was more deeply into
politics than ever as he was seriously being considered as a
presidential candidate. He arrived in Huntsville several weeks
later, laden with gifts for the children and handsome fabrics
and a gold locket for Margaret.

In 1853, Margaret's chronically troublesome asthma was
bothering her, and the Houstons began to think of moving to a
higher altitude. Nancy Lea had been singing the praises of
Independence to them for some time; in fact, since she and one
of Margaret's sisters had moved there several years ago, Mrs.
Lea was especially fond of the strong Baptist congregation
there. Another consideration was the education of the
children. Sam, Jr. was ten, and Nannie at seven was exceptionally bright. Baylor Preparatory School and Co-
educational University would offer them opportunities for a
good education.

In October of 1853 a caravan left Huntsville for Independence. Houston and his son led the way in a buggy,
Margaret and Eliza and the girls followed in the yellow coach,
and the servants and baggage packed in wagons brought up
the rear. The home the Houstons bought was on a hill next to

the preparatory school. It was a sturdy log house set in a beautiful grove of oak trees; the cost of $4,000 included 200 enclosed acres and 165 acres of timberland.

During another senatorial term — six more years — Houston followed the pattern of spending his winters in Washington, D.C., and his summers as a family man in Independence or at Huntsville or at Cedar Point. He was always a restless person and liked to move about among their homes. Margaret as usual made every effort to please him, and it was said that she could have their large family and group of servants ready to roll in the yellow coach to any of their homes on an hour's notice.

In 1854, two joyful events occurred for Margaret. Their long-awaited second son was born on June 21. He was named Andrew Jackson, and Sam, Jr. was overjoyed, as he had long ago told Margaret that he had enough sisters and requested six brothers for companions.

The second event fulfilled a long-awaited dream of Margaret's, when Sam Houston knelt at the altar of the Baptist church at Independence to accept Christ as his personal Saviour. The bell that Nancy Lea had presented to the little church tolled the glad tidings through the rolling hills. On November 19, 1854, the convert was baptized in the chilly waters of Rocky Creek, just outside Independence. The Reverend Mr. Rufus C. Burleson, famous Baptist educator and pastor, was in charge of the service. Baptists from miles around came to witness the event. A well-known painting of the ceremony (now in the foyer of the Baptist Foundation of Texas in Dallas) shows Houston and Burleson, robed in white, earnestly performing their roles in the ritual while a crowd watches from the banks of the creek. Margaret is nowhere to be seen in the picture; as usual she preferred to stay in the background. But she rejoiced that another step in her reform program was completed. In a poem about Independence she wrote:

> Sweet "Rocky!" of what hallowed joys
> Shall mingle with my dreams of thee!

Houston, who never did anything halfway, undertook to pay half the minister's salary and made other generous contributions to the church, for he said his pocketbook was "baptized too."

During the long months of Houston's absence from Independence Margaret occupied herself as usual with music, books, church work, poetry, instructing the children in religious matters, and writing long letters to her husband. He was an affectionate father, and she wrote him minute details of their daily lives. She told him:

> Dearest, perhaps you may suppose from the multiplicity of things I have had on hand that I find no time to pine for you. Then you are mistaken for there is everywhere a void, which nothing can fill but the presence of my darling husband.

He kept her informed of his involvement with the growing crisis over the issue of slavery and states rights. But his heart was with her. He told her:

> When I reflect on the distance from this to where you are and our flock, I feel that I am indeed an exile . . . our sunny home appears to me more bright and lovely than it has ever done . . . .

He wore a miniature likeness of her entwined with a lock of his own hair "in his bosom."

In 1857 Houston entered the gubernatorial race against Hardin R. Runnels. As usual Houston put on a good show and undertook a strenuous speaking schedule that gave all of Texas an exciting summer — except for Margaret, who remained at home with the children, following the campaign on a map and through the papers and Houston's letters. They were in Huntsville when they learned that Houston had lost to Runnels.

In November Houston returned to Washington, D.C., to complete his Senate term. Margaret returned to her waiting, but it was made more endurable this time by the knowledge that her husband would soon be returning to Texas for good. She was also awaiting their seventh child, and on Sam Jr.'s fifteenth birthday, May 25, 1858, he got his wish for a second brother. William Rogers was not as sturdy a baby as her other children had been, and both Margaret and Houston lavished special care and attention on this child.

To add to their problems, the Houstons now found themselves in financial trouble. Margaret was a good manager, more concerned with spiritual than with worldly wealth, but Houston could be a free and easy spender, especially during campaigns. It was finally decided that Woodland should be sold to pay their debts; and Margaret once more packed herself and the children into the yellow coach for a move back to the Independence home.

When Houston vowed he would become a sheep rancher at the end of his Senate term, Margaret probably didn't put much faith in it. And it's well that she didn't, for in 1859 he again ran against Runnels for Governor. His popularity had reached a new peak, and although he made only one campaign speech (in which he opposed the slave trade), he was swept into office by 10,000 votes more than Runnels received. Houston was sixty-six and Margaret forty.

In December of 1859 they moved into the impressive Governor's Mansion that had been built during the Pease administration. Margaret was again the First Lady of Texas. But her first night in Austin was a miserable one. When they arrived she was suffering a bad attack of asthma brought on by the dust of the trip and perhaps by the emotional strain of the move. In writing of that night, Jeff Hamilton, one of the twelve slaves the Houstons had while in Austin, reported that he got no sleep because the General had him pick leaves and put them in dishpans and buckets and keep them burning all night to relieve the attack.

Their short stay in the mansion was not a happy time. Austin citizens, remembering that Houston had once moved the capital, were cold to the family. Perhaps fortunately, Margaret's eighth pregnancy allowed her to avoid appearing in public after the first few months. Also, Houston was involved in an increasingly unpopular cause. While he strongly supported the Union in the face of a growing clamor to withdraw and join the Confederacy, Margaret tried to watch over his diet and his health.

Sam, Jr. was sent to nearby Bastrop Military Institute; Margaret and Houston (in spite of his busy days and nights) wrote him long letters. The younger children were lively and mischievous, especially six-year-old Andrew, who gave the Austin gossips plenty to talk about. Some were amused and some were not when he locked the door of the Senate Chamber while the Senators were in session and hid the key. Only his father's threats of a whipping and a jail term made him reveal where the key was. Out of Andrew's hearing, the Governor boasted that his son had better control over the Senators than he did.

In spite of, or perhaps because of, the pressures of state business, Houston found time for fun with his children. A story is told of his forgetting the dignity of office to join them in learning the "pigeon wing," a new dance craze, but Margaret soon appeared on the scene to put a stop to the unseemly behavior of the chief executive.

Nancy Lea came to help Margaret prepare for the birth of her last child — the first baby to be born in the Governor's Mansion. The birth took place on August 12, 1860, in the huge, square four-poster walnut bed that Houston had ordered made to duplicate one he had enjoyed sleeping in at a friend's home in Seguin. The baby was named Temple Lea after Margaret's father.

About this same time, to Margaret's relief, Houston withdrew as a potential candidate for the presidency of the United States. She was seriously ill for about two weeks after the birth, and this may have influenced Houston's decision. He put aside everything he could to stay with her.

The days of the Houstons in the mansion were numbered. In his last years as a Senator, Houston had shown himself a statesman, willing to support his beliefs about the importance of maintaining the Union at whatever cost to his personal political fortunes. Now in the bitter days of disunion he stood by his convictions, knowing that he was supporting a hopeless cause. Margaret listened to his nightly pacing and gave him all

the support she could. But she was realistic about their future
and wrote to her mother:

> Truly the present appearance of things is gloomy enough . . .
> General Houston seems cheerful and hopeful through the day, but
> in the still watches of the night I hear him agonizing in prayer for
> our distracted country . . . I cannot shut my eyes to the dangers
> that threaten us. I know that it is even probable that we may soon
> be rendered to poverty, but oh, I have such a sweet assurance in
> my heart that the presence of the Lord will go with us wherever
> we may go.

Houston refused offers from supporters to keep him in office
by force. A similar offer of federal aid from Lincoln he is said
to have burned in a fireplace of the mansion. When the
Secession Convention decreed that all state officials must sign
an oath of loyalty to the Confederacy, Sam Houston paced the
floor all night. Early the next morning he declared, "Margaret,
I will never do it." He had put his principles above expediency,
well aware that the price was political exile.

Friends helped the Houstons pack, and one day in late
March the yellow coach took the ex-Governor and the ex-First
Lady out of Austin. They stopped in Independence long
enough to leave Nannie, Maggie, and Mollie with Grandmother Lea so they could attend Baylor's Female Department.
From there they went on to Cedar Point where Sam, Jr. was
managing the farm.

Sam, Jr. was not happy to be spending his time counting the
livestock and supervising the hoeing of the corn while there
was a war going on. Houston cautioned him to wait until Texas
needed him, and Margaret begged him not to go, but he was
his father's son and at the first opportunity joined a unit in his
neighborhood.

It was Dr. Ashbel Smith's Bayland Guards. When the company was sent to Missouri, Margaret wrote to Nancy Lea, "I
thought I would lie down and die."

But instead she summoned up her "fortitude" and wrote him
encouraging letters. In one she said:

> As it is the Sabbath, I do not feel at liberty to write any secular
> details; so, I will beg you to answer the all-important question:
> Have you given your heart to God?

Sam Houston added, "My dear Son, I only send you a fond father's tender blessing and assure you of his prayer at the Throne of Grace for your safety and salvation."

In the same company with Sam, Jr. was Charles Elliot Jones, the son of Anson Jones, former political crony of Houston's but later one of his severest critics. Margaret had known Mary Jones at Independence and in their mutual trouble, politics meant nothing. Both of their sons were reported missing after the Battle of Shiloh. When Mary passed on a letter to her saying that Sam was a prisoner and Charles only slightly wounded (the wound proved to be a mortal one), Margaret returned it with a note congratulating Mary on her good fortune and adding, "My heart is still crushed with anguish and suspense."

Later Margaret was to learn that her concern for her son's spiritual welfare had probably saved his life. Before he left she had given him a Bible to take with him, inscribed "from Margaret Lea Houston to her beloved son." A Union chaplain who found Sam saw the inscription and nursed the boy back to health with special care instead of allowing him to be treated as an ordinary prisoner. Many months later as she was working in her flower garden at Cedar Point, a thin Confederate soldier stopped at her gate. As was her custom, she started to ask him if he wanted food or water. Sam, Jr. laughed. "Why, Ma, I don't believe you know me!" he said.

The war brought economic hardship to the Houstons as it did to other Southern families. To earn an income, they were forced to cut down much of the timber around Ben Lomond and sell it for firewood. In spite of their financial straits, Houston, in his usual extravagantly generous manner, surprised Nannie on her birthday with a beautiful rosewood piano that had cost $1,500.

In the fall of 1862 Galveston Island was cut off by a federal blockade. The Houstons decided to move to Huntsville, but they owned no home there now. In vain Houston tried to buy back Woodland; it was not for sale, so they rented the strange building called "Steamboat House" because its builder had modeled it after a Mississippi River steamboat. In this house Houston passed the last few months of his life.

Margaret was concerned by her husband's increasing feebleness and protected him in every way possible, even from problems concerning the children. She wrote to Sam, Jr., now in school in Independence, "I do not think your father has the remotest idea that you have made any bills. Do not get anything more, I beseech you."

She urged Houston to go to Sour Lake to take the mud baths and prayed that they would restore his strength. They did seem to help temporarily, but early in July of 1863 he went to bed with chills and fever. He was physically weak and spiritually depressed to see his unhappy forebodings about the outcome of the Civil War coming true. Margaret watched in despair as he developed pneumonia; medical aid could do nothing for him. She stayed by his side, reading passages from the Bible. Shortly after six p.m. on July 26, Margaret was reading the 23rd Psalm to her semi-conscious husband. He roused and said, "Texas — Texas — Margaret," and with her name on his lips he died.

In her two-volume Bible Margaret made the entry:

> Died on the 26th of July 1863, General Sam Houston, the beloved and affectionate husband, father, devoted patriot, the fearless soldier — the meek and lowly Christian.

The responsibility she had assumed when she married Sam Houston was over — her task successfully completed. But another one, perhaps more difficult, lay ahead.

In his will Sam Houston appointed "My dearly beloved wife Margaret guardian of my children." The formal appointment was unnecessary, of course, for Margaret had long ago accepted that responsibility. In a poem she had written, "My beauteous gifts, how carefully/Their tender branches I must train!"

Crushed by grief, the 44-year-old widow had to put her mourning aside to think of her eight children. What was best to do for them? Back to Independence she went to be near her aging mother and other relatives. She bought a two-story house made of hand-hewn cedar, near her mother's house and near the Baptist church.

She had hoped that Sam, Jr., now twenty, would be her "prop." But Sam had other ideas; he left school to join the army again. The smaller children were sometimes hard for her to manage by herself, especially Andrew, who loved to tease his grandmother and his sisters. One of his minor pranks was to crawl under a sofa and pin the skirts of Mollie and a visiting friend together. At times Margaret felt he was too much for her. She wrote to Sam, Jr., "Andrew [age 10] is growing rapidly. He is boisterous and unmanageable. I need you home with him very much."

Margaret's great comfort as always was her religion. She and Nancy Lea loved the little Baptist church at Independence. Now Margaret found that her mother was preparing for death. She had bought a metal coffin and built herself a stone vault across the street from the church. She prudently kept her coffee and sugar, scarce wartime items, in the coffin to save them from being pilfered by the servants.

Only six months after Houston's death, Margaret was writing Sam, Jr. of the death of his grandmother. She reported that a large crowd attended Nancy Lea's funeral. Her spirits were depressed, but would have been even more so if she could have forseen the circumstances of her own bleak burial in that same tiny plot. At least, in the services for her mother, the family had all the consolations that religion could offer.

The war ended and the hardships of reconstruction began; cash was difficult to come by for Margaret, as it was for most Texas families. One day, Joshua, a former Houston slave, appeared with his life savings — $2,000 in U.S. gold and silver. He had saved the money from his income as a blacksmith, a sideline that Houston had allowed him to pursue, and now he offered it to Margaret, who had taught his children to read and write along with her own. She told Joshua to use it for the Christian education of his children, which he did.

There were happy events to dispel Margaret's sense of loss.

Nannie and Maggie were married in the little Baptist church within a three-month period of 1866, and Margaret used her decorating and entertaining talents to make the weddings memorable. In June of 1867 Nannie presented her with her first grandchild and namesake, Margaret Houston Morrow. Margaret was delighted and insisted on sending Eliza to stay with Nannie to help take care of the baby.

But now Margaret's time had come. Late in 1867 the dreaded yellow fever plague swept over Texas. Margaret was busily packing in the happy anticipation of spending Christmas with Nannie and her six-month-old grandchild in Georgetown when she became ill.

Helplessly, Mollie and Nettie watched as the fever consumed her. She begged them to take the younger children and go on to Georgetown, but they would not leave her. On December 3 she died. That same evening, according to medical regulations, she was buried deep in the earth beside her mother as soon as a coffin could be constructed.

Only the two daughters and two servants attended the burial. For fear of contamination, no minister would conduct the services. Ironically, the devout Margaret, who had devoted so much of her life to her religion, was laid to rest without the rites of her beloved church.

Her only memorial was in the hearts of her children. Daughter Nettie wrote that while other things might be forgotten:

> . . . the words of my mother still lingered
> Like the echo when songs die away.

3

"To Forget Is Guilt"

Tabitha Jordan Lamar

The most romantic of all Texas' presidents, Mirabeau Lamar, was always fond of the ladies, and they of him. A dreamer and a poet, he often expressed his feelings for attractive females in verse. One of his early poems (written in 1816 when he was eighteen) is a graceful compliment to five girls in Eatonton, Georgia, near Lamar's hometown of Fairfield. Entitled "No Girl Can Win My Stubborn Breast," the theme is that he could not love any girl unless she combined the virtues of all five of the young women to whom the poem is addressed.

Lamar was a widower when he occupied the office of President of the Republic of Texas. He would marry again toward the end of his life, but at the time of his presidency he was still very much under the sway of his feelings for his first wife, Tabitha, and of the grief that he suffered after her death from tuberculosis. In fact, if her death had not sent him into a state of bitterness and depression, he might not have come to

Texas at all. It seems appropriate, therefore, to include a brief sketch of Tabitha Lamar because of the influence she had on the third President of Texas, even though she was not actually a First Lady.

The circumstances of Lamar's first meeting with Tabitha, who was the fourth of five daughters in the Jordan family, are uncertain. According to one report, Lamar saw her for a brief moment when she was only fourteen. Three years later he is supposed to have encountered her unexpectedly at a party in Eatonton, and to have impulsively proposed, only to be turned down. Their next meeting supposedly occurred when she passed through Milledgeville, Georgia, where Lamar was serving as secretary to Governor George Troup. Tabitha was on her way to live with a sister in Alabama after her father's death. Evidently the results of this meeting were more encouraging, for in the only extant letter from Lamar to Tabitha (December 3, 1825), he addresses her affectionately, reminds her of their "plighted faith" and worries about a rival who he fears is going to visit her.

Being a romantic *and* a poet, Lamar wrote many verses to his sweetheart, but after her death he destroyed them all. On January 1, 1826, Lamar and Tabitha were married, probably at her sister's home in Perry County, Alabama. He was twenty-eight; she was seventeen.

While the newlyweds were traveling back to his home, an accident almost ended their marriage — and the bride's life. During a moment when Lamar had left the carriage in charge of the Negro servants, the horses became frightened, bolted, and smashed the carriage against a tree. Tabitha was thrown onto some rocks, where her face was cut to the bone. According to legend, Lamar carried her to a nearby Indian hut, trimmed the ragged wound with his razor and sutured the cut with an ordinary needle and thread. Tabitha said to him, "You loved me for my beauty — it is gone forever."

But she was wrong. Lamar quit his job to nurse her and the wound healed, leaving only a tiny white line. However, Tabitha's health continued to be delicate, and she began to

have the first symptoms of what would later be diagnosed as
consumption (tuberculosis). Blissfully unaware of the serious-
ness of the insidious disease, the happy couple celebrated the
birth of a daughter in November of 1827 and named her
Rebecca Ann after her two grandmothers.

A short time later the family moved to Columbus, Georgia,
where Lamar put his writing talent to work by founding *The
Columbus Enquirer*, which became an outspoken state's rights
journal. Lamar bought a lot near the Chattahoochee River at
an auction in Columbus and built his wife a wide, one-story
wooden cottage. Tabitha, Lamar, and Rebecca loved to stroll
along the expansive walk on the river bank in the evenings.
Here, too, Lamar sat to compose songs, most of which were
destroyed later.

Although Tabitha's health continued to be frail, for a time
the affairs of the little family seemed to be going from good to
better. The paper prospered; Lamar ran for a State Senate
seat and won by a sweeping majority. After a successful term,
he was preparing to run again; victory seemed certain. And
then disaster struck. On August 20, 1830, Tabitha died
unexpectedly at the age of twenty-one, a victim of the treach-
erous tuberculosis. Lamar never completely recovered from
the emotional shock of her death.

He withdrew from the Senate race, sold his interest in the
Enquirer, left Rebecca Ann in his mother's care, and spent the
next two years in restless travel. It was sometime during this
period that he destroyed all of the love poems and songs he
had written to Tabitha. In a later poem he said:

> *When she died and left me here*
> *My soul in desolation —*
> *I broke the shell she loved so well*
> *Destroyed the songs I wrought her.*

In 1832 Lamar was back into Georgia politics, but when he
moved back to Columbus he stayed in a hotel, not feeling able
to live with his memories in the cottage near the banks of the

Chattahoochee.

In 1835, after being defeated for Congress, Lamar again felt the need for a change. Exciting stories about the Texas frontier were pouring into Georgia, and Lamar's good friend, James W. Fannin, had already left for that western land. The chance for action and a change of scenery remote from the memories associated with Columbus proved irresistible.

Before he left Georgia, Lamar had a simple obelisk of white marble erected over Tabitha's grave. It was inscribed:

> Erected by Mirabeau B. Lamar in
> memory of his wife whose death
> has left him no other happiness
> than the remembrance of her virtues

On the trip to Texas Lamar stopped in Mobile to visit a cemetery, an act that was to become a habit with him as he continued to nurse his grief, for he wrote in his journal:

> I never read upon the marble tablet of a young and beautiful wife
> ... fading into dust like a drooping rose in the bloom of loveliness,
> but what I mourn afresh the loss of my own sweet flower ...
> there is bliss in tears shed for the loved. To forget is guilt, and not
> to weep is worse than ingratitude.

By a strange coincidence, while in New Orleans he bought a sermon by John Newland Maffitt, the father of the woman Lamar would take as his second wife twenty years later.

Soon after arriving in Texas, Lamar joined the Texas Army and traveled with it to San Jacinto, where he led the cavalry with reckless courage and became a part of Texas history. Within ten days he had risen from private to Secretary of War under Burnet, and four months after the Battle of San Jacinto he was elected Vice President under Sam Houston.

Lamar was a glamorous figure in the newborn republic and the target of many unattached ladies, but his deepest personal feelings were for his little daughter back in Georgia and for her dead mother. When Houston's term expired and Lamar was elected President by a large majority, he arranged for a visit by Rebecca Ann before his inauguration. The visit was a happy one for them both, although the frail child was already

showing signs of the disease that had killed Tabitha. Reluctantly, Lamar sent his daughter back to Georgia where she
could receive a better education than was possible in Texas.

Although concern for his daughter weighed heavily upon
him, the business of government demanded Lamar's attention.
His administration from 1838-1841 was marked by four
objectives — defending the frontier from Indians and
Mexicans, gaining recognition of Texas' independence by
leading powers, organizing a strong government, and laying
the foundation for a public school system for Texas. His
greatest long-range success came in the last area.

Rebecca Ann made a second visit to her father during his
administration and expressed obvious admiration and love for
her important parent in her childish letters. This visit was cut
short by the threat of yellow fever in Texas, and she was
hurriedly sent back to Georgia.

During Lamar's presidency, the capital was moved from
Houston to Austin. A colorful (but unverified) story is told of
Lamar's choosing the site while on a hunting trip. According
to the legend, he chased a buffalo up what is now Congress
Avenue and shot it on a hill (where the capitol is now located).
Looking down the slope to the Colorado River, he said, "This
should be the seat of empire." Whether he influenced the
decision or not, the commission in charge of making the
decision did decide that the place where the little town of
Waterloo was then located was the right spot, and amid great
celebration the capital of Texas was finally permanently
located.

Lamar finished his term, as Burnet and Houston had theirs,
under heavy critical fire. He spent the spring of 1843 in
Georgia with Rebecca Ann, who was sixteen and a lovely
replica of Tabitha as she had looked when he had married her.

Almost immediately after his return to Texas, Lamar
received from his brother a letter that dealt another
catastrophic emotional blow. Rebecca Ann had died soon after
he left her. For a time his family and friends feared for
Lamar's sanity and for his life. Finally, in a poem "On the

Death of My Daughter" he poured out his grief and seemed to find some relief. Stanza XII says:

> *She was the last enchanting ray*
> *That cheered me here below —*
> *The only star that lit my way*
> *Through this dark world of wo;*
> *And now, bereft of that sweet light,*
> *Oh, how shall I sustain*
> *The shadows of that awful night*
> *Which must with me remain!*

Another period of restless wandering followed Rebecca Ann's death. Some of Lamar's time was spent in working for the annexation of Texas, about which he had reversed his attitude since leaving office, but a great deal of it he spent in visiting with literary people and in writing.

When the Mexican War began, Lamar stopped his travels and hurried back to take part in it, and again distinguished himself in battle. After the war ended, Lamar traveled again in desultory fashion until he met the beautiful Henrietta Maffitt. He had met her family and Henrietta before, but this time he courted her with poetry. And although she had been engaged to another man, they were married in 1851; Lamar was fifty-three.

At last Lamar had the happy domestic life he longed for and had not known since Tabitha's death. Henrietta encouraged his writing and persuaded him to have some of his poetry published. When their daughter, Loretto Evalina, was born, he wrote:

> *Like yon declining sun, my life*
> *Is going down all calm and mild,*
> *Illuminated by an angel wife,*
> *And sweetened by a cherub child.*

Although he had to spend twenty months away from his family as Minister to Nicaragua, affectionate letters bridged the geographical separation, and great plans were made to celebrate the first Christmas following Lamar's return to Texas. By-passing offers of official entertainments to honor his return, he hurried home to their Richmond plantation to help prepare for a joyous holiday. But on December 18, 1859, he suffered a heart attack and was dead the next morning. For the last time fate had turned Lamar's expectations of happiness to tragedy.

The second Mrs. Lamar died October 6, 1891, and was buried beside her husband in Richmond, Texas.

4.

"The Last Leaf"

Mary Smith McCrory Jones

When President McKinley visited the city of Houston on May 3, 1901, he addressed the Daughters of the Republic of Texas. At the end of the President's speech, Governor Sayers of Texas gave his arm to an aged, feeble woman and introduced her to McKinley, who bowed to her with deep respect. She proudly presented to the President a small silk flag of the Lone Star State; its staff, she explained, was made of wood from the old Capitol Building at Columbia. The President was touched and complimented her on her long and distinguished life.

"Yes," she replied, "I am the last leaf on the tree."

The leaf would not fall for a half-dozen more years.

As the nineteenth century faded into history, Texas, along with the rest of the world, paused to look back in wonder at the changes the last few decades had brought. For many Texans the fragile woman on stage with President McKinley epitomized in her life span the sweep of Texas history

— from Mexican territory into an independent nation which had chosen to become a member of the United States, then into secession with the Confederacy, and finally back into the Union. Few living Texans had experienced as intimately as Mary Smith McCrory Jones, widow of Texas' last President, the drama and trauma of those years.

The pioneer fortitude and resolute calmness of Mary's personality were forged both by her heredity and by her environment. She was born in Lawrence County, Arkansas Territory, on July 24, 1818, to John McCutcheon Smith, a Virginian, and his wife, Sarah Pevehouse Smith. Her earliest memories were of her childhood in the blue mountains of Conway County, Arkansas, where the family moved when Mary was three.

Her childhood years from eight to fourteen were spent in the secure poverty of the family's small farm near Little Rock. When Mary was fourteen, her father died and her mother found it difficult to make the farm yield a living for herself and her five children. Attracted by notices offering free, fertile land in the Texas Brazos Valley, Sarah Smith sold the Arkansas farm, packed her household goods and five children into a wagon, and joined a wagon train bound for Texas territory in November, 1833.

The weather was unusually cold for November, and the caravan was drenched by heavy rains. When the group at last reached the Sabine River, they found it too swollen to ford. However, travelers in those days were used to obstacles. The men of the caravan hacked down wild mulberry trees and made a raft on which the twenty families and their possessions were precariously transported across the flooded river.

Once across, they still faced almost 300 miles of trackless territory to reach their promised land. And who knew what dangerous wild animals and even more dangerous wild Indians those miles contained?

Although their worst fears were not realized, the discomforts of the trip were harrowing enough, and it was a weary group of travelers who reached the farmlands near

Brazoria at the end of January, 1834.

Mary, only 15, was probably totally unaware that her future, in the person of Dr. Anson Jones, had arrived in Brazoria in October of 1833 — about a month before she and her family left their Arkansas home for Texas. Nor did the busy 36-year-old doctor have much time to notice a sunbonneted, barefoot teenager, because for the first time in his life his practice was bringing him a good return and requiring all of his attention.

The energetic Widow Smith set about making her farmland productive. Doing the heavy outside work herself, she turned the household management and the education of the four younger children over to Mary.

Not far from the Smiths' new home was the farm of John Woodruff, a widower with six children. The laws of propinquity and practicality took effect, and in October of 1835 Widow Smith and Widower Woodruff combined their households and made bond to be married by a priest, whenever one should appear. In the eyes of the community this constituted marriage. Four new children were eventually added to the eleven who already belonged to the couple, and Mary would find herself in charge of a covey of fifteen whole, step, and half brothers and sisters.

While this merger of households was taking place, the "war-dogs" were busy stirring up the sparks that would flame into revolution. As 1836 dawned, even conservative residents of Brazoria like Anson Jones had to admit that Texans must do whatever was necessary to win independence from the intolerable Mexican rule.

On a cold March morning in the village of Washington-on-the-Brazos, fifty-nine brave men signed a declaration of independence for Texas, knowing that they might well be signing their own death warrant. In Brazoria, Dr. Jones turned his practice over to his cousin, Ira Jones, and set off to join Houston's army as a private. The Smith-Woodruff family anxiously listened to reports that daily grew blacker. Mexican troops were approaching from the west, and the Texas government and army were retreating toward the east.

Panic followed the disasters of the Alamo and Goliad, and the family joined the thousands of retreating pioneers who fled for their lives with whatever possessions they could carry on wagons, oxcarts, sleds, horseback, or on foot.

The misery and desperation of the participants in the Runaway Scrape were to remain vividly in Mary Smith's mind. She recalled it later:

> We camped two weeks in pouring rain and then the sufferings of those without shelter were terrible. Many women and children walked. All along the route evidences of alarm and hasty flight were visible. In one place an open trunk from which some articles had been hastily snatched; in another a looking glass hung on a tree, showed where some toilette had been rudely interrupted.

Arriving at the San Jacinto River, the Brazoria fugitives found Santa Anna and his men camped at the river crossing. Not knowing what else to do, they stayed in the swamps adjacent to the battle ground and listened to the sounds of battle. Mary remembered, "We heard the cannon's roar with blanched cheeks and trembling nerves, for what fate awaited us in case of defeat?"

Fear turned to joy when the Battle of San Jacinto led to the war-ending victory for the rebels, and Mary heard clearly the triumphant yells of the Texans. In a few days her family was plodding slowly back to their farm near Brazoria.

But the war had changed things; the old way of life could not be recaptured. The Mexican General Urrea and his troops had plundered the deserted farms. So had looters, who took advantage of the hasty departure of the fleeing families to scavenge whatever moveables were left behind. In addition, strangers looking for cheap land and full of get-rich-quick schemes disturbed the peaceful community.

The Woodruffs decided to leave Brazoria and make a new beginning. In the fall of 1836 they moved to the site of the brand new city of Houston, which at the moment was only a scheme in the minds of two brothers named Allen. On the banks of Buffalo Bayou, the family camped with other pioneer settlers. There, under trees dripping Spanish moss, on benches carved by a whip saw, members of the tent city attended church services led by the Woodruffs.

The new house built by the Woodruffs was cramped and lacking in comfort, but so were most of the other homes in the new city, including the President's "mansion." In spite of the crowded conditions, John Woodruff decided to add to the family income by taking in boarders. Since Sarah was taking care of a newborn infant, most of the work of managing the household fell on Mary's shoulders. She was eighteen now and an attractive young woman. No picture of the young Mary has been found, but a description of her says:

> Her features are clearly defined, her dark eyes bright and steady, expressing at once sincerity and vivacity, her mouth and chin evince firmness tempered with sweetness. Her voice . . . soft and her enunciation peculiarly distinct. There is nothing vague or vacillating in appearance, manner, or character about her.

Somehow she managed to find time to take part in such social life as existed in the primitive city and to meet one of the most eligible bachelors — Hugh McCrory.

Hugh was an adventurous young Kentuckian who had come to Texas to help the Texans win their independence from Mexico. He arrived too late to join the fight, but decided to settle in the new capital of the infant nation. He helped establish the firm of Wright and McCrory and bought lots in the middle of Houston. Then he married Mary Smith.

Theirs was the first marriage license issued in Houston. The day before Mary's nineteenth birthday, they were married by a visiting Methodist minister.

Mary had good reason to take pride in her husband. He was a success as a business man and was also a popular young man about town. He was elected one of the first aldermen in the city. The young couple stayed in the Woodruff home while they collected household goods and made plans to build their own home. Their future looked bright.

Then suddenly Hugh became very ill. On September 13, 1837, less then two months after their marriage, Mary's husband was dead. Wearing her mother's black mourning clothes, Mary again took up her role as chief overseer of the large Woodruff brood and manager of the family boarding house. Less than two weeks after Hugh McCrory was buried in City Cemetery in Houston, Congressman Anson Jones of Brazoria came to stay at the Woodruffs'.

Life was hectic for the new statesman — so many problems needed to be solved all at the same time for the young country. And Jones was determined to do everything he could for Texas, where he had finally achieved a measure of success after a past filled with failures. The thirteenth of fourteen children, he had had a sketchy education, learning medicine under the apprentice method, and interrupting his studies to eke out a living selling drugs and teaching school. When he finally received the degree of doctor of medicine from the medical department of Jefferson College, Canonsburg, Pennsylvania, he opened an office in Philadelphia, but few patients came. In disgust, he decided to try business, and became a junior partner in a New Orleans mercantile establishment. Unfortunately, he had chosen an unscrupulous partner, with the result that the business soon failed, and Jones was left with debts he could not pay. He again tried medicine — with no better luck than before. The puritanical Jones was disturbed by his increasing penchant for gambling and drinking. When a friend, who was a ship captain, urged Jones to try his fortune in Texas and offered him cheap passage to Brazoria, the thirty-five year old doctor unenthusiastically accepted the offer that was to change his fortune and his destiny.

It is doubtful that Mary and Jones knew each other more than casually when she was a barefoot adolescent and he a well-to-do, dignified physician in Brazoria before the Revolution. Now Mary was a handsome, efficient young woman who could appreciate the gentleness and tact of Anson Jones that set him off from many of the rougher frontiersmen who gathered at the Woodruffs' table.

Gradually, as they spent more time together, they became

more attracted to each other, but both Jones and Mary respected her mourning and did not rush into marriage. However, before Congress adjourned, she had promised to marry him the next June.

Dr. Jones returned to Brazoria to prepare his cottage for his bride-to-be and to re-establish his medical practice. But fate in the shape of a letter from Sam Houston upset his plans. Reluctantly, Anson accepted the call to serve his country as Minister from the Republic of Texas to Washington, D.C. The wedding would have to be postponed.

Mary waited patiently during Anson's long stay in Washington. Fortunately, she was too far away to hear rumors that he had proposed to an attractive young lady named Jeanette and had been rejected. However, she must have wondered why his letters faded away until the two were completely out of touch.

When Anson Jones was dismissed as Minister by President Lamar, he returned to Texas determined to remain a private citizen. But his friends in Brazoria had other plans for him. Upon his arrival in Galveston, he was greeted with the announcement that he had been elected Senator from Brazoria to replace his old friend William Wharton, who had recently died.

While Anson was away in Washington, John Woodruff had again transplanted his family. Anticipating a new capital for Texas, he moved to Austin. This time he moved almost too soon; Austin was on the edge of civilized territory and Indian raids and scalping parties were a nightly hazard. Again the family lived in tents and ate buffalo meat.

By October a number of cabins had been built and the legislators were moving into town. Among them was the newly-elected Senator from Brazoria, Anson Jones. Apparently he was in no hurry to see his sometime fiancee. The first record of their meeting in Austin is his cryptic diary notation for November 1: "Attended sale of town lots. Saw Mary." However, by the end of the legislative session he was again courting Mary. Something — perhaps the marriages of his friends, the passing of his forty-second birthday, Mary's charms, or plain loneliness — had turned his thoughts toward matrimony again.

In March he moved into the Woodruffs' home as a boarder and began building a house for Mary on Pecan Street, on one of the lots he had shrewdly bought when he first arrived in Austin. The house itself cost a little more than $2300.

Although Mary had had three years to collect her trousseau, an oxcart had to be sent to Houston to bring back the final items necessary to complete it. On May 16, 1840, the County Clerk of Travis County sold the second marriage license issued in the county to Anson Jones and Mary McCrory. The next day Anson and Mary were married by Chief Justice J. W. Smith, whom Anson paid $50 for solemnizing the ceremony. Anson's comment on the event in his memoirs was, "On the 17th of May I was married, and spent the summer principally in making improvements on my place, or in doing nothing . . . ." The idle period did not last long, for he had his lots, loans, and medical practice to attend to. He and Mary also took part in what social life there was in the budding capital until she became pregnant.

Displeased with the quarreling in the new government, Anson Jones took his seat in the Fifth Congress determined to leave politics for good at the end of the session. He arranged to sell the house on Pecan Street (for a nice profit) and bought a $900 carriage to take Mary and their expected child back to Brazoria.

On the 26th of February, Dr. Jones delivered his wife of their first son, who was named Samuel Houston Jones. A month later the family left Austin in the new carriage for Brazoria. When they reached Brazoria County on April 11, Mary and the baby stayed with friends in Columbia while Jones went to Houston and Galveston to collect medical supplies and inevitably to talk politics. When Jones returned to Columbia, he assured Mary that he was through with politics and began to devote himself to his medical practice.

They had reckoned again without considering Sam Houston. No sooner had he been elected President than he wrote to

Jones urging him to serve as Secretary of State. Again Jones answered his old chief's call. There were rumors that Sam Houston, who had never liked Austin as a capital site, would soon move the seat of government again, so Mary agreed to stay in Brazoria County with the baby. Anson told her that having her in Brazoria would give him a good excuse to take "a leave of absence" from his often onerous duties.

However, during the four-month period between October, 1841, and February, 1842, the Secretary of State could not find time for a leave to visit his family. When Congress adjourned he and Mary looked forward to a reunion and time to take care of their private affairs. They planned to meet at Cousin Oliver Jones' plantation at Burleigh. Actually, Oliver was not related. "Cousin" was adopted by them both through a strong feeling of friendship.

Scarcely had Mary welcomed her absentee husband back when another call came from Sam Houston. There was threat of a Mexican invasion, and the President wanted his Secretary of State with him. Jones kissed Mary and Sam good-bye and followed the government to Galveston, where Houston had moved it to be handy to incoming news.

The Mexican "invasion" turned out to be only a raid, and Anson returned to Burleigh loaded with gifts of chinaware, jewelry, and toys for Mary and Sam. The Mexican issue was not solved, though, and the Secretary of State made several more trips at the call of President Houston as the Mexicans continued to raid, and the Texans to retaliate.

In October, answering yet another call from the President, he learned enroute to Houston that Sam Houston had packed up the government and moved it to Washington-on-the-Brazos. Disgusted, Jones turned around and went back to Mary "until the government took a notion to light."

A month later Mary settled at the Woodruffs' on Mill Creek in Washington County, while her husband went to Washington-on-the-Brazos and decided whether he wanted to be in or out of politics — again. After a few weeks, Jones had his fill of leading a bachelor's life and returned to Mill Creek to help Mary pack for a move to Washington.

The Brazos River chose this time to go on a rampage. Jones and Mary waited it out until the waters receded at the end of January. Then they moved to the Farquhars' farm, three miles from Washington, where they boarded temporarily for $75 a month. They both took advantage of the opportunity to study the techniques used by the Farquhars in managing their prosperous plantation, for Mary and Jones had a dream of owning a plantation of their own.

When Mary made trips into town, she sometimes stayed with Margaret Houston, who had married Sam Houston about the same time Mary was marrying Jones. Although their backgrounds were quite different, they had much in common. Each was well-educated for her time; each was the wife of an important Texas statesman; each had the same problems to cope with in making a life for herself and her family in the primitive capital of the new nation. And each was expecting another child.

When the President and the cabinet vacated Washington-on-the-Brazos for the summer, Anson had an unusual amount of time to devote to Sam and Mary, who was nearing the end of her pregnancy. Mary's mother, Sarah, came to help out and on September 4th a second son was born to Mary and Anson.

There was much discussion over choosing a name for the child. Mary had never liked naming their first child after Sam Houston; she had wanted to name him after his father. Finally it was agreed to name this son after the British charge d'affaires — Charles Elliot — who was a close friend of the family.

The Jones' plantation house (plus two log cabins) was being built three miles out of town by a Mr. J. Campbell for "200 acres of land, $200 in cash, and $100 in stock at market prices." They named it Barrington, after Anson's birthplace in Massachusetts.

Much of the supervision was left to Mary because two important matters claimed her husband's attention. First, there was his nomination and candidacy for the office of

President of the Republic; and second, there was the complicated problem of securing annexation of Texas to the United States or recognition of Texas' status as an independent nation by Mexico and leading European countries.

However, the cautious Secretary took time to keep his eye on family affairs. One hopeful entry in his diary reads, "Wed. Jan. 24th Mrs. J. says she will not want another dress until next fall." A careful line drawn through the notation proves again that Robert Burns was right about "the best laid plans of mice and men," especially when they concern a woman's wardrobe.

In March Jones explained his lack of action in connection with his candidacy to his campaign manager by pleading deep involvement in matters pertaining to annexation and the "illness of Mrs. Jones and the baby." She must have recovered in time for spring planting, for the plantation's garden flourished that summer under Mary's supervision, and the family enjoyed their own peas, Irish potatoes, beets, cucumbers, and squash.

Mary was expecting their third child when Texas elected Anson Jones its President on September 2, 1844 — ten years after he had arrived at Brazoria a penniless immigrant. Since her time was nearly due by Inaugural Day, December 9, she did not attend the inauguration or the ball that evening above Hatfield's saloon. Thus she missed seeing the highlight of the ball when a "very attractive, very popular, rather large" young woman began to sink through the floor boards to the saloon below. Sam Houston had had the stairs moved outside to stop lawmakers from slipping down to the saloon and carpenters had failed to nail down the boards that covered the empty stairwell. Fortunately, the lady was pulled to safety by some of the gentlemen present.

Mary's concern with her husband's worrisome political problems had made her anxious and unusually nervous during this pregnancy. Also, the burden of doing most of the planning for the plantation had taken its toll of her normally robust constitution. Anson dropped all official business to be with her during the birth of their daughter, Sarah, and remained close at Barrington until he felt reassured about her health.

Helplessly Mary watched as the steamroller of feeling for immediate annexation crushed the four years of delicate diplomacy her husband had practiced in order to give the people of Texas their choice of independence or annexation on the best possible terms. With him she suffered as the impatience of the people who misunderstood his motives led to threats of impeachment.

But a more personal tragedy claimed her attention just as annexation was accepted by the Senate. Her mother lay seriously ill in Houston. On July 4, Anson, Mary, the children, and a servant left Barrington for Houston. But courageous, enduring Sarah had fought her last fight. Nothing could be done for her, and they held her funeral on July 9. Sadly, Mary returned to Barrington, taking four of the young Woodruffs to stay there for a while.

Although affairs of state were at this time disappointing to the President and his wife, their personal affairs were in splendid condition. The slave quarters, stables, barn and Anson's office in the yard at Barrington were finished. The field hands were harvesting fodder, corn, and excellent Cuban tobacco. Many distinguished guests were entertained at Mary's table, including General Houston and foreign and domestic diplomats.

Mary stayed at Barrington to care for the household while her husband made his last official appearance and delivered a poignant speech surrendering "the power and authority which we have some time held" to the government of the United States. Perhaps only she understood fully the struggle that had led to his closing words, "The Republic of Texas is no more."

For the next decade Mary was the wife of a successful planter. Their cotton brought premium prices on the market, and their corn and tobacco, which Jones experimented with, were of fine quality. The vegetables and fruits raised at Barrington were also known for their excellence.

Jones's sister Mary had come to supervise the education of the children, who were handsome, healthy and now four in number. Cromwell Anson (named after Jones's famous ancestor, Oliver Cromwell) had been born at Barrington.

The Joneses were among the founders of St. Paul's Episcopal parish at Washington, which Bishop Freeman said was the handsomest church in Texas. Mary invited the Bishop to be their house guest at Barrington on the visit during which he confirmed her into the church and baptized the children. Anson agreed to their contributing heavily to the church and served as a warden, but did not become a communicant member.

The Joneses also helped found St. Paul's College at Anderson. At least the two older boys attended the college, and Mary carefully preserved their letters. In his first letter Charles said he was pleased with the school but added, "I want to see you and pa very much . . ." In other letters he spoke of being anxious to come home. But he must have gotten over his homesickness the next year because he reported to his mother "the place has improved a grate [sic] deal." Mary and Jones tried to raise money to keep the school going, but they failed and it closed its doors for lack of funds.

In spite of these activities, Mary watched her husband grow increasingly depressed and restless. Their old friends were far away from Washington; Anson had little to talk about with his German neighbors except crops and livestock. After having been one of the architects of a nation, being a planter and occasionally a physician did not satisfy Anson Jones as he had once dreamed it would. Life on the plantation was predictable and unexciting.

He turned to reading and a study of the carefully preserved documents of his years as a statesman. The more he studied the history he had helped make, the more he became convinced that Sam Houston was behind all his problems and had always been his enemy. He published bitter denunciations of Houston and changed the name of his first son from Samuel Houston to Samuel Edward.

One day in 1849 Mary was horrified to see the slaves carrying Jones into the house unconscious. He had been thrown from his horse, and his left arm and hand were left permanently withered and discolored. From that time on, he wore a glove on his left hand.

Mary had the satisfaction of seeing that the accident at least had the effect of pulling her husband out of his apathy. In search of medical aid he went back to Philadelphia and New York. He didn't find any help for his injury, but he became involved in industrial schemes and again became interested in Masonic and Odd Fellows activities. He also renewed his interest in Texas politics. He wrote jokingly to Mary about Senator Rusk, who was reported to be drinking heavily, "If he dies, please have me appointed to the Senate."

After Rusk committed suicide in July of 1857, Mary encouraged Anson when he responded with enthusiasm to the suggestions of a few friends that he might be elected Senator. Eagerly he went to Austin to await the election by the legislators "in case" they wanted to ask him any questions. But they ignored him completely, giving him not even one vote.

In vain Mary assured him that it didn't matter; they were much better off at Barrington than in Washington, D.C. But his reaction to the rebuff by the legislators was to give up all that he and Mary had created at Barrington and make a new beginning. Vaguely he talked of practicing medicine in Galveston. Sadly she watched as he quickly sold their plantation for only a part of its value.

Christmas, 1857, passed bleakly, and as the new year dawned, Mary watched with a sinking heart as the sixty-year-old Anson set off through rain and mud to find a new life for them. In a few days she received a letter that did little to relieve her mind about him. He told of renting a house in Galveston and reported that he had deposited the manuscript he had been writing for the past ten years with his bankers. Prophetically he added, "I merely mention this for your information, in case of any accident to myself."

From Galveston he went to Houston where a letter from

Mary reached him. He read it in his room in the Old Capitol Hotel, which was the same building where he had begun his public career. Mary wrote to "My Ever Dear Husband":

> I feel confident this little trip will be of service to you . . . being among more congenial spirits . . . will have a good affect at least I hope so . . . I trust we will soon be together again.

> Blot out the past, forget you were ever engaged in the promotion of the best interests of Texas and above all, try to forget her ingratitude toward you — I pray God you will do this . . .

> . . . I feel so anxious . . . .

Jones answered Mary's letter immediately saying, ". . . for fear of accident or delay I write you today," and mentioning friends he had met and plans he was considering. Before the letter reached her, he had put his pistol to his head and shot himself to death.

On January 15, W. D. Smith wrote to Mary telling her that Jones had invited him to his room on January 6, and that Jones, who appeared "quite unwell," had deposited with him $80, requesting that he pay Jones's bill and return the balance. Smith reported to her that her husband's bill at the Old Capitol was $39 and that the coroner's inquest had cost $21. He returned $20 to Mary plus her husband's trunk in which he put his wallet, watch, spectacles, cane, umbrella, and pistol.

Letters of condolence poured in on the new widow from friends and relatives. Some were from Masonic friends such as Col. Eben Allen of Galveston, who wrote that he was sending his wife to console Mary. He invited her and the children to stay with the Allens for as long as they liked, and begged her to call on him for any "service or counsel" in his power.

The person with whom Mary shared her deepest feelings was Anson's sister, Almira Blachford, in Missouri. There is a question as to whether they had met. Almira speaks of being "strangers personally" but of having a strong spiritual kinship with her sister-in-law. In their long letters to each other, they poured out their grief and shock at the death of Jones. On the first anniversary of his death, Almira wrote to Mary saying, "I am glad you can speak so freely." Mary and Almira comforted each other with strong religious sentiments.

With mixed emotions, Mary received the news that the same legislators who had refused to acknowledge her husband's existence in November, voted in January to create the county of Jones and declared, "The county seat thereof shall be called Anson."

Mary was only thirty-nine when Anson died, and she would live another full and active half century. First, there were the children to care for. Within a year after Jones' death, she had moved from the house he had rented in Galveston to a farm near Lynchburg.

Her training at Barrington and her natural ability as a businesswoman enabled her to run the farm skillfully and profitably. Her business letters are courteous, clear, and to the point. With some help from friends such as Dr. Ashbel Smith, she made "excellent trades" for land and slaves. Letters to Margaret Kemp, a friend who was a teacher, show her interest in trying to establish a school in the area near Lynchburg. Mary offered to arrange for a building and lodging if the teachers were willing to come there.

In late 1858 Mary fell victim to a yellow fever epidemic that swept over Galveston Island, but her strong constitution enabled her to survive the attack. "Cousin" Oliver Jones wrote to Mary from Burleigh advising her to get someone else to superintend the farm until she had fully recovered. On his letter she noted, "God bless such a friend," and kept right on with the work of overseeing the farm.

With the help of Dr. Ashbel Smith and Eben Allen, Mary arranged to have the bulky manuscript that Anson had written published by a New York publisher. She wrote a preface which said:

> As these pages will pass through the Press, so too, will mingled feelings of pain, pleasure, & regret, pass through my heart . . . In the high minded Author of the foregoing "Memoirs" etc, etc, may be traced the resignation of a heart too sensitive to battle success-

fully with the bitter Sorrows, with which his eventful and varied life was strewn.

... I only deem it, my most sacred duty - one I owe to his memory, to his orphan Children, to myself, and the Truth of History, to submit those "Records" to the Public. They must judge —

In 1904 she noted on her copy of the preface, "Was not used. Someone will be able to burn this — I can't."

In addition to taking care of her own family, Mary often took care of her neighbors. She had picked up nursing skills through necessity in her early life when she was in charge of the health as well as the education of her numerous sisters and brothers and also through living with a pioneer doctor. In her new setting she found that skill in much demand. Along the coast her neighbors called upon her regularly day or night until her medical calls were "as numerous as if she had been a regular practitioner."

Like other Texas women she endured the hardships and tragedy of the Civil War as best she could. Samuel Edward and Charles Elliot fought as members of Dr. Ashbel Smith's company in the Confederate army. Charles was mortally wounded at the battle of Shiloh. Samuel, after "meritorious service," returned home to study dentistry and was successful in that profession.

The youngest son, Cromwell Anson, became a lawyer and Judge of the County Court of Harris County. In 1888 Mary suffered another crushing sorrow when this son died suddenly at the peak of his career.

Sarah (nicknamed Sissy) married R. G. Ashe. In the latter years of her life Mary made her home with them in Houston.

During those years one of Mary's chief interests was the Daughters of the Republic of Texas. Quite appropriately, Mary was president of the group from the time of its organization in 1891 until her death in 1907. She was very active in the affairs of the association as long as she was able. Even after she was physically unable to attend meetings, members turned to her for advice and counsel. She was a link to Texas' past, and in her position she worked long and hard to gain from the State a more generous recognition of the services of the founders of the Republic and to bring about the purchase and preservation of various historic monuments.

In 1898 she sent an address to the Daughters to be read at the meeting commemorating the anniversary of the Battle of San Jacinto. In it she recalled her feelings as she huddled in the swamp listening to the sounds of the battle. She also spoke of the efforts of the society to purchase San Jacinto Battlefield, which she felt would soon be successful. She mentioned the frustrated attempts of the organization to preserve the first Capitol Building at Columbia and the successful plan to place a statue of Stephen F. Austin in Statuary Hall at Washington, D.C. Generously (in view of her husband's feelings), she recommended that a statue of Sam Houston also be placed in the Hall.

She asked for help in collecting books of "patriotic Texas songs and recitations" for use in schools, and for renewed efforts to locate and mark graves of Texas heroes. She concluded her address with a strong plea to the members to teach their offspring that the idea of dividing Texas was "nothing short of a crime" and urged them to send "echoing down the corridors of time our clarion cry of 'Texas one and indivisible.' "

The public recognition that had been denied her husband fell on Mary Jones as her life neared its end. Each birthday, illness, or public appearance was marked by long news stories detailing her part in Texas' early history. Her children and grandchildren gave her loving attention, and her last years were filled with marks of honor and respect.

When she died at 89 on the last day of 1907, her family was gathered at her bedside. The funeral service, under the auspices of the Christian Science Church, was held at the Ashe home, which overflowed with floral tributes. Representing the San Jacinto chapter of the Daughters of the Republic of Texas, whose members attended as a group, was a great floral star made of red, white, and blue blossoms. A drumbeat of rain accompanied the eulogies for the last First Lady of the

Republic of Texas. She had outlived most of the friends, most of the neighbors, and most of the acquaintances who had shared the terrors and the triumphs of the infant days of Texas. But many of those attending her last rites were the descendants of her fellow pioneers.

Through a steady downpour slowly rolled the hearse bearing her coffin, draped in the Lone Star flag. Despite the rain, a long line of carriages followed to Glenwood Cemetery in Houston. And a host of mourners gathered to watch as mounds of fragrant Texas flowers were heaped above the frail earthly remains of this woman who had helped pioneer Texas' independence.

In San Antonio the flag above the Alamo flew at half-mast. The last leaf had fallen.

5

First Lady, Extraordinary

Frances Cox Henderson

If the Women's Liberation Movement could choose a representative from the First Ladies of Texas, their choice would almost certainly be Frances Cox Henderson, wife of the first Governor of Texas. Brilliant mathematician, musician, linguist, author, church organizer, social worker, Biblical scholar, lawyer (in all but name), and international traveler (she crossed the ocean fifteen times), she was an extraordinary woman for her time, or for any time.

Her ancestry and excellent background account for some of her accomplishments. Frances Cox's maternal grandfather, General William Lyman, was an officer of the Connecticut forces in the Revolutionary War and a Consul General of the United States under Thomas Jefferson.

She was born in Philadelphia on July 21, 1820, to Martha Lyman Cox and John Cox. Mr. Cox was president of the Lehigh Coal and Navigation Company, which pioneered in developing the anthracite coal business in America. Later, he acted as the European agent for the company. In this capacity he traveled often to Europe and had an opportunity to observe that the educational system there was far superior to the system in America at that time — especially when it came to educating girls.

When Frances very early showed signs of her unusual intellect (she was reading the Bible at six), he decided to move his family to Switzerland.

A few years after the family had moved, Martha Cox died, and Mr. Cox decided to move his three children to Paris. Here Frances was to live until she married. French became the language used by the family, and soon she was reading the Bible in French. She and her sister Julia corresponded in French all of their lives.

John Cox's determination to give his children every advantage was a strong influence on Frances' life. A family story further illustrates this trait and his sense of humor. When his children were grown, and he had come back to Philadelphia, Julia, Frances' older sister, kept house for him and refused many offers of marriage. Afraid that she was remaining single on his account, Mr. Cox threatened to get married himself if she refused another suitable offer. Julia eventually married Thomas Biddle, a wealthy young stockbroker.

Frances took full advantage of the opportunities her father provided for her education. She proved to be brilliant in mathematics, often astounding experts by her ability to do problems in her head, which they found it necessary to work out with paper and pencil. She also learned to play the piano and harp expertly and excelled in swimming and horseback riding.

By the standards of any day, Frances' command of languages grew to be phenomenal. She learned to speak eighteen languages fluently, and knew seven others well. The best evidence of her linguistic ability is the book of short stories she compiled and translated into English from Swedish, Hungarian, Italian, Russian, Slovak, Spanish, Dutch, German, Polish, Czech, Flemish, Portuguese, French, Croatian, Danish, Serbian, Slovenian, Norwegian, and Roumanian. The stories she chose were ones she felt that

English-speaking people should know. The book was called *An
Epitome of Modern European Literature*, and was published
by J. B. Lippincott & Co. in 1881. Her genius for using her
opportunities to learn is illustrated in a story that tells of her
exchanging English lessons for Russian lessons with a priest
of the Orthodox Church.

While Frances was growing up in Europe and developing
her skills, a brilliant young North Carolinian, James Pinckney
Henderson, was maturing and passionately pursuing his
education. So industriously did the young man study in his
chosen profession of law that he received his license to
practice when he was barely twenty-one. However, he also
weakened his health by studying eighteen hours a day, and he
showed signs of incipient tuberculosis.

But frail health did not slow the handsome young lawyer
with the musical, hypnotic voice. His sympathies, like those of
many residents of the United States, became caught up in
Texas' struggle for independence. He went to Velasco, Texas,
in June of 1836, where President David Burnet commissioned
him a brigadier general. Returning to North Carolina,
Henderson used his persuasive speaking ability to raise a
company, which he sent to Texas at his own expense.

Henderson had planned to set up a law practice in Texas,
but his natural talents soon caused him to be drafted for
service to the young Republic. Sam Houston chose him to
serve as Attorney General, and when Stephen F. Austin died
in December of 1836, Houston appointed Henderson to
succeed Austin as Secretary of State.

When President Houston put his seal on the papers naming
James Pinckney Henderson as the Republic of Texas' Envoy
Extraordinary and Minister Plenipotentiary to the Court of
St. James in London and the Tuilleries in Paris, he also sealed
the fate of Frances Cox. The attraction between the two
intellectual young people seems to have been swift and
mutual. Shortly after they met, Henderson added a postscript
in a letter to President Lamar (who had been elected in the
meantime):

I could not very well tell you in the body of this letter which is semi-official, that I am about to be married, which you may be surprised to hear, considering my bad health. But do not be surprised that one of your constituents is to be married in Paris, because it is not to be a French or even an European lady, but one of our own country, a native of Philadelphia, who has been in Europe for eight or ten years.   J.P.H.

He was wrong, however, about being wed in Paris, where there was much red tape involved in the marriage of foreigners. The Church of England was (and always would be) the church to which Frances was devoted; therefore, they decided to cross the channel for their wedding. On October 30, 1839, in St. George's Chapel, Hanover Square, London, their vows were said before the highest level of British society, reputedly including members of the royal family. A picture of Frances in her wedding gown shows a slender young woman with chestnut hair and hazel eyes; the gown is satin, trimmed with narrow black lace and black velvet ribbon; and the headdress is of lace.

Henderson succeeded politically as well as romantically. He secured recognition of Texas as an independent country by France and negotiated a trade treaty, which was signed by France's foreign minister, by Henderson, and by King Louis Phillipe. The King made a speech on the occasion praising Henderson's diplomatic abilities. Possibly not even Frances knew what the long, strenuous hours of negotiating had cost him physically.

Texans were delighted with their minister. When he landed at Galveston with his bride in June, 1840, the city turned out to welcome them with a gala ball and banquet, where Henderson was hailed as another Franklin. Other cities wanted to honor them with similar affairs, but the young couple were anxious to begin their life in San Augustine, where he planned to set up a law practice.

For Frances, the cultural shock of changing from a life style that had included the literary salons and music rooms of Paris to that of the rough and ready Texas frontier must have been great. San Augustine, however, was one of the oldest and

most civilized towns in the Republic at that time, and although
her first home was a log house, they soon began building a
large two and one-half story home modeled after a Virginia
mansion.

The house had upper and lower galleries supported by
massive Greek columns. The half-story under the roof could be
converted into a ballroom or used as a playroom for children.
Downstairs, large folding doors between rooms allowed them
to be used for parties and for church services. A rambling
lawn shaded by large oak trees made a gracious setting for the
house that soon became a social center in East Texas.

But entertaining graciously was not enough to occupy the
energies of Frances Cox Henderson; she wanted to help her
husband in a more practical way. With his guidance she
studied law, and soon she was going beyond his teachings to
do the legal reading he did not have time for. In a short time,
she had mastered the fundamentals of law so well that
Henderson could safely trust her to take care of his practice
when he was away at court.

In 1845 Henderson was called upon to serve as a member of
the Constitutional Convention, and in 1846 he was elected the
first Governor of the new state of Texas. Austin was still on
the edge of the frontier, subject to Indian raids and vulnerable
to Mexican invasion. It was considered a place for men to
conduct the business of the government, but not a desirable
place to settle families. So Frances remained in San Augustine
during Henderson's term of office and served as First Lady
from their pleasant home. Her early training and talents
equipped her to fill her role with ease and grace.

Her education and linguistic ability were so superior to
those of most of the people of her time that she probably had
to be careful not to seem snobbish. Fortunately, tact and
genuine friendliness seem also to have been among her
talents, and references to her as the Governor's hostess
describe her as being hospitable and charming. Not only did
she entertain the statesmen, judges, lawyers, and
businessmen whom her husband brought home, she also gave

dinners, receptions, dances, and children's parties so that
every group in town shared in her hospitality. In addition, she
shared her talents by giving speech and music lessons to
children of the town.

Three daughters — Frances, Julia, and Martha — were born
to the Hendersons while they were in San Augustine. Julia
was apparently most like her mother. A newspaper article
tells of her introducing the "novelty of swimming to the fair
sex of the town." Also, like her mother, she learned to speak
several languages fluently and was an excellent horseback
rider.

Perhaps the most outstanding contribution Frances made to
East Texas during the nineteen years she lived there was to
single-handedly import the Episcopal Church to that area. She
began by bombarding the Secretary of the Committee on
Domestic Missions of the Episcopal Church in Philadelphia
with requests for a missionary to come to San Augustine. The
Committee was reluctant to send one of its shepherds into the
wilds of Texas; it probably doubted that there could be much
of a flock in such a wilderness. But the Committee under-
estimated the determination and organizing ability of Frances
Henderson. Her endless requests wore down their resistance,
and at last the Reverend Mr. Henry Sansom appeared in May,
1848, to be the minister for San Augustine and Nacogdoches.
Sadly, his first service was a funeral for his young son who
died the day after they arrived of scarlet fever contracted on
the trip to Texas.

Now that she had a minister Frances determined that the
little parish must have a suitable church. Using her
connections in Philadelphia, she secured plans for a Gothic
church with arched ceilings and stained glass windows — and
several hundred dollars toward a building fund. Energetically
she set about increasing the fund with donations from the local
populace until she had enough for the building and
furnishings, including a small reed organ. She and Henderson
gave generously to the church fund and also contributed linen
and silver. In addition. Frances organized a choir for the

church and played the organ for services.

Events in connection with Frances' church activities show the frontier spirit of cooperation that often existed among different denominations. While the Episcopal church was being built, the Methodist church members offered their building to the Reverend Mr. Sansom to use. And Frances worked with Mrs. Littleton Fowler, wife of the Methodist minister, and Miss Fannie Rankin, a staunch Presbyterian, to keep a Sunday School flourishing in San Augustine.

Although she was in earnest about her church work, Frances revealed her sense of humor when she included in her *Ms Sketch of Christ Church, San Augustine* a quotation from one of her fellow townsmen, who was amazed by the use of the prayer book in the church service. "Come on," he said to some friends, "let's go up to the Episcopal Church and hear the parson read his prayers out of a book and his wife jaw back at him."

In 1851, Mr. Sansom left to take charge of another church and was replaced by the Reverend Mr. Elisha Downing, who was full of good intentions but sadly lacking in adaptability to rural life. One morning he examined the vegetable garden of his landlady and decided that her beans were growing all wrong. Carefully he turned each plant upside down so that the beans were under the ground — like the potato plants he was evidently familiar with. If he handled his parishoners as ineptly, it's not hard to understand why they decided not to renew their agreement to support him.

Again Frances sent pleas to the Committee on Missions in Philadelphia, but the members were still dubious about the Texas mission and failed to send a replacement. Undaunted, Frances obtained a letter from her vestrymen granting her power to call a minister to fill the parish vacancy. She proceeded to Philadelphia and shocked the Bishop almost out of his senses by producing her credentials and insisting on being allowed to address the clergy of the diocese — a thing no female had ever done. Again through courage and action she won her goal, and a new minister was sent to East Texas.

While the Reverend Mr. Downing was still the minister in San Augustine, Frances had traveled with him to Rusk and Palestine to help establish Episcopal parishes at those towns, taking her little daughters along with her. Since the Nacogdoches parish was formed in conjunction with the one she established at San Augustine, she also deserves credit for it. And, as we will see, she helped found a church in Marshall. Truly, Frances Henderson left her imprint on the religious life of East Texas.

In the meantime, while Frances kept busy with the children, church work, and community affairs, James Henderson was struggling with the complicated affairs of the new state. The treasury, as usual, was not only bare but deeply in debt; the court system badly needed improvement; a public school system needed to be established; and Indian raids continued to plague the settlers. But more immediate was the fact that Mexico was putting into effect her threat of war in retaliation for the annexation of Texas by the United States. Governor Henderson was appointed a major general in command of Texas Volunteers. Also serving with the Volunteers were two future Governors of Texas — Edward Clark and George T. Wood.

Turning the reins of government over to Lieutenant Governor A. C. Horton, Henderson took direct command of a Ranger unit. Although he had recently risen from a sick bed, he played an active and courageous part in the Battle of Monterrey. For his services in the war the United States awarded him a gold-hilted sword. This sword was cherished by Frances, and after her husband's death was passed down to the oldest son of their oldest daughter, according to her husband's wishes.

Frances and her husband were happy when his term came to an end in December of 1847; they thought he was "retiring" from politics at thirty-one. And for ten relatively peaceful years they did pursue the lives of private citizens. In spite of Henderson's fragile health, they were busy, fruitful years. Both Frances and Henderson took an active part in conducting

his law practice, in community and church affairs, in rearing
their children, and in the social life of the community. In 1856,
perhaps seeking a less active life because of his health, they
moved to Marshall. There Frances found a struggling
Episcopal parish, and again she took the initiative — raising
funds, building up the congregation, and eventually directing
the building of Trinity Church.

James Henderson was not to be allowed to end his days in
political retirement. When his old friend and law partner,
Thomas J. Rusk, one of Texas' first United States senators,
committed suicide in 1857, Henderson was elected to fill the
vacant seat. The strain of the move and the difficult trip to
Washington, D.C., proved too much for his waning strength.
Frances watched over him anxiously as he became
progressively weaker and finally died on June 4, 1858, at the
age of fifty. A state funeral was held for Henderson in the U.S.
Senate chamber of the Capitol. The President of the United
States attended and eulogies for the dedicated statesman
were given by Sam Houston and Jefferson Davis, among
others.

For almost twenty years Frances had shared her husband's
service to his chosen state. Along with him she had given
generously of her wealth, talent, time, and energy to promote
the welfare of her community. Now the primary concern of the
new widow was to do the best thing for her daughters. Civil
war loomed ominously and her sympathies were divided:
Philadelphia was the place of her birth and many of her
kinsfolk still lived there, but Texas was her adopted home and
most of her friends lived there. The deciding factor, however,
in her removal from Texas was probably her desire to give her
daughters the best possible educational advantages. Like her
father, she felt that Europe offered better opportunities than
America. If girls weren't permitted to enroll in the larger
universities there, at least there were plenty of excellent
private schools they could attend. With income from sales of
her Texas properties she could do as she chose!

Consequently, soon after her husband's death Frances took

her three daughters to live in Europe. For the next few years they spent the spring and summer months traveling extensively through Italy, Switzerland, Germany, France, Austria, in the Mediterranean area, to the island of Sardinia, and to other places. In the fall and winter months the family settled down, usually in Germany, and the girls attended school.

In a personal diary that Frances kept between 1860 and 1863, she showed her continued devotion to "the English Church." Almost every Sunday the entry in the diary is a report of a sermon she heard. On February 28, 1860, she took a guided tour of some Italian catacombs and noted:

> I believe these are the only three story catacombs known. There is a very small stone pillar to which it is said the ancient martyrs were fastened to be tortured. The guides assured me that I greatly resembled the wife of Leopold Prince of Salerno and Uncle of the late King. They said I had the same dignity of deportment. I did not know which to do — feel flattered by resembling an archduchess or hurt by reminding them of so old a lady as she must now be.

At the age of eighteen Martha died in Schwalbach, Germany. The grief-stricken mother built a permanent memorial for her young daughter in the form of a chapel.

While the girls were in school, Frances followed her own intellectual pursuits. One diary entry made in Geneva comments:

> I began to take Swedish lessons as, though I could read the language, I had never heard it spoken. . . . I have amused myself writing a german novel. . . . Besides I went to the music store and got new music to read.

Numerous Shakespearean dramas which she and the girls attended are commented on, and at the back of the diary is a long list of musical performances that she attended.

Frances' namesake and oldest daughter, Fanny, became a social belle, well-known in the capitals of several European countries. According to various diary entries, the family was on a familiar, friendly basis with royalty in a number of European countries. Frances Henderson would have been respected as the widow of a diplomat, but she no doubt also won friends through her linguistic ability and her personality.

Fanny acquired a title when she married Reichsfreiherr Clemens von Presuschen von und zu Liebenstein (Baron of the Holy Roman Empire), who fought in the army of Emperor Franz Joseph of Austria. Fanny never returned to America after she left it at the age of fourteen, and her descendants are still living in Europe.

Julia was also married in Europe — to an American, Edward White Adams of Louisiana, who had a sugar plantation there. He was in Europe engaged in the production of wine, but Frances didn't approve of his wine-making business and persuaded him to give it up and return to his Louisiana plantation.

After the marriages of her children, Frances Henderson returned to the United States and lived with Julia and Edward for the last sixteen years of her life. Her mind and energy were unimpaired to the day of her death. While she was staying at the Adams' Louisiana plantation, she became interested in the plight of the Negroes, who had so recently won their freedom from slavery. The result of her interest was a study of one black woman's development which resulted in a book that she called *Priscilla Baker: Freed Woman.* She also, without being militant about it, was a strong supporter of women's suffrage.

When Edward became a stock broker in New York City, he and Julia bought a home on High Street in East Orange, New Jersey. Frances moved with them and continued to play a vigorous role in civic affairs. She was President of the Bureau of Associated Charities for many years. She originated the House of the Good Shepherd for aged and infirm women, and a laundry for older women capable of working. She also was active in the work of the East Orange Free Library and in religious work in St. Mark's Church.

Early on the morning of January 25, 1897, she fell down a flight of stairs in her daughter's home and ruptured blood vessels in her head. That same evening she died. After funeral services in her beloved Episcopal church, she was buried in

Rosedale Cemetery in East Orange.

Although in connection with most of Frances Cox Henderson's work we have no description of her beyond the cold facts of her accomplishments, it is clear that she was a woman of rare intellect, vigor, and humanitarian instincts. The first First Lady of a Governor of Texas left behind an exceptional record of achievement.

6

A Generous Heart

Martha Evans Gindrat Wood

On February 6, 1839, Captain John Steib, owner of the sloop *Marshall*, signed a charter agreement with one George T. Wood to "sail with the first fair wind and weather that shall happen after the sixteenth day of the present month . . . from Apalachicola to Galveston in Texas . . . with family consisting of man and wife and four children, and such wares, chattels, or merchandise as said George T. Wood may load on the said sloop." The family was to have the cabin, and they and the slaves, about thirty, were to be furnished transportation, food and other necessities for the total sum of $650.00.

In addition to the family members mentioned in the charter, also on board were George Wood's widowed mother and a freed slave, Uncle Tony, for whom the Woods acted as guardians (and who was never known to do any work other than fishing during his 107 years). Three of the children mentioned — David, Henry, and Elizabeth Gindrat — belonged to Martha through her first marriage. The fourth child, little Martha Anne Wood, had been born in Cuthbert, Georgia, almost a year after the wedding of George Wood and Martha Gindrat at her home in Milledgeville.

When Martha met George she was a vivacious twenty-eight-year-old widow, and he was a tall, handsome forty-two-year-old successful merchant and a hero who had won fame in the Battle of Horse Shoe Bend in the Indian Creek War. He was also a member of the House of Representatives for the State of Georgia. Martha was still living in the large family home built on land that one of her ancestors received under a grant from General James E. Oglethorpe, the famous colonizer. The thirty slaves transported to Texas on the *Marshall* were hers, as was a large part of the baggage, including a number of mulberry trees. She was a good businesswoman and intended to continue the silk culture at which she had become an expert, having sold her woven silk material for ten dollars a yard.

Exactly why the Woods decided to leave their successful mercantile business in Cuthbert and move their family and worldly goods to the primitive new Republic of Texas is not known. Perhaps it was a desire for adventure and new opportunities, and perhaps it had something to do with the fact that Wood had met and admired Sam Houston at the Battle of Horse Shoe Bend.

At any rate, as they neared Texas shores the Gulf of Mexico was in its usual turbulent state. A gale which blew them off course added to the miseries of the seasick travelers. They were happy to reach Galveston, although it must have seemed tiny to them. Aside from the hotel where sailors gathered to get their grog, it consisted of some scattered farm houses. Spanish gold pieces were occasionally picked up out of the sand, perhaps dropped there by Jean Lafitte and his buccaneers, who had recently headquartered on the island.

Martha stayed in Galveston with the children and some of the slaves while Wood set out with other slaves to explore the Brazos, Colorado, and Trinity Rivers in search of a home site. He finally decided on a spot on the Trinity in the area that is now Pointblank (Point Blank then) in San Jacinto County, where the soil was rich and the forest primeval. Here the Woods and their slaves set about to build a plantation. Logs were carefully hand hewn and put together with wooden pins to construct a sturdy main house that would last until it would be torn down in 1916. Numerous other log cabins dotted the farm land — to be used for the slaves, for guests, for storage purposes. Large areas were cleared and crops planted, along with Martha's cherished mulberry trees (which thrived in the alien soil). A landing was built, as was the custom with river planters. Wood's Landing would become a frequent stop for steamboats, which would unload supplies and foodstuffs, bring precious letters and newspapers to the isolated settlers, and take on loads of cotton.

After a year of hard work, the plantation was in good running shape and Wood began to get interested in other things. He studied law briefly in Houston and advertised in the *Houston Telegraph and Texas Register* on December 30, 1840, that he would practice law in the district courts of the counties of Liberty and Montgomery. (San Jacinto County was then a part of Liberty County.)

Wood had a warm, outgoing nature and made friends easily. He soon became a popular and well-known figure and in 1841 was elected to represent Liberty County in the Sixth Congress of the Republic of Texas. Martha stayed at home to manage the plantation and to take care of the children. Like Sam Houston, Wood seems to have found a mule better transportation than a horse, for he traveled between the capital and Point Blank on his faithful mule Pantellete. At night with the reins tied to his feet and his saddle for a pillow, he slept under the stars. He also saved on laundry, if the rumor is true that he was the only Texas governor never to wear socks.

On January 5, 1843, another daughter, Mary, was added to the family. Sometime during those early years, Martha, the baby born to the Woods in Georgia, had died. For two years after the Sixth Congress adjourned, Martha had her husband home to help with the plantation and with the children. The Woods were relaxed, loving parents and many years later their children remembered the happy times on the plantation.

Everyone was permitted and encouraged to keep as many dogs, cats, horses, and other pets as they wanted. The food was good and plentiful; deer, turkey, and bear were common and often appeared on Martha's table. The hospitality of the Woods was lavish and boundless. In later years Mary said that she could never remember a meal "not shared with guests."

Especially pleasing to Martha was the close relationship that developed between her husband and his stepson, David Gindrat. George Wood was a devoted and indulgent father to all of the children, but David was the one he called his "closest friend and counselor."

In 1845 Wood was once again called to Austin, this time to serve as a member of the Annexation Convention. After the convention, Wood was elected to the Texas Senate. He barely had time to become acquainted with his new son, George Tyler Wood, Jr., born on January 25, 1846, before he had to leave to take his place in the Senate in mid-February. Although neither Wood nor Martha would live to know it, this son would become a victim of the Civil War, dying of typhoid fever contracted while serving in the Confederate Army.

The year 1846 was to be a memorable one for the Woods. After he had successfully introduced a bill into the Senate for the creation of Tyler County, the people of the county named its county seat Woodville to honor him.

When the Mexican War was activated by the annexation of Texas, Martha probably knew that her husband would not be able to keep out of it. He resigned from the Senate to become colonel of the Second Regiment Texas Mounted Volunteers, and commanded the regiment from July to October. Often he fought near Colonel Jefferson Davis and formed a lifelong friendship with him. Wood fought with outstanding bravery in the Battle of Monterrey, in which Governor James Henderson also took part. Wood's men declared him a hero, but there are conflicting stories about just what part each man played in the fight.

Some authorities feel that the fact Henderson failed to give Wood credit for his action in the Battle of Monterrey may have

influenced Wood's election as governor in 1847 when the
people — particularly soldiers — reacted against the "unfair"
treatment of their hero. Whether this was the deciding factor
or not, Wood was elected and took up quarters in the famous
Bullock Hotel in Austin for his term, the old "President's
home" having burned down some time before.

Aside from one trip to Austin, Martha stayed home to take
care of the plantation and the five children. As a result of her
efficiency and encouragement, the governor was free to
devote his time and attention to the serious problems that
faced his administration. Among these problems were the
public debt, frontier defense, the continuing Indian problem,
and the boundary dispute with New Mexico.

Wood insisted that the state debt be paid, saying, "The
honor of the state must stand without a blemish." He
demanded Texas Rangers for frontier defense, sending his
message through Senator Sam Houston, who told the Federal
government, "Give us 1000 Rangers and we will be
responsible for the defense of our frontier." The governor
shared the popular thinking of Texans of his time that the only
good Indian was a dead one, and he threatened that if the
Federal government couldn't handle the problem, Texas could
and would. He was also outspoken in his opinion about the
boundary dispute with New Mexico, involving 98,000 square
miles. He promised that Texans would defend their right to
every mile of it; however, his term expired before he could
carry out his threat.

The records show that Wood was frequently absent from
Austin during his term as governor, which is not surprising
considering the length of a trip between Point Blank and
Austin by mule or horseback — and considering the great love
Wood had for his farm and family. His saddlebags were always
bulging with gifts when he arrived at the plantation, and he
never failed to stop at the big gate that was the entranceway
to distribute candy to the children — black and white — who
came running to greet him. Martha set the cooks to preparing
extra food as soon as he arrived, for she knew there would be a

continuous stream of guests as long as he was home.

One of these guests was Sam Houston, who was living at Raven Hill, only about five miles from the Woods' plantation. The two men were close personal friends, although at times they disagreed on political issues. Houston actually worked behind the scenes to help defeat Wood in his bid for re-election in 1849. Ironically, many people voted against Wood because he was known as a "Houston man" and the anti-Houston forces were growing strong.

After his defeat, Wood tried once again unsuccessfully for the governorship in 1855. If the voters did not welcome him, his family and friends did, and the eight years of his retirement were happy ones for him and Martha. The plantation overflowed with animals, children, and the never-ending stream of guests who traveled long distances to enjoy Wood's congenial company and Martha's lavish hospitality. And there were the arrivals of the steamboats to look forward to, with the steamboat officers to entertain and the fun of being entertained by them. One day, fifteen years after Martha had left Georgia with her new husband, a steamboat captain delivered to her an heirloom Bible that she had left behind among other treasures to be forwarded when an opportunity arose.

Remembering his earlier calling, Wood again became involved in the mercantile business, commuting from the plantation to Galveston to help run the firm of Wood & Powers. It eventually grew to be an important and successful company. But for his family, Wood's trips to Galveston meant a joyful reunion when he returned bringing all kinds of luxuries in the way of clothes and food and bright, blooming plants for Martha and the girls.

In addition to feeding and entertaining their friends, Martha and Wood shared their prosperity in other ways. When the field workers reached the edge of the Woods' fields adjoining a poorer neighbor's, they were instructed to cultivate his field too. In 1858 the Woods began to build a larger house on a hill two miles from the Trinity River. Asked why they were building so large a house, they answered that it was for their friends.

Before the house was completed, Wood became ill and died in September of 1859. Martha was left with a fairly large estate, including several thousand acres of land plus a lot in Austin, numerous slaves, and a half interest in the company of Wood & Powers. She continued to care for Wood's aged mother, who survived him a year, and for her five children.

In January, 1861, she died and was buried beside her husband on their beloved plantation. For over fifty years their graves were unmarked and almost lost to memory and to the tall pines that surrounded them. Finally, in 1911 a marker of Texas granite was erected at their resting place. The naming of Wood County after Texas' second Governor is an additional memorial to the couple from Georgia who adopted the new state as their own and helped to settle it.

7.

A Connecticut Yankee in Texas

Lucadia Christiana Niles Pease

"We have just killed six hogs and I am deep in the business of lard making and curing of hams. We shall put up twelve hogs this winter and hope to have enough — last year they had to buy pork while I was away —"

So wrote the First Lady of Texas on February 10, 1857, to her sister in Connecticut. The letter was datelined Austin and written from the elegant new Governor's Mansion, of which Lucadia Niles Pease was the first mistress. In the same letter she reported having planted peas, Irish potatoes, and "most of the early vegetables."

Like Margaret Houston, Lucadia Pease always had slaves or servants to help with her domestic duties, but never for a minute did she consider turning the management of her household over to them as Margaret gladly did. Lucadia's yankee know-how, thriftiness, and capacity for physical labor never ceased to amaze her easy-going southern friends. But if she was imbued with the Puritan work ethic, she lacked their dourness of spirit, for she was to become the social leader of Austin, noted for her fun-loving nature and ingenuity in entertaining.

Lucadia Christiana Niles was born in Poquonock, Connecticut, in 1813 to Richard and Christiana Griswold Niles. With her three sisters she enjoyed a happy childhood in the heart of the large, affectionate Niles family. The Niles girls received a better-than-average education for their time, attending Hartford Female Seminary, where the principal was the sister of Henry Ward Beecher. While at this school, Lucadia became acquainted with a distant cousin, Elisha Marshall Pease, who was a clerk in the post office at Hartford.

Lucadia grew to be an attractive, dark-haired, dark-eyed young woman with a quick, inquisitive mind. For a few years she was a governess to a family on a Virginia plantation. After her father died, her uncle, John Milton Niles, helped Mrs. Niles look after the children, and they became very fond of him. When he became a United States Senator and later Postmaster General of the United States, Lucadia, along with other members of the family, visited him in Washington, D.C., where she observed with great interest the nation's capital and the many important people she met there. She attended President Polk's inauguration, which she described as "wild and wooly."

In the meantime, Marshall Pease had also been doing quite a bit of traveling and observing. In New Orleans he heard exciting stories about Texas, and in 1835 he came to Mina (now Bastrop) to study law. He was soon a strong supporter of Texas' independence movement and joined the Texans at Gonzales, where he fought in the opening round of the Texas Revolution. In the following years he held a number of positions in the Texas government and is credited with writing many of the laws that came into being during the early days of the Republic. He established a successful law firm in the town of Brazoria. At last he felt "settled" and ready to take a wife; and he had her picked out.

Over the years, Lucadia and Marshall had kept in touch through his infrequent visits to Connecticut and through the erratic mail service between that state and Texas. Finally, on August 22, 1850, they were married in Poquonock. Although

Lucadia was thirty-seven and had lived away from her home for short periods of time, the prospect of the long trip to her Texas home in Brazoria and the inevitable lengthy separation before she would see again any members of her family was frightening. Marshall's sister, Carrie Pease, went along on the trip with them to give Lucadia a female companion.

During the trip they shopped for supplies for their home as the opportunity arose. In New York they purchased furniture and silverware; in New Orleans they bought a long list of groceries and medical supplies; and in Galveston they bought a fireplace outfit, including fenders and tongs.

Lucadia wrote home to her mother and sisters long, detailed letters of the trip, describing the weather, Niagara Falls, cotton and cane fields, towns along the Mississippi, the French Catholic cemeteries in New Orleans, their fellow travelers and everything else that caught her observant eye. She was surprised to find four churches in Galveston, "considering the first house was built here only fourteen years ago." Lucadia and Carrie remained in Galveston with some friends of Pease while he attended to urgent business. The trip to Brazoria was made by carriage along the beaches of the Gulf of Mexico to Velasco and then through the prairie to Brazoria. There was a delay in getting aboard the ferry to the mainland from Galveston Island, and Lucadia and Carrie clung to each other in terror as the carriage hurtled through the night, often up to its hubs in the waters of the Gulf, which were at high tide.

After the long journey of almost two months, Lucadia was glad to arrive at her Texas home, even though it was only a plain four-room dwelling in a still relatively primitive frontier town. Energetically she set about making it attractive with her New York furniture and silverware. But the yard was in terrible shape, as were most yards in the town, because of a shortage of labor. Since her husband was busy catching up with affairs connected with his law practice, she proceeded to cut the weeds and grass and to cultivate the flower beds herself, working hard to make them resemble the well-kept New England beds she was familiar with. The southern ladies

of Brazoria watched with amused amazement the activity of
their little yankee neighbor, who stubbornly planted the
northern bulbs, vines, clippings, and cuttings in soil that
frequently refused to nourish these foreign bodies.

Carrie was quite popular with the bachelors and widowers
of the area, but entertainments were few and consisted mostly
of "calls" made by the inhabitants on one another. One of
Carrie's beaus, and a frequent caller, was the ubiquitous Dr.
Ashbel Smith, who played an important role in Texas'
formative years as a republic and as a state.

There was a "preaching" by the Methodists once a month
and Catholic mass occasionally. Camp meetings were exciting
events, and the Peases sometimes drove a long distance to
spend a couple of days at one. Sundays were usually very
quiet, even dull, for the white folk, for it was not considered
proper to do any work or to have any kind of lively entertainment on this day. For the Negro slaves, however, Sunday was
the high point of the week, the day when families that might
be scattered among several homes or farms dressed up in
their best clothes and visited each other.

Lucadia found her slaves to be a mixed blessing. Emily
cooked and did general housework, Mary waited on the table
and helped Emily, and big Sam worked in the garden. Lucadia
felt they needed constant supervision to do things "right," and
she never learned to relax and overlook things undone or not
done to her standards. Consequently, she often did much of
their work herself. Too, they had to be cared for almost like
children — food and clothing and living quarters had to be
provided for them, and they had to be looked after when they
were sick — as they frequently were — with a wide variety of
ailments they called the "miseries." She reported to her
mother that she treated most of their complaints "very
successfully" with ginger and molasses.

Pease realized how homesick Lucadia often was for New
England and her family, and he planned for them to make a
trip back in the summer of 1851. But plans were cancelled
when it was discovered that Lucadia was pregnant. The baby,

a girl, was born two months prematurely and was at first sickly. Pease, who had been away from home campaigning for Governor at the time of her birth, was so distressed over Lucadia's and the baby's health that he withdrew from the contest. But before long Lucadia was describing Baby Carrie in her letters home as "fat," with a mass of pretty hair and a "bright, wise face."

In the summer of 1852 they made the postponed trip to Poquonock, where Carrie was duly admired by all of her relatives. Juliet Niles, Lucadia's older sister, made the trip back to Texas with the Peases for a visit. (Carrie Pease had returned to her home.) Although Brazoria was considered a thriving frontier town and port by Texans, Juliet was less than enchanted with it. She wrote to another of their sisters, Augusta:

> ... I shall go home as soon as I can in the spring ... We do not go out much & live as quiet as snails, that is I do. L had enough to busy herself superentending [*sic*] her housekeeping, which is no slight matter I assure you, being four of the niggers to keep in slow motion .... the mud is a great drawback on these pleasant days — & as I fear to get stuck beyound the power of extrication, & maybe take root & grow in this boasted productive soil, a "consummation" *not* devoutly to be wished — I do not venture out much.

One of the first carriages in Brazoria belonged to Lucadia, and she was generous enough to lend it to her friends for special occasions. When it rained, as it often did in South Texas, and streets became ribbons of mud, all of the ladies rode horseback.

In spite of her sharp comments about the environment and her sweeping indictments of "shiftless" southerners, Juliet was a good companion for Lucadia and a great help when there was sickness or any other kind of emergency. After the birth of a second daughter, Julia Maria, on March 14, 1853, Lucadia was confined to her bed for two weeks. Juliet proved indispensable because there was no nurse to be hired in the vicinity.

That year Pease's friends urged him to run for Governor, and Lucadia, feeling that he had withdrawn from the previous race on her account, added her encouragement to theirs. It was arranged that Lucadia and Juliet would take the two children to Connecticut for a visit so they would not have to spend the summer alone while Pease was away from home campaigning. During this long separation, letters, which were often three or four weeks old, were their only means of communication. These letters reveal that they were a loving, close, and extremely devoted family. They became anxious when each mail did not bring a letter; often they dreamed of each other; constantly they worried over the health of the other and of the children; each letter contained assurances of love, affection, devotion and a longing to be together again. Pease censured himself "for having left my happy home to run after such a bubble as the office of Governor."

At this time their plans for the future were uncertain. They owned some acres in Brazoria that they called the "place," where they had a vegetable garden and where they had planned to build a larger home. But in many ways Lucadia liked Galveston better than Brazoria, and they talked of moving there; of course, if Pease won the election, their home for the next two years would be Austin. Just in case they did build, Lucadia consulted with her relatives and friends about house plans, and collected information on building techniques, including how to oil bricks and how to mix wall paint.

When Lucadia wrote to Pease that Juliet was suffering from malarial chills and fever, he immediately wrote back detailed instructions for her treatment, which consisted mostly of eating lightly and taking quinine in Madeira wine or French brandy. Whether or not she followed his directions, Juliet continued to have recurrences of malaria for a long time, and her misery during these attacks did not improve her opinion of Texas.

The election took place on August 1, but it was weeks before a complete tally of the votes showed Pease to be the winner. A yellow fever epidemic raged at New Orleans and Galveston during August and September of 1853, and Pease wrote to Lucadia repeatedly warning her not to begin the trip home until there had been several "hard frosts" in these places, after which it would be considered safe to pass through them. On the twenty-fifth of October, Lucadia started for Texas with a nurse named Jane whom she had hired to help with the children. She soon found she had made a mistake; she could not trust the children with Jane, who drank brandy and camphor whenever she could get it and proved such a great annoyance that Lucadia could hardly wait to send her packing back to New York.

Most of the Peases' carefully selected furniture had to be sold. It was not practical to transport it overland from Brazoria to Austin by ox cart. Therefore they arrived in the capital city with only their small possessions and the family silver. They boarded with a Mrs. Susan Ward, wife of Thomas William (Peg Leg) Ward, who was serving as United States Consul in Panama.

Lucadia was pleased with the accommodations at Mrs. Ward's and with the Austin area in general. She wrote to Juliet:

> ... I often wish you were here at breakfast that you might disclaim what you used to say, that you had never seen a good beef steak in Texas, for I never ate anywhere better broiled & buttered steaks than we have daily, nor better light bread. Then we have mince pies and crullers and many northern dishes ....

She enjoyed daily drives in the hills around Austin, describing it as being "more like New England than any other place I have seen in Texas." It struck her "oddly" that the women dressed extravagantly in brocade silks, velvets, and satins although they lived in crude log houses. For both of her husband's inaugural balls she wore a plain black silk that she felt was good enough "to answer for all purposes," including weddings, funerals, and balls.

When Mrs. Ward moved from Austin to be nearer her family, the Peases continued to rent her house and bought some of her furniture. Lucadia had big Sam plant a garden in which they raised sweet corn, tomatoes, and other "common garden vegetables." She was rather pleased that her third pregnancy allowed her to forego some of the ritualistic calling that was the foundation of social life in Austin.

She found the heat enervating in the summer months and missed the Gulf breeze that had made hot weather tolerable in Brazoria. But she didn't miss the "stinging creatures" that had been so abundant there — mosquitoes, flies, fleas, and red bugs. In her letters home, she reassured her mother about the dangers of Indian attacks, which were sometimes described graphically in the New England papers. However, she told Juliet about entertaining a Mrs. Wilson, who had been captured the previous fall by Comanches and treated in the most "inhuman" manner before she escaped and was rescued by a group of Mexicans.

On November 28, 1854, Lucadia gave birth to a third daughter, weighing ten pounds. After months of indecision, she was finally named Anne. The Peases were anxious to have a home of their own for their growing family and bought some lots in Austin in the hilly section, which they referred to as the "new place." But again their planning had to depend on the outcome of other events. The Sixth Legislature voted to erect in Austin "a suitable residence and out-buildings for the Governor of the State," and Pease was appointed one of the three commissioners who were to furnish a plan and superintend the erection of such a building. They were allowed $14,500 for the buildings, plus $2,500 for the furnishings. The lowest bid (by $90) was submitted by Abner Hugh Cook, a pioneer architect-contractor of Austin. Slaves made bricks on the banks of the Colorado, and huge pine logs were hauled from Bastrop to begin construction. Lucadia was not satisfied with the location chosen for the Governor's Mansion, and there is good evidence to suggest that she chose the present site, diagonally across from the Capitol, on grounds with beautiful old trees. It was obviously a better location than the one first chosen, and the legislators raised no objections.

Abner Cook encountered delays caused by weather and labor problems, and the building, scheduled for completion by

December, 1855, was not ready for occupancy until the middle of June, 1856. Mr. Cook had to pay $435 to cover the rent for the governor's family during the six extra months of construction time.

An Austin merchant, S. M. Swenson, was assigned by the commission to go to New York to purchase furniture, drapes, rugs, etc. for the Mansion. He used the $2,500 allotment to purchase "plain, neat and substantial furniture" for the parlor, the family sitting room, one bedroom, the hall, and the dining room, but completely overlooked providing kitchen furnishings and accessories. The commission found it necessary to ask for an additional $6,000 for the kitchen necessities, additional furniture, landscaping the grounds, and digging a well.

Mr. Cook did his job well, and when the stately house in classic Greek revival style was completed, Texans, including the Peases, were proud of it. Lucadia delayed her long-anticipated visit to Connecticut, hoping to be on hand to supervise the move into the Mansion. But as completion continued to be delayed, she finally left at the end of May with the children, taking a boat at Galveston for the long trip to her mother's home.

On June 8, Pease wrote to her, ". . . I shall commence moving into it [the mansion] tomorrow and hope before the close of the week to have everything properly arranged." He was overly optimistic, and for the rest of the summer he and Lucadia exchanged letters about the placement of the furniture and other domestic arrangements in connection with the move. He also consulted her about the details for a party, "a levee," that he planned to give in August to allow the public to see their new Executive Mansion.

The invitation to the open house read:

Governors Levee

A levee will be given at the Executive Mansion on the twenty-third inst., at eight o'clock, P.M. The executive presents his respects to his friends and the public and will be pleased to meet them on that occasion

Austin, August 20th, 1856

The party was a huge success. The *Texas State Gazette* reported:

> On last Saturday evening, at the invitation of the Executive, a large party of citizens, strangers from abroad, and members of the Legislature, assembled at the Mansion, near the Capitol. It was a gay and brilliant affair the ladies in large number enlivening the occasion with their presence. Among the young folks, dancing was kept up to a late hour. Refreshments were on hand in abundance, while at the hour of supper, a most sumptuous repast was spread out to all the guests. The occasion was one of great hilarity.

The bill for the affair included six turkeys, six ducks, two dozen chickens, two shoats, forty loaves of bread, five pounds of butter, cakes, ten pounds of candy, ten pounds of almonds and amounted to $121.80, including $8.30 for "broken crockery."

Pease reported the details of the levee to Lucadia in a long letter. He was well pleased that the party was called "the best one ever got up in Austin." At least five hundred people attended and although he had a nervous stomach and was not able to eat anything himself, he thought the table the "finest I ever saw set in Austin." Lucadia's friends had helped him with the arrangements and they had all wished that she was there, but he added, "I wished for you much more than they did." He assured her, "Though absent your labors contributed greatly to the excellence of the supper, for all the brandied fruit and most of the preserves were of your making."

While Lucadia was visiting her family in Connecticut, she prudently provided for the winter in Texas by picking and drying apples from the Nileses' trees and by canning the vegetables that her husband was so fond of. She was greatly distressed, though, when a jar of sweet corn exploded in one of her suitcases and ruined several of her dresses.

In spite of its elegance there were a number of housekeeping problems in the new mansion. The detached kitchen, with its dirt floor, was difficult to keep clean. The only semblance of a bathroom was a lean-to on the back of the house with a tin bathtub. The spacious high-ceilinged rooms collected moths and spiders, and Lucadia worried about getting flowers to grow in the soil around the mansion.

In their new home Lucadia became more involved in the social life of the town. She loved people and entertaining, but never came to like the making of obligatory calls and leaving of cards. She noted in her diary: "The practice of calling on New Years day is not observed here, tho' Ashbel Smith with his Frenchified manners gave me a call that morning . . . ."

When Sam Houston came to Austin to speak at a Know Nothing Party meeting, she gave a dinner for him, but had a hard time deciding on a guest list. She felt he would not like to meet his former Democratic friends, and her husband did not want to entertain Houston's new Know Nothing ones. She finally chose a small number of men like Dr. Smith who, she said, "is not much of a partizan [sic]."

Among the common forms of entertaining were table rapping, card games, especially euchre or whist, and germans (cotillions involving a special kind of dance called the german). In a letter to her sister Augusta, Lucadia described a "tableaux" she had arranged and given in the front parlor of the mansion on an improvised platform. After the performance, which went off with "great eclat," she served chicken and lobster salad, custards and jellies, hams and turkeys and pyramid loaves (cakes). The table, she thought, looked "very handsomely" with her good crystal and silver containers. Probably without being aware of it, Lucadia was establishing a tradition for elegant entertaining that would be followed by succeeding First Ladies. Nor did she consider how extraordinary it was for this kind of occasion to take place in a little Texas village of about 5,000 inhabitants who still went to bed at night listening for sounds that might indicate Indians were making a raid to steal goods or kidnap children.

In 1856 at the age of forty-three, Lucadia's teeth were giving her so much pain that she had all of the upper ones extracted — at one sitting. Then she had false ones made. At about the same time she began to worry that her hair was turning gray very fast and wrote to her sisters asking them to send her a recipe for "hair wash" to restore it to its original color. She also frequently asked them to send her patterns of the newest fashions for gowns and bonnets. Whenever possible she prudently had her old dresses made over into the latest styles.

Whatever their official or social responsibilities, the Peases first concern was always the welfare of their three daughters. When Carrie fell from the top to the bottom of the front steps of the Mansion and broke her collar bone, she was kept in bed for a week and anxiously nursed until it had completely knitted.

The letters that the Peases exchanged during their periods of separation, besides showing their deep and constant affection for each other, indicate that he often consulted her about his important decisions of state.

As a result of these decisions, the years 1853 to 1857 were marked by a number of important improvements for Texans. When the United States government paid Texas $10,000,000 for lands it gave up claim to when the present boundaries were established, part of this sum was used to set up a permanent school fund and to found institutions for the "deaf, dumb, and insane." Railroad construction, a crying need, was pushed, with Pease proposing big land gifts to the railroads. And the first free schools were finally funded. At the end of Pease's second term, Texas was almost free of debt, and the state tax had been greatly reduced.

When Pease's second term ended, the family moved back into the Ward house temporarily, still thinking of building on their "new place." However, when Woodlawn, an imposing home of red brick and white columns, was offered for sale, they decided to purchase it. It was situated in the rolling hills on the west side of Austin and was surrounded by great Spanish oaks. Abner Cook had built it on the same general plan as the Executive Mansion, except the rooms in Woodlawn were larger.

Many guests, including the famous sculptress Elisabet Ney, were entertained in the gracious building. Lucadia frequently cooked for them herself — chicken pies, loaf cakes, and pumpkin pies. She also did her own preserving and jelly making, which she did not consider that southerners knew how to do "nicely." She found time to read, and along with many other Americans waited impatiently for chapters of Charles Dickens' latest novels to cross the Atlantic.

As the secession issue became hotter, Sam Houston became a frequent visitor at Woodlawn. Previously, he and Pease had been at odds on many political issues, but now they worked together to try to keep Texas in the Union. When that became a lost cause, Pease retired from politics for the duration of the war. Lucadia's letters show her sharp disapproval of those who voted for Texas to secede from the Union.

A great personal grief for the Peases during the sad years of the Civil War was the loss of their youngest daughter, Annie, who died of a childhood disease. Lucadia turned her energies and inventiveness into finding ways to help others survive the hardships of the war years.

Under her direction, the carpets at Woodlawn were taken up and sewed into overcoats for the slaves. And the Peases' stately home became the one place in Austin where the slaves could hold religious services. In 1913, Julia Pease wrote her memories of Christmas fifty years earlier in 1863:

> The Christmas tree was just a common cedar, cut by old Tom. Sprawling it certainly was, making it difficult to attach the many bundles done up in wrapping paper and home-made twine. The ladies worked for days stringing popcorn, making cornucopias and pasting on them the bright prints which had been saved for months. My mother cut out a pair of slippers from the kid skin and my sister and I embroidered them as a gift for my father.

Texas ports were blockaded and all of the gifts were homemade and home grown, but Julia added, "Patience and love redeemed all."

In August of 1865 Lucadia described in a letter to her family the spirited way in which she and other women in Austin met the difficulties of the war years:

> You would be amused to know to what expedients we resorted . . . to supply ourselves with the many necessaries which the blockade deprived us of. This ink . . . is made of sumac berries boiled and

strained — The bonnets and hats for men and women have all been homemade, some of corn shucks or husks or rye or wheat straw bleached split grain — then our gloves, if we had any, were spun, knit, colored, and all done by ourselves, in shoemaking I became quite adept particularly in the art of cobbling — We made our own soda, much of our toilet soap, and in all the different varieties of tallow candles I most particularly prided myself that I excelled my neighbor, the prickly pear hardening, alum clarifying, small twisted wicks, were all topics of conversation with visitors. But coloring was the great art of arts, the leaves, berries, bark and roots of every tree were tried, the long moss, short moss simmered and boiled . . . If sometimes when we expected a yellow or grey color, it came from the dye green or brown, we had only to try again with the hope of better luck . . . Then I had all the sewing for my family, including mending, and you can understand I had not many idle moments.

The war finally dragged to a close and Lucadia took the girls to Connecticut to enroll them in schools which were much more stable than those in Texas at the time. In 1866 Pease ran for Governor on the Republican ticket, but was defeated by James W. Throckmorton. Throckmorton's governorship, however, lasted only a year. When he clashed with General Philip Sheridan, military commander of Texas, Sheridan ordered Throckmorton to vacate the office and appointed Pease Provisional Governor. Lucadia left the girls in charge of her sisters and returned to Austin to be with her husband during this trying time.

Pease worked hard to modify the harsh measures imposed on Texans by the military government. He refused to use his office for the personal satisfaction of getting even with any who had opposed him on the secession issue, saying:

I would blush to use my office to punish wrongs done me individually . . . I want every Texan to forget the bloody past and unite all our energies to make Texas the grandest state in the Union.

Lucadia hadn't the heart to reopen Woodlawn without sufficient help and without the children, so the Peases boarded with friends in Austin. Finally, in 1869 Pease found he could not agree with the military commander about reorganization of the state government and resigned his post. In search of a happier environment, Lucadia and Pease moved to Connecticut. While they were gone, General George Custer and his troops used the Woodlawn acres as winter headquarters. Friends of the Peases asked Custer to leave the main house alone and he did.

In spite of the bitterness of Reconstruction, the Peases were by this time thoroughly Texan at heart and were drawn back to Austin in 1870. Julia stayed up north to enter Vassar in Poughkeepsie, New York, from which she graduated in 1875. Lucadia again made Woodlawn a social and cultural center, introducing such New England customs as high tea to her friends. But her habits of thrift, hard work, and practicality still dominated her life. She did much of her own shopping and food preparation and kept a weather diary to help direct her in planting crops. She also wrote long letters of advice to Julia and warned her not to waste her "precious eyesight on fancy work."

In January of 1875 the parlor at Woodlawn was the setting for the wedding of Carrie to George Graham. The newlyweds lived with the Peases for a few years and soon there were grandchildren romping through the spacious gardens and rooms of Woodlawn.

In 1879 and 1880 Pease served as Collector of Customs at Galveston. He, Lucadia, and Julia stayed at the famous old Tremont Hotel there. Lucadia enjoyed the ever-changing Gulf and wrote into her notebook detailed instructions for cleaning and polishing the shells which she collected.

After they returned to Austin, Pease became vice-president of the First National Bank of Austin. Once again Lucadia settled into her busy life of social, home, and civic activities. Then, within the space of a year, a double tragedy struck. First, Carrie died in childbirth in 1882, and after a short illness Marshall Pease died in 1883. Julia, the social belle of Austin, proved to be a daughter worthy of her mother. She took over the care of Carrie's three surviving children, one of whom was the newborn baby, and also was Lucadia's greatest comfort during her remaining years.

Together the two women continued to make Woodlawn an intellectual and social center of Austin. Lucadia lived to see the little village, in whose development she had played an important role, grow into a sprawling, complex city. She was still active enough at eighty-eight to enjoy an European tour. Her health was good until she fell in 1903 and broke a hip; from that time on she was a semi-invalid, but her mind remained sharp and her spirits cheerful. In January of 1905 she died and was buried in the town to which she had brought so many "civilizing" influences.

8.

Sister-in-Law
to a
Governor

Martha Caroline Adams Runnels

Hardin Richard Runnels never married, but three women influenced him greatly. The reason he remained a bachelor may have been because his fiancee jilted him like the poet's true love in Tennyson's *Locksley Hall*: "Puppet to a father's threat, and servile to a shrewish tongue!"

At thirty-three "Dick" Runnels, as he was always called by his family and friends, finally found the girl he wanted to marry. When he and Miss Eliza Smith of Clarksville, Texas, became engaged, he couldn't do enough for his bride-to-be. Near Old Boston, Texas, he built her an ante-bellum mansion of the finest material available; he ordered furniture from the East and had it shipped to Jefferson and brought from there to Old Boston by ox-cart; he bought her a fine coach. But he had a richer rival who owned many slaves and much land and lacked the risky political ambitions of Runnels. And so her parents persuaded her to break her engagement and marry the man with the larger fortune.

This unhappy ending of his love affair undoubtedly left a deep impression on Runnels, but the woman who influenced him most was probably his strong-minded mother. Martha

"Patsy" Darden Runnels, the daughter of a Revolutionary soldier (George Darden, Sr.), had married Hardin Dudley Runnels in 1814; he was the son of Harmon Runnels, also a veteran of the Revolution. Tiny, blonde Patsy was a direct descendant of Sir John Washington of England, brother of the Reverend Mr. Lawrence Washington, an ancestor of George Washington. Through this line she could also claim Alexander the Great as an ancestor. With such illustrious forefathers, it's not surprising to learn she was a woman of great wit, courage, and determination.

This last quality, plus her capacity for inspiring devotion, is shown in a story handed down by her family. A thirteen-year-old black boy, said to have been a prince in his own land, was brought to Mississippi and purchased by the Runnels family. He was given the name John Runnels but later was affectionately called "Black Daddy," after he grew to be seven feet tall. In 1833 when Patsy's brother-in-law, Hiram G. Runnels, was a candidate for Governor of Mississippi, he and Patsy's husband were off on a campaign trip when an important message for them was brought to the house. She and John set out on horses to deliver it, but heavy rains had flooded a river they needed to cross. John suggested he swim the river with Patsy on his back. She agreed, the crossing was made, and they continued on foot to deliver the message.

In 1839 when her husband died, Patsy set out for Texas with her four sons, about one hundred slaves, and her money in gold, hidden in the false bottom of a wooden meat box. She bought 2,000 acres of black land on the Red River in Bowie County and established a successful plantation. As she grew older she remained independent in planning her life. When her son defeated Sam Houston for the governorship of Texas, she refused to move to Austin with him, preferring to stay in her beloved Red River country.

Like Mrs. Clark, she could have said that governors were "nothing new" in her family. Her sister Elizabeth had married Colonel Stephen Heard, the first Governor of Georgia, and her brother-in-law Hiram Runnels had been Governor of

Mississippi and later helped frame the Texas Constitution of
1845. (Runnels County, Texas, is named after him.) Patsy,
however, chose to continue to live her own life rather then
share the limelight as First Lady during her son's administration.

His mother's refusal to move to Austin with him led Runnels
to invite his sister-in-law, Martha Caroline Adams Runnels, to
act as First Lady during his administration. Martha was
delighted to accept his invitation to become his hostess. She
was only twenty-one at the time and had married Howell
Washington Runnels the year before her brother-in-law
became Governor. Since her husband was serving in the State
Senate, it was a convenient arrangement. A description of
Martha says she was tall, slender, and graceful, with an erect
carriage. She had black hair, fair skin, large gray eyes, and
was poised, witty, and gracious. Dick Runnels admired his
charming sister-in-law, and she seems to have been a happy
choice for First Lady.

Martha's background also helped fit her for her role. She
was born in Zebulon County, Georgia, on March 6, 1836, to Dr.
Jonathon Adams and Mary Gray Adams. Among her
ancestors were General David Adams and James Adams, who
served in the Revolutionary War. As a child she came to Texas
with her family in a wagon train. The Adams family brought
with them, in addition to their household goods, a number of
slaves and quantities of flowers and bulbs. Martha early
acquired a love of flowers and all of her life had a flower bed
that she kept up herself. The Adamses settled in Marshall,
then a cultural center of Texas, and Dr. Adams became one of
the largest land owners in that part of the state. When Martha
became her brother-in-law's hostess, she took with her to the
Executive Mansion the fine china and crystal she had received
as wedding gifts.

Bitter controversy over slavery and secession marred
Runnels' two-year administration. In addition there were
Indian problems, Mexican raids, and rampant cattle rustling
and lynching. The Texas Rangers were hard-pressed to keep

the peace. Men still wore guns as a part of their dress; the Governor himself carried two six-shooters at his side — and wore a diamond pin in his tie. In these turbulent times, Martha provided an atmosphere of serenity as she entertained cheerfully and ran the Governor's Mansion with tact and grace.

At the end of his term Runnels retired to his farm, where he died suddenly on Christmas Day, 1873. After the Civil War, Martha and her husband built a white, frame Victorian house outside the new village of Texarkana. Fourteen children were born to them, but only six lived to adulthood. Martha's great generosity of spirit is exemplified in the naming of their first child. Before his marriage to Martha, Howell Runnels had been married to Smithia Jane Hooks (the daughter of Colonel Hooks for whom the village of Hooks near Texarkana is named). Smithia Jane died in childbirth, and the baby boy died a few days later. When their first child was born, Martha named the baby girl Smithia Jane for her husband's first wife.

Another testimonial to Martha's character is the relationship she had with her daughter-in-law, Kate Neely, who married Howell W. Runnels, Jr. The couple came to live with Martha, and Kate became devoted to her mother-in-law, speaking of her as a "noble woman." Even after she was eighty, Kate liked to recall and chuckle over some of Martha Runnels' witty remarks. On July 19, 1907, Martha died and was buried in Texarkana's Rose Hill Cemetery, exactly fifty years from the time she had so capably answered her brother-in-law's request to serve as First Lady of the Governor's Mansion.

9.

Pacifist in a World at War

Melissa Evans Clark

With burning face and clenched hands, the young matron listened to Governor Sam Houston flay her husband with sarcastic eloquence. She was a large, plump woman whose most attractive feature was her abundant, glossy hair, although she wore it in the unbecoming "skinned back" fashion of the day. When the language became increasingly scathing, a friend turned to the embarrassed woman and suggested that they leave. But Melissa Clark shook her head and remained in her seat until the bitter end of the denunciation delivered to the Secession Convention. The time itself, February, 1861, was bitter, and perhaps Melissa dimly understood that the Old Lion was attacking the secessionist policy of his Lieutenant Governor and not the man himself. It was a time for the breaking of old friendships, family ties, and political alliances.

It seemed the people of Texas hardly understood what they wanted in the way of leadership. In 1857 they had elected Hardin Runnels over Sam Houston, and in 1859 they did an about face and elected Houston over Runnels by almost the same majority by which Houston had been defeated two years before. Running with Houston on the Independent ticket,

Edward Clark had won over F. R. Lubbock by a narrower margin.

In the midst of such turbulence and mercurial changes, mild, sweet-tempered Martha Melissa Clark must often have felt like a displaced person. Born on May 21, 1829, in Madison County, Tennessee, she was one of fourteen children. When she was thirteen, her father, Dr. William Evans, moved the family from Tennessee to Marshall, Texas, where he was the first licensed physician to practice in Harrison County. He also became a successful planter and built one of the finest homes in the community. There Melissa lived a sheltered life, waited on by slaves in as much security and luxury as was available in Texas in the middle of the nineteenth century.

Just as Melissa reached maturity, Edward Clark, a dashing young major, returned to Marshall, fresh from the Mexican War in which he had distinguished himself. Her relatives approved the friendship; Clark came from a fine family and his grandfather and father had been governors of Georgia. He himself was a lawyer and had been a member of the 1845 Texas Annexation Convention and a member of the first House of Representatives. He had been married, but his young wife had died soon after their marriage.

Friendship deepened into love, and Melissa Evans and Edward Clark were married at her home on July 28, 1849. During the ten years that followed, the Clarks lived in Marshall while he held the positions of Senator in the Second Legislature, Secretary of State under Governor Pease, and State Commissioner of Claims. Four children were born to Melissa and Clark, three boys and a girl; the oldest son died in infancy, but John Evans, Alfred, and Nancy lived to maturity.

As long as Melissa was living in Marshall near her family and her strong-minded mother-in-law, she managed with their aid to cope with the children fairly well. But she did not understand them, and after her husband was elected Lieutenant Governor on the Houston ticket in 1859, she and Clark bought a home in Austin. On her own, she was quite helpless to manage her rambunctious offspring, and their behavior was the topic of much gossip and severe criticism.

When Sam Houston refused to take the oath of allegiance to the Confederacy and was deposed, gentle Melissa found herself mistress of the Governor's Mansion. Unquestionably she would have preferred to stay at home and work peacefully at her loom on the counterpane she was making for a friend. But fate had willed otherwise, and she dutifully prepared to attend the inaugural ball for her husband.

At the ball, however, she was eclipsed by her mother-in-law. When the elder Mrs. Clark was congratulated on her son's accession to the governorship, she replied, "It is natural to have Governors in my family. The dress I have on now was worn at my father's inaugural ball in Georgia, later at my husband's inaugural ball in the same state, and now I am wearing it at my son's inaugural ball in Texas." With a toss of her head, she added, "Oh, no; it is nothing new to have Governors in our family." History does not record what Melissa wore to the ball.

Edward Clark's term lasted from March to November of 1861. His major concern was to mobilize Texas in the Confederate cause. Plans had to be made to prevent Federal invasion, to organize resources of men, supplies, and arms for defense, and to care for families of Texas soldiers. Camps of instruction were set up to train troops for the Confederacy. One of Clark's hardest jobs was to convince the horse-oriented Texans that some must serve in the infantry instead of the cavalry. He succeeded, and Texas supplied more soldiers and officers to the army than any other state in proportion to population. Proudly, Clark announced, "Twenty thousand Texans are battling for the rights of our new-born government." Under Clark's leadership, Texas also furnished the southern army with guns, powder, lead, cloth (made in the penitentiary), and salt.

While her husband was struggling with the problems involved in mobilizing men and materials, Melissa struggled with the problems of managing the Governor's household and children. In the graceful, curved banister of the stairs in the entrance foyer of the mansion are some filled-in nail holes. Guides tell visitors that the nails were placed there by some Governor to prevent his children from sliding down the railing. They might well have been put there during the Clarks' residence as a means of enforcing the discipline lacking in Melissa's laissez-faire attitude.

Since it was a time of war, few social demands were made on the First Lady, and Melissa was content to see her few close friends and church acquaintances. She was an ardent member of the "hard shell" branch of the Baptist Church, which had between fifteen and twenty members in Austin during her stay in the mansion.

When he had served the remainder of Houston's term, Clark ran against Lubbock for the governorship. He was defeated by one of the narrowest margins in Texas' elections, 21,854 votes to 21,730. As soon as the election returns were known, Clark set out to raise a regiment, the Texas 14th Infantry, which he commanded as a colonel. His regiment fought in Arkansas and Louisiana to prevent Federal troops from invading Texas from those states. He was wounded in the leg during the bloody Battle of Pleasant Hill in Louisiana, while he was leading a charge six feet in front of the first wave of troops. He continued in the service and rose to the rank of brigadier general.

Melissa had no desire to remain on her own in wartime Austin. As soon as Clark left, she gathered up a few faithful slaves and the children and started for East Texas in a carriage and covered wagons. En route the little procession was stopped by soldiers who commandeered one of the carriage horses. But they reached Marshall safely, and Melissa enjoyed the security of being among friends and family while her husband was away.

His absence was extended for a year after the war when he, along with other Confederate leaders, fled to Mexico to escape possible vengeance from Unionists. When Clark returned home to Marshall in the difficult postwar days, he tried several unsuccessful business ventures. Then he resumed the

practice of law, with much better luck. The last years that he
and Melissa had together were quiet ones as the harshness of
the Reconstruction years gradually abated. In May of 1880
Clark died.

Melissa lived for ten more years, perhaps the most peaceful
ones of her adult life. The children were grown, and after her
husband's death there was no social pressure on her. She was
free to devote herself to her sewing, work in the Baptist
Church, and visiting with her small circle of friends. In May,
1890, peace-loving Melissa died and was buried beside her
militant husband in the cemetery at Marshall.

10

"My Creole Wife"

Adele Baron Lubbock

"From the moment my wife entered the house they were all delighted with her, and she grew day by day upon my mother's heart by her gentleness and tender care for her. As for me, while I could but grieve over the occasion of my visit, I was proud to see how they all admired my young Creole wife, and I was happy to know . . . I had been fortunate enough to select a companion, a perfect stranger to my people, whom they could love as a daughter and a sister.

Thus, in his memoirs, Francis R. Lubbock recorded the first meeting of his sixteen-year-old bride with his family. The sad occasion for the visit was the fatal illness of his mother. He was only nineteen himself, but already was beginning to realize that he had been wise in choosing the woman who would be his companion for almost fifty years.

When she met and fell in love with Frank Lubbock, Adele Baron was living in New Orleans, where she had been born in 1819. All of her short life had been spent in the heart of her large, lively family. Her father, N. A. Baron, Jr., a former Parisian, was a prominent sugar and cotton dealer. Her mother, Laura Bringier Baron, was the daughter of one of the earliest cotton planters and sugar growers in Louisiana.

Numerous aunts and uncles owned plantations near New Orleans, and young Lubbock, who had come from North Carolina and established himself as a partner in a wholesale and retail drug supply business, was amazed at their way of life. He called them "the most luxurious livers I have ever known . . ." and described their luxuries in detail:

> They had fine plantations, good houses, well-kept grounds, excellent horses, well-trained servants, and tables laden with the best of everything . . . excellent beef and mutton, game of every kind, fish, terrapin, tropical and other fruits, elegant sweetmeats, wines of every vintage, from table claret . . . to Burgandy and Champagne, old Cognac . . . with cordials of every description . . . .

Lubbock was critical of the Federal protection (through high tariff laws) that enabled these planters to live so lavishly, but he was completely enchanted by Adele Baron.

The petite Adele was a vivacious girl with gray eyes, light brown hair, and a beautiful voice. Most of the songs she knew were in French, since the family always used that language among themselves. Lubbock counted this an asset; he noted, "The very fact that she spoke little and poor English made her more interesting to me." They exchanged language lessons, but she learned much more English than he did French.

He was far from bored by the lessons, though, for he recalled, "I was soon very desperately in love with the Creole girl." After their marriage he referred to her affectionately as "my Creole wife," and he was careful to explain the term to those who might not understand it: "Creole means a native, so that children born of French parents in Louisiana are designated as French Creoles; those born of American parents as American Creoles; of Negroes, as Negro Creoles. Chickens, eggs, and such things are called Creole chickens, and so on, and these are preferred."

Adele's family were Catholic, and when Lubbock was making wedding arrangements with a priest, he could not recall being baptized. So he insisted on being christened on the spot rather than delay the wedding. They were married on February 5, 1835, and set up housekeeping near Lubbock's business with Adele's mother and two of Adele's brothers living with them. Fortunately, Lubbock was fond of his mother-in-law and of French cooking.

In May of 1835 Lubbock's mother became seriously ill, and the young couple took a ship for Charleston. Adele's first long trip was a disagreeable one because they were constantly buffeted by heavy winds and storms. She would never forget her first sight of the city of Charleston: a great fire was raging and "the entire center of the city seemed wrapped in flames." Lubbock's mother lingered for two weeks. During that time Adele won his family's affection by her sincere warmth and considerate behavior.

Tom Lubbock, Frank's brother, who wanted to try his fortune in new territory, made the return trip to New Orleans with them. They decided to travel overland by railroad and by stagecoach part of the way. The stagecoach was crowded and hot and not much more comfortable than the boat had been. Between Columbus, Georgia, and Montgomery, Alabama, their stage was upset and several of the passengers were injured. Lubbock suffered a severe wrist sprain, and Adele was so seriously hurt that they were delayed several days in Montgomery while a doctor took care of her. She never completely recovered from her injuries. In Lubbock's memoirs there seems to be a faint hint that this accident may have been the cause of their inability to have children — which they both so earnestly wanted.

Back in New Orleans, Lubbock found that his drug business had become shaky. And it did not improve, even though with Adele's consent he used her dowry to shore it up. All sorts of disasters occurred: barrels of castor oil (worth $80 to $100 each) leaked away; a number of large collections could not be made; markets were depressed. Pressed by creditors, the firm closed its door and settled its debts. "I reserved nothing but my household furnishings and my horse," Lubbock said. Soon, however, he found employment as a dealer in watches, jewelry, silverware, and firearms at the very handsome salary of $2,000 a year.

Tom, always restless and eager for action, decided to heed the distress calls that were coming from Texans who were struggling to free themselves from Mexican rule. Reluctantly, since they felt responsible for the seventeen-year-old, the Lubbocks helped outfit him. He became the first volunteer in the New Orleans Grays and sailed with that outfit, arriving in Texas in time to take part in the Battle of Bexar in which 300 Texas volunteers routed and captured 1,100 Mexicans.

Adele and Lubbock completely lost touch with Tom and became concerned about him, so Lubbock decided to make a trip to Texas to try to locate his young brother. Always the canny businessman, he took with him flour, coffee, and other staple groceries to sell to the Texans. After some difficulty he located Tom, who because of poor health had left the army to take a job on a Brazos River steamer. This trip showed Lubbock that there was a demand for goods in Texas, and he returned to New Orleans full of exciting ideas.

For months Adele and her husband agonized over whether to stay with the relative security of his job in New Orleans or to move to Texas in search of new opportunities. The lure of adventure won, and a few days before Christmas in 1836 they set sail on the schooner *Corolla* for the newly independent republic. Again Lubbock took supplies with him; at Velasco he sold ten barrels of flour to the government at thirty dollars per barrel. He accepted government certificates for it; fifteen years later, after the sale of the Santa Fe territory to the United States, he finally received payment for the certificates.

The Lubbocks decided to try their luck in the brand new village of Houston. But to give Adele a rest after their long trip, they spent a few days in Brazoria at the boarding house of Mrs. Jane Long. Mrs. Long had had some thrilling experiences as a pioneer in Texas, and Adele listened wide-eyed to recitals of Jane Long's encounters with the Karankawa Indians and other dangerous adventures. The Lubbocks also encountered interesting guests at the boarding house, such as Vice President Mirabeau Lamar, still being acclaimed for his heroic action at the Battle of San Jacinto.

Having lived all of her life in the relatively sophisticated city of New Orleans, Adele must have found the raw village of Houston strange. From the landing she could see a few tents (the largest one was the saloon) and farther on several small log and clapboard houses — and that was all there was to her new hometown. Lubbock purchased a lot for $250 from the agent of the Allen brothers, the founders of the town, and paid another $250 to have a clapboard house built.

Adele's new home consisted of one twelve-foot-square room plus a shed room. There were no windows; a board was removed when air or light were needed. The floor was made of rough boards which did not extend under the bed because the bedstead was made by driving forked sticks into the ground and laying poles across with boards on top to hold the moss mattress. "Brother Tom" came to stay with them, and life must have been uncomfortable, to say the least, for the young bride who had been used to every comfort and many luxuries in her family's home. But apparently she didn't complain, for Lubbock recalled: "We were young and happy, . . . we took cheerfully every inconvenience and hardship, looking with hope to the great future of Texas."

There were some memorable entertainments, too. On April 21, 1837, the first anniversary of the Battle of San Jacinto, a large ball was held in Houston. People came from as far as fifty to sixty miles away, by horseback and rowboat. Frank and Adele Lubbock were in the small group that accompanied President Sam Houston to the dance. Houston, of course, was the star of the occasion, but Adele was one of the belles and danced in the same cotillion as Houston.

When the problem arose of a suitable dwelling for the new President in the city of Houston, which was now the capital, Lubbock offered to sell the government a building he had built as a warehouse. Possibly as a result of supplying the first "White House," (located near the site of the present Rice Hotel), he was appointed chief Clerk of the House of Representatives.

During this period Lubbock practiced a deception on Adele which was to prove beneficial in a surprising way, many years later. Because of her upbringing as a Catholic, she was strongly opposed to the Masonic organization. Lubbock became interested in Masonry and secretly devoted many hours to it while Adele thought he was working at his duties as Clerk of the House. When Adele discovered his deception, she became more than ever prejudiced against the order, and for a time it was a matter of unhappiness for them both.

At the age of twenty-two Lubbock was appointed Comptroller of the Republic by Sam Houston. The salary, $2,000 per year, enabled the Lubbocks to buy better furnishings for their house. Adele now had two Mexican prisoners for servants, and the young couple often entertained the outstanding men of the town, including President Houston, Dr. Ashbel Smith, Surgeon General of the army, and the Allens.

In his memoirs, Lubbock recalls a fifty-mile trip he and Adele and a Mrs. J. G. Welchmeyer made in the spring of 1838 to visit friends. The ladies rode in a gig with a leather top and Lubbock rode a "Texas" pony. They "nooned" at a friend's house where part of the refreshment was rich, cool, delicious buttermilk. Being extremely thirsty, they all enjoyed it, but Lubbock drank seven large tumblers full. That afternoon on his hard-trotting pony, trying to keep up with the gig, he was "transformed into a churn full of buttermilk." In pity, Adele slowed the gig's pace to ease her husband's suffering, but the episode later furnished much material for joking at his expense when they had reached their destination.

The next day, showing off in front of the ladies, he cracked a whip at a skunk, but the skunk proved better at long range than he. The ladies were highly entertained but not anxious for his company and rode home well ahead of him. Adele met him at the gate with a change of clothes held at arm's length and orders to retire to an outhouse to put them on.

On the return trip a more serious accident occurred at a rest stop. Lubbock carelessly let the bridle fall from the head of the horse pulling the ladies' gig. The horse started off at full speed, dragging Lubbock with it until the gig hit a stump. Adele and Mrs. Welchmeyer were dumped out, but luckily were only shaken up. The gig, however, was a complete loss. Lamar recited the lessons he learned on the trip:

> Never take more than two glasses of buttermilk at a time; never take the bit out of your horse's mouth when he is hitched to a vehicle containing the wife whose life is as precious as your own; and most emphatically never fight a skunk . . . .

When his term as Comptroller expired, Lubbock was elected District Clerk for Harris County. Sometimes his fees were paid in livestock, and perhaps this was what motivated him to go into ranching. At any rate, in 1846 the Lubbocks paid seventy-five cents an acre for a 400-acre ranch six miles from Houston on Sim's Bayou. Here they built a spacious home and many outbuildings. The few cows that Lubbock had taken (along with pigs and sheep) as fees were eventually built up into the largest herd between the Brazos and the Trinity. The cattle were shipped by steamer to New Orleans' markets.

Adele experimented with raising fancy Asiatic poultry, but was so generous in giving away chicks and eggs that it wasn't a profitable venture. The ranch took on an exotic appearance in 1858 when forty camels were grazed there before being sent to West Texas to be used by the United States War Department in an experiment to test them as a means of desert transportation.

This country home was popular with visiting friends such as Sam and Margaret Houston. It was the visiting children, however, whom Adele went out of her way to please, and they were always sure of an especially warm welcome. She was a kind, competent mistress and the cheerful, orderly atmosphere of her home is shown in the description by a friend's daughter, who was often a visitor there as a child:

> How well I remember the young negro girls busy at work polishing brass door knobs and the brass balls on which Mrs. Lubbock's bedstead rested, one or two of the women engaged in the simplest of needlework hemming towels or sheets, sometimes with a half-

grown one taking lessons in overcasting, all under the eye and directions of the mistress of the household.

Lubbock could not stay out of politics and helped organize the Democratic Party in Texas in 1856. The next year he ran for Lieutenant Governor, winning over Edward Clark. Two years later he was defeated for re-election by Clark, but in 1861 he defeated Clark for the office of Governor, by a scant 124 votes, thereby becoming Texas' first elected Confederate Governor.

Adele often accompanied her husband on his political campaign tours. They drove their own pair of fine horses, and during one campaign they visited more than one hundred counties. Her warm personality and her soft, southern voice with its tinge of foreign accent charmed the voters.

When they moved into the Governor's Mansion, the Lubbocks brought with them two pairs of carriage horses, Lubbock's saddle horse, two men to care for the horses and two well-trained girls for housework. In spite of restrictions caused by the Civil War, Adele managed to do a great deal of entertaining. Soon after they were settled in the mansion, a levee was held for the Austin citizenry and the legislators. "It was a jam and everything was served in profusion," Lubbock reported. They "invariably" had from two to a dozen members of the Senate or House of Representatives dining with them. Luckily, turkeys were only fifty cents each and in plentiful supply — at first. After a drought in the summer of 1862 created scarcities of food in Austin, Adele bought fowl and vegetables from farmers twenty miles away to keep her table supplied for their numerous guests.

While Adele dealt with household problems, the Governor had his hands full with a twofold war. The Indians had picked this time to become aggressive, and his first step was to organize a defense against them. Lubbock also liked being known as the "War Governor" and gave one hundred percent support to the Confederacy. He urged the drafting of all men between sixteen and sixty and sent quantities of valuable supplies to the Southern army.

A personal tragedy for the Lubbocks during the Civil War was the death of Tom Lubbock. He had won fame as the co-organizer and leader of Terry's Rangers but then had become ill and died in 1862. Surviving members of his regiment would later name the city of Lubbock and Lubbock County in his honor.

A revealing insight into Adele's character is shown by a letter written in 1862 by William Lount to his family in New York. He wrote of the rather sudden death of his young wife, who had settled in Austin with him and their little daughter, Mollie, less than a year before. He mentioned that his wife had counted among her intimate friends the families of ex-Governor Clark, ex-Governor Pease, and the present Governor Lubbock, "whose kind Lady was with her during the most of her fatal illness, and at her bedside at her death when she wept as none but a mother could have done. Mrs. Lubbock is an elderly lady [she was forty-three] without children and from her first acquaintance with Naomi loved her with a mother's love and never seemed as happy as when Naomi was with her either at the mansion, in her carriage or at our rooms at the avenue . . . ." He went on to mention little Mollie's bereavement and added, "Mrs. Lubbock begs me hard for her and promises that the Gov. will make her his sole heir but I cannot give her away."

Lubbock did not run for re-election in 1863. Instead, the day his term ended he joined General John Magruder's staff as a colonel. This unit moved about frequently and Adele, back on the plantation near Houston, suffered greatly, not knowing where her husband of nearly thirty years was, or in what danger. As often as possible Lubbock sent her long, cheerful letters to relieve her anxiety.

In 1864 he became aide-de-camp to President Jefferson Davis. He soon became a close personal friend of the Confederate leader and of Mrs. Davis. When Davis was captured in May of 1865, Lubbock was taken with him. Adele suffered a long, tense period of waiting for news. Finally, the letter that he had written almost immediately after his capture reached her. It was datelined Macon, May 13, 1865, and said:

> My Dear Wife: I am at this place a prisoner of war. The President, with a small party making their way to the Trans-Mississippi, was captured on the 10th near Irvinsville, Ga., about 100 miles south of this place. . . . .
> Do not be uneasy, my dear wife. I am in fine health and about as well treated as could be expected . . . . Keep up your spirits, my sweet wife. All will yet be well.
> You had better sell cattle if you can occasionally for specie and secure it in case you should need it. . . .
> I can not say much at present. God bless you and all at home. Give my love to all. Kiss the children for me . . . .

The children referred to were their nieces and nephews, of whom they were both very fond.

From Macon, Lubbock was sent to Fortress Monroe and then to Fort Delaware, where he spent the remaining seven months of his imprisonment. Here he was kept in solitary confinement and not allowed to write. Adele didn't know if he was alive or dead. The next thing she heard of him was from a newspaper clipping sent to her by a friend. It was a notice that appeared in a twenty-five cent advertising column and said only:

> To Mrs. Lobock of Texas - Your husband, Col. Frank Lobock, is confined at Fort Delaware in good health and spirits - A.T. Texas papers please copy.

The notice was the result of Lubbock's having taken the opportunity while he was exercising on a parapet to shout down to a passer-by, asking him to let Mrs. Lubbock of Texas know "her husband Frank is a prisoner here and in good health and spirits." This scrap of paper Adele kept among her "sacred treasures." Through bribery and Masonic connections, Lubbock managed during his last months in Fort Delaware to smuggle letters in and out and to obtain some comforts for himself.

In August of 1865 Adele wrote ex-Governor Pease and Governor Hamilton seeking help in securing her husband's release. She told them, "I have been hoping for and expecting his return so long that I am nearly crazy with despair." She was afraid that Lubbock would have to stand trial now that the war was over. She begged them to suggest anything she could do and offered to come to Austin if it would do any good, although her health was "very feeble." At last, in November, with the help of Masonic friends, he was released. From that time on Adele was reconciled to Masonry and found no more fault with the order.

On his return to Texas, Lubbock went back into the mercantile business, first in Houston and then in Galveston with a branch office in Houston. He and Adele lived in Galveston for about ten years. When he suffered heavy losses through speculating in beef packing, he decided to give up business and get back into politics. He ran for State Treasurer in 1878 and was elected.

Again Adele packed to move to Austin, where they bought a large, two-story house near the Capitol Building. Here she renewed old friendships, and again her home became a gathering place. The last four years of her life were happy ones in spite of her failing health. Because she was so greatly admired, many children were named after her, and the childless Adele became a loving godmother to many infant namesakes. People who had met her never forgot her; business letters to her husband, including those from Jefferson Davis, frequently contained affectionate messages for her.

Adele died in 1882 and was buried in Houston, where a number of relatives of the Lubbocks lived. Lubbock continued to be re-elected Treasurer through six terms. He served on the Board of Pardons during the James Stephen Hogg administration and retired from public life at the age of eighty to write his memoirs, *Six Decades in Texas*. He lived to be ninety and married twice more before he died of a stroke in June of 1905.

In a letter to the Texas Veterans Association he made several requests concerning his funeral arrangements. He asked that his body, dressed in his Confederate uniform, lie in state at the Capitol and that his services be conducted by Holland Masonic Lodge of Houston. And he also requested that the remains of Adele be placed beside his in the State Cemetery in Austin, remembering as he had said earlier of her, "I had in truth and in fact a helpmate, God bless her."

11

"The Sad, Beautiful Face of Poor Miss Susie"

Sue Ellen Taylor Murrah

The life of Sue Ellen Taylor Murrah can only be told as a short, tragic mystery, full of unanswered questions. Why did she and her husband spend their wedding night apart? Why did Pendleton Murrah treat his gay, beautiful wife so coldly? Was there another woman (or women) in his life? What happened to Susie Murrah in the few blank years she lived after her husband left her and rode off to Mexico to die?

At the time of her wedding, Susie Taylor, like Adele Baron, was very young (fifteen and a half) and the adored daughter of a large family. She also was petite, vivacious, and even more beautiful than Adele. She, too, had a large wedding at her family's home (in the country near Marshall) with music, dancing, delicious foods, wines and laughter. But there the similarity ends. Instead of settling into a happy, companionable marriage as Adele did, Susie experienced only coldness and estrangement from her husband — with one brief exception.

Probably any guest at the wedding of Susie Taylor and Pendleton Murrah in 1850 would have prophesied a happy future for the couple. Both were well-known and well-liked in their home town of Marshall, even though there was a mystery connected with Murrah's background. It was known that he had been educated by the Baptist Church at Brown University in Rhode Island, but that was all. Actually, he had been born out of wedlock in a cabin on the old Choctaw trail in what is now Chilton County, Alabama.

His mother was a Murrah; her father was a bishop in the Methodist Church. She later married a man named Harper and was a respected member of her community, but Murrah was always deeply ashamed of his mother. He shunned her publicly; however, he visited her secretly and gave her money at intervals. There were rumors of his illegitimacy in Marshall, but he had proved himself in the eyes of his fellow Texans as a hard-working, dynamic attorney and politician. So the townspeople were happy to see him marry the popular Susie Taylor.

What happened on their wedding night remains a puzzle. After the guests had left, the young bride waited in her bedroom for the groom to come up to her, and the groom sat in the parlor waiting for his bride to come down to him. No one seems to have told him where she was. Evidently some kind of misunderstanding had taken place. It seems incredible that such a fiasco could continue all night, even if shyness on her part and pride on his were the cause. But it did.

The next morning, stern and unforgiving, Pendleton Murrah took his bride away from her family home. During the next thirteen years while they lived in Marshall, Murrah built up a thriving law practice, made money, and dabbled in politics. There is strong evidence that he also had time for some extra-marital activity, including an aborted plan to elope to Mexico with a young sister of his wife. Whether Susie knew anything about this scheme is questionable. In 1855 Murrah was defeated in a campaign for a seat in Congress, but in 1857 he was elected to the Legislature. Susie stayed at home, managed their household, took care of an orphaned child, and kept her loneliness to herself.

Sometime during those hard-working years Murrah

contracted tuberculosis. After the Civil War began, he tried to work as a quartermaster in East Texas but had to quit because of his health. When he was elected Governor to succeed Lubbock in 1863, he was already a dying man. Susie was twenty-eight when she became mistress of the mansion, and whatever unhappiness she felt inside, to the public she appeared as a bright and charming addition to the bleak wartime city. Formal social life had almost come to a standstill in Austin; restrictions and scarcities had reached all levels of society. The traditional state inaugural dinner was held for the Murrahs; however, the cakes were made of corn meal.

Murrah took over the leadership of a state seething with turmoil. As he told the Legislature:

> In some sections society is almost disorganized; the voice of the law is hushed . . . Murder, robbery, theft, outrages of every kind against property, against life . . . are frequent and general. Whole communities are under a reign of terror, and they utter their dreadful apprehensions and their cries of distress in vain . . . .

Indians, outlaws, deserters, Federal troops threatened on all sides along a 2,000-mile hostile frontier, border, and coastline. There were at least 74,000 dependents of soldiers who needed help. And still the Confederate government demanded more troops. Murrah got the harsh conscription laws modified and put the safety and needs of the state first; but he could not work miracles, and problems increased as the war neared its end.

The one redeeming moment in Susie's unhappy marriage happened in the midst of all this. One sleety night in the winter of 1864 she was lying ill in bed. Fires had been lighted in the mansion's fireplaces to counteract the cold, and one of the big logs rolled out onto the floor of the library, setting the room ablaze. As cries of "Fire!" broke out, the Governor rushed into his wife's bedroom, wrapped her in a quilt and carried her across the street to a neighbor's home, where he placed her on the bed of the woman of the house.

When he left to return to see about the fire, Susie, ill and weak, broke into tears sobbing, "He called me 'my dear.' "

Then for the first time the love-starved wife poured out the story of the wedding night mix-up and of her husband's coldness to her during their marriage. The words he had spoken to her under the stress of the fire were the first terms of affection she had heard from him since their wedding. In the face of his indifference over the long years, she had been able to cover up her hurt, but one word of kindness in her weak state broke through her defenses.

The mansion's most persistent ghost story grew out of a family tragedy that happened while the Murrahs were living there. During a time when a beautiful young niece of the Governor was a guest, a nephew of Murrah's (not her brother) came to visit. He fell madly in love with his cousin, and apparently she led him to believe that she cared for him too. But when he proposed, she laughed at him. It was more than the impetuous young lover could bear. That night, from the little north room of the mansion, a shot was heard. The horrified family rushed in to find the dead youth's body sprawled across the bed and the wall splattered with blood.

Some months later, after the Murrahs left the mansion and it was being taken care of by the black servants, Jake and Malvina Fontaine, their daughter, sixteen-year-old Melissa Fontaine, and a friend decided they wanted to sleep in the Governor's house in the "white folks" bed. In the middle of the night the girls heard strange moans and groans; then they felt the hair rise on the back of their necks (a sure sign of the presence of a ghost) and they fled back to their own quarters.

Over the years, many other people staying in the mansion have heard strange noises and seen strange sights, such as doorknobs that turn of their own accord. Next to the shade of Sam Houston, whose ghostly footsteps are heard pacing as he returns to haunt the scene of his bitter decision, the shade of the romantic young lover is most often thought of as being the source of these unexplained phenomena.

As the war ended, wild rumors began to fly that rebel leaders would be taken prisoner and severely punished. Many Confederate officials crossed over into Mexico seeking refuge;

Murrah decided to go with them. His tuberculosis had become severe during the sixteen strenuous months of his administration. He must have been aware that he was near the end of his life when he put on his old gray·uniform and rode away from the shattered capital — and from the woman he had married. Less than two months later he died in Monterrey and was buried there in an unmarked grave.

What happened to Susie after Murrah's departure can only be guessed from a few known facts. The capital was a dangerous place to be. The night that Murrah left, forty bandits broke into the treasury and succeeded in stealing almost $2,000 before they were finally subdued by a group of citizens whom a patrolman summoned by ringing church bells. Apparently Susie left Uncle Jake and Aunt Malvina Fontaine in charge of the mansion and returned to Marshall. There is only one trace of her life there — a number of large, beautiful old trees that she planted on her home grounds and which testify to her love of nature and beauty.

The only other fact known about her is that she died in 1868 in Tyler and is buried there. And so, at thirty-three the tragic life of Susie Taylor Murrah ended, still shrouded in mystery. Her story is a haunting one to many people besides Melissa Fontaine, who could never forget "the sad, beautiful face of poor Miss Susie when she told us good-bye."

12.

Wife
of a
Southern
Unionist

Mary Jane Bowen Hamilton

In the last months of 1846 an elegant barouche made the long trip from Talledega, Alabama, to a farm near La Grange, Texas. The outside front seat of the carriage was occupied by two slaves — Old Henry, who was driving, and Rachel. On the rear seats, which faced each other, sat Andrew Jackson Hamilton, his wife, Mary Jane, and their two small children, Mary and Frank. They were an attractive family. Twenty-eight-old Mary Jane had dark hair and sparkling dark eyes that were her most striking feature. She was tall, but not so tall as her six-foot husband, whose black hair contrasted with his light blue eyes. All of the family were dressed in well-made clothes of quality material, which Mary Jane preferred to showy outfits. Since the distance was long and their progress slow, Mary Jane had plenty of time to think about the events of her past that had led to this trip — and of her future in the brand new state of Texas.

She had moved twice before in her life: from South Carolina, where she had been born in 1826, to Mississippi and then to Weldona, Alabama, near Talledega. Her life had been pleasant and easy, for her father was Judge John David Bowen, a

well-to-do lawyer and plantation owner. There had always
been slaves to do the hard work; in fact, the slaves in the
barouche were hers. When Andrew Jackson Hamilton arrived
in Talledega to take his law degree, she was impressed, as
were most people, with his rich vocabulary and remarkably
resonant voice.

After Hamilton went into partnership with her father, he
and Mary Jane were often together, and soon they were
engaged to be married. The wedding took place on September
3, 1843. Mary Jane enjoyed her new position as a young
matron and Hamilton practiced his profession of law
successfully. In January of 1845 their first child, Mary, was
born, and the next year brought the birth of a son, Frank.
Seemingly the Hamiltons were happily settled for life. But
Andrew J. Hamilton shared the questing spirit of many
adventurers before him who had responded to the appeal of
Texas as a land of opportunity.

The opportunity they responded to was a more specific one
than many Texas pioneers enjoyed, for it was a tempting offer
made by his older brother, Morgan Hamilton. Morgan had
done well during his nine years in Texas, and he owned many
acres of the new state. When he offered his younger brother
and Mary Jane a farm in Fayette County near La Grange, they
decided to accept his offer, and that was why Mary Jane found
herself in the barouche on the long, slow trip to her future in
Texas.

The Hamiltons' pioneer life began in a small log house on the
farm that Mary Jane soon came to manage so that Hamilton
would be free to set up a law practice. His practice thrived,
although he was often paid in farm produce or slaves instead
of money. During the two and one-half years the Hamiltons
lived on the farm near La Grange, another son, John, was
born. Again, it seemed the couple was well-settled; but again,
more exciting prospects beckoned.

The countryside was quiet compared to Austin (where
brother Morgan was now living). Looking for a more
stimulating environment and perhaps with an eye on politics,

Hamilton moved his family to Austin in the spring of 1849. While they were living in temporary quarters there, another daughter, Betty, was born. In the state's capital Hamilton's talents as a lawyer and as an orator brought him to the attention of Texas' top leaders, and in 1850 Governor Peter Hansborough Bell appointed Hamilton Attorney General of Texas.

With assistance from Morgan, the Hamiltons bought a 200-acre farm with a home on it. (Part of this land Hamilton later donated to the state, and it is now occupied by the State Cemetery.) The house, which they named Fair Oaks, was palatial for its day. Across the front, two huge rooms opened into each other, and behind them was a twenty-five foot dining room which was flanked on either side by bedroom wings. A large gallery extended across the entire front of the house. The kitchen, as usual, was detached, but Mary Jane had servants to do the cooking and serving. There were solid blinds at the windows with loopholes through which to fire at Indians in case of a siege.

Two more daughters, Lillie and Katie, were born to the Hamiltons in this home. Mary Jane found the large house with its spacious entertainment areas useful as the family increased in number and as her husband got deeper into politics and their circle of friends and acquaintances grew.

During this time Mary Jane became aware of a problem that was to plague them both for as long as Hamilton lived. Because of his outstanding ability as a orator, Hamilton was often invited to make speeches around the state. These occasions were frequently followed by trips to the nearest saloon for an informal review of the evening, accompanied by copious liquid refreshment. Although Mary Jane could influence Hamilton to practice restraint when he was at home, she had no control over his habits during these times away from home. Always convivial, Hamilton took every opportunity to celebrate and thereby earned a reputation as a heavy drinker.

However, among early Texas settlers such a reputation was

quite often more admired than condemned. Hamilton's popularity grew, and in 1851 and 1853 he was elected a member of the Texas House of Representatives from Travis County. In 1856 he was a Presidential elector on the Democratic ticket, and in 1859 he was sent to the Thirty-sixth Congress as an Independent in the United States House of Representatives. During the campaign for this office he acquired, because of his size and eloquence, the nickname that was to stick to him — "Colossal" Hamilton.

The Hamiltons decided to take advantage of the opportunity to get a better education for the older girls than was available in Texas at that time. Consequently, Hamilton took the two oldest daughters, Mary and Betty, with him to Washington to put them in school there. Mary Jane stayed in Austin to take care of the farm and the other four children. Hamilton's letters to Mary Jane during this time of separation show his deep love and concern for her and the children and his homesickness. He wrote:

> You cannot imagine how much I want to hear from you. I will not enjoy myself here. Oh how much rather would I be sitting by your side with Lilly and little Kate on my knee. But I must drop this subject for my eyes fill and my heart aches.

He told her that Frank and John must write to him every week and begged her to write every few days and tell him all about "the children, the Negroes, the horses, the ponies, the cows, the dogs and anything about our Home that you think will interest me." He advised her not to expose herself to cold weather and to wear good thick shoes when she went out. He asked her to tell him about the inauguration of "Old Sam" (Houston) and wanted to know what she thought of him. Unfortunately we don't have her reply to this question. A letter dated May 6, 1860, refers to the birth of a child during his absence and its death but gives no more details. He worried when Mary Jane didn't write often enough, saying, "I began to think I would never hear from you anymore. You can't imagine how it [her letter] gladdened my heart."

When Congress adjourned in June, 1860, and Hamilton

came home for the summer, Mary Jane and the children were delighted, even though he was busy campaigning for Stephen A. Douglas — urging voters to support him to keep Lincoln out of the presidency.

The Texas Secession Convention met soon after Hamilton returned for the second session of the Thirty-sixth Congress, and he had to take his stand. He did so by coming out strongly for the Constitution of the United States and the Union. As the southern states began to secede, other Congressmen returned to their home states, but Hamilton kept his seat until Congress adjourned in March, 1861. Back in Texas, he was elected to the Legislature on a Union ticket. However, like Sam Houston, he refused to sign the oath of loyalty to the Confederacy and so could not take his seat.

With these events a time of anxiety and social ostracism began for Mary Jane. Unionists became increasingly unpopular in Austin. There were few friends who dared be seen with her, but she continued to support staunchly her husband and to care for the farm and their children. In 1862 disasters multiplied for her. First Katie became ill and died. The war news was grim for the South at this time, and Katie's funeral was scarcely over when rumors reached the Hamiltons that a force was coming to capture and lynch him. He fled first to a spot in the hills west of Austin called Hamilton's Pool because it was on land that had been owned by Morgan Hamilton. There he hid for days, living partly on berries and roots until friends helped him escape to Mexico and then to New Orleans. As his ship left the shore of Texas, it was pursued by a small boat of armed men, but they failed to overtake him.

Mary Jane, waiting for news at Fair Oaks, probably was happy to read even the derogatory reports printed about her husband in the Texas papers. At least they told her he had reached safety in Union-held New Orleans. The news that Hamilton had been made a brigadier-general in the Union army and that Lincoln had appointed him Military Governor of Texas made Texans even more hostile toward her and the children. Also, in his capacity as Military Governor Hamilton was located in Brownsville — a long, long way from Austin in those uncertain times. Mary Jane and the children survived mainly on what they could produce in their garden and on the poultry and cows on the farm. The Hamilton boys learned to make shoes and the girls to help make clothing because there was little, if any, to be bought.

Hamilton worried about his family and wanted desperately to get them out of Texas to the safety of New Orleans. He enlisted the help of some high-ranking Mexican officials, who asked Governor Lubbock to allow Mrs. Hamilton and the children to leave the state. Lubbock passed the decision on to the military, which meant that it was suspended in red tape for months.

Mary Jane was kept under surveillance to prevent her from communicating with her husband. In a letter from Hamilton to President Lincoln, dated August 22, 1863, Hamilton says of the condition of his family that one of his sons (presumably Frank) was "like his Father, an outcast from home, hiding in the mountains to escape conscription or death — the other in effect a prisoner with his mother and little sister."

Mary Jane, however, was not confined to the house, for in the summer of 1864, while she and the children were visiting one of the few friends they had left in Austin, Fair Oaks was burned to the ground by rebels. Since furniture, clothing, and all of their other possessions were destroyed, the next few months were spent in the home of friends. Finally, two years after Hamilton's first request, Mary Jane and the children were allowed to leave for New Orleans in the late fall of 1864.

Their boat was met at the dock by Hamilton, and a joyous reunion took place on December 14. Mary Jane had her husband with her for Christmas and the rest of the winter of 1864-65. There is no record of where they stayed or what they did, but it must have been a time of great happiness for the reunited family. Lucadia Pease, Mary Jane's close friend, remarked in a letter to her sister Juliet that Hamilton was "very affectionate and indulgent to his family, and they had such a high appreciation of his talents, they almost idolized him."

When the war ended the Hamiltons returned to Austin. On July 21, 1865, Hamilton was appointed Provisional Governor by President Andrew Johnson, and Mary Jane moved her household into the Executive Mansion. The early months of reconstruction were a difficult time to be Governor (or First Lady) of an ex-Confederate state. Hamilton had to convince the Negroes that the government had no intention of giving each of them "forty acres and a mule"; he had to work to get Texas back into the Union as a full-fledged state; and he had to find ways to fend off attacks on the population by both Indians and carpetbaggers.

An example of Hamilton's lack of bitterness and vindictiveness is shown in his reply to a request from Adele Lubbock to go north to join her husband, who was a prisoner at Fort Delaware. Hamilton not only granted the request promptly but also offered all aid possible to Mrs. Lubbock, in spite of her husband's lack of response to a similar request made in behalf of Mrs. Hamilton during the war.

Mary Jane shared the common problem of finding ways to get around shortages created by the war and to educate her children. A minor, unique problem for her was that the superstitious servants refused to enter the still blood-spattered north room of the mansion where Murrah's nephew had shot himself. The Hamiltons had five servants while they were at the mansion, and Mary Jane spent much time planning social events, especially levees. At times these parties became somewhat strained when formerly bitter enemies met, but Mary Jane tactfully smoothed over rough situations and helped promote the healing of old wounds.

She had to use all of her patience and genuine friendliness, as did Hamilton as he struggled to win the confidence and cooperation of Texans, many of whom still thought of him as a traitor. Nevertheless, he was a surprisingly successful Governor, and his moderate policies won him many friends. But a year was not enough time to convince the majority of the people that a "Union man" was a desirable leader, and when Hamilton ran against Throckmorton in the 1866 gubernatorial race, he was defeated.

The year that followed was an unhappy one for the Hamiltons. Frustrated over his political defeat and debts, a lawyer without clients, Hamilton began to drink heavily. Marshall Pease and other friends came to his aid and managed to get an appointment for him as a register in bankruptcy in Brookhaven, Mississippi. Mary Jane and the children settled in New Orleans, eighty miles from Brookhaven, so the children could attend the superior schools there. Unhappily, an outbreak of yellow fever swept over New Orleans, and the Hamiltons' younger son, John, contracted it. In a few days he was dead. It was a crushing blow for his devoted parents, and perhaps because of a desire for the comfort of being together, Mary Jane and the other children moved to Brookhaven to be with Hamilton for the rest of his time as register of bankruptcy there.

In the late fall of 1867, Hamilton was appointed an Associate Justice of the Military Supreme Court of Texas. The Hamiltons again returned to Austin where he served with distinction in his new role. The next year Mary Jane was busy preparing for the wedding of their oldest daughter, Mary, who married W. W. Mills and moved with him to El Paso where he was a customs collector. (Later, President McKinley appointed him consul at Chihuahua City, Mexico, where he served for ten years.)

Also in 1868 Hamilton was a member of the Texas Constitutional Convention at which he was effective in gaining suffrage for both blacks and ex-Confederate whites. He still felt a strong urge to get back into politics. His friends and supporters urged him to run against E. J. Davis for Governor in 1869. His defeat in this contest was a bitter blow for the Hamiltons, especially since the counting of the votes was highly questionable and the results very close. It was more than a month after the election when the count was announced as Davis 39,901 and Hamilton 39,092. Hamilton and Mary Jane always believed that he had won.

After this disappointment, Hamilton decided to retire from politics. Over the years, Hamilton's brother Morgan had become wealthy, and in the late sixties and early seventies he generously began distributing his money among his relatives. With their portion, Hamilton and Mary Jane decided to rebuild Fair Oaks in a new location in a grove of huge old oak trees on their farm. The home they built was as spacious and palatial as the first home they had there, and Mary Jane had a garden filled with white and purple wisteria, snowy bridal wreath, lavender mountain laurel, and fragrant jasmine.

Fair Oaks became a favorite spot with young people who were friends of the Hamilton children and with visiting northerners, who were still treated with hostility by many Texans. General George Custer was among the guests while he was stationed at Austin. Dances and dinners were held frequently and were well-attended. The Virginia reel and the card game of euchre were popular ways for the Hamiltons and their guests to amuse themselves. Hamilton wrote to his daughter Mary that he was living the life of a farmer and mentioned his continuing fight against his liking for hard liquor, saying that he had swapped whiskey for ale, buttermilk, and ice water.

Life was more tranquil for the Hamiltons than it had been in years. Mary Jane had her family around her living in the security of their beautiful home, which they enjoyed sharing with their friends. But her serenity was not to last long. Soon after his retirement Hamilton developed tuberculosis. He was treated by a San Antonio doctor who specialized in respiratory ailments and for a time seemed to be improving. On April 10, 1875, Hamilton met his friend Marshall Pease in town and told him he felt better and thought he was recovering. However, the next morning he had an attack of coughing, hemorrhaged, and died. He was sixty years old. Old conflicts were forgotten as Hamilton was honored by large numbers of the people of Austin at his funeral services in the Capitol.

Mary Jane continued to operate the farm for years after her

husband's death. After the children married and left Fair Oaks for their own homes, she moved into Austin to live with Mary, whose family had returned to that city. She remained alert and active into advanced old age. When she was more then eighty years old she was often seen on the streets of Austin driving alone in her buggy. She enjoyed visits from her friends, children, grandchildren, and great-grandchildren and remained in excellent health until shortly before her death in April, 1916.

13.

Duty
into
Pleasure

Annie Rattan Throckmorton

The tall, handsome woman stood in the door of her log cabin home, the sun glinting on the red gold of her hair, her blue eyes narrowing as she watched a group of Indians approach. She glanced nervously from the men dressed in buckskin and beads to the baby sleeping in its cradle behind her. In spite of the fact that these were Indians known to her and her husband, she turned cold with fear, for she was alone and she knew that "friendly" Indians could become hostile without warning.

Masking her feelings, she greeted the group with a smile which she forced to remain on her face as the giant chief bent over the cradle, his fantastic headdress trailing on the floor, lifted the child and fondled it. She knew she must not offend the visitors in any way. Years later the incident and her feelings remained vivid in her memory. She recalled, "I thought I should die of fear and loathing, yet for the sake of peace it must be endured."

Annie Rattan Throckmorton acquired her courage through necessity. As a young girl she was considered high-strung, but frontier Texas was no place for a temperamental woman, and she quickly learned self-control as a means of survival. She had been born at Carrollton, Illinois, on March 5, 1828, to Thomas and Gillian Hill Rattan. Her father was a descendant of Nathanael Greene, a famous general in the American Revolution.

Annie received the meager education available for girls in her time, but she continued to educate herself all of her life. She was a voracious reader of books, newspapers, magazines, and any other material she could get her hands on. She was familiar with most of the classics, including Shakespeare, and kept up with the popular writers of her day, such as Dickens, Thackeray, and Eliot.

At the age of nineteen in March of 1847 she was married in Illinois to a distant relative — Dr. James W. Throckmorton. The young doctor had recently been discharged from the army after serving as a surgeon with the Texas Rangers during the Mexican War. The couple started for Texas immediately after their marriage. With them traveled Annie's older sister and her family and some friends; the long trip was made in wagons.

The Throckmortons settled in Collin County near McKinney where his father had practiced medicine and become well-known locally. (The county of Throckmorton was named after him.) James Throckmorton built his bride a log cabin and set up his own medical practice in the area. Sometimes he would be gone for several days at a time on his widespread rounds in the thinly populated region. Annie, who was the youngest in a family of sixteen, had come from a good-sized town, and she was terribly afraid of the wild animals and Indians that roamed near her isolated Texas home. So when she became pregnant, Throckmorton built her a room on her sister's house, which was some distance from the Throckmortons' log cabin. There Annie stayed until her first child was born. Then she moved back to her log cabin home and endured the loneliness and fear that were a part of her life there.

Annie's humanity is shown in an incident that occurred during her early days in Texas. Since distances were great and transportation difficult, Dr. Throckmorton sometimes brought home with him patients who required long and repeated treatment. At these times Annie turned their home into a hospital and became a nurse. On one occasion he brought home a ten-year-old girl who had an eye ailment. She remained in a darkened room two months while Annie nursed and took care of her. When her parents came for her, the girl cried and clung to Annie until she was almost forcibly removed by the embarrassed couple, who were kind people with a comfortable home. The girl grieved so much for Annie that she endangered her eyes and returned to the Throckmortons for treatment. She remained in their home for almost a year, and it was only Annie's influence and loving persuasion that convinced her finally to return to her parents' home.

Within a few years, Annie's loneliness was erased by an abundance of company. The Throckmortons' own children arrived regularly until there were ten: Hugh, Jennie, Tollie, Edward, Hattie, Benjamin, Lulie, Annie, James, and Florence. In addition, the Throckmortons added two sisters, six and four years of age, to the family when their father, who was James' brother, was killed by a man he had jailed while he was a State Marshal in Arkansas. The little girls considered "Aunt Annie" their mother, and she always treated them exactly as she did her own children. Years later, one of them recalled that she never allowed selfishness among the children. "If there was a stick of candy, everyone shared alike."

A niece of Annie's and a nephew of Throckmorton's also came to live with the expanding family. Perhaps because she had come from a large family, Annie managed to create a smooth-running household. The girls learned to do housework by being organized into partners to do the necessary jobs. The joy Annie took in her family was infectious and there was much laughter with the work. Again, inspired by Annie's boundless hospitality, the family welcomed a constant stream of visitors as the community grew. One of their favorites was Uncle Scott McKinney, the minister of the Methodist church

in McKinney which the Throckmortons attended. All
members of the family went to church faithfully, and they
must have made up a large part of the congregation in the
little town.

Household duties did not quench bookworm Annie's hunger
for reading materials. During the long spells when her
husband was away, she devoured his medical journals. The
knowledge she acquired proved valuable when their children
needed medical attention while he was gone. Once one of their
sons jumped on a broken broom weed that pierced the
bottom of his foot and broke off. Her husband was away on his
rounds, and the child was feverish and almost in convulsions.
Getting a Negro servant to hold the boy, she took some of her
husband's old instruments, opened the wound, removed the
stick, and put a dressing over the opening — possibly saving
the child from lockjaw.

In spite of the fact that he was a charter member of the
Texas Medical Association, Throckmorton detested practicing
medicine. But for years he continued to work at the job he
hated — partly because his father had wanted him to follow
the profession, partly from a sense of loyalty to an uncle who
had helped him get a medical education, and partly because he
needed to earn a living. In a letter to a cousin he explained his
feelings:

> In boyhood I had a yearning for the farm. I commenced life with
> my family without a home and without a dollar. I had studied
> medicine to gratify your grandfather. The profession was
> exceedingly distasteful to me, but an unrelenting necessity forced
> me to follow it.

Throckmorton's own health was not strong, and the life of a
rural doctor was extremely rugged. In 1851, with Annie's
blessing, he decided to give up his medical practice and turn to
law and politics to earn their living.

Annie was pleased that he was happier with the change,
although she was probably sometimes puzzled by the due
process of law. Throckmorton did not want any of the family to
attend court when he was presenting a case. However, once

when he was defending the son of a widow, who was a neighbor of the family, two of the children (possibly with Annie's knowledge) slipped in to hear the case. The young man, Ben, was accused of cattle thieving, a serious crime at that time, and the children watched spellbound while Throckmorton wept openly for the widow and Ben. While the jury was out, the children slipped out of the courtroom and ran home to report to their mother. When Throckmorton got home, Annie asked how the case turned out. Her husband answered, "Ben got off; I cleared the devil, though he was as guilty as sin!"

Through his own practice of medicine and law and through Annie's open-handed friendliness and hospitality, Throckmorton became well-known and popular in their area. He was elected to the Legislature and for the next ten years served in that body as either a Representative or a Senator.

While her husband was in Austin, Annie remained in their Collin County home, managing the farm, bearing children, and taking care of them and of the various relatives who came to stay with her. But she didn't allow her world to become limited to domestic concerns. She read everything she could to keep up with the news of the day in order to be interesting to her husband.

And there was exciting news to keep up with as the Civil War loomed nearer. Throckmorton was a member of the Secession Convention in 1861, where he was one of the "immortal seven" who voted against secession, saying, "In reverence to God and my country, unawed by the wild spirit of revolution around me, I vote *no!*" However, when the war became a reality, he was among the first in Texas to take the oath of allegiance to the Confederacy. And he served the Confederacy in several ways: as a soldier in Arkansas and Louisiana, as commander of the Third Military District of Texas, as brigadier general of the Frontier District of Texas, and as Confederate Commissioner to the Indians. In appreciation of his helpfulness, the Indians presented him with a richly embroidered leather coat and later affectionately dubbed him "Old Leathercoat."

Like other soldiers' wives, Annie waited anxiously for letters. Throckmorton was faithful in writing often, but the mails were uncertain and the waits were long.

After the war ended, Throckmorton served as president of the Constitutional Convention of 1866, and in the summer of that year he became the first postwar elected Governor of Texas, overwhelmingly defeating former Governor E. M. Pease. Annie did not move into the Executive Mansion, for she and her husband knew that his term of office was unpredictable. Throckmorton told the people who had elected him:

> ... I shall have the consolation of serving my country faithfully ... But I am harrassed by ... a heart lacerated with a knowledge of wrongs imposed upon an outraged and suffering people which I may witness, but have no power to avert.

He was right about his lack of power. The conflict of authority between the military and the civil handicapped him as it had Hamilton. His policies were too conservative to suit the Congress, and on July 31, 1867, General Philip Sheridan removed him from office as "an impediment to Reconstruction" and replaced him with his old rival, ex-Governor Pease.

Throckmorton returned home to practice law and to continue to fight against radicalism in Texas. For about a half-dozen years Annie had her family intact. But in 1874 her husband was elected a Representative to the United States Congress from the Third District and for the next fourteen years served intermittently in Congress. Annie stayed on the farm to take care of things. With nine girls and five boys in various stages of growth and the crops to manage, she was not very mobile.

Her reading matter now included the Congressional Record so she could be knowledgeable about the ideas that occupied her husband's mind. Once when one of her daughters asked her how she could read such dull material, she answered, "I began it as a duty; now I find it necessary and really enjoy it." Her devotion to her husband seems to have made her interests and pleasures always connected with things that were close to him and his work.

That Throckmorton appreciated and loved his wife is shown in his affectionate letters and in a story that tells of a conversation that took place between Throckmorton and a friend at a large reception in Washington, D.C. A renowned beauty passed by and the friend asked, "Is she not the most beautiful woman you ever saw?" Throckmorton replied, "No, indeed, I was just thinking of a more beautiful one — my wife." Annie herself was entirely unpretentious about her appearance, never wearing any jewelry other than a brooch and her wedding ring.

In 1878 Throckmorton was a candidate for Governor of Texas but was defeated, although many people felt the state owed him a term because of his unjust removal from office in 1867 and because of the outstanding record he had made in Congress in promoting the railroads. Again in 1890 he tried for the nomination but was swamped, as were other candidates, by the enormous wave of popularity that swept James S. Hogg into office.

The health of both Throckmorton and Annie weakened after 1890. Annie became quite deaf during this period. Her husband was distressed because one of his chief pleasures in life was in talking to her. When a new doctor came to town and discovered that her "deafness" was caused by impacted wax, which he removed, the family was delighted. Even as she became increasingly feeble, Annie loved to entertain her numerous children and their families and old and new friends, who found her a fascinating conversationalist because of her wide reading.

Throckmorton died on April 21, 1894. A few months later Annie suffered a stroke and remained unconscious and paralyzed until she died on October 30, 1895. She was buried in the McKinney Cemetery beside the man to whom she had devoted her life.

14

A Wife
for All
Seasons

Anne Elizabeth Britton Davis

Legend has it that when Elizabeth Davis learned President Grant had refused to send troops to keep her husband in the Governor's office, she climbed on a chair, yanked the President's picture from its place of honor in the Governor's Mansion, and stomped her French slipper through Grant's face. In later life Lizzie denied this story, but it might well have happened, for it symbolizes the spirit of this strong-minded wife of a strong-willed husband.

Anne Elizabeth Britton was an "army brat," born on a military post in Arkansas on April 9, 1838, and educated at the Visitation Convent in Baltimore. Her father, Major Forbes Britton, was a West Point classmate of Ulysses S. Grant and served in the Mexican War with Generals Winfield Scott and Zachary Taylor. After that war, he settled his family in Corpus Christi, Texas, where he became a well-respected businessman and a wealthy rancher. One of the pieces of land he owned was eight miles southwest of Corpus Christi at a place that came to be called Britton-Mott.

By the time the Davis family moved to Corpus Christi, Lizzie had become a pretty, vivacious young lady; and she soon became a popular belle, skilled at playing the piano, harp, guitar, and noted for her abilities in singing and dancing. Her silver stirrups and silver-mounted saddle are reminders that she was said to have been the best horsewoman of her day in Texas. She liked to travel and delighted in visiting the plantations of relatives in Maryland and Louisiana, where she was as much a favorite among the young people as she was in Corpus Christi.

The gay, high-spirited girl caught the attention of Judge Edmund J. Davis, a lawyer from Brownsville, who was District Judge for all of the Texas portion of the lower Rio Grande Valley. Some years earlier he had settled with his family in Galveston, where his father was buried. (He did not move "with his widowed mother to Texas" as stated in the *Handbook of Texas*.) Now he was a tall (six feet, two inches), slender man, whose refinement and courtly manners contrasted with the behavior of many of the rough and ready young pioneers of Lizzie Britton's acquaintance.

Apparently she approved of what she saw, for he moved to the number one spot in her parade of suitors and they were married in Corpus Christi in April of 1859. Dr. Britton gave the newlyweds a comfortable house with dormer windows; it was located just north of the present post office.

As questions connected with slavery and secession became more urgent, Lizzie found herself in an unhappy situation. Almost all of her immediate family, including her twin brother, Edward, favored the Confederate side, while her husband was an ardent Unionist. Her father was opposed to secession but said that if his home state (Virginia) seceded, he would go with it. He died in 1861, however, before he had to make a choice.

Two years after their marriage a son, Britton, was born to the Davises. And in 1862, just as the Texas climate was becoming untenable for supporters of the Federal government, another son, Waters, was born.

When Davis refused to take the oath of allegiance to the Confederacy, he was removed as District Judge. Threatened with being forced into the Confederate service, he left Texas aboard a blockader for New Orleans, where he organized a regiment of cavalry composed mostly of Unionist Texans.

Lizzie remained in Corpus with her mother, since both she and Davis believed that the United States would take possession of Texas immediately. Britton was not quite two years old and Waters was still a nursing infant of only seven weeks. Three months later when it became evident that the war would not end as quickly as they had expected, she obtained a pass to leave the state.

With a Negro nurse and the two small children, she started for the Rio Grande. After thirty-six hours of traveling they reached Brownsville where she was brusquely told by the authorities that she must return home. When she pleaded that she was too fatigued to start back at once over the 175 miles to Corpus Christi, adding that it would kill her, an officer spit out an oath and told her: "It makes no difference whether you are killed one way or another, and if you attempt to cross the river, you will be shot, and your body will float down the river, and be like so many deserters, you will never be heard of again!" To add to the bitterness of her situation, the man who spoke these words to her had been a close friend of her father and of her husband and had been at her wedding.

Lizzie was sent back to Corpus Christi in the care of a Confederate soldier, who treated her virtually as a prisoner. She was not allowed to stop at the ranch houses, as was her custom, to rest. For five nights she slept kneeling in the bottom of the carriage with her head on her hat box. The baby slept on the carriage seat and the nurse slept with Britton on the ground under the carriage.

After reaching home, she began to receive threatening and insulting letters. Another former friend, Colonel Hamilton Bee, who also had been one of the guests at her wedding, turned into a deadly enemy. She reported in a letter to one of her father's close friends:

> He also told me to my face, that my husband was reported coming to Texas, and that he was only coming for the purpose of murder-

ing the loyal citizens, and robbing them of their property, and when he came I must be prepared to have my throat cut first. Now this speech to me in the presence of my mother, made to a lone woman with two helpless children, and my only and twin brother in the Confederate service, I thought unbearable.

Her reply was that when her husband came for the purposes Bee named, she would be prepared and he might come and cut it.

When it became definitely known that Davis was organizing in earnest to come to Texas, the Confederate authorities sent Lizzie another pass. She was well aware that this action could be part of a plot, but again she made the tedious trip to Brownsville with the small children. There she stayed at a friend's house until night; then she put a change of clothing for the children and herself into a carpetbag, threw a Mexican blanket over her shoulders and set out for Mexico. Two friends went along to help her with the children; one of them was a member of the Home Guard. The border patrol thought she was a member of her friend's family and let her cross the ferry in safety. When she stepped on to Mexican soil, she dropped her carpetbag and blanket and cried, "Is it possible I am free!"

She remained in Mexico from December 24, 1862, until the next March before her husband could reach Matamoros from New Orleans. When he finally came, they went to the mouth of the Rio Grande, from where they planned to take a ship for New Orleans. But they had to stay there several days waiting for a tide high enough to enable vessels to cross the bar. While they were waiting, on the evening of March 14, a group of southerners crossed the Rio Grande and surrounded the house where they were staying.

The Confederates entered and demanded Davis' surrender. It was obvious they hoped he would resist and they would have an excuse to kill him. Lizzie begged them not to murder him, reminding them that she was the daughter of a respected Confederate and had a brother fighting for the Southern cause. In response to her pleading, the soldiers took Davis away alive. But they returned later and captured Captain

William Montgomery, a friend of Davis, who had come to the house looking for him.

Lizzie soon learned with horror that Montgomery had been hanged from a mesquite tree as soon as the raiders had crossed the river back into Texas. For three days she did not know where her husband was or if he was alive. Her friends did not believe that he would be allowed to live and urged her not to be too optimistic, but she refused to give up hope, although she was in misery. She wrote of the experience:

> I walked the floor day and night like a raving maniac, eating nothing for three days and nursing a young infant. I became so weak I could hardly walk without support.

The fourth morning she could stand the uncertainty no longer and prepared to cross the river to discover her husband's fate. Before she could leave, he walked into their bedroom. Almost in a state of shock, she heard his explanation.

The Mexicans had reacted violently against the violation of their neutrality by the southern raiders and had demanded the release of Davis. They threatened to close the border to all trade, to burn the city of Brownsville, and to arrest southerners in retaliation. The Confederates decided it would be wise to release Davis and brought him back to the Mexican shore.

One more frightening experience awaited Lizzie before they got under way to Louisiana. The little boat taking her and the children out to their steamer nearly capsized in the breakers, and for a few minutes she thought they were all lost. But they finally arrived safely in New Orleans, where they remained for the duration of the war. In 1864, Davis led the unsuccessful Union attack on Laredo, and the next year he was made a brigadier general.

When the war ended, the Davises returned to Corpus Christi, where he took up his law practice, and ventured into real estate by buying Mustang Island for $1,000, a purchase his family thought foolish. General Philip Sheridan, military commander of the Southwest, offered Davis an appointment as Chief Justice of the Texas Supreme Court, but Davis declined. However, it was not long before he got into political action and became involved in reconstructing the Texas government. He served in two Texas Constitutional Conventions — as a delegate in 1866, and then as President in 1868-69.

The contrast between Davis' behavior in political positions and his behavior in his private life made him a difficult person to understand. For example, in a fever epidemic in 1867 in Corpus Christi he served as a kind and willing nurse among the poor. When a woman dying of the fever wanted to spend her last moments with her mother, he helped carry her cot the three blocks to the home of the mother, who was also stricken with the fever.

But his ultra-radical policies at the conventions did not improve his popularity with Texans. Among other measures, he advocated the disfranchisement of former Confederates and unrestricted Negro suffrage. He also led the almost-successful movement to divide Texas into three states. Lizzie naturally felt much of the criticism aimed at her husband, but she never made excuses for his actions nor apologized to his critics for his behavior. On the contrary, she was outspoken in his support. Despite her background, she became every bit as much a radical as he.

In 1869 Davis ran against the more moderate Unionist, A. J. Hamilton, for Governor. The election contained many irregularities, but the military commander for the subdistrict of Texas, J. J. Reynolds, declared Davis the winner by 800 votes. The returns were bitterly disputed. Consequently, Lizzie moved into the Governor's Mansion in a somewhat less than harmonious atmosphere. The general unwillingness to accept her husband as Governor included a reluctance to accept her as First Lady. Lizzie's dreams, however, went far beyond their present situation. Before she left Corpus Christi for Austin she confided to a friend that this journey was only "the first step to the White House."

During the four years of her husband's term as virtual

dictator, martial law, riots, and temporary reigns of terror were the order of the day. Among the flood of name-calling that she shared with her husband, Lizzie perhaps resented most the term "carpetbaggers." Since both had been Texas residents for over twenty years, she felt it was grossly unfair. Although she could be imperious in manner with her husband's critics, her warm-heartedness and generous nature won her many loyal personal friends, so she was not isolated. There was, however, little formal social life in Austin.

Given the temper of the times, there was virtually nothing Lizzie could do that would not be misinterpreted. An Austin paper reported that Davis was trying to get a certain measure passed by the Legislature and that his wife was feasting the members on champagne toddies and chicken salads because "she knew a man was like an alligator, the way to his heart was through his stomach." Lizzie's sense of humor was a saving grace, and she found the report highly amusing.

An exception to the usually somber atmosphere that enveloped the mansion during the Davises' tenure was provided by the first wedding to take place there. A niece of the Governor, Mary Goodwin Hall, who was living with the Davises, married George W. Sampson in January of 1872. The ceremony was read in the double parlors of the mansion. (The grandson of this couple, George Nalle, would marry one of the daughters of the Fergusons.)

Such bright spots were few, though, as a vicious cycle existed during Davis' term of office. As the people became more discontented and uncooperative under his high-handed rule, he became more arbitrary and determined to bring about order through punitive measures, which of course increased the discontent. Lizzie unflinchingly endured the unpopularity created by her husband's policies, for she believed in him and had faith that history would justify his actions. In later years she recalled, "I was for him first and last, right or wrong."

In 1874 her husband's tumultuous rule came to a stormy conclusion when Democrat Richard Coke was elected by a large majority over Davis, who was running for re-election on the Republican ticket. Davis put up a last-ditch fight to keep control of the government. He declared the election illegal and, surrounded by his militia (composed mostly of Negro troops), barricaded himself with the old Legislature on the first floor of the Capitol while Coke and the new Legislature conducted business on the second floor. Davis appealed to President Grant for Federal support, but Grant refused to interfere. This, according to reliable witnesses, is when Lizzie reacted by smashing the President's picture.

After 1874 the Davises continued to make their home in Austin, where he practiced law and remained the Republican leader. They built a beautiful home, and as time began to heal the wounds of war and reconstruction, their lives became more serene. Lizzie gave large entertainments, which she called "hops," that were attended by a variety of people. To one of them came a man who had been a member of the raiding party that had captured her husband and threatened his life while she watched helplessly less than a dozen years before.

An incident from these post-gubernatorial years illustrates Lizzie's capacity for friendship in the truest sense of the word. Perhaps because the Davises had no daughters, Lizzie became very fond of a young woman named Jessie Davidson Rhea, often lending Jessie her fine saddle horse and inviting her frequently to their home. Jessie married and became pregnant, but when she went into labor, no doctor was available. Lizzie stayed with her young friend during the long hours of labor, and when the time came delivered the infant, a healthy baby girl.

When the Davises' own children reached college age, the older son, Britton, went off to West Point; and the younger son, Waters, went to Ann Arbor, Michigan, to study law. Meanwhile, Davis made two more political essays — both unsuccessful. In 1880 he ran against Oran Roberts for Governor and lost by more than a hundred thousand votes. In 1882 he was an unsuccessful candidate for Congress. The majority of Texans wanted no more rule by the old "Reconstruction gang."

The year after his defeat for a seat in Congress, Davis caught pneumonia and after an illness of only ten days, died on February 7, 1883. Lizzie's grief was eased somewhat as she had the satisfaction of seeing the highest civic and military honors paid to her husband. His body lay in state in the chamber of the House of Representatives. Governor John Ireland led the tributes, and even old enemies like the *Austin Statesman*, which had so often blasted his political actions, paid him homage. Its February 8th editorial column said:

> In social and domestic life he has been one of the best and purest of men . . . He was a gentleman of culture and refinement, courteous, gentle, and refined in his bearing, devoted to his family, true to his friends.

Lizzie buried her husband beside her father in the State Cemetery. A few years later one of Davis' brothers had a tall monument erected over the grave; today it still towers above the other tombstones there.

After her husband's death, Lizzie moved from their large home and boarded at a Mrs. McGowan's in Austin. She remained impetuous and charming to her friends. One day she found young Lillie, Mrs. McGowan's daughter, in tears because she couldn't finish the dishes in time for a matinee. Lizzie shooed Lillie off to the show and took over. Other women in the house came to help with the drying while Lizzie entertained them with anecdotes from her life. One listener later said she "never spent a more pleasant hour."

For a time Lizzie went to stay with an uncle and his wife, Dr. and Mrs. Millard in Grand Cateur, Louisiana. She had often been a visitor at their plantation before she had married, and many of her old friends came to call on "Miss Lizzie," who had been the belle of numerous balls. Among the callers was an old suitor, Alexander Smith, now nicknamed "Pots" Smith because he was in the business of making pots and pans.

Lizzie's sons brought her satisfaction and pride as they matured, but they were far away from her physically. Britton, who had graduated from West Point the same year his father died, was stationed in California; and Waters had passed his bar examinations and was on his way to becoming a distinguished lawyer in El Paso.

In spite of the difficulties through which she had passed, Lizzie was still filled with a zest for living. When Alexander Smith asked her to marry him and go to Washington, D.C., to live, she agreed. She joined Trinity Catholic Church, Georgetown, and lived a quiet but busy life among new friends. In the later years of her life, she continued to support her first husband's actions. In a letter written in 1907 to James T. DeShields (author of *They Sat in High Places*), she pleaded with him to treat Davis' administration "more objectively" than others had done.

A fleeting glimpse of Lizzie in her old age is handed down by a granddaughter who recalls a ritual that took place when her grandmother came to visit. An old Negro, who had been a slave of the Davises, always came in to pay his respects to his former mistress. He and Lizzie each took a glass of port. She raised her glass and drank "to the Old South"; then he raised his glass and drank "to the good old days and to you, Miss Lizzie."

Alexander Smith died when Lizzie was in her early eighties, and she continued to live in Washington until her own death at the age of eighty-seven, on May 5, 1925. She was buried in Rock Creek Cemetery, District of Columbia, far from the husband at whose side she had remained with fierce loyalty all of his life.

15

The
Durable
Invalid

Mary Evans Horne Coke

The young Waco lawyer watched appraisingly as the slender girl stepped into her carriage. In the ascent she revealed her dainty ankles and feet. "I'm going to marry that girl," he declared. He kept his vow, and for the next half-century took pleasure in buying shoes for his wife's tiny feet.

Those captivating feet belonged to Mary Evans Horne, who was born in Georgia in March of 1837. At the age of ten she moved with her family to Mississippi. Three years later, her father, a physician, decided to move his practice to Texas. The family settled in Waco, a frontier village in McLennan County, where other pioneers such as the Ross family were establishing themselves. Mary was only fifteen when she met and married Dick Coke, who had first fallen in love with her feet and then with the whole girl. The vows were read by Dr. Rufus C. Burleson, the great Baptist preacher who baptized Sam Houston.

Richard Coke, the twenty-three-year-old bridegroom, had been born in Williamsburg, Virginia, and was a graduate of William and Mary College. After graduation, he studied law and was admitted to the bar in 1850 when he was only twenty-one. Unable to decide where he wanted to practice, he had gone to Washington, D.C., to talk over the problem with his uncle, Congressman Richard Coke, for whom he was named. His uncle introduced him to Senator Sam Houston, who dazzled young Coke with glowing descriptions of Texas as a land of opportunity. The old warrior made it sound irresistible. Armed with letters of introduction from Houston, Coke packed his law books in his saddlebags and found his way to McLennan County and young Mary Horne.

Soon after their marriage, the Cokes built a home and started a cotton plantation on the black waxy soil by the banks of the Brazos River near Waco. Mary would live in or near that town for the rest of her life, except for the years spent in the Governor's Mansion. Through hard work, her young husband made a success of the plantation and built up a substantial law practice. In a biographical sketch of Coke, Dr. Burleson points out that he was not gifted with any outstanding talent, such as brilliant wit or eloquence, but that he achieved his goals by plodding hard work and unshakable integrity.

And he adored his fragile wife. Mary Coke was never a strong woman, but in spite of her consistently frail health, she bore four children and outlived all of them, as well as her husband. In January of 1856 the Cokes' first child, Amanda Eliza, was born; but she died before she reached her first birthday. The next year another child, Jack, arrived and Mary was greatly comforted that he was a strong and healthy infant.

The Cokes became prosperous in the years immediately preceding the Civil War. By 1860 they owned approximately 2,700 acres in McLennan County and several lots in the town of Waco. In addition to the plantation, Coke was using about 300 acres on the Brazos River to raise swine. They had personal property valued at over $17,000 and owned fifteen slaves.

When the war began, Coke enlisted as a private in the Confederate Army and served throughout the war. Soon after he left home with his company, Mary gave birth to a third child, Mary Victoria. But the following year this baby also died. As she endured the long months of waiting for news of her husband, Mary found great consolation in the company of Jack, now a toddler. When news came, it was usually exciting but not particularly soothing, for Coke, who was promoted to the rank of captain for gallantry in action, always seemed to be where the fighting was the hottest. As one of his company remarked, when the bullets were flying, he was in the middle of them, "his bald head shining, hollering, 'Come on, boys!' "

On May 31, 1864, Coke wrote a letter to his commandant asking for a leave of sixty days to visit his family "on the following grounds:"

> About the first of April last my overseer who managed my plantation and attended to all my business enrolled in the Confederate service . . . My family consisting of a wife and one child are living on my plantation and no white male on the place . . . My wife's health is so bad as almost to unfit her for attention to her domestic duties . . . More than nineteen months have elapsed since I was at home and saw my family.

The request was granted immediately, and Mary had her husband home for most of the summer. Then he returned to his unit to remain until the war ended the next year.

Back in Waco, Coke was appointed a District Judge, and for convenience he and Mary purchased a house on the corner of South Second and Clay Streets. In 1866 another promotion came as Coke was elected Judge of the Texas Supreme Court. Fortunately, Mary did not move to Austin with him, for the following year he was one of those swept out of office by General Philip Sheridan as "an impediment to Reconstruction."

For six years, along with the rest of Texas, the Cokes suffered the hardships of Reconstruction. During this time, on July 30, 1869, Richard Coke, Jr. was born. Like most Democratic Texans, Mary and Coke hated the thought of four more years under Davis and his "carpetbag regime." Friends and admirers urged Coke to enter the gubernatorial race in 1873, and with Mary's consent he agreed. Ex-Confederates rallied to elect him by a two-to-one majority over Davis.

Davis, however, was not ready to vacate the Governor's chair; he had his hand-picked Supreme Court declare the election void because of "illegal voting." Texas seemed on the verge of its own civil war as Davis and his State Police — mostly Negroes — entrenched themselves on the first floor of the Capitol while Coke, his Lieutenant Governor, Richard Hubbard, and their supporters gathered to organize the new administration on the second. Austin began to fill up with armed men, and Davis' backers drilled holes for small arms fire in the ceiling under the roof where the inauguration was to be held.

How much Mary knew of her husband's danger is not recorded, but it was an ugly situation. If President Grant had sent the Federal aid that Davis requested, the casualties might have been serious. As it was, the only blood-letting occurred through the use of fists against noses as Davis and his troops reluctantly vacated the building when the President refused to support them.

Texans responded enthusiastically to Coke's inaugural address, which he began at midnight of January 15, 1874:

Let the hearts of the people throb with joy, for the old landmarks of constitutional representative government, so long lost, are this day restored and the ancient liberties of the people of Texas reestablished.

To celebrate deliverance from the plague of Reconstruction, a grand inaugural ball was held on the night of February 5, 1874. The Austin *Weekly Democratic Statesman* reported that 1,500 people attended the ball, which was held in both the legislative halls where a "grand array of beauty and splendid costumes graced for many hours the halls of the Capitol." The event began at 9:30 and opened with a grand march in which the Governor, the Lieutenant Governor, and other state officials took part.

No mention is made of the Governor's wife in this account, and it is not likely that she took an active part in the affair, even if she attended it. For Coke's entire term as Governor, Mary's health was so poor that she was considered an invalid and took little or no part in social events. Her gentle, retiring nature contrasted dramatically with the personality of her predecessor, the forceful Elizabeth Davis. However, Mary's kindness and concern for others won her a circle of loyal friends.

One social happening of note during Mary's time as mistress of the mansion was the wedding of Coke's widowed cousin, a Mrs. Hook. She had been staying with the Cokes, and when she married General Jerome Robertson, theirs was the second wedding to take place in the Governor's Mansion.

Although Coke was a popular Governor, his term was troubled by difficulties including debts owed by the state, Indian and Mexican raids, and disputes over the railroads. An important task was the calling of a Constitutional Convention, which in 1876 adopted the constitution under which the state has operated for more than a century. Under this new constitution Coke's term was cut from four to two years, but he successfully ran for a second term in 1876.

While her husband struggled with these administrative problems, Mary stayed quietly and patiently in the background carrying out her two-fold duty as she saw it — to support her husband in every way that she could and to provide a pleasant home atmosphere for him. These duties she performed well in spite of her poor health. When Coke decided to run for the U.S. Senate, she encouraged him, even though she realized it almost certainly meant long periods of separation if he were elected.

He did win the election, and in 1877 resigned as Governor to assume his seat in Congress. Mary returned with Jack and Dick, Jr. to Waco, where Coke bought her a palatial home on South Eighth Street. Here she lived with the children while Coke served a total of three terms as a U.S. Senator. She made occasional trips to Washington when her health permitted. However, for most of this time she remained at home, going out very little socially, using her strength and energies for charity and church work.

As they grew up, her two sons, who were devoted and solicitous in looking after her needs, became her greatest comfort during her husband's long absences. In 1880 Jack, the oldest boy, contracted a "disease" (possibly meningitis). A few months later, on June 5, he died. At the time of his death Mary was described in newspaper accounts as being "seriously ill" herself. Twenty-three-year-old Jack, a law student at Baylor, was a great favorite of many people in Waco, and the longest funeral procession ever seen in that city (more than a mile in length) followed his coffin from the Cokes' home on Eighth Street to Oakwood Cemetery.

Senator Coke was delayed in reaching home; he sent a wire from St. Louis asking that services be postponed until he arrived, and a later wire from Sedalia, Missouri, ordering that interment take place immediately "should such course be deemed best." He finally reached Waco by train, the evening after the funeral.

Dick, Jr. was only eleven at the time of his brother's death, and all of the Cokes' hopes now centered on him, their only living child. When it was time to choose a career, he was offered opportunities to enter the legal field, but he preferred farming and chose to learn to manage the family's cotton plantation. Mary and her husband looked forward to the time when their son would marry and produce grandchildren for them to enjoy. But that day would never come.

In 1895 Dick acquired a "lingering disease" — probably tuberculosis. His illness was a great blow to his parents and may have been the reason that Coke resigned from the Senate that year. Within a twelve-month period Mary suffered a double tragedy. In 1897 Coke died after a brief illness. In January of 1898 Dick, who had a cold, rode fourteen miles to the lower end of the family farm and back. The exertion and exposure resulted in pneumonia and within two weeks he was dead.

Mary's life must have seemed very empty as she looked at the graves of her four children grouped around the snow white, lifelike statue of her husband which she had erected in Oakwood Cemetery. Ironically, she, the chronic invalid, had outlived all of those who had watched so carefully over her health and who had been nearest and dearest to her.

Her only close surviving relative was her younger brother, James E. Horne, who came to live with her and take care of her during the last two years of her life. Financially, she was well off. Her husband had acquired business buildings in Waco as well as the prosperous cotton plantation; in all, his estate was valued at over $250,000. But all that she truly valued was gone and her days were sad.

There was a little comfort in the tributes paid to her husband, including the naming of Coke County after him. And she continued to take an interest in performing acts of charity where she saw a need. One of her last public actions was to endow a medal for the Rusk Literary Society of the University of Texas, to be awarded annually to the member who proved to be the best debater.

On October 29, 1900, after a short illness, she died at her home. Her funeral services were conducted by Dr. Rufus Burleson, who had officiated at her marriage nearly fifty years earlier. A large crowd attended and the floral offerings were lavish. One of the most sincere and spontaneous tributes occurred when the casket lid was raised for friends to view her remains. Some of the former slaves of the Cokes fell on their knees in front of it and cried for "young mistress."

Prominent men sent messages of condolence to James Horne, Mary's brother. These included a telegram from ex-Governor James S. Hogg, who said that for her loyalty and devotion Mary deserved to share the honors of her husband. He commended her "modest, patient life."

16.

From Tyler to Tokyo

Janie Roberts Hubbard

Preceded by military and civil authorities in glittering uniforms, the Emperor's royal carriages drew up to the ancient walls of the Japanese palace. As the procession paused in front of the gates, bugles sounded and a drawbridge was lowered over the moat. While the guards stood at attention, the golden carriages slowly entered the magnificently manicured grounds and stopped at the front entrance. An American woman of regal bearing stepped from one of the carriages and was met by princesses and ladies-in-waiting, who escorted her through the massive doors and into the throne room.

The American woman bowed low three times as she approached the imperial presence of the Empress of Japan. When the two women stood face to face, the tiny Empress looked up at the figure in front of her and made a brief but earnest speech of welcome in which she paid tribute to all American women. After an English translation of the speech, the visitor bowed once more, made a short, formal response, and slowly backed from the imperial presence the full length of the reception room.

The year was 1885 and the American woman was Janie Roberts Hubbard, wife of Richard Hubbard, envoy extraordinary and minister plenipotentiary to Japan — and ex-Governor of Texas.

Janie Hubbard had not been eager to make the trip to Japan; it was such a long distance from home and friends, and her health was not good. But during the sixteen years of their marriage she had been her husband's hostess and companion, and she intended to continue in those capacities as long as she was able.

Born Janie Roberts on August 9, 1849, in Georgia, she had spent most of her life in Tyler, Texas. Like her father, who was a member of the Georgia Senate, she had a brilliant mind and the tact of a skilled politician. While his daughter was still a very young girl, Willis Roberts moved the family to Smith County, Texas, where he became a prominent planter. The family bought a home in Tyler, a town that Janie came to love and always considered her home, no matter where she might live temporarily. Here she came to know Richard Hubbard, a widower and a lawyer.

Although there was seventeen years difference in their ages, the two had much in common. Janie, at twenty, was quite poised and dignified. Physically she had a large, stately figure; Richard was also imposing in appearance, being a huge man weighing close to three hundred pounds. They were also well-matched intellectually, both having sharp, quick minds. Janie's heart went out to the big, sad man, who had suffered more than his share of tragedy, having lost his young wife and four of his children.

At the age of thirty-seven, Hubbard had already distinguished himself in a number of ways: he had served in the House of the Eighth Legislature of Texas and had commanded the Texas Confederate 22nd Regiment of Cavalry as a colonel during the Civil War. For his eloquence and the powerful voice that matched his size, he had earned the title "the Demosthenes of Texas."

Turning his persuasive powers on Janie, Hubbard talked

her into becoming his bride. They were married in her home in Tyler on December 2, 1869, and settled in Lindale, a few miles north of the city. With them lived Hubbard's children by his previous marriage — Serena (Rena) and Richard, Jr. — and Hubbard's mother. They were relatively well-to-do for the postwar South. The 1870 census showed that they owned real estate valued at $10,000 plus $5,000 of personal property.

In 1873 and again in 1876 (at least partly because of his brilliance as a speaker) Hubbard was elected Lieutenant Governor on a ticket with Richard Coke. During Hubbard's first term, a son, Charles, was born to the couple. An insight into child psychology of the day is revealed in an anecdote that tells of an occasion when Janie was visiting a friend and Charley got his head caught between the banister rails of the hostess' stairway. Janie sighed, "I knew Charley would do something which he ought not to do. I generally punish him before I leave home to assure his good behavior." The preventive punishment was to stand Charley on a chair and switch his little stockinged legs. Being a normal child, Charley probably felt he was due some mischief since he had paid for it in advance.

In October of 1875 the family was saddened by the death of Hubbard's eight-year-old son Richard, Jr.

The year 1876 was eventful for Janie. In May she gave birth to a second son, Clarence. In September she basked in the praise for her husband that poured in after he was appointed Centennial Orator of Texas and delivered an outstanding address at the World's Exposition at Philadelphia. And when Coke resigned as Governor in December, she suddenly found herself elevated to the position of First Lady of the state. She was only twenty-seven, but her stately bearing and gracious manners won her the approval of Austin society.

During and after the war had stretched long years that were barren of formal entertaining, and townfolk were delighted with Janie Hubbard's elegant teas and dinner parties. The conversation was as sparkling as the women's gowns. Among the titillating topics of conversation at Janie's distinguished dinner table were the daring train robberies and bank holdups being made by organized groups of outlaws. For Hubbard and his administration, crime was one of the major problems, and the Rangers were kept busy. Sam Bass, the "Robin Hood" bandit, met his nemesis during Hubbard's term when he planned one bank robbery too many. Bass was reported headed with his gang toward Austin, but he was betrayed to the Rangers by one of his own men and received a mortal wound in the ambush that took place in Round Rock, a few miles north of the capital. Tales of the capture provided dinner table talk at the mansion for weeks.

During her term as First Lady, Janie had the pleasure of arranging the third mansion wedding. The bride was of more than usual interest to Texans, for she had been a resident of the mansion when her father, Sam Houston, was Governor. On March 1, 1877, Nettie Houston married Major W. L. Bringhurst, a teacher at the Military Institute in Austin. It was a cold, rainy spring night and only a few people were present, but the bride wore white satin and borrowed orange flowers (there were no florists in Austin) and was given away by Governor Hubbard. Long afterward, Rena Hubbard remembered sitting on the stairs watching the impressive ceremony in awe. Janie superintended the preparation of a wedding feast for the young couple and their guests.

In the somewhat overwrought prose of the period, the *Democratic Statesman* of March 15, 1877, commented:

> There was a singular propriety in having such a marriage celebrated in such a place. The daughter of Sam Houston, inheriting certainly the most poetical attributes of his genius, wedded to Texas by a thousand memories, could hardly begin the new life without the benediction of the commonwealth which Houston having protected and saved, ever owes a roof-tree to his children.

With the end of his term approaching, Hubbard sought renomination by the Democratic Party in 1878. He was challenged, however, by former Governor Throckmorton and Colonel W. W. Lang, Master of the Farmers' Grange. After the nominating convention had argued inconclusively for five days in the August heat, it took the unusual step of appointing a committee to select a nominee from the leading men in the state. The committee chose Judge Oran Roberts; so in 1879 the Hubbards returned to Tyler, where Hubbard resumed his law practice.

On August 14 of the following year a daughter, Searcy, was born. Janie was never strong after this birth, but she settled down contentedly to rearing her children and raising flowers in the town where relatives and friends lived. The Hubbards were faithful members of the First Baptist Church of Tyler. A happy event in 1871 was the naming of Hubbard City in honor of Richard Hubbard. (The name was later shortened to Hubbard.)

In the opening months of 1882 a double tragedy struck the family. The Hubbard family Bible records the death of "Charles Freeman Hubbard on the 30th day of January A.D. 1882, aged 8 yrs. 6 mo. 17 days." The next entry records the death of "Clarence Roberts Hubbard . . . in February A.D. 1882, aged 6 yrs. 9 mo. 9 days." Like so many other children in the nineteenth century, the little boys were victims of the dreaded diphtheria.

Frederick Mansfield, Hubbard's personal secretary, was a great comfort and help to the family, and they were all pleased when Serena became engaged to him. The wedding took place at the Hubbards' home on September 23, 1884. The next year the Mansfields added a son to the family — Richard Bennett Mansfield.

Possibly to help ease his grief over the death of his sons, Hubbard had become involved in politics again. In 1884 he was a delegate to the Democratic National Convention that nominated Grover Cleveland for President. Impressed by Hubbard's oratorical ability, the convention elected him temporary chairman. In the campaign that followed, he made a number of effective speeches for the Democratic ticket in various states. When Cleveland won his election, he showed his appreciation of Hubbard's efforts by appointing him the United States minister to Japan. Although Janie's health was poor, she packed to accompany her husband on the long trip to the Orient aboard the Pacific liner *Tokio*. It was a comfort to her that Searcy, Rena, her husband, and their young son, Richard, were to accompany them.

The ship sailed from San Francisco, and after a tedious journey of twenty-three days, the shores of Japan finally came into view. The Hubbards, along with the other passengers, watched the sun set over their long-awaited destination. Then they retired to their stateroom to finish packing and rest in anticipation of an early morning disembarkation. They were aroused at midnight by a ship's officer who reported that the ship had run onto "a granite shelving rock" and was in imminent danger of breaking in two. For a time it seemed that the ship would sink with everyone aboard. Hubbard later wrote of the courage of his wife, and of his daughter who prayed during the tense moments while Janie calmly helped others put on their life jackets.

After this frightening beginning, Janie found life in Japan colorful and interesting. The American Embassy was spacious and luxurious; the formal diplomatic routine with its elegant entertainments was quite a contrast to social life in Tyler, Texas, in the 1880's, but it pleased the adaptable Janie.

The men's bright military uniforms, glittering with gold braid, and the exquisite gowns and elaborate hairstyles of the doll-like women fascinated her. And she was delighted with the beauty of the well-kept gardens with their shrubs shaped into forms of birds and beasts, vine-covered tea houses, miniature waterfalls, and gorgeous flowers. The huge variety of many-colored chrysanthemums especially impressed her, and one of the entertainments she liked most was the imperial chrysanthemum garden party held in the beautiful palace grounds. Other not so enjoyable experiences were the occasional earthquake tremors that shook the walls of the legation.

In the spring of 1886, the Hubbards were saddened by the news of the death of Janie's father in February and of her mother's death in April. Janie was quite ill for a time herself after she received the news of her mother's death, and in May Hubbard took her and Searcy to a picturesque mountain resort where they enjoyed the hot baths. (He was dieting and hoped the baths would help him reach his goal of getting his weight under three hundred pounds.)

Back in Tokyo the Hubbards tried to lead as normal a life as Janie's health would permit. They joined the Union Church, which was made up of several Protestant denominations. Janie had a Chinese cook named Yin whom she was more or less successful in teaching to cook "American style." In addition to making the formal diplomatic calls that were expected of them, they visited tourist sites, exhibits of Japanese art, and went on shopping expeditions.

Cholera was prevalent in Japan in 1886, and in June the Mansfields' son, Richard, became ill with it. Rena was pregnant, and therefore not allowed to nurse him, so Janie took over the task. The doctors despaired of his life, prayers were offered for him in the church, and Janie watched over him day and night. On June 28, Hubbard recorded in his diary, "Mrs. H. nearly broken down with nursing." Richard slowly recovered, but there was a cholera epidemic at Yokohama. When Hubbard asked for permission to move the entire legation to the mountains, the request was denied. However, soon after the Mansfields' second child, Louise, was born, Hubbard did take the family to Ikao, a watering place.

From this time on Janie's health was poor. In the diary that Hubbard kept during the remainder of the year, he comments daily on the state of her health. When he could report that she showed improvement, he wrote, "delighted!" Her condition was of more concern to him than anything else in his life — every church service, official function, or social affair is mentioned in relation to whether or not Janie was able to attend with him.

On Hubbard's fifty-fourth birthday, November 1, she was well enough to join in the celebration which included a dinner and a ball. But during the fall she missed several of her "days at home," which were Wednesday afternoons when she usually received visitors. At Christmas she was feeling fairly well and on December 31 Hubbard wrote, "Family circle in Japan is unbroken and the insatiate archer has retained his arm for the time."

But Janie's time was becoming short, and she must have realized that she would not recover her health. She had a dread of dying and being buried in the foreign land, for she had seen this happen to other Americans who had succumbed to cholera. Her husband promised that he would not let it happen to her, and he was faithful to his word.

After months of increasing weakness and suffering, Janie died on July 9, 1887 — exactly a month before her thirty-ninth birthday. The Hubbards had been in Japan not quite a year and a half.

The Japanese government gave Janie Hubbard an elaborate funeral ceremony with all the pomp and honors at its command. Her body was embalmed and placed in an above-ground vault where it remained until her husband returned to the United States two years later. During those two years Rena Hubbard served as her father's hostess and took care of her little half-sister, seven-year-old Searcy.

As he prepared to return to the United States in April of 1889, Hubbard recorded in his diary, "Now it is I feel my great bereavement and the loss to little Searcy of her devoted mother, God help us!"

On June 9 Janie was buried beneath the pines and cedars of Tyler's Oakwood Cemetery near the graves of her two young sons, Charley and Clarence.

Hubbard lived for twelve more years. During this time he gave lectures on the Orient and wrote a book, *The United States in the Far East*, which was published in 1899. Two years later he died and was buried beside his faithful wife, who had followed him wherever his career had led.

17.

Coffee Beans and Turnip Greens

Frances Wickliffe Edwards Roberts

Two smartly-dressed matrons descended from their carriage in front of the Governor's Mansion in Austin and walked sedately up the steps. They had put on their best clothes and best manners to pay a call on the mistress of the mansion. A plainly dressed woman, her silver hair pulled back in an unfashionable, no-nonsense bun, beckoned to them from the garden at the side of the building. They stared in shocked disbelief as the First Lady of the state put aside the turnip greens she had been picking, wiped her hands on her blue-checked apron and welcomed them warmly. Before their visit was over the callers had come to appreciate Frances Edwards Roberts for the down-to-earth naturalness and sincere friendliness that characterized her, no matter what her circumstances. Plain, practical common sense and a deep religious faith gave her confidence that there was a right and wrong in every situation. Acting in accordance with her strong sense of right gave her a serene self-confidence that was felt by all who met her.

Born in the Greenville District of South Carolina to Scottish and English parents on March 4, 1819, Frances Wickliffe

Edwards combined some of the best traits of the two national-
ities. While she was very young her family moved to Ashville,
Alabama, where they purchased a home about a mile from the
farm of a widow, Mrs. Margaret Roberts. Frances came to
know Mrs. Roberts' son, Oran, who from the time he was ten
did a man's work on his mother's farm. With six children (all
girls) in her own family, Frances early learned to work hard,
too. Both youngsters grew up used to plain living, imbued
with the idea that duty can be pleasure, and with an
abhorrence of being in debt.

At sixteen, Oran Roberts faced a serious problem: he didn't
want to spend the rest of his life as a farmer, but he had no
formal education. He began to make the long trip to
Tuscaloosa to earn a high school degree. Sometime during the
years while he was acquiring his education, he realized he had
another problem: he was in love with his pretty brown-haired
neighbor, but he felt awkward around girls because he had
had little contact with them during his hard-working
childhood. In his practical way he began to attend a dancing
school at the local hotel in Tuscaloosa in order to acquire some
social graces.

Before he finished high school he had gotten Frances'
promise to wait for him — until he became a lawyer! Their
early training had conditioned both of them to work and wait
for the things they wanted. Oran graduated from the
University of Alabama at twenty-one, studied law with a
friend, and a year later passed the bar examination in record
time. As soon as he achieved this goal he "redeemed a long-
standing pledge" when he and Frances were married on
December 12, 1837.

Others besides Frances were quick to appreciate Oran
Roberts' worth, and he was elected to the Alabama
Legislature the year after their marriage. He had a successful
term and his popularity increased in Alabama. He probably
could have had a distinguished political career in that state,
but the new Republic of Texas with its exciting challenges
beckoned. In 1841 the young couple set out for San Augustine

and a new beginning.

San Augustine was a flourishing East Texas town known as a social and political center of the newly independent country. Roberts set up a law practice and again quickly came to the attention of state leaders. Within a little more than two years after the Robertses had moved to Texas, Sam Houston appointed him District Attorney, and two years later Texas' first Governor after annexation, J. Pinckney Henderson, also a San Augustine resident, named Roberts a District Judge.

At some time during these years the Robertses bought a farm in Shelby County near San Augustine. When her husband's official duties took him away from home, Frances managed things. Three of their children were born here: Sarah Jane, Oba, and Robert Pinckney. With Frances' approval Roberts served as President of the Board of Trustees and as a lecturer in law at the recently opened University of San Augustine. In 1857 he was appointed an Associate Justice of the state Supreme Court. About this same time the Robertses moved to another farm near Tyler. Here four children were born to them — Margaret Eliza, Peter, Frances Una, and Oran Milo, Jr.

Always firm in his convictions, Roberts was instrumental in calling the Secession Convention which met in 1861; when it convened he was unanimously elected its President. In 1862 Roberts raised a regiment, the Eleventh Texas Infantry, and served as its Colonel.

Frances took over a small vacant house on a lot adjoining their home and fitted it as a hospital for the wounded and sick members of the Eleventh Infantry. Sarah Jane helped her with the nursing duties while their two oldest sons served in the war with their father. One of Frances' few self-indulgences was in satisfying her fondness for coffee, which became practically unobtainable during the war. She had no taste for the substitute mixture of rye and barley that so many people were using. On a trip to Houston, Roberts managed to get her a sack of coffee beans and brought it to her, urging her to use it sparingly because it would probably be the last she would

get until the war was over. When Frances saw how much the
sick and homesick soldiers in her hospital enjoyed a steaming
cup of the precious brew, she generously shared it, giving
away much more than she consumed herself.

Frances could not card raw fibers because of an asthmatic
condition, but she did the weaving for four soldiers during the
war.

In 1864 Roberts was appointed Chief Justice of the Supreme
Court of Texas, and served until he was removed by the
military authorities during Reconstruction. He served in the
Constitutional Convention of 1866, and that same year the
Texas Legislature elected him and David G. Burnet to the
United States Senate. However, the radical Republican
Congress refused to seat them, and Roberts told Frances that
he "imitated Moses" as he gazed from the gallery at his empty
promised seat.

Like many other southerners, the Robertses found
themselves in financial difficulties after the war, and Frances
insisted that they sell their home to pay their debts. From
1866 to 1874 while Reconstruction was in full swing. Frances
moved her household about in East Texas as Roberts
practiced law in Tyler and then in Gilmer (where he organized
a law school), farmed in the lower end of Shelby County, and
then returned to practice in Tyler, In 1874 Governor Coke
again appointed Roberts Chief Justice of the Texas Supreme
Court. This time he served four years, winning acclaim for the
careful research and analysis that went into his decisions.

As a result, when the Texas Democratic Convention of 1878
met and found itself in a deadlock between the supporters of
ex-Governor Throckmorton and Governor Hubbard, a
committee was formed which chose Roberts as a compromise
candidate. The Robertses were on their farm near Tyler when
the telegram arrived announcing his selection. Securing
Frances' agreement, Roberts put on his Prince Albert coat
and rode into town on his fantail spotted pony, smoking his
corn cob pipe. In Tyler he borrowed fifty cents from a
bartender friend to wire his acceptance to the convention.

Roberts was sixty-three and Frances was fifty-nine when they moved into the Governor's Mansion. All of their children except Oran, Jr. had grown up and left home. The Robertses brought with them their simple, unpretentious manners and life style. Roberts was called the "cob pipe" Governor because he and his pipe were inseparable. When he stood up to be sworn into office, he handed his cob pipe to a friend while he raised his hand to take the oath. For all state occasions, such as the inauguration ceremony, Frances wore a good, plain, black silk gown.

The people of Texas expected Governors of that day to begin their terms with two big social events—an inaugural ball and a levee for the Legislature. Everyone paid five dollars to attend the dance, for which the music was provided by a string band that played mostly waltzes and Virginia reels. A few days after the ball, Frances had to provide a supper for the levee to which the legislators would bring their families and friends. And they expected to be well fed! Pigs, chickens, turkeys, vegetables, salads, pies, cakes and gallons of coffee had to be prepared and served, at a cost of between $400 and $500 (paid by the Governor). Frances must have done her job well because a story goes that when one of the lawmakers first met Frances he told friends, "Mrs. Roberts is rather plain and I don't know how I will like her." After the levee he said, "Old Mrs. Roberts will do. I never ate such a supper!"

In spite of the fact that Frances' health began to fail from the time she moved into the mansion, she worked hard at her new job. In her view the Governor's Mansion belonged to the people of Texas, and as many of them as wanted to were always welcome to visit. The stately house became a homey place under her management. She worked in her vegetable garden, and turned the back parlor into a bedroom in order to have more room for visiting constituents. When the Capitol Building burned and blackened and water-soaked pictures were sent to the mansion for safekeeping, she gave them careful attention and did all she could to preserve them. And always she gave a warm welcome to the steady stream of visitors from the poorest favor-seekers to well-known personalities such as Dr. Ashbel Smith and Elisabet Ney. It would be interesting to know what the conservative Frances found to talk about with the liberal Miss Ney.

The pay-as-you-go policy that Roberts put into effect on a statewide basis was the same policy that Frances had always insisted they follow in their own affairs. Texans liked having the Robertses in the mansion, and when he ran against ex-Governor Davis in 1880, they re-elected their "cob pipe" Governor by an overwhelming majority.

Again Frances put on her good black silk and again gave Austinites a levee to remember. She continued to tend her turnip patch and to make visiting Texans feel welcome to their Austin "home," even though her health progressively deteriorated. A corps of about ten young society women from Austin sometimes helped her with the entertaining. Among them was the young lady who would later become the wife of Colonel E. M. House, who helped manage several guberna-torial campaigns and later became a trusted advisor to President Woodrow Wilson. It is quite likely that Colonel House was introduced to his wife by Frances during one of the official state entertainments.

Educational legislation was important during Roberts' administration, and the University of Texas finally became a reality during his last year in office. When his term ended, he became one of the first professors of law at the University.

As Frances' tenure as First Lady came to an end, so did her strength. The unexplained illness that had plagued her during her days in the mansion finally brought about her death on November 27, 1883. The people of Austin turned out in great numbers to show their feeling for the plain, warm-hearted woman who had lived among them as a friend, and modest Frances Roberts had one of the most impressive funerals ever held in Austin. The entire law class of the University of Texas acted as an honorary escort, marching on either side of the hearse. Massive, costly floral designs covered the coffin in which Frances lay — dressed for the last time in her good black dress.

After his wife's death, Roberts continued to teach at the University of Texas for ten years. He came to be thought of as a link between Texas' distant past as a Republic and her present, which Roberts had helped shape. His pupils affectionately called him "the old Alcalde," and the ex-students magazine of the University of Texas took its name, "The Alcalde," in his honor. He was one of the "Robertses" for whom Roberts County was named. In 1887 Roberts married Mrs. Catherine E. Border of Austin. After he retired from teaching in 1893, they moved to Marble Falls, Texas. In his later years he did a great deal of writing about Texas and served as an organizer and the first president of the Texas State Historical Association. He died in Austin on May 19, 1898.

An interesting twist of fate caused descendants of the thrifty, plain-living Frances Roberts to become enormously wealthy through her estate based on seventy-two blocks in New York City. The property came to her through Toberts Edwards, original owner (from whom she was a direct descendant). If the money had been available to her during her lifetime, it's hard to imagine that it would have changed her way of living — except that she would probably have enjoyed being able to share it.

18

Lady
of
Good Deeds

Anne Maria Penn Ireland

"The dampness of the walls, the exhalations from vapory and various cellars, the leaky roof, and other notable faults, make it unfit for human beings to dwell in."

Following this dismal description of the Executive Mansion, the Austin *Daily Statesman* of February 7, 1883, advised Governor and Mrs. Ireland against moving into the twenty-seven-year-old building. The editorial warned that disease had "taken hold of every family occupying it," that the Hubbards' children became infected with "miasmatic poison" and later died from its effect, and that diphtheria, chills, and fever prevailed among the members of Governor Roberts' family as long as they occupied the building.

Notwithstanding these dire foreshadowings, the Irelands (after some renovations had been made) survived four years in the mansion. Since Anne Maria Ireland had plenty of servants, she probably had little occasion to go into the "vapory" cellars. And, in any event, she was much less concerned with physical comforts than she was with the spiritual welfare of herself and those around her.

Anne Maria Penn was born on July 7, 1833, in Henry

County, Virginia, to Columbus and Frances Rives Penn. Later
the Penns moved from Virginia to Mississippi where they
remained until Anne Maria was in her early twenties. One of
Anne Maria's close girlhood friends in Mississippi was Mary
McKay. By a strange coincidence both girls in later life would
live for a time in the Governor's Mansion in Austin — Anne
Maria as its mistress and Mary McKay Bruner as a guest
while her daughter, Mrs. Thomas Campbell, was the First
Lady of Texas. But those times were far in the future.

In 1855 the Penns moved to Ruterville in Fayette County,
Texas. A short distance away in Seguin lived a young lawyer,
John Ireland, the son of Patrick and Rachel Newton Ireland.
He had spent his early days in Kentucky where he served as a
constable and sheriff before being admitted to the bar. In 1853
he arrived in Seguin with only two silver dollars, a watch, and
the clothes he was wearing. The following year he represented
a young widow, Mrs. Matilda Wicks Faircloth, in Probate
Court. Two months later he married his client, and the next
year a daughter, Matilda (Tillie), was born to them. The
following January Mrs. Ireland became ill with a fever and
after a short illness died at the age of twenty-nine.

Sometime during these two years Anne Maria Penn and
John Ireland had met. Now he found consolation in being with
the deeply religious Anne Maria, who at twenty-four was
quite mature. A little over a year after the death of Ireland's
first wife, he and Anne Maria were married — on May 21,
1857. They moved into a large house in Seguin and the
following year he became the town's mayor. Anne Maria spent
the majority of her time working for the Methodist Church
and in performing private charitable acts. All of her long life
she enjoyed personal contact with the needy and delighted in
giving them sympathy and understanding as well as material
things. She cared little for any kind of ritualistic social life but
loved to fill their home with friends and her husband's
associates. Over the years four children were born to the
Irelands: Mary, Katie Penn, Rosalie, and Alva.

In 1861 Ireland was a delegate to the Secession Convention;

when it ended he volunteered as a private in the Confederate Army. Advancing to the rank of lieutenant colonel, he organized a company that was sent to protect the Texas coast. Anne Maria closed their comfortable home in Seguin and moved with the children to a residence near her husband's camp. She was a splendid nurse and because of her sympathetic nature became the "angel of mercy" to many of the wounded young men to whom she gave friendship, advice, and mothering along with nursing care.

When the war ended, the Irelands moved back to Seguin where Ireland became deeply involved in affairs of state. He served as a member of the Constitutional Convention of 1866 and as a District Judge — until he, like other ex-Confederates, was removed from office by General Sheridan as an impediment to Reconstruction. He served in the Thirteenth and Fourteenth Legislatures, where he won the nickname "Oxcart John" for opposing grants of land and subsidies to railroads. He also served as an Associate Justice of the Texas Supreme Court. In 1876 and 1878 he made unsuccessful campaigns for the United States Senate and House of Representatives. But in 1882 he was nominated for Governor by the Democrats without opposition, and he won the election, defeating the Greenback party's strong candidate, George Washington Jones.

Anne Maria had little interest in politics, but she never opposed her husband in his career. Because of her religious beliefs, she disapproved of dancing; therefore, she did not attend the inaugural ball for her husband. A friend wrote urging her to come to Austin for the affair and added, "If you do not, I will represent you in the grand march." But Anne Maria replied promptly, "If you represent me, you will stay at home; that is what I am doing."

However, after the inauguration, in spite of the warnings from the *Statesman*, Anne Maria dutifully moved into the mansion and assumed the obligations of First Lady. She had splendid assistance from her stepdaughter Tillie, who had married the Governor's private secretary, Shelby Carpenter.

Together the two women planned the elegant, dignified entertainments that were characteristic of the times.

For convenience, the Carpenters and their baby, Patrick, lived in the mansion with the Irelands. During Ireland's first term, Tillie became pregnant again and gave birth to the second baby to be born in the mansion (Temple Lea Houston had been the first). But this baby lived only a short time.

At the time that the Irelands occupied the mansion, daughter Rosalie was a lively, beautiful young woman with a large circle of friends. She apparently didn't share all of her mother's religious scruples; one evening after a supper party, she began playing gay waltzes for her young friends to dance. Anne Maria asked Rosalie to stop playing, declaring there would be no dancing in her house. For insurance she put the piano key in her pocket, after locking the instrument.

Sometime after this incident, Rosalie became the fourth "mansion bride" when she married E. S. Hurt, a student at the University of Texas. The ceremony was read by Dr. Goodwin, pastor of the Austin Methodist Church, on New Year's Day of 1887.

During her husband's first term, Anne Maria was among those who attended the ceremonies marking the laying of the cornerstone for the new Capitol. Quite probably because of her influence, the Reverend Mr. Thrall of the Methodist Church of Seguin gave the invocation. She could take pride in the fact that it was at Ireland's insistence that the Capitol was to be built of Texas materials.

One of the most persistent and distressing problems during Ireland's administration was the emotionalism generated by the use of the newly popular barbed wire — and the strong reactions, including wire cutting, by those who wanted open ranges. It finally took legislation and Texas Rangers to stop the fence-cutting war. While this furor was going on, strikes by the Knights of Labor also plagued Ireland's two terms.

But aside from fulfilling her duties in connection with official entertainment, Anne Maria remained detached from political and economic conflicts. Nor did she have any desire to lead

Austin society — in any direction. The parties that she truly enjoyed were those she gave for Confederate veterans. The refreshments at these affairs were always generous and extra help was employed. Once a waiter had to leave in the middle of one of these entertainments. Anne Maria put on her apron and helped with the serving, brushing aside a comment that such work was beneath her dignity. Probably the activity she enjoyed most while she was First Lady was to fill her carriage with baskets of food and clothing which she distributed personally to the needy. It also gave her pleasure to help young people financially when she found an opportunity.

Although the Irelands were proud of their daughters, they never stopped wishing for a son. As time passed, they became extremely fond of the Carpenters' little boy, Patrick. Eventually they persuaded the parents to let them "adopt" him. To please the Governor, friends in the Legislature introduced a bill stating that the child would become "in name and by law, his adopted son, and bear the name of Patrick Carpenter Ireland." The bill was passed and the Irelands had a son. Pat became the spoiled darling of the mansion and seldom heard a discouraging word. The only exception on record occurred when he was punished for riding his pet donkey up the steps and into the building. Later Pat attended West Texas Military Institute in San Antonio where one of his fellow cadets was Douglas MacArthur.

When his second term as Governor expired in 1887, Ireland ran for the United States Senate, but he was defeated by the popular Judge John H. Reagan. The Irelands returned to Seguin where he again took up his private law practice. Anne Maria happily reopened their hospitable home and resumed her work connected with the Methodist Church and her private charities.

Paradoxically, some unfortunate ventures in railroad holdings marked the last years of the man who had been dubbed "Oxcart John" for his support of measures to block railroad expansion. Poor health also plagued him. In March of 1896 he made a business trip to San Antonio; young Patrick as usual was with him, but Anne Maria stayed at home because she was not feeling well. When Ireland became ill, he was put to bed at the Maverick Hotel where he and Pat were staying and a doctor was called. But on March 15 he died of what the papers called "neuralgia of the heart." His funeral services were conducted from the State Capitol, and he was buried with honors in the State Cemetery.

Anne Maria lived fifteen years after her husband's death. For a few years she remained in Seguin; then she moved to Austin to live with her daughter Mary. Mary's son, Ireland Graves, was a student at the University of Texas, and their home was a gathering place for young people. Anne Maria became a substitute grandmother for many of the homesick youths, and she often spent whole afternoons contentedly darning socks for Ireland and his friends. She delighted in the successes of her "University boys."

On May 28, 1911, a couple of months before her seventy-eighth birthday, Anne Maria died in Austin. The flag flew at half-mast on the State Capitol, and memorial services were held for her in Austin churches. But Anne Maria Ireland was buried, as she had requested, in Seguin, the Texas town that she thought of as her true home.

19

The Knight's Lady

Elizabeth Dorothy Tinsley Ross

Waco had never seen such a procession. Five hundred horsemen wearing red sashes, the Fireman's Band, the Waco Light Infantry, groups of civic organizations and hundreds of noisy, jubilant citizens followed the handsome carriage drawn by four large white horses. When the carriages and foot marchers in the vanguard of the parade had turned from Austin Avenue into Eleventh Street, the participants in the rear had not even left the square. The destination of the marchers was the home of General Lawrence Sullivan Ross, one of the men in the lead carriage. The Democratic Party had just chosen him as their gubernatorial candidate, and the town had turned out en masse to celebrate the event.

Another throng awaited the paraders at the Ross home, where hundreds of Chinese lanterns lighted the grounds. As they came within sight of the house, the candidate's eyes traveled over the crowd to the porch where a large, dark-haired woman stood watching. Around her clustered six children, transfixed into unnatural stillness by the scene. When Sul Ross joined his beaming wife and children, the watchers split the night air with exultant shouts. Ross was so overcome by the demonstration that it was many minutes before he could thank his friends and well-wishers.

Lizzie Tinsley Ross would witness many other ceremonies honoring her husband, but she would always remember this night as a high point in her life. She had cherished the belief that her husband was a man of heroic stature, and this spontaneous outpouring of approval confirmed that belief. Even when they were children, she had had the feeling that there was something special about Sul Ross. Whenever possible she had chosen him to be her partner in the games they played.

She had been born in Augusta, Georgia, on November 29, 1845, and christened Elizabeth Dorothy Tinsley. Her father was a well-known physician and planter who moved his family to Texas while Lizzie was still quite small. The inhabitants of the brand new town of Waco (a former Indian village) were delighted to have a competent doctor settle among them. They were even more pleased when it was discovered that he was willing to travel many miles to outlying farms to visit the sick and that all got the same careful treatment, regardless of their financial status.

For his part, Dr. Tinsley was so impressed with the opportunities for settlers around Waco that he persuaded his brother to move to Texas and go into a farming partnership with him. Together the Tinsley brothers became the largest landowners in the area, sharing over 4,000 acres of rich Brazos bottom land.

It was inevitable in the small village that the Rosses and the Tinsleys would come to know each other. The Rosses were "old-timers," having been among the twenty-one original white settlers of Waco. Shapley Ross was a well-known Indian agent — and sometimes an Indian fighter — when he moved his family to Waco. By that time eleven-year-old Sul Ross had already had more exciting adventures in his young life than most people experience in a lifetime. Before Sul reached his first birthday, his father had moved the family from Iowa to Texas, where they settled first on Little River at about the place where Cameron now stands. Indian raids were frequent in the area, and during one fight Shapley Ross fought and killed the famous Indian warrior Big Foot.

The Ross children had been well-drilled on how to behave in case of danger. On one occasion when Shapley was lying ill in bed, a band of Indians came to the cabin demanding food. They forced little Sul to show them where the corn and melons were growing. He marched ahead of them, reminding himself of his father's instructions never to show fear in the presence of Indians. And although they beat his legs with the shafts of their arrows until he was bleeding, he did not cry or whimper. When they returned to the cabin, the Indians told Shapley that he had a brave son and left without doing further damage.

At another time when Sul and his father were returning to the cabin on foot, they found themselves surrounded by fifteen or twenty mounted Comanche warriors. Shapley Ross took Sul on his back and ran a zig-zag course, dodging arrows until they arrived home safely. Sul said his father "fairly flew."

When Sul was about eight, Shapley moved his family to Austin in order to give the children some formal schooling. Three years later the founders of Waco offered Shapley several inducements, including town lots, bargain farmland, and the ferry rights, if he would settle there and help protect the town against hostile Indians. It was too good an offer to turn down.

A few years later the Tinsleys came from Georgia to settle in the growing village, and Lizzie became acquainted with Sul Ross. He had thrilling tales to tell about his life on the frontier, and she thought he was the most exciting boy she had ever met. He remained her hero for as long as she lived.

Although the Rosses' big log house had become the town's chief hotel and social center, Sul soon began to spend as much time as possible in the Tinsley home, which was located in what is now the heart of downtown Waco. For the times it seemed a mansion. Outside, wide galleries ran across the entire front of its two stories. Inside, the big, airy rooms were hung with pictures and filled with comfortable furniture.

Honeysuckle and white roses planted by the tall, white pillars perfumed the air. The immense front yard contained giant old oaks and was surrounded by a bois d'arc hedge. Orchards full of fruit trees attracted multitudes of birds. It was a delightful setting for young people to get to know each other in. There were plenty of servants to do the work, so there was leisure for parties, music, games, and long walks and talks.

When she reached her teens, Lizzie was sent to Miss Lambdin's Select School for Girls to learn the social behavior expected of a Southern belle. And at fifteen, Sul was sent to Independence to attend Baylor, then the largest college in the state with nine teachers and 260 students. Here he came under the influence of Dr. Rufus Burleson, who was greatly impressed by young Sul and prophesied that he would one day be Governor of Texas. Dr. Burleson joyfully recorded the fact that during a revival meeting he was conducting, Sul Ross "embraced the plan of salvation" very near the spot where Sam Houston was converted just two years before. Sam Houston was a longtime friend of the Ross family and may have influenced their decision to send Sul to Baylor.

After a year at Baylor, Ross attended Wesleyan University at Florence, Alabama, then one of the best schools in the South. Here he acquired a deep interest in higher education and the polished manners that concealed the bold, fighting spirit that was to make him a legend in his own lifetime.

During vacations Ross returned to Waco where he saw as much of Lizzie as possible. Again there were gay parties and long afternoons of talking about the future, to the accompaniment of the music furnished by the locusts and whippoorwills on the Tinsley plantation. A good friend of theirs was Richard Coke, a struggling young lawyer, who had come to Waco a few years earlier.

In 1858, during the summer vacation, Lizzie came close to losing her sweetheart. Shapley Ross, who was ill at the time, was serving as United States agent of the Brazos Indian Reservation near Waco. He asked nineteen-year-old Sul to lead a company of his reservation Indians against the

Comanches, who were causing a great deal of trouble. In a wild battle that took place in the Wichita Mountains, Ross rescued a little white girl of about eight years. Later in the melee he was seriously wounded by both a bullet and an arrow. For five days he lay on the battlefield tended by his faithful Caddo Indian friends.

When he could be moved, they made a litter and carried him to transportation. He brought the little girl home to his mother to care for. Having tried in vain to trace her family, the Rosses decided to adopt the child. She was christened Lizzie Ross in honor of Lizzie Tinsley, with whom Ross had an "understanding" although Lizzie Tinsley was only thirteen at that time. Lizzie's namesake was educated and treated by the Rosses as though she were one of their daughters. She later married a Los Angeles merchant and died in that city, never knowing who her real parents were nor how she came to be a Comanche captive.

As soon as Ross recovered from his wounds, he returned to Wesleyan University for his final term. Lizzie was left to dream of her sweetheart and to take pride in the ballads and stories of the Wichita Mountains battle that soon sprang up to commemorate his heroism.

When he had earned his degree, Ross sold his books and extra clothes, bought a horse and headed for Waco. Almost immediately Governor Sam Houston appointed him captain of a company of Rangers. He was only twenty, and Lizzie received the news of his appointment with mingled apprehension and pride.

Her fears were justified when he again came close to being killed in December of 1860. He had led a force of Rangers up the Pease River to a large Comanche village where the famous Peta Nocona, longtime scourge of white settlers, had his headquarters. After a wild horseback chase, Ross caught up with Nocona, who shot a series of arrows at him, wounding his horse. Clinging to the pommel of his saddle, Ross fired a pistol shot that broke the chief's right elbow. The warrior still refused to surrender and continued to thrust at Ross with his spear, until Ross' Mexican servants shot him.

Ross captured the chief's wife, and to his amazement saw that she had blue eyes. He discovered that she was the long-lost Cynthia Ann Parker, who had been captured at Fort Parker when she was nine — two years before Ross was born. He brought her back to Waco, but she was never happy there and constantly tried to rejoin the Comanches and her two sons. Frustrated in her efforts she died in 1870.

This decisive battle with the Comanches broke their power and was a great relief to settlers along the frontier. It also freed many fighting men from frontier patrol and allowed them to join forces in the Civil War, which was imminent. Ross himself left the Rangers to enlist as a private in his brother's Confederate company.

But before he went off to battle again, he and Lizzie decided they would wait no longer to marry. In May, 1861, a month after the opening guns were fired at Fort Sumter, Lizzie was married to her childhood sweetheart and hero. The spacious Tinsley home was filled with friends of the young couple and gaily decorated for the occasion, but the festivities were touched with sadness because everyone was well aware that the newlyweds would soon be parted. A few short weeks after the wedding, Lizzie was telling her husband good-bye as he left for the war.

Soon he was writing to tell her, "I think of you by day and dream of you by night." He assured her that he would be home in three or four months and promised to settle down quietly since "prominence does not suit my inclination." He proved to be a poor prophet on both counts. The four months were to become four years as he served for the duration of the war and took part in 135 engagements.

Lizzie eagerly read the news dispatches telling of his bravery and of his promotion to brigadier general, but his long, newsy letters were what she lived for. He told her in detail the events of his days, depicting encounters and men vividly, often with considerable humor. She was thankful that his life seemed charmed, for he was always at the center of any battle. He had seven horses shot out from under him and yet came out of the war unscathed.

During the four years he fought in the war, his leaves were few and far between. Several times Lizzie threatened to come to see him, but they both knew that was impractical. Their first reunion was a joyous one during Christmas of 1862. About nine months later their first child was born, but it died soon after.

As the fighting grew more intense, so did his longing for her. In March of 1864 he wrote, "I am nearly dead to see you. It's hard . . . to be parted from Wife and love . . . ." Lizzie spent much of her time writing him detailed letters of news about her days, their families and their friends. The delivery of letters was at best uncertain and precarious, which of course made them all the more precious. As the time of their separation lengthened, the letters became the only link that made them seem "real" to each other.

In September of 1864, Ross was delighted to have a much-delayed packet of Lizzie's letters catch up with him at his company's camp about eleven miles outside of Atlanta. Even though General Sherman's troops were in the vicinity, Ross sat down under a tree to read the long-awaited letters. In a few minutes shots rang out as a patrol of Sherman's company came up to within sixty feet of the camp. All of the group jumped on their horses, including Ross. But as he mounted, his horse shied, causing him to drop the letters. Calmly Ross dismounted and with bullets whining around him, picked up every one of the scattered pages before riding off to find a more peaceful place to read the priceless documents.

At the end of the war, a joyful reunion was followed by the necessity of facing the grim aftermath of Reconstruction. The Rosses turned to farming as a means of livelihood. But it was not their destiny to live a quiet life. The lawlessness that followed the Civil War called for strong leadership, and the people of McLennan County petitioned Ross to become their sheriff. He filled this role with the bravery and daring that had made him a successful Indian fighter, Ranger, and soldier. As always, Lizzie prayed for his safety while she admired his courage.

During the decade following the war, the Rosses' children began to arrive regularly, until there were seven: Mervin, Lawrence, Florine, Bessie, Frank, Harvey and Neville. Another baby died in infancy. Lizzie's hands were full managing this brood while her husband became more deeply involved in politics.

The sheriff's job led to his being named a member of the Constitutional Convention of 1875, which meant that he had to be in Austin for several months. Lizzie stayed in Waco to take care of the children, and they kept in close touch with letters. Ross's letters were full of messages to the children, reminding them to do well in school, to be helpful at home, and promising that he would bring them presents.

Richard Coke, their friend from their early courtship days, was now the Governor of Texas, and Ross was often entertained in the mansion. In a letter written in October of 1875, he urged Lizzie to return to Austin with Mrs. Coke (who was visiting her family in Waco). He suggested that Lizzie's mother would be willing to keep the children and reported that he was nearly "dead" to see her. Whether or not Lizzie was able to make the trip is not recorded.

In 1880 Ross was elected to the Senate of the Seventeenth Legislature, and again each of them suffered during the weeks and months of separation. He told her, "I never hated to leave Waco or Home so badly in my life . . . ."

In the spring of 1881 Lizzie's mother died. Soon afterward their son, Mervin, also died. Ross was concerned for his wife's health and wrote to a friend saying:

> The incessant watching, anxiety — and trouble seriously impaired the health of my wife and her situation has given me such serious concern as to render me entirely incapable of attending to business interests.

In time she recovered her strength, and with her husband took delight in watching over and training their lively brood. She was also a help to her husband as he moved upward politically. In addition to entertaining for him, she served as his confidante and advisor. He gave her credit for making friends for him that he was unable to reach on his own.

His popularity continued to grow, and in 1886 the enthusiastic parade took place that marked his nomination for Governor by the Democratic Party. He easily won the election, and after a series of celebration parties, Lizzie packed up their household for the move to Austin. It appeared that most of the citizens of Waco wanted to accompany them on the train to the capital city. In spite of a delay that caused the train not to arrive in Austin until nearly 1:00 a.m., a large crowd was on hand at the station to give them a rousing welcome that seemed to warm the chilly January air. In a carriage drawn by a handsome team of four black horses, Lizzie with her husband and their six wide-eyed offspring rode to their apartments in the Driskill Hotel.

The inaugural reception was also held at the Driskill, which was elegantly decorated with rich draperies and luxurious furnishings. Wearing a heavy black silk dress trimmed in jet ornaments and ending in a train, Lizzie presided at an elaborate supper, featuring boned turkey and other delicacies. The crowd was so great that it was daylight before everyone had his fill and departed.

On the whole, the times were peaceful and prosperous during the Rosses' stay in the Governor's Mansion. It was a time for progress in the state. Aid was given to educational institutions, and four eleemosynary establishments were founded. There was even time for such domestic matters as declaring an "Arbor Day."

The new State Capitol was finished, and of course there had to be a suitable dedication. Lizzie acted as hostess for the State at the most elaborate reception and ball that Austin had ever seen. It had an international scope: Mexico sent ambassadors and the Mexican National Band to take part in the festivities. Over the years Lizzie had grown plump and matronly, and for this occasion she made an impressive figure in a gown of black lace over moire antique silk with jet trimmings and ruby accessories. Florine, now a young lady, was also an object of admiration in a decollete train dress of blue moire silk, draped with lilies of the valley and diamond ornaments. The high point of the evening was the grand march led by the Governor and First Lady.

During the two terms of Ross's administration, the mansion was a noisy, lively place, filled with laughter, music, and young people. Florine and handsome young Lawrence Ross were especially popular and fond of entertaining. Lizzie encouraged the children to invite their friends, and she liked having personal as well as political friends over for an evening's amusement. The Austin *Statesman* reported in August, 1890, that the Whist Club held its first meeting in the Governor's Mansion. Sixteen "society folks" took part and enjoyed light refreshments. The club was to meet every two weeks, and the reporter predicted that it "will be one of the most prominent society factions of the coming season."

A reminder of the days of the Rosses in the Governor's Mansion is an intricately designed octagon-shaped table, still in the possession of members of the family. A Mexican man, who was sentenced to life imprisonment in the state penitentiary for a murder committed when he was a young man, began the table at the age of eighty. He used fourteen different kinds of Texas wood and a total of 75,000 pieces in constructing it. It took him four years to complete the complicated inlaid pattern. The old man had a passionate desire to spend his last days in his home in Mexico, and he sent the table, covered with roses, to Lizzie Ross. Under the flowers was a note begging her to persuade her husband to grant his pardon. Whether or not his plan succeeded is not known.

At the close of his second term in 1891, Ross was asked to become president of the Agricultural and Mechanical College of Texas, which had been without a formal president for eight years. The college had many problems and was barely clinging to its existence. An editorial in the Galveston *News* suggested that the academic functions of the school be transferred to the

University of Texas at Austin and the buildings be converted to use as a normal school or as a lunatic asylum.

True to that trait in his character that would cause the cadets to dub him a "knightly gentleman," Ross accepted the challenge of saving the school. Lizzie found she had some challenges to meet too in setting up housekeeping in their new home. In a letter to a friend Ross said:

> When we arrived everything looked cheerless about the new home. The house had been long vacated, was damp and the rain steady. No beds, no comfort in any respect . . .

Quite a change from the mansion! But soon carpets and furniture were installed and the house took on a more homelike atmosphere.

Under Ross's leadership the faltering school did an about face and became one of the strongest institutions of higher education in the state. An extensive building program began and improvements in many areas were made, including a large brick dormitory, a wood shop, blacksmith shop,· electric light and ice plant, steam laundry, water works, and natatorium (equipped for students' baths when "necessary"). The school periodical, "The Battalion," proudly issued its first volume. Other firsts for the college under Ross's leadership were the acquisition of a football coach and the founding of a fraternity that was the forerunner of A&M's strong Association of Former Students.

When Ross assumed the presidency, the most elite company of the cadet body renamed themselves the "Ross Volunteers." Lizzie became a co-sponsor of the group and enjoyed giving elaborate receptions and dances for the handsome young men in their dazzling white uniforms. In return the company annually presented her with a keepsake (on one occasion a pair of opera glasses) and offered to her the "love, the protection, and the constancy of the Company."

Entertaining for this group and for many others in her role as college president's wife became easier when the school gratefully built its savior a handsome president's home on the campus.

Seven years after the Rosses moved to College Station the future looked bright for the college and for the family of its president. Then in January of 1898 Ross became ill while on a hunting trip. He was taken back to his home where he lay in a coma for some time, watched over by several physicians, his children, and Lizzie. At six o'clock on the evening of the third day he roused a little. A doctor asked, "Governor, how do you feel?" Ross closed his eyes and said, "Well, I feel like a new man, and I guess I am one." In five minutes he was dead.

For many years, the cause of his death was thought to be pneumonia. But in 1929 a nephew of Ross, Clint Padgitt, revealed that his famous uncle had died of accidental poisoning. According to his story, rat poison had been put into one of the barrels of flour taken on the hunting trip because the rats in the woods were numerous and destructive. The cook had made the mistake of using flour out of the poisoned barrel in making biscuits, and Ross had eaten one. He warned the others that it tasted "queer" and then became deathly ill.

If this was the case, his death must have seemed doubly tragic to Lizzie. She took the body of her husband back to Waco, where they had spent so many years together. A large portion of the personnel of A&M accompanied her, and with much pomp and ceremony helped honor their beloved "Sully" as he was laid to rest. Many of the friends who attended the ceremony had gathered in the same place eight months earlier to mourn the death of the Rosses' good friend, Richard Coke.

After the funeral, Lizzie returned to Bryan to live with Florine and her husband, Dr. Henry Hill Harrington, professor of chemistry and mineralogy and later president of A&M. Although she was surrounded by her children and friends, she was saddened and lonely; no one could fill the place of the man who had been her hero — long before the world recognized him as a man of outstanding bravery and daring. Many tributes and memorials were made to him during her lifetime, but some she did not live to see, such as the naming of Sul Ross State College at Alpine in 1919.

Her mourning continued to the day of her death, June 8,

1905. The next day her children took her body to Waco for services at the Austin Avenue Methodist Church. Then a large group of friends watched as the modest Lizzie was buried beside the "knightly gentleman" whose lady she had so gladly been.

20.

The
Perfect
Chatelaine

Sarah Ann Stinson Hogg

Native Texans in the northeast part of the state expect a considerable amount of moisture in the spring, but during the month of April, 1874, the rains seemed to be trying to wash away the countryside around the little town of Quitman. Normally placid streams became raging torrents, and crossing them and the bridgeless sloughs was a risky business.

On the Stinson farm, some fifteen miles from town, a bride-to-be peered anxiously through the curtains of rain. It was the 22nd, the date set for the wedding, and there was no way to notify the invited guests of a delay — even if the bride had wanted one, which she didn't; at least not after the bridegroom arrived, soaked but safe. One by one the carriages and buggies straggled up to the door, and the dripping guests scrambled out. They competed in telling horror stories about having to swim horses through high water and getting bogged down in deep mud.

When everybody had more or less dried out, it was well past time for the ceremony to begin, but the Methodist minister who was to officiate had not arrived. After a wait of two or three more hours, Mr. Stinson sent a runner for a Primitive

Baptist preacher who lived nearby. Without stopping to
change from his work clothes, the Reverend Mr. Pressly Davis
hurried back with the messenger. They made their way with
difficulty over the turbulent Big Sandy River at a place still
called the "Press Davis Crossing." After the minister was
sufficiently dry, he proceeded to unite Sarah Ann Stinson and
James Stephen Hogg in wedlock. It was midnight when the
wedding feast took place, and since it was too dangerous for
the guests to risk returning to their homes in the darkness,
the whole wedding party stayed at the Stinsons' until the next
day.

And so began twenty-one years of a remarkably happy
marriage for a couple who were remarkably different in many
ways. Even their physical contrast was striking. James Hogg
was six feet, three inches tall, and Sallie little more than five
feet. Their difference in size would become more marked in
later years when he weighed about 300 pounds and she less
than 100 as she became increasingly frail and wasted. But in
Sallie Stinson's small frame was a large spirit, and from the
time he first met her at Mr. Baggett's country school a few
miles east of Quitman, gray-eyed Sallie was the only girl for
James Hogg.

Six years after Sallie Ann had been born in Troup County,
Georgia, to Sarah Leander and James A. Stinson, the family
moved to Texas and built a large, comfortable home near
Quitman. Colonel Stinson became a prominent farmer,
lumberman, and horticulturist, experimenting in the
improvement of fruit trees. Sallie grew up surrounded by
many luxuries in the spacious Stinson home, which had a wing
on the second floor that was one large room suitable for
religious services, Grange meetings, dances — and weddings.
She was an accomplished pianist and seamstress, and had
acquired extraordinary skill as a homemaker, which she would
put to full use in her marriage.

Colonel Stinson wanted the best education possible for his
talented daughter and sent her to Looney's Seminary, an
excellent boarding school for young ladies in Gilmer. There

Sallie continued to develop her musical ability. Her fair skin, dark brown hair and dainty features gave her a sweet, refined appearance, and her tiny, beautifully formed hands were her distinguishing feature. Her feet were so small that she had to have her slippers specially made. In spite of her modest nature, the petite Miss Stinson began to attract many suitors. But after she met James Hogg, she never seriously considered marrying anyone else.

Her father at first didn't share her enthusiasm for the young man, although he came from a good family background and, like the Stinsons, could trace his ancestors back to the Revolutionary War. Both of James Hogg's parents had died during the Civil War, and Mountain Home, the family plantation, had gradually been sold to pay taxes and to provide food, clothes, and books for the children. James's education had been acquired chiefly through his work as a newspaper apprentice. When he met Sallie he was the editor of his own paper, the Quitman *News*, and had entered politics by successfully running for justice of the peace. Neither of these occupations seemed to Colonel Stinson to promise a secure future for his daughter, but when Sallie turned her persuasive powers on her father, he soon yielded. Later, he would come to appreciate his son-in-law.

The "Honeymoon Cottage" where the Hoggs would live for six years was much less impressive than the home where Sallie had spent most of her life. It was located on the Gilmer road in the east part of Quitman, and consisted of only four small rooms. However, both Sallie and James were nest-builders, and the little house soon became a comfortable home. James cut trees and built a fence to enclose a large garden, and Sallie canned and preserved the fruits and vegetables they raised. While her husband pored over books, studying to become a lawyer, Sallie kept busy turning the cottage into a model home. The energy and concern with which she attended to every detail of homemaking would be characteristic of her all of her life.

The young couple were delighted when their first child,

William Clifford, was born on the last day of January, 1875. Like the Houstons, the Hoggs were adoring parents who rejoiced at the birth of each child and reared them with great pride and love and respect for their individuality. Spurred by the desire to provide more security for his growing family, Hogg intensified his law studies after the birth of Will and a few months later had passed his bar examination.

Sallie was never very interested in politics except as they affected her husband. But she wanted him to do whatever would bring him satisfaction, so when he decided to run for a seat in the Texas Legislature in 1876, she did not object. And she shared his disappointment when he suffered his only political campaign loss in this race. Two years later, however, they had reason to celebrate when, at twenty-seven, he was elected County Attorney of Wood County. The citizens of the Seventh District were impressed by his honesty and efficiency in this office and in another two years they elected him District Attorney, a position he was to hold for four years.

The new position required Hogg to travel to six different county seats. Neither he nor Sallie liked the periods of separation this travelling involved, so they decided to move to Mineola, a railroad junction town. There they bought a small white house whose most attractive feature was a large dogwood tree in the backyard. Sallie set to work to make a comfortable home in the raw railroad town, and soon they were entertaining new friends. Wherever his weekday duties took him, Hogg always made a special effort to be with his family on weekends. One of their favorite pastimes in the evenings was hymn singing. A worn copy of *Gospel Hymns Consolidated*, owned by the Hoggs from the time they lived in Mineola and now on display in the Governor's Mansion, bears mute testimony to many years of hard use.

On July 10, 1882, a daughter was born to the Hoggs. She was named Ima, after the heroine in the book *The Fate of Marvin*, which was a novel of Civil War times written by Hogg's older brother, Thomas, whom he greatly admired. Hogg expressed their elation in a letter to another brother:

Our cup of joy is now overflowing! — We have a daughter of as fine proportions and of as angelic mien as ever gracious nature favored a man with, and her name is Ima! Can't you come down to see her?

In spite of a boom for him to run for the United States Congress after his term as District Attorney ended, Hogg decided to go into private law practice in Tyler. He and Sallie wanted to have more time together, and the cultural and educational advantages of the larger town were appealing. Sallie particularly looked forward to being able to enjoy more musical events. In the fall of 1884 they moved into a small house near the town square in Tyler, where for two years they enjoyed a happy, domestic life while his practice grew until he was, as he put it, making "more than a living." In April of 1885 they treated themselves to a vacation trip to the World Exposition in New Orleans. After seeing the fair, they joined former Governor Lubbock in a trip to Biloxi to visit Jefferson Davis, the ex-President of the Confederacy. When the Hoggs admired a big rooster, Davis insisted on giving it to them and had it sent to their home in Tyler. The rooster was, of course, named Jeff Davis. Even more exciting was another addition to the family, Michael (Mike), born on October 28, 1885, and joyfully welcomed by father, mother, brother, and sister.

When friends urged Hogg to run for Attorney General in 1886, he was hesitant to disturb the tranquility of their domestic life. He consulted older friends, including former Governor Roberts, before making a decision. Finally, with some reservations, he entered the race, which he won. The victory meant another move for the Hoggs — this time to Austin, where they settled first in an excellent boarding-house which faced the side yard of the Governor's Mansion.

Both of them wanted their own home, though, and as soon as they could find a suitable house they bought it. It was a large two-story dwelling on 14th Street, and Sallie energetic-ally set about once again using her talents to create a comfortable place for her husband to return to in the evenings after the arduous duties of his new job. He was truly appreciative of her efforts; no matter how great the pressures and problems he dealt with during the days, he shed them and reveled in the quiet time spent with his family in the evenings. During this time Sallie began to keep clippings about her husband in a scrapbook which he gave to her and inscribed "to my dear wife Sallie." Her poor health was the one cloud on their happiness.

She was in her fourth pregnancy and suffering from several complications. Although her health was never hearty, she was always active, and it worried Hogg when she became obviously ailing. On August 20 she gave birth to a third son, who was named Thomas Elisha after Hogg's oldest brother. Sallie was quite ill for a long time after the birth of the baby and was unable to nurse him, which distressed her because he appeared puny and weak. However, after a wet nurse was obtained, the Governor was soon describing Tom as "frolicsome, fat and fine." But his mother never again regained even her normal strength.

Hogg encouraged Sallie to take frequent trips to health resorts and to visit relatives in different parts of the state, hoping that the change would benefit her, although he missed her and the children. In February of 1887 he wrote to her while she was on a visit to her family home in East Texas, "Enjoy yourself in every way possible. Make your stay at your Pa's to suit yourself, and write me often." Three days later she received another letter from him saying, "I am nearly dead to see Mike, Sallie, Willie, and Ima."

During 1890 Sallie's health remained frail, and she sought cures at Sour Lake, Wooten Wells, and other resorts, without much effect. In December Hogg wrote to his sister in Pueblo, Colorado, that Sallie had been feeble all year, but he added, "She heroically stands all her ailments."

Sallie supported her husband when he entered the gubernatorial race in 1890, although she must have dreaded knowing that the campaign would take him away from home for long periods of time. It was a hard fight, and she was often upset by the name-calling and denunciations of her husband as an enemy of free enterprise and capitalism. But the little people loved him and believed him when he told them that "the people must rule the corporations or the corporations will rule and ruin the people." The main plank in his reform program called for establishment of a commission to regulate the railroads, and the plain people swept "Hogg and Commission" into office.

The weather was rainy and chilly on January 20, 1891, but the House chamber of the Capitol seemed warm and bright to Sallie as she sat with Will and Ima listening to retiring Governor Ross introduce her husband as the new leader of the state government of Texas. She could see that all the nooks and crannies of the room, including the window sills, were filled with the common people who had come to see "their" governor take office. She knew that the occasion was even more historic because it was the first time an inauguration had been held in the new and present Capitol Building, and also because her husband was the first native-born Texan to become Governor.

The day was filled with other exciting events such as the traditional torchlight parade up Congress Avenue with the participants wearing oilcloth coats to protect themselves from flying sparks and oil drippings. The lavish inauguration banquet and ball were also held in the new Capitol Building. The following morning an Austin paper carried an account of the event:

> Dignified matrons, gay young girls, befrizzled old men and rising young men pressed their way through embankments of silks, satins, decollete gowns and broad white shirt fronts for hours, and tried to talk above the blasts of the bands that were filling every nook and corner of the building . . .

It was a thrilling but exhausting day for the new First Lady.

The excitement turned to dismay when the meticulous Sallie prepared to move her family into the Governor's Mansion. She discovered that the calcimine walls were cracked from top to bottom, the curtains were raggedy, the carpets worn out, and there was practically no furniture. After the Rosses removed their own furniture and accessories, it was a bare and comfortless house. In addition, there were no state funds available for the extensive renovations that were obviously needed.

Using her talent and ingenuity as a homemaker, Sallie met the problem head-on and accomplished maximum results with minimum expense. Before the family moved in she had the walls canvassed and new wallpaper put on, the woodwork scraped and painted, the worst of the carpets replaced, and the windows hung with new lace curtains. She chose inexpensive but fashionable rattan furniture to replace the worst looking pieces. And she spent days supervising the scraping of hardened chewing gum from under tables, chairs, and even the door moldings. Under her fastidious supervision the old building acquired a bright and clean aura.

Another, more serious, problem for the frail First Lady was the lack of adequate heating facilities. There was no central heat and the ceilings were seventeen feet high. There were five grates downstairs for coal; upstairs only three rooms had fireplaces. The coal supply was sometimes short, and since Sallie had pneumonia several winters, the arctic climate of the rooms and drafty halls was a real threat to her survival.

There were other discomforts in the aging building. The bathroom was a lean-to affair attached to the back of the house. Upstairs was a seven-foot tin bathtub built especially for Sam Houston. It was a hard task to pump up the water to fill it. Members of the family could choose between bathing in cold cistern water, or they could wait for gallons of water to heat on the back of the stove. Sallie had only one maid and a cook (paid by the Hoggs) for inside help and one gardener (furnished by the state), who also drove the carriage.

However, in spite of all its drawbacks, the mansion became an attractive, comfortable home for the new First Family under Sallie's watchful eye. Back of the ironing room next to the kitchen was a large smokehouse-storeroom. Here the family's provisions were kept — barrels of flour, 100-pound cans of lard, sugar, sides of bacon, a dozen hams, and smoked chickens that were purchased live by the dozen for twenty-five cents apiece. Under Sallie's prudent supervision the supplies were used wisely but well. She carried around with her the keys to this and other storage cupboards so that she was dubbed "the Chatelaine" by her family.

To help with preparations for formal occasions, such as the huge obligatory New Year's receptions, neighbors, friends, and many of the young people of Austin came in to help with the cooking and decorating chores. Sallie planned these events minutely, even though she sometimes had to issue her orders from a sick bed.

The Hoggs were a zestful, fun-loving family, and although Sallie performed her required duties as First Lady with exemplary skill and poise, she much preferred the informal entertainments that were frequent during the Hoggs' tenure in the mansion. These invariably included the children and their friends. Almost every Saturday night the music for square dancing, Virginia reels, schottisches, and polkas could be heard pouring from the stately house. In the back parlor, tables were set up for card games. Euchre was a favorite, as popular as bridge is now, and Sallie, who was a good player, usually euchred her husband, exclaiming, "James Hogg, I've got you!" He probably replied, "By Gatlins, so you have!"

The high good spirits of these gatherings were generated solely by the happy, relaxed atmosphere created by Sallie and James Hogg and their lively offspring. On rare occasions champagne was served to the adults, but Sallie did not care for any kind of alcohol and preferred serving cider or some other soft beverage to her guests, even on state occasions. As always with the Hoggs, singing was a favorite pastime. The Governor loved to hear Sallie play the piano accompaniment, but on the evenings when she had one of her severe headaches, Ima was an able substitute.

The gaiety and high spirits with which the Hoggs filled the mansion were similar to the atmosphere that Theodore Roosevelt and his family brought to the White House a few years later. The children recalled the four years in the mansion with pleasure after they were grown; they always felt they had everything they needed. It was only in thinking back over little details that they realized their mother had kept things running smoothly by careful management and attention to small economies, such as taking the buttons, hooks, and eyes off outworn garments for use on new ones.

The children's growing years were guided mostly with love and by example, although Sallie did keep a slender switch handy to use on little legs, usually when one of the three younger acrobats did something she considered hazardous to their lives or limbs. Tom was generally the object of her concern. Like many other Governors' children, he couldn't resist sliding down the polished stair banister and once fell off midway and hung, bleeding, by his chin from a stair. On another occasion he caused a furor by starting a fire too near one of the wooden fences on the grounds.

The grounds around the mansion were fascinating for the children. There was a croquet lawn, a fish pond, a vegetable garden, a stable, and fruit trees, including figs, peaches, plums, and quince. The vegetable garden was the Governor's special delight; he liked to experiment in it. Sallie was an ardent flower gardener, specializing in coleus, begonias, and geraniums. Each morning she put a blossom in her husband's buttonhole before he left for work. (This was a custom he would continue in her memory after she died.)

Behind the stable was a large plot intended as a running ground for horses, but also highly suitable for the running and jumping games in which Ima and the two younger boys delighted. Here, too, circuses could be given with Ima providing guitar music.

There were always plenty of animals for these performances. A number of Governors' families have had pets, but none had so many or such a variety as the Hoggs. Probably the favorite was a Shetland pony which delighted in pitching would-be riders off his back, fortunately without seeming ever to injure any of them. In addition, each child had a dog or cat, and in a large cage on the north side of the mansion were rabbits, cockatoos, possums, raccoons, parrots, and whatever creature had recently been "rescued" and was being nursed back to health.

Jane, a red-headed parrot, roamed the house and grounds as she pleased and apparently thought she was one of the family. When the Governor came home for dinner at noon, she waited for him at the front door; as he entered the gate, she ran to greet him, flapping her wings and calling "Papa, Papa!" in imitation of the children. She also liked to listen in on conversations and mimic the laughter she heard. Once when Sallie, after much persuasion, had talked her husband into buying a full dress suit and accessories, Jane got into the closet and peeled the patent leather off his new pumps.

Sallie's exquisite taste in fashion can be seen in her pictures, and Hogg liked to see his dainty wife wear elegant clothes. His salary was meager, but by careful management Sallie was able to have some handsome dresses made from the magnificent damask and brocade dress lengths that the outstanding Austin merchant Hatzfeld brought back from Paris. If the dresses were not sewed exactly to suit her, she would take out the stitches and remake them to meet her own exacting standards.

She always had ready a piece of embroidery, or handwork, which she could do while talking with visitors. In those days it was the style for little girls to wear white aprons over gingham or woolen dresses, and Sallie often made Ima's exquisite aprons of finest muslin, dimity or swiss with rolled and hand-whipped ruffles edged with real lace trimming or eyelet embroidery. All of her own fine muslin or linen underwear was made with the same care. She usually chose the soft, quiet grays, buffs, blues, and lilacs that her husband preferred, but her last reception dress (now in the Governors' Wives collection at Denton) was pink with a pearl passementerie. Of her other gowns, only a few basques remain, but the materials in these are still quite beautiful.

Hogg felt that a wife should be in every way a complete partner, and Sallie was his confidante and advisor on all questions. He depended on her intuition and judgment about people and was pleased that she "never got me into any trouble by tattling, or talking too much," as he once told Will.

When Hogg ran successfully for reelection in 1892, Sallie was distressed over the derogatory stories that were a part of the rough-and-tumble campaign that was impressive even in a state noted for hot and close elections. During his second term, she kept up with the intense social and family life in the mansion on nervous energy and sheer determination. While her husband had become a symbol of a reform champion to the people of the state, she had become a symbol of the perfect homemaker and hostess.

People who came to receptions expected to be fed something much more substantial than cookies and punch. The standard fare was chicken salad, baked turkey and baked ham, beaten biscuits, salted nuts, especially almonds, and many varieties of cakes and pies — marble, spice, fruit and Lady Baltimore were favorites.

The ordeal of standing in reception lines was especially fatiguing, so a tall stool was placed behind Sallie for her to sit or lean on at intervals. And she continued to perform her duties as First Lady with her customary perfection, even when the strain on her strength was great. As her severe headaches and fatigue became chronic, Hogg sent her to various watering places in Texas, hoping that in one of them she would find a cure for her mysterious illness. By 1894, the Hoggs felt gratified when Sallie's health could be described as even "fair."

In the summer of 1894 when social life in Austin was at a low point, Sallie took the children to her family's farm. Hogg missed them greatly. He wrote:

> Have a nice time and enjoy yourselves . . . I'll be there by watermelon time. Then we'll go fishing and have a big frolic . . . I am like a ghost in a two story barn *deserted*.

In 1895 Hogg left office in debt and "with one silver dollar," as he put it. It was reported that he had to borrow $100 to move his family out of the mansion. They settled temporarily in a comfortable boardinghouse on 8th Street, but Hogg was anxious to be able to buy their own home. In an essay he had expressed his feelings about the importance of having a home:

> For many years, my advice has been is yet and will continue to be that every man in this State, either in the country or in town, should acquire a home . . . Home! The center of civilization . . . Home! The ark of safety to happiness, virtue and Christianity . . . Every man should have a home!

Setting up a legal practice in Austin, Hogg soon had accounts that required him to go to Boston and New York to take care of some of their business. He was reluctant to leave Sallie, but she insisted he make the trip and wrote him reassuringly. In a letter dated May 8, she told him an Austin doctor had found her lungs to be "all right" and diagnosed her trouble as "bronchitis and catarrhal affection." She added, "Now take your time, I am perfectly satisfied, contented, and not impatient at your long stay. I know you are doing your best to succeed, and I *fully* appreciate it." With a touch of humor she added that there was some political unrest in Austin, and it was fortunate he was out of town or he would surely be blamed for it. The letter ended with "a world of love-kisses." Hogg wrote to Will, urging him to take care of his mother, and to see that "she gets everything she wants and goes where she pleases."

In June Sallie gathered up the children and went to her father's farm, hoping the change would help her. But when Hogg arrived at the end of the month, she was showing little improvement. They decided to have her consult Dr. Adolph Herff, a well-known San Antonio doctor. He told them that she had tuberculosis and recommended that she get away from the intense Texas summer heat. Hogg's sister in Pueblo, Colorado, had a son who was a physician, and it was quickly arranged for Sallie to go to stay with them. Ima went along as a companion to her mother. At first Sallie seemed to show a slight improvement in the cooler climate. Her letters to her husband, sweltering and worried in Austin, were cheerful and optimistic.

But she must have known how seriously ill she was, for she

had long talks with thirteen-year-old Ima to prepare her to face a future in which she must be a guide to her younger brothers. By the first of August Sallie became much sicker, and Hogg and the three boys were sent for. Nothing could be done to stop the ravages of the insidious disease, and on September 20, 1895, with her children and her husband at her bedside, Sallie quietly drew her last breath.

Governor Culberson made arrangements to have services held at the mansion, which she had so recently left. Then Sallie Hogg was buried in Oakwood Cemetery in Austin. Of the many eulogies made for her, the best one is in a letter that her grieving husband wrote on October 14, 1895, to his sister Julia:

> In all the storms of an eventful life the severest shock that I ever received was the death of poor Sallie . . . It is all over, except now and then — almost hourly — when memory recalls the past and with it my wife's suffering and death compared to her gentleness and virtues . . . She never spoke an unkind word to me in her life and never had I to account to others for a word or act of hers. God knows if all men were so blessed the earth would be more like heaven. My ambition is to raise my children after her model. If I succeed the world will be much better for it.

He succeeded very well, and the world, especially the part of it that was his native state, is better off for it. Sallie would have been happy to know that after the family became wealthy through Hogg's investments in city property and oil lands, the children became philanthropists, supporting organizations and projects that have made outstanding contributions to education, the fine arts, mental health, and historical preservation and conservation in Texas.

21.

The Darling of "The Darling of Texas Politics"

Sallie Harrison Culberson

Pearl Cashell Jackson relates the story of a lanky mountaineer who, seeing Governor Culberson sitting on the Executive Mansion porch one sultry afternoon, stopped to chat. "Be youse the Guvner?" he asked.

"I am," was the reply.

"Wa'll I've never seed a Guvner, and I've never seed the house he lives in."

"Come in and see me and the house," the hospitable Culberson returned.

After an inspection tour of the entire mansion, the man was introduced to Mrs. Culberson and her sister, who had come to the front hall to try to catch a breeze. The man ambled out and turned to the Governor as they came to the front steps. "Wa'll, I like you, Guvner, and this house is the purtiest one I ever seed, but (with an expression of great self-satisfaction) my wimmin folks can sure take the shine off of your'n."

The frail First Lady dressed in dark mourning clothes (for her father) obviously struck the mountaineer as being too puny for much physical effort. He was right about her fragile strength; however, he didn't understand Sallie Culberson's method of operation. Like her predecessor, Sallie Hogg, she was a perfectionist, but unlike Mrs. Hogg, she was content to let others carry out the details of her carefully made plans. Petted and spoiled by those around her — and especially by her husband — she made the most of her semi-invalid condition and thoroughly enjoyed her years in the mansion.

Sallie was a native Texan, born on July 25, 1861, in Clarkesville to William M. and Elizabeth Ann Harrison. Her father served as a captain in the Confederate Army during the Civil War, narrowly escaping death when his horse was shot from under him in the Battle of Shiloh. After the war he moved his family to Jefferson where he engaged successfully in the wholesale grocery and banking business.

The same year that Sallie Harrison was born, the Culberson family, including six-year-old Charles, had moved to Jefferson from Gilmer, Texas. After the Civil War, the father, David Browning Culberson, would become well-known in Texas politics and would serve as a United States Congressman for twenty-four years. (Culberson County would be named after him.) Two such prominent families must have soon become acquainted in the small town, but just when Sallie and Charles became friends is not known. Since most accounts of his life refer to her as his "childhood sweetheart," it must have been while they were quite young.

However, when they reached their teens, there were long years of separation while they attended widely scattered schools. Sallie went to Ward's Seminary at Nashville, Tennessee, and Charles, after graduating from Virginia Military Institute, entered the law school of the University of Virginia, from which he graduated in 1877. By this time Sallie was an attractive young belle, used to being waited on and surrounded with the best of everything. Charles was quite handsome in his young and middle years and always dressed immaculately, but at this time he was only a beginning young lawyer without much money — which may be the reason they waited five more years to marry. The elaborate wedding finally took place on December 7, 1882, in Jefferson.

After spending five more years in their hometown, the young couple moved to Dallas. Here Culberson entered politics with almost immediate success. In 1890 and again in 1892 he was elected Attorney General of Texas, serving as James Hogg's right-hand man and defending some of the reforms Hogg had enacted into law — such as the law establishing the Railroad Commission.

Sallie's health was poor at this time, so the Culbersons settled into quarters in the Driskill Hotel to save her the effort of housekeeping. She had little interest in politics and did not pretend what she did not feel. She chose friends whose company she enjoyed and didn't go out of her way to encourage those who might help her husband's career. In some ways her frail health was convenient. She never returned calls and seldom accepted invitations, except those from friends she particularly wanted to visit. Once when it was remarked that she could be more tactful, she replied, "What is the use? Charley is equal to that."

And he was quite equal to the political challenges that came his way. For more than a quarter of a century he would be known as the "darling of Texas politics." With the support of the influential Colonel E. M. House, Culberson was elected Governor in 1894.

Sallie had her handsome rugs, valuable pictures, and other luxurious accessories moved into the mansion. She also had a big iron base burner installed in the lower hall, changing the temperature there from "arctic to temperate" in winter.

Because she was considered an invalid, the Legislature appropriated forty dollars a month for a housekeeper. Also Sallie's widowed sister, Mrs. Mary Schleuter, came to live in the mansion to help with the First Lady's social obligations. Sallie liked her role, and when some state occasion demanded an entertainment, she would have nothing but the best. Her insistence on perfection kept those who helped her running. Once when preparations for a state reception were under way, and Sallie was lying on her couch issuing orders, her sister remarked, "Sallie can lie there and keep forty women busy."

Luncheons were her favorite way of entertaining, and she spent hours planning them down to the last painstaking detail — for others to carry out. One of her triumphs was to be the first hostess in Austin to serve cranberry sauce in individual molds. Many were the trials and tribulations of the women researchers who labored in their kitchens to bring about this miracle. Of these luncheons a contemporary said, " . . . everything is formal, everything is beautiful, and everything is delicious."

Culberson was devoted to his frail wife and loved to carry her in his strong arms from room to room to give her a change. He never passed her room without stopping to ask, "How is my darling feeling?" Several times during his term as Governor she went to Battle Creek, Michigan, for medical treatment. If a day went by without word from her, Culberson would call his private secretary and ask, "Have I anything from Battle Creek today?" If the answer was "no," he would immediately send Sallie a telegram asking, "How are you today, my dear?" Several times when the answer did not satisfy him that she was feeling well, he dropped his work and caught the next train to Battle Creek.

Although Sallie usually stayed out of politics and did not try to influence her husband, it would be interesting to know if she was one of the women who protested the Robert Fitzsimmons-James Corbett world championship boxing bout scheduled to be held in Dallas in 1895. At any rate, in one of the most spectacular actions of his first term, Culberson called the Legislature into special session (the shortest in history) to enact a law which made holding a prize fight in Texas a felony. For this action he was labeled "the great Christian Governor" by many Texans, and this action may have helped in his reelection in 1896.

During Culberson's second term Sallie's health improved, and she was able to take a more active part in social events. One notable occasion was the New Year's reception held on January 1, 1898. The mansion was open to callers from six to ten. The Austin *Daily Statesman* reported that the Governor and his lady "surrounded themselves with a corps of most beautiful ladies who added materially to the success of the evening." The ladies were described as being "superbly gowned," and Sallie may have worn her silver shoe buckles set with marcasites that are now displayed in the memento case at the mansion. The drawing rooms, dining room, and hall were decorated with palms, bamboo, and flowers, and a substantial feast was laid out in the dining room. Among the guests was the Honorable William Jennings Bryan. All in all the *Statesman* concluded, "The reception was one of the most brilliant in the history of the Capital City."

A highlight of Culberson's second term was the United States' declaration of war against Spain. When President McKinley called for volunteers, Texas furnished four regiments, which were sent to Cuba from Galveston. The most famous of these was Teddy Roosevelt's "Rough Riders," organized at San Antonio. This unit included men from all over the United States as well as many Texans. For weeks mansion guests talked of little else but their exploits.

As her time as First Lady came to an end, Sallie had mixed emotions. Her husband had been elected to the United States Senate, and she was pleased for his sake, but she felt now — and always would feel — that her days in the Governor's Mansion in Austin were the happiest of her life. She looked about her for some lasting contribution she could make that would be a reminder of the time she had spent there. She was dismayed at the casual way furniture was brought into and removed from the mansion, and she decided to insure that the priceless Sam Houston bed would be preserved and easily identified by future generations. So she had a silver plate fastened to the footboard reading:

> This bedstead was used in the Executive Mansion by Governor Sam Houston and this tablet placed thereon by Mrs. Charles A. Culberson to identify and preserve it for future generations. January 16, 1899.

As Sallie supervised the packing of her belongings for the long trip to Washington, D.C., she could not have known that this would be the last time she would have to move them. For her husband was to serve twenty-two years in the Senate, only two years short of the record his father had set. Again her sister, Mary Schleuter, accompanied the Culbersons to help with the duties of running the household.

Before the next year was over, her help was doubly welcome; after eighteen years of marriage Sallie was pregnant. In 1900 the Culbersons' first and only child was born. Culberson wired their friends in Texas, "It is only a little old girl." But Mary Harrison Culberson became the idol of her father's life. He taught her to ride, swim, and to love baseball, which he considered the finest of all American sports. Sallie had to be firm to keep Mary from becoming a complete tomboy. She persisted in wearing bloomers until her mother insisted on dresses and at twelve was begging to drive her father's seven-passenger Pierce-Arrow.

Culberson's appreciation of women and his recognition of their rights extended beyond his family. He explained his support of the Nineteenth Amendment by saying:

> I regarded the natural and inherent rights of women as citizens as paramount . . . Accordingly, I favored the submission of the 19th Amendment, extending the right of suffrage to women, upon the broad grounds . . . that women . . . are of right entitled to full and complete citizenship and should therefore enjoy equal political rights with men.

Culberson was a political favorite in Washington as he had been in Texas. Colonel House, who had as much political insight as anyone of his time, felt that Culberson would have been nominated for President in 1912 if his health had been stronger.

For now, ironically, it was Culberson's health that needed to be guarded, and Sallie, who had always leaned on her husband for strength, began to watch over him anxiously. However, during World War I there was little she could do to keep him from overworking as he helped frame the war measures of Woodrow Wilson's administration. The result was that he permanently damaged his health. Any physical effort became difficult for him, and in 1922 he was forced to retire.

The Culbersons decided to remain in Washington, which had been home to them for more than twenty years. Culberson's greatest pleasure was to take long automobile rides around the city, once in the morning and once in the afternoon. Usually Sallie accompanied him on these trips. Another diversion that she provided for him as often as possible was the entertaining of old Texas friends in their home.

Early in 1924 Culberson went to New York City to consult a noted physician. He remained there for two months and seemed somewhat benefited from the electrical and Swedish treatments that he took. During the summer of that year he and Sallie and the two Marys took a cottage in Atlantic City, hoping he would benefit from the sunshine and salt air. They enjoyed the resort city, but his health did not improve. Always solicitous and thoughtful of Sallie, he never complained of his own weaknesses but asked each morning, "How is my darling today?" as if her health was of more concern than his own.

He remained mentally alert but gradually lapsed into a more feeble state physically, and Sallie expended her own strength in nursing him and in worrying over his decline. Early on the morning of March 19, 1925, Culberson sank into a coma, and a few hours later he died.

Sallie took her husband's body home to Texas and buried him in the Harrison family plot in Oakwood Cemetery in Fort Worth, where two of her sisters and a brother were living. Some years earlier her parents had been buried in Oakwood, where Culberson had asked to be placed when he died so the mockingbirds would "sing over his grave."

After the funeral Sallie returned to Washington to the home and friends she had shared with her husband for a quarter of a century. Her sister and her daughter were with her, but life was empty without the man who had watched over her so devotedly for more than forty years. Sallie could not recover from the blow of his death, and exactly a year and a month later, she suffered an apoplectic stroke and died. Her body was taken by train to Fort Worth, where she was buried beside her husband.

When Culberson died he made no public bequests but willed everything to Sallie. His assets plus those she had inherited from her family made her estate relatively large for those times — $635,174.58. In her will Sallie left $25,000 as a Charles A. Culberson Memorial Endowment to the Baptist Hospital at Dallas and gave $10,000 for a student loan fund to the University of Texas.

Early sketch of Governor's Mansion. Courtesy The Austin-Travis County Collection, Austin Public Library, Austin.

Governor's Mansion, 1880. Note gazebo at left. Courtesy of Barker Texas History Center, Austin.

Governor's Mansion, early 1900's. Courtesy The Austin-Travis County Collection, Austin Public Library.

Governor's Mansion, picket fence added. Note clothing hanging from second-story window. Courtesy The Austin-Travis County Collection, Austin Public Library.

Governor's Mansion, iron fence added. Courtesy Austin-Travis County Collection, Austin Public Library.

22.

The Dolly
Madison
of the
Mansion

Orline Walton Sayers

In 1967 a resolution was introduced into the Texas House of Representatives proposing that:

> In as much as Governor Sayers' labours as a soldier, lawyer, statesman and public servant inured to the lasting benefit of the entire state of Texas, it seems proper that his grave and that of his beloved wife be placed at last at the seat of government of this state amid the other sleeping heroes thereof, readily accessible to the homage of all citizens of Texas.

What the resolution meant was that the Sayerses' remains should be moved from Fairview Cemetery in Bastrop to the State Cemetery in Austin. But the relatives of the Sayerses and the citizens of the town of Bastrop objected. The couple were buried in the community where they had met and where they had married; it was also the place they had called home (even though much of their time had been spent in Washington, D.C.) for the first twenty years of their married life. They had been faithful members of the Methodist Episcopal Church, South, of Bastrop.

The protestors overrode the House resolution, and the graves remain serenely undisturbed inside the old-fashioned iron fence in the quiet cemetery. In the plot are three graves in a row; the carving on them tells a story. The center one is inscribed:

Joseph D. Sayers
1841-1929

Lena - Ada

To the right is a tall, weather-aged stone, which says:

Ada
wife of Joseph D. Sayers
Sept. 19, 1846
Married
March 5, 1868
Died
Feb. 25, 1871

To the left is a smaller, more modern stone on which is carved:

Lena
wife of
Joseph D. Sayers
1851-1943

Nearby are graves of the parents of Lena and Ada Walton and of the parents of Joseph Sayers. The close proximity of the family plots indicates the closeness of the two families. And Joseph Sayers' position between the two Walton sisters shows the love he felt for each of his wives. Lena's tombstone callously reveals a secret that she zealously guarded from even her closest friends all of her life — her age.

Born in Aberdeen, Mississippi, on August 12, 1851, to Maria and James Walton, Orline had come with her parents, her brother, George, and her sister, Ada, to settle in Bastrop just after the Civil War. In Mississippi she had studied with tutors because her health was considered too frail for her to attend school. In Bastrop she was fortunate to have an inspiring teacher — Mrs. S. J. Orgain. Lena had a bright, inquiring mind; she was an avid reader all of her life. Mrs. Orgain recognized her pupil's potential and encouraged it. After Mrs. Orgain had attended Chautauqua meetings in New York, she and Lena and a few other women held weekly meetings to study and discuss classical literature.

The young Lena also had artistic talent. Many fine pieces of beautifully painted china, family portraits, and drawings of personalities from literature still exist to attest to her skill. In addition, she became an accomplished pianist, a talent that was to bring her husband hours of pleasure in later years.

In the spring of 1868 an exciting event happened in the Walton family. Ada, who was five year older than Lena, married Joseph Sayers, a handsome young Civil War hero. Like the Waltons, the Sayerses had originally lived in Mississippi, but Dr. David Sayers had brought his children to Bastrop after the death of his wife in 1851. Dr. Sayers, who soon became a highly respected member of the little village, had chosen Bastrop partly because of its good schools. The Sayers boys were enrolled in the Hancock School in Bastrop.

Then Joseph Sayers went on to become the first student to receive the degree of bachelor of arts from Bastrop Military Institute. At the graduation ceremony on June 7, 1860, Governor Sam Houston handed him his diploma and commissioned him a lieutenant in the United States Army. Sam Houston, Jr. was a classmate of Sayers. Young Joseph Sayers opposed secession, but when the war actually began, he joined the Confederate Army as a private in the Fifth Texas Mounted Volunteers and made an outstanding record.

He was given a series of promotions for gallantry in action. Seriously wounded, he refused to leave the company. Governor Lubbock comments in his memoirs that Sayers was the only man he ever saw on crutches in active military service. He left the service in May of 1865 with the rank of major — a title he always preferred above all the others that he would eventually acquire.

Returning to Bastrop, he opened a school and studied law at night. The following year he passed his bar examination. Now that he had a profession, he was ready to settle down, so he courted and married the older of the two attractive Walton sisters.

He built his bride a comfortable Greek Revival style frame
house. The foundation was of hand-hewn pine logs; and it had
walnut handmade doors, walnut mantles on its four fireplaces,
and a built-in walnut china cabinet. The newlyweds were
proud of their new home and seemed ready to begin a satisfying life in the community where their families were firmly
rooted. The Waltons were happy that Ada had made such a
good match. But as the relatives on both sides were preparing
to welcome the first addition to the new family, Ada died in
childbirth.

The grief-stricken young husband threw himself into
political activity and was elected to the State Senate in 1873.
He kept in close touch with the Walton family and especially
with his wife's sister, Lena. She was sensible, attractive,
intelligent, and witty; and although he was ten years older
than she, they had a great deal in common, including their
shared grief for Ada.

In 1878 Sayers was elected Lieutenant Governor on the
Democratic ticket along with Governor Oran Roberts. One
month after the inauguration ceremony, he and Lena were
married — on February 20, 1879. Their honeymoon was spent
in Austin so Sayers could attend to his official duties.
Governor and Mrs. Roberts entertained the newlyweds with a
reception at the Executive Mansion.

It wasn't long, however, before Sayers disagreed with
Roberts on several issues regarding public lands and support
of public free schools. Consequently, he decided to try for the
office of Governor himself. But when Roberts was nominated
by the Democratic Convention at Dallas in July, 1880, Sayers
cheerfully supported him and the whole Democratic ticket.
For a short time after this effort, the Sayerses settled down in
the Bastrop home that Sayers had built for Ada, but he didn't
stay out of politics long. In 1884 he was nominated without
opposition and by unanimous vote of the Democrats of the
Ninth Congressional District to represent that district in the
United States Congress.

This was the beginning of fourteen years of alternating

between Washington, D.C., and Bastrop for the Sayerses. At thirty-four, Lena was slender and dainty with an appealing oval face and a clear ivory complexion. She eagerly took advantage of the opportunities offered by the capital city, studying French in the Berlitz School of Languages so she could communicate more easily with the diplomatic corps. And she also studied art, developing her knowledge and her talent. She quickly became a favorite in the government social circle.

One particular friend with whom she remained in close touch to the end of her life was the brilliant Señora Romero, the Mexican ambassador's wife. The Mexican legation was one of the most splendid and elegant in Washington; at dinner parties the guests ate from a dinner service of solid gold. Undoubtedly, the young neophyte from Texas learned from Señora Romero many of the social skills that were to make her famous later in life.

When her husband was made chairman of the Appropriations Committee, the Sayerses' position in the political pecking order rose even higher. Lena became intimately acquainted with Mrs. Grover Cleveland, the wife of the President. The formality and rigid rules governing entertaining and calling in the official circles in which she moved did not daunt Lena now. It was all a game she had learned to play with consummate grace and delight. She never grew arrogant in her position, but was always helpful to the wives of newly elected congressmen, guiding many of them gently through their first unsure essays into the confusing social world of official Washington.

Recognition of her husband added to her happiness as over the years he became one of the most respected and influential men in the House. Lena was as pleased as he was when the battleship *Texas* was named in his honor, because of work he had done in Congress on behalf of the Navy.

Lena and her husband had much in common, sharing especially a love of reading. On many occasions — birthdays, anniversaries, Christmas, Valentine's Day — he gave her books of poetry, which she treasured. A book of Elizabeth

Barrett Browning's poems given to Lena by her husband is in the permanent memento collection at the mansion. Other talents which he did not share, such as her musical and painting ability, he appreciated and admired.

When Sayers decided to run for Governor of Texas in 1898, Lena was willing for him to do so in spite of her love for the friends and life they had established in Washington. When he was elected (without having to campaign, thanks to the help of E. M. House) she expressed no regret at leaving the life she enjoyed so much. Long afterwards she said that the years in Washington had been her training for the mansion and added, "It was the Major's ambition to be Governor of Texas, and I was perfectly happy when that ambition was realized."

With this spirit of pride, she set out to be the best First Lady possible for her husband. Of course, there was much curiosity about this new mistress of the mansion, who had spent so many years among the sophisticated folk in the East. The curious were not disappointed in their first glimpse of her at the inaugural ball. She was poised and elegant in a gown of white Batenburg lace with simple pearl accessories.

Diplomatically she went about systematizing the social life connected with her position. The rules she set up were of great value to her successors. Tuesday afternoons were set aside as "at home" days when callers at the mansion could expect to find a gracious hostess, assisted by a large house party, and excellent refreshments awaiting them. Calls were punctiliously returned. She used the forty dollars allotted her for a housekeeper to hire two maids, and did her own overseeing of household affairs.

Lena asked for and received permission from the Legislature to have a general overhauling of the house grounds. The amount given her was small, but she made it go a long way. The outside of the building was painted; the fountains on either side of the front walk were removed; and great rosebeds were planted on the south lawn. She was a dedicated gardener and liked to work in the flower beds herself. The dilapidated old stable was replaced with a model up-to-date one, where her beloved carriage horses, King and Prince, were kept. They recognized her footsteps and voice and always came to her to rub their heads against her sleeve until she produced the sugar cubes they knew were in her pockets.

On the inside of the mansion, she retouched the historical pictures herself, and then had them reframed and hung in the hallway. Lena had the Sam Houston bed upon which Mrs. Culberson had placed the silver marker put into the hands of an expert cabinet maker for needed repairs. And she had other suitable colonial furniture placed in the room so that it was appropriate for use as the state bedroom for important guests.

Sayers' unmarried sister, Miss Jessie Sayers, lived in the mansion during their stay. She had her own pink and white room opposite their quarters. Jessie, who was noted for her intellect, taught in the Austin public schools during this time.

The initial reception given by Lena at the mansion was pronounced "brilliant" by society editors. They were especially impressed by its democratic nature — "everybody was invited, and everybody went" — legislators, university professors, university freshmen, aging Confederate soldiers, little businessmen, millionaire bankers, grandmothers, society belles, whole families, including babies in arms. One father was observed sitting on the floor in a corner of the dining room feeding his youngest on ice cream and cake. Lena had a way of making each person who came feel at home and welcome.

Hardly a week of her husband's two terms passed without some official or semi-official affair being held at the mansion. The papers soon began calling Lena "the Dolly Madison of the mansion." The Governor was dedicated to his job, and the Sayerses took no vacations during his first term. It was only after he had been renominated by acclamation at the Democratic Party State Convention in Waco in 1900 that they finally left Austin for a ten-day visit to Rockport.

A number of distinguished guests from out of the state were entertained by the Sayerses. They included the William

Jennings Bryans and two different Governors of Mexico. When the Jay Goulds were touring their railway lines in the South, Lena give them a memorable reception at the mansion. The Gould family was charmed with this break in their schedule and felt it gave them a better idea of Texas than they could get from inside their private car.

Lena particularly enjoyed entertaining guests from Washington, D.C., with whom she could share news and memories. President and Mrs. Theodore Roosevelt visited, as did President and Mrs. McKinley in May of 1901. The McKinleys were given a parade through the city in which Lena and Mrs. McKinley rode in the second carriage behind the carriage containing the President and the Governor. After the parade an elegant "Ladies" reception was given Mrs. McKinley in the Senate chamber.

At the mansion Lena arranged a dinner for the McKinleys and their party. She planned every detail with the utmost care. The parlors were decorated with smilax and roses, and the dining room looked like a floral grotto. Mrs. McKinley, who was a semi-invalid, had to rest on a couch during the meal. The delicious food and pleasant atmosphere pleased President McKinley so much that he dubbed Lena "the governor of the Governor." She loved the compliment and often recalled it in later years to tease her husband. Lena remained in Austin while the Governor accompanied the presidential party to Houston where McKinley paid tribute to a former First Lady — Mrs. Anson Jones, wife of the last President of the Republic of Texas.

In addition to planning entertainments and returning calls, Lena found time for worthwhile service activities. There were a series of disasters in Texas while the Sayerses were in the mansion — the burning of the Huntsville prison, the Brazos River flood of 1899, and the devastating Galveston hurricane of 1900. After the Galveston storm, while her husband slept on a cot in the hallway night after night and directed the rescue work personally by telegraph, Lena headed the Austin Relief Society and worked strenuously to help the storm's victims.

Lacking children of her own, she showed her concern for young people through her interest in the Young Men's Christian Association. She served as president of the local auxiliary of the Austin YMCA. When she left the mansion, the Board of Directors of the YMCA gave her a beautiful engraved silver pitcher.

She also found time to do church work. In Bastrop the Sayerses had been active members of the Methodist Episcopal Church, South, and they always felt a warm affection for this church. For years Sayers had served as Sunday School superintendent there. In Austin they became members and workers in the University United Methodist Church. Their regular attendance at services impressed at least one young university student. Later in life, after he became a judge, he recalled being influenced by seeing these two busy, important people walk down the aisle faithfully every Sunday morning.

The one great disappointment shared by the Sayerses was the fact that they had no children, but as the years passed, they grew closer in their relationship to each other. Unpretentious to the point of appearing almost careless in his dress, Sayers was proud of his wife's social skill and her ability in managing the household, a job he left strictly up to her. He loved to have her play soft, soothing music while he worked on knotty governmental problems, with her cat, Beauty, impudently strolling over his desk and sitting on important state papers. For Christmas of 1902, Lena gave her husband a dessert set consisting of a plate, cup, and saucer of Haviland china that she had painted for him. The arts of painting and playing music were "mysteries" to him, but he enjoyed her mastery of them.

Sayers was well-known for his economy in governmental affairs. But as a result of Lena's influence, he encouraged and signed a bill appropriating funds to have two life-size models of Sam Houston and Stephen F. Austin cast in marble and placed in the Capitol Building. The fragile plaster casts of these figures had lain in the studio of their creator, Elisabet Ney, for five years while she and friends had vainly tried to secure the money necessary for their completion. A warm friendship grew up between the famous sculptor and the Sayerses, and out of gratitude for their help in making it possible for her work to be put into permanent form, she made a bronze bust of the Governor. Many critics consider it one of her best works. It is on display in her museum today.

As Sayers prepared to leave office, he was lauded by many groups for his diligence, integrity, and success in generating good will during his administrations. But as Pearl Cashell Jackson says, " . . . how much of Major Sayers' political success is due to her [Lena's] charming personality the world will never know."

The office of Governor was the last political position that Sayers sought. He returned to the practice of law and remained active in that profession until his death. For a short time after leaving office, he practiced in San Antonio, but within a few years the Sayerses returned to Austin where they built a stately cream brick home on the corner of Eighth and Rio Grande Streets. All the rooms were large and airy, and the house was obviously planned with entertaining in mind.

The entrance hall was flanked by a reception room on either side and between the dining room and the kitchen was a large pantry with numerous shelves for ample storage of china and supplies. The dining room itself held a big mahogany table with at least a dozen chairs. An attractive guest room was always ready for company. In the Sayerses' bedroom was an enormous bed, elaborately carved by inmates of the Huntsville prison as a gift to the Governor and his wife. The wood was of Bastrop cedar, and Lena was proud of this piece of furniture. A huge chest of the same wood and design was also in the room. In this comfortable and gracious home Lena and her husband were to spend their remaining years.

A frequent visitor to the home was the Major's only sister, Jessie. She had been teaching mathematics at Southwest Normal College in San Marcos since it opened in 1904, but she continued to spend much time with her brother and sister-in-law.

Lena now added a number of new activities to her old ones. Because she was fond of animals, she gave much time to the Humane Society. She served on the state committee that paved the way for the establishment of the Young Women's Christian Association in Austin and in other Texas cities. She served the Austin YWCA as its president for four years and then held various other offices in the organization, and came to be called the "Mother of the Y" by its Austin members. Her love of children was manifested again in the time and interest she put into the YWCA's project of caring for Central European children when World War I broke out.

Lena also tried to be helpful to incoming First Ladies. In 1915 she gave a tea to introduce Miriam Ferguson to Austin society. As always the event was exquisitely planned down to the pink candles with rose-colored shades, silver filigree bonbon baskets, and arrangements of flowers in various hues of pink and rose. She also helped Mrs. Ferguson with some of her first entertainments in the mansion.

Ironically, Sayers had been appointed a member of the Board of Regents of the University of Texas in 1915, and in the controversy that arose between Governor Ferguson and the University he was appointed chairman of the Citizens Committee formed to present the University's case to the people. As a consequence of his work in marshalling the facts against Ferguson, Governor Dan Moody's first appointment after his induction into office in January, 1927, was that of Major Sayers as Chairman of the Board of Pardons and Paroles.

The Sayerses kept in touch with their Bastrop friends, and in 1926 presented their prized Bible, bound in heavy red leather, to the First Methodist Church there when it was dedicated. In the Bible was written:

> The last present of poor Ada to her husband. The M. E. Church, South from Joseph D. Sayers and Orline Walton Sayers
> May 20, 1926

In the Bible were carefully recorded the dates of the

marriages of the two Walton sisters to Joseph Sayers, his
birth date, and Ada's birth and death dates. There was no
record of Lena's birthdate. She considered it no one's business
but her own and guarded the secret all of her life. She once
refused to give it to a census taker, commenting to a friend
after he left, "How impertinent!"

In 1929 the Sayerses celebrated their Golden Wedding
anniversary. A snapshot taken about that time shows them to
be a handsome couple in their old age. Sayers had grown
portly, but he still had abundant white hair and a full
moustache. Lena's figure had become matronly, but not obese.
She wore her hair pinned in a bun on top of her head with soft
curls and waves framing her face. Sayers never retired from
his law practice and was still putting in a full day's work until
the time of his death. Three months after their fiftieth
anniversary, on May 15 just after he had finished breakfast, he
suffered a heart attack and died. He was eighty-seven. Lena
took her husband's body back to their hometown of Bastrop
for burial in the family plot. She did not complain of the
loneliness she must have felt after his death, but rather
expressed gratitude that they had had fifty good years of life
together.

Although her health was frail, and she was more or less
house-bound for the rest of her life, Lena remained cheerful
and interested in many things. She kept up a lively
interchange with the members and minister of her church and
enjoyed visits from numerous friends and relatives.

She did not lack for care and attention as she grew more
feeble. A companion lived with her, as well as a housekeeper
who did the cooking. Until she died in 1939, Jessie Sayers
visited frequently and helped keep the household running
smoothly. After Jessie's death, a nephew, Thomas Sayers, and
his wife, Irene, moved to Austin and helped look after Lena.

Her mind remained clear and her hearing perfect until the
end of her life. Her face in old age had a serene, contented
expression, reflecting her often expressed feeling of thank-
fulness for a full life that had left her with pleasant memories

for her old age.

In December of 1943, at the age of ninety-two, she fell from her chair and was taken to Brackenridge Hospital. There she received excellent nursing care and attention during the last few weeks of her life. She died the day after Christmas in 1943. Her funeral services were conducted by her minister, the Reverend Mr. Edmund Heinsohn of the University United Methodist Church. Then she was laid to rest beside her beloved "Major" in the little community where they had met and married more than half a century before.

23

The Governor's Teacher

Sarah Beona Meng Lanham

On October 9, 1866, a group of pioneers, consisting of thirteen single men and four married couples, met at Woodruff, South Carolina, to make a start for Texas. In the aftermath of the Civil War, they were all seeking greener pastures. Among the travelers was a young honeymoon couple — Sam and Sarah Lanham — who had been married scarcely a month.

The newlyweds were better off than some of their companions, for they had a little cloth-covered wagon, two mules, some cooking pots, bedding, a tent, clothing, a small amount of food, and about two hundred dollars in gold. As the procession crept westward across Carolina, Georgia, Alabama, Mississippi, Arkansas, and Indian Territory into Texas, the bride had plenty of time to remember the past and to dream about the future.

She must have felt regret at leaving her parents, Garland and Suzanna Meng, who had reared her in their comfortable home on the family plantation until the Civil War had destroyed their way of life. Even then they had managed to send her to an excellent school while the war was going on.

Since they were of the Moravian religion, she attended the fine Moravian Convent School headed by the Reverend Mr. Colon Murchinson in Unionville. After leaving the convent, she was engaged by her future father-in-law to teach school for the benefit of his own and the neighbors' children in a room over his store in Spartanburg.

From the Lanham children Sarah heard about their brother Sam, who had enlisted in the Confederate Army at the age of fifteen. His family was proud of the distinguished record he had made, and were eagerly looking forward to his coming home soon. When Sam Lanham was mustered out of the army at the end of the war and returned to Spartanburg, he realized that although he was a hero in the eyes of the townspeople, he was a poorly educated one.

His war experience had taught him a great deal, but he was well aware that he needed more formal training. Consequently, he began studying in the little school above his father's store. The teacher was only one year older than he and so attractive it was hard to keep his mind on his books. Sarah Meng was sympathetic toward this mature student, who was so eager to learn that he studied the dictionary while walking behind the plough on his family's farm. The attraction grew, and in a little over a year pupil and teacher had become man and wife.

Now she was on her way to a new home in a remote place called Texas and a life she could not really imagine. Had they made a mistake in following Horace Greeley's advice to "Go West"? Sometimes she must have wondered as they plodded on day after day.

Their diet was limited and the slowness of the journey was tiresome. Once they almost suffered a severe loss when one of the mules — either Union or Spartanburg — decided it didn't want to be a pioneer and headed back for South Carolina. It had covered quite a few miles of the return trip before Lanham, riding the other mule as fast as it could go, caught up with the runaway.

As the emigrants pushed on week after week, the weather

turned cooler and finally became cold. Their money dwindled as they paid for supplies and repairs, but hope, courage, and religious faith sustained them. They never broke camp on Sundays and practiced a spirit of tolerance and brotherhood in their relationships with each other. When they reached Arkansas, a few of the weary travelers decided to stop there to make their homes.

During the last week in November the remainder of the group reached Texas, crossing over the Red River by the Mill Creek Ferry. They received a cold welcome in the form of the first "blue norther" they had ever experienced.

More distressing to the new arrivals than the chilly weather was the discovery that the saloons and gambling houses were "running full blast" on the Sabbath. A few of the pioneers were so shocked that they decided to turn around and go back to the more "civilized" state of Mississippi to seek their fortunes. The Lanhams took stock of their remaining supplies and cash and decided they could not afford to join the retreat.

By the time the nomadic honeymooners reached the small town of Old Boston in Red River County, they were almost out of money. So they sold the wagon and team of mules; however, Sarah kept the wagon sheet to use to make shirts for her husband. She was pregnant by this time, and they decided to teach school to gain some income. When their first child was born, they named him Claude, but he only lived a few months. Discouraged by their loss and a scarcity of pupils, the Lanhams decided to move on after about a year in Old Boston.

They settled in Parker County in Weatherford, a small village on the edge of the frontier. The closest railroad point was Dallas, sixty miles away. Here they built a double-room log cabin. One room was for the school they planned to start, and the other was their living quarters. In June of 1868 an advertisement appeared in the Weatherford paper with this information:

A MALE AND FEMALE
HIGH SCHOOL
under the combined tutorship of
S.W.T. Lanham and Wife

Will open in the town of Weatherford on
Monday 22nd day of June.

Our past experience as Teachers warrants a confidence in our
ability to give satisfaction in the advancement of students, and
general scholastic system. We expect to merit a share of the public
patronage, and respectfully solicit a trial. We have located here
with the intention to remain and establish a permanent school.

RATES OF TUITION

Primary class, per month, specie,	$2.00
Intermediate, per month, specie,	2.50
First, per month, specie,	3.00
Latin, etc., per month, specie,	4.00

Students charged from admission to close of session except in case
of protracted illness. Session to last 20 weeks.
Weatherford, June 20th, '68.

Sarah realized that if they were to present a respectable
appearance, their wardrobes needed replenishing. She took
her trousseau dresses of imported English broadcloth and
made suits for her husband to wear. Homespun material
would do for her dresses better than for his pants and jackets.
At night she taught him the lessons he would need to teach his
pupils the next day. When a difficult problem came up during
the day, Lanham would tell the young scholar, "Take it home
with you, and if you really can't work it out yourself, I'll help
you tomorrow." That night Sarah would show him how to do
it, and the next day he would be able to solve the problem for
the student.

Life was primitive in Weatherford, compared to what Sarah
had known before she had married. Indians still staged
occasional raids, making it necessary to keep supplies and
valuables locked up. Since no woman in the village had enough
dishes to feed more than her immediate family, when company
came it was necessary to send all over the neighborhood to
borrow dishes.

Over the years in Weatherford Sarah gave birth to seven
children. They were named Sam, Hood, Howard Meng, Edwin

Moultrie, Fritz Garland, Grace, and Frank Valentine. The two oldest boys, Sam and Hood, died in infancy, but the other four boys and one girl grew to adulthood.

In addition to learning his lessons at night, Lanham studied law and in 1869 was admitted to the bar. One of his first cases involved an old man and his wife who were charged with stealing corn. The couple had traveled to Texas from one of the eastern states, and by the time they reached Weatherford were destitute, cold, and hungry. The old man, who could not bear to see his wife suffer for lack of food, broke into a barn and took some ears of corn. He was an inexperienced thief, and the snow on the ground had enabled the owner of the barn to track the couple and have them arrested.

From his own recent experiences, Lanham could well understand how the couple had felt, and he volunteered to represent them without fee. Returning home to prepare his case, he asked Sarah if there wasn't a verse somewhere in the Old Testament that fitted the case. She took down the Bible and found for him the thirtieth verse of the sixth chapter of Proverbs: "Men do not despise a thief, if he steal to satisfy his soul when he is hungry." Using this quotation as his basic argument, Lanham spoke so persuasively and so eloquently that he had the spectators and the jurors in tears. Without leaving the box, the jury handed down a unanimous verdict of "not guilty."

The vocabulary Lanham had studied with Sarah as his teacher enabled him to prepare convincing briefs and to present cases eloquently. He soon became noted for his ability as a lawyer, and within a year he held the position of District Attorney. Sarah, along with the rest of Texas, watched with interest as her husband prosecuted the two Kiowa Indian chiefs, Satanta and Big Tree, for their part in a murderous attack on a wagon train. The assault, during which most of the twelve teamsters were killed or wounded and the mules stolen, occurred between Jacksboro and Fort Griffin. The jury was convinced by Lanham to return the death penalty, but Governor E. J. Davis commuted the sentence to imprisonment.

In 1882 Lanham was elected to the United States Congress to represent the Eleventh District, called the "jumbo district" because it was composed of ninety-eight West Texas counties. Pleased with the chance to send the children to good schools in the East, Sarah packed to go with her husband. Unlike Lena Sayers, Sarah Lanham was not captivated by Washington society. But like Lena, she took advantage of the cultural opportunities offered by the nation's capital.

After the children were enrolled in the local schools, she studied German and learned to speak it fluently. She also studied art, developing her talent so that she painted in oils and on china with considerable skill. For four years she studied literature in a Chautauqua course and read widely, especially in the classics, history, and the Bible.

Sarah was a very private person who only entertained and mingled socially as much as was necessary to keep her husband in the good graces of his colleagues. Although he was much more of an extrovert, Lanham accepted Sarah's preference to lead a quiet life. And he continued to ask her advice and counsel on thorny problems.

After he had served five terms in Congress, the Lanhams retired to Weatherford where he resumed his law practice for four years. But the voters would not let him rest; again in 1896 they reelected him to Congress, and again Sarah and the children went with him to Washington.

Although he enjoyed the life of a Congressman, Lanham had a secret desire to play a different role. Finally he told Sarah and then the rest of the world his cherished dream — he wanted to be the Governor of Texas. In 1902, with her consent, he decided to try to make his wish come true.

His candidacy was based partly on an appeal to the veterans of the Civil War. Audiences were stirred to tears by his touching accounts of his war experiences. Many of his fellow veterans were influenced by the realization that he would almost certainly be the last ex-Confederate Governor of Texas.

His campaign was successful, but like many other mortals, he discovered that when his dream became a reality, it did not match his expectations. At sixty and sixty-one years of age, neither he nor Sarah was in very good health. "I made a great mistake when I became Governor of Texas," he later admitted. But in spite of disappointment, he and Sarah fulfilled their roles with dignity and integrity.

When she became First Lady, Sarah had silvery hair which she complemented by wearing orchids and grays. She wore soft styles that suited her rather than following those prescribed by fashion, and she cared little for jewelry but liked rich lace as decoration on her clothes. She had an erect bearing that some of her contemporaries thought gave her a "royal" air. This impression, added to her natural reserve, caused some people to label her as haughty.

Sarah did not try to match the energetic social life of her predecessor, Lena Sayers; for she had neither the interest nor the strength to do so. Her preference for a quiet, retired life — contrasted with the continuous round of entertaining and visiting of Lena Sayers — again made many people think of her as cold and distant. But when she was stirred by some event, she could be forceful. Once when she became convinced that a certain prisoner was worthy of freedom, she went in person before the Board of Pardons with an application and presented the same appeal to her husband. The man won his pardon.

On another occasion when she learned of the death of a servant who had been in the family for years, she took the first train to Weatherford to attend the funeral.

She held strong religious beliefs against drinking and never allowed liquor to be served at the mansion while she was its mistress, to the displeasure of some people.

The bright side of life at the mansion for Sarah and her husband was that their three youngest children — Fritz, Frank, and Grace — were with them. They all three became interested in theatrical performances, and Sarah enjoyed going to the theater and occupying a box with her husband

while they watched the children perform. Fritz later spent a
year as an actor before he followed his father into politics. He
felt that he had inherited his talent from his mother as well as
from his father. He commented that she had a keen sense of
the ridiculous and was a good mimic. This side of her
personality was revealed only to those closest to her.

The most elaborate entertainment that Sarah planned while
at the mansion was the wedding and reception for Grace and
Edward Connor on January 1, 1907. Edward was a graduate
student at the University of Texas, and Grace, who had
graduated from Winston College at Salem, North Carolina,
was a music student there. Austin society came to see the
popular young couple marry, knowing that this affair also
marked the end of the Lanhams' stay in the mansion.

Lanham's administrations were conservative. The times
were relatively peaceful and prosperous, and he had won
reelection with little trouble. One of the most important laws
passed during his tenure concerned the holding of primaries
for parties polling more than a hundred thousand votes in the
last general election. He suffered from diabetes, and during
his second term was increasingly unhappy. He wrote:

> I was very happy for years and years serving the people in my
> district as their congressional representative. Then I became
> governor. Office-seekers, pardon-seekers, and concession-seekers
> overwhelmed me. They broke my health and when a man finds his
> health gone, his spirit is broken.

Sarah also was relieved to leave Austin for Weatherford in
January of 1907. In September of that year, Governor Thomas
Campbell appointed Lanham a regent of the University of
Texas, but because of his failing health, Lanham attended only
two meetings of the board.

Sarah lived only a year and a half after their return to their
home. On July 2, 1908, the birthday of their daughter Grace,
she suddenly became very ill and died the same day. Her grief-
stricken husband buried her on his own birthday, July 4.
Complicated by depression, his condition became rapidly
worse following Sarah's death, and he died within the same

month — on July 29. Pupil and teacher were buried side by side in the Weatherford cemetery.

Her son, Fritz, who perhaps understood Sarah better than any of her survivors, wrote of his mother, "The more I think of her the more I marvel at her accomplishments. She was equal to any occasion."

24.

The Reluctant Sweetheart

Fannie Irene Bruner Campbell

When Mary McKay and Anne Maria Penn were children growing up in Mississippi, they were fast friends. After they matured, Mary McKay watched with interest as the serious young Anne Maria married the widower John Ireland and became the First Lady of Texas. Mary didn't dream that two decades later she herself would be an honored guest in the Executive Mansion of Texas as the mother of another First Lady of that state.

The McKay clan was large and well-known in Mississippi. Among their members were lawyers, doctors, and well-to-do planters. When Mary McKay and William Bruner of Vicksburg, Mississippi, married they had no plans to leave their native state, especially after their daughter, Fannie, was born on March 17, 1856, at their plantation.

Then the Civil War came along and Bruner served the Confederacy with gallantry. After the war, the family moved to Clinton, Mississippi, to give the children (of whom there were thirteen by this time) better educational advantages. Here Fannie attended Central Female Institute, a school for young ladies established in 1853, and acquired the polished manners and knowledge of etiquette expected of young ladies of her day.

Life in Mississippi was difficult and depressing after the war, and Bruner decided to move his family to Shreveport, Louisiana. Young Fannie never forgot the excitement of the trip to their new home via steamboat on the Mississippi and Red rivers. Her father served Shreveport as city comptroller for ten years and became a large property owner there.

Fannie grew into a graceful belle whose creamy, magnolia complexion was set off by her dark brown hair and eyes. Many young men of the area came to court her. Among these was Thomas Mitchell Campbell, a Texan whom she had met on a trip to Longview, where he was just beginning law practice. He and James Hogg had been born on neighboring farms near the town of Rusk in Cherokee County and remained lifelong friends. As adolescents both had vowed to become Governor of their native state.

Campbell's attraction to Fannie was instant, deep, and permanent, but Miss Fannie was much slower in surrendering her heart. For the next two years after their meeting, the couple sent a blizzard of letters over the sixty miles that separated her home in Shreveport from his in Longview. His letters became more ardent in tone with every passing week, but to his despair hers remained "friendly" but "distant." Even so, she was reluctant to have him let anyone see the letters she wrote, and it is possible that to please her he destroyed them.

In any event, we can reconstruct the nature of the correspondence by reading his side of it, which reveals his warm, emotional nature. He called the days spent with her "the happiest of my life." He often declared words inadequate to express his feelings and resorted to underlining even his greetings: *My Own Darling Fannie, My Dear Dear Fannie, Darling of All.* He passionately poured out his feelings for her and told her everything he thought could possibly interest her, but lamented that she kept things from him, saying, "That's the way my 'Little Girl' *always* does, just tells me half, *if that much.*"

As often as he could he met trains coming from Shreveport in hopes of having a letter from her. And he never stopped trying to elicit more feeling from her in her letters. He told her:

> ... for me to ask you to write to me as though you loved or even admired me is as I now conceive *all all* in vain ...

> Now I don't think you ought to continue that *cold formal* way of closing your letters — "Yours truly." Oh! it is too distant, and I do think it is *too much like disinterestedness* — I could never get my own consent to leave you with the inexpressive term "Yours truly"
> . . . .

As he came to know her family, he became genuinely devoted to them and they to him. In fact, Campbell seems to have won the affection of Fannie's family long before he was sure of hers. He soon began to refer to her parents as "our" Ma and Pa, her sisters as "our" sisters, and her aunt as "our" aunt. Mrs. Bruner visited relatives in Longview frequently, and he gave her every help and attention in his power. Apparently Mr. Bruner and Campbell were also quite compatible. They advised and encouraged each other and in later years exchanged warm, affectionate letters.

Even though Fannie's letters lacked the show of affection Campbell craved, she began to give him advice on his personal life, which he dutifully tried to obey. He played croquet because she suggested it; he tried to be home by dark because she told him he should; and he went or did not go to social functions such as picnics and balls according to her directions.

Much of his time was spent in planning so he could get to Shreveport or in begging her to come to Longview for a visit. When a yellow fever outbreak struck Shreveport in the summer of 1878, he worried frantically about Fannie and her family. He wrote to Mr. Bruner and persuaded him to move the family out of the city before railroad service was shut off as a precautionary measure against the spread of the disease. As a result, Fannie came to stay in Longview during the epidemic, and it was some time during this stay that she and Campbell made definite plans to marry. However, she refused to set a date and continued to refuse although he begged her in every letter to "tell me when I can be married." He promised not to tell the date, but she evidently didn't trust him to keep a secret and withheld her decision from him until the last minute.

He fretted over every cold or sore throat she reported and warned her against spending too many hours sewing (on her trousseau) for fear of hurting her health. For each letter she wrote he thanked her fervently, and when she at last concluded one with "affectionately" he went into raptures. After the wedding invitations were printed, he made the mistake of showing them to his friends without asking her permission. In reply to her scolding, he said, "You must tell me better the next time we get married."

What others thought of his behavior in connection with his "love affair" he cared not at all, even though he realized how it must seem to them. Shortly before their marriage he wrote to Fannie, "I sometimes think I am foolish about you, and very often act very simple, but I just don't care; and I am glad of it — for you are so true, so good and kind to me, and always seem willing to pass my many defects by unnoticed, for which I will always love and respect my Fannie." By the time the wedding was held on December 24, 1878, Campbell already seemed like a member of the family.

The day after the ceremony, the couple returned to Longview, which was to be their home for the next fourteen years. Over these years five children were born to them — Mary, Fannie, Thomas Mitchell, Jr., Sammie Belle, and Maydelle. The oldest daughter, Mary, died of some kind of chest disease (diagnosed as consumption) at the age of four.

During these early years of her marriage, Fannie's center of interest was in her family, but she also took an active part in the affairs of her town. She seems to have had a natural leadership ability that was soon recognized in whatever group she joined. She enjoyed working for the United Daughters of the Confederacy and in the local literary club and devoted much time to church work. Her family had been strong

Presbyterians — her father was an elder — in Shreveport, and this no doubt influenced her decision to join the Presbyterian church in Longview and to persuade the rest of the family to go along with her, although Campbell had been regularly attending Methodist services before their marriage. A surviving grandson, William Bruner Campbell, remembers that she saw to it that he became a Presbyterian at an early age. She became president of the Ladies Aid Society of the church in addition to her other duties.

Over the years Campbell became a prominent attorney in Longview, and one of his cases led him to become the receiver for the International and Great Northern Railroad when it was thrown into litigation. The receivership was closed in 1892, and he was appointed general manager for the line. His acceptance of this position made it necessary for the family to move to Palestine.

It was during this time that financier Jay Gould was trying to gain control of the railroads in Texas; Campbell opposed his efforts. Learning that Fannie was fond of fine china, Gould presented her with some pieces of exquisite Sèvres. He also entertained the Campbells lavishly in his special railroad car. Fannie prized the porcelain and enjoyed the elaborate entertainment, but her husband did not yield in his opposition to Gould's efforts to monopolize the railroads.

As the wife of the general manager of the International and Great Northern Railroad, Fannie had a ready-made place in the social life of Palestine. The old-fashioned railroad mansion provided by the company was the center of much social activity, and many notables in the railroad world and in state government were entertained there. When Governor Hogg visited the city, he stayed there as a guest of his old friend Campbell. He was accompanied by his small daughter, Ima, who displayed her already marked talent as a pianist.

Again Fannie showed a lively interest in local affairs. She was a member of the John H. Reagan Chapter of the United Daughters of the Confederacy, which was responsible for the erection of the handsome Reagan Monument in Palestine. She also served on the state committee of the organization and had an active part in the movement which resulted in the building in Austin of the Home for the Wives and Widows of Confederate Soldiers. She was a charter member and president of the Acorn Club, a literary organization founded in 1899, and with the exception of the four years she spent in Austin, continued an active member until her death. She also served as treasurer of the Library Board under the City Federation of Women's Clubs that worked toward the founding of the present Carnegie Library in Palestine. Somehow she also found time to pursue her hobbies with such diligence that she became known as an excellent cook, fine china painter, gardener, and needlewoman, especially of needlepoint, which was cherished by those fortunate enough to receive a piece as a gift.

The busy, pleasant life in Palestine was interrupted when Campbell, at the urging of Hogg and others, decided to enter politics for the first time. He entered at a high level by joining the gubernatorial race, announcing his candidacy in 1906, six weeks after the death of his friend, James Hogg. Campbell promised to revive Hogg's crusade against big business; the time was ripe, and the people of Texas elected him Governor on this platform. His campaign song was, of course, "The Campbells Are Coming." The citizens of Palestine gave a big reception for "Governor Tom" and his wife when the returns were in. And the newspapers reported "the honor was a joint affair in which Mrs. Campbell was equally an honoree with her husband." In November, Sarah Lanham, her predecessor as First Lady, gave a reception in Austin for Fannie.

The Campbell family left Palestine for Austin on January 14, 1907, to prepare for the inaugural ceremonies and other festivities that were to take place the following day in the Capitol. For the inauguration that took place at noon on the fifteenth, Fannie wore a rich wine-colored velvet gown and matching hat that emphasized the beauty of her dark hair and eyes.

The inaugural ball was held that evening in the Capitol. It

was preceded by a reception in the Senate Chamber, which was decorated with palms, vines and cut flowers. Here Fannie and other dignitaries received the distinguished guests who were attending the ceremonies. At ten-thirty the grand march formed, led by Governor Campbell and Mrs. Lanham, followed by ex-Governor Lanham and Mrs. Campbell. It proceeded to the House of Representatives, where the Grand Ball took place. Fannie wore an exquisite long-trained gown of white satin, with brocaded empire wreaths of roses; the bodice had an entire yoke of duchess and rose point lace with a bertha of the same lace cascading to the waist back and front and finished with pearl pendants and belt. She carried a huge bouquet of La France roses.

When Fannie became Texas' First Lady at fifty, she was stepping into a role that suited her perfectly. She loved to organize and plan formal entertainments, and she had dignity and poise in abundance. She also had a strong sense of obligation to the people of Texas. When an appropriation was made by the Legislature for improvements to the Executive Mansion, the decision as to how to use the money was left up to the Campbells. Various conveniences and comforts that could be added to the interior of the mansion were discussed by the family. Then Fannie decreed, "I say no! Any of these things would benefit only us and the Governors' households following us. That money should be put where the people generally would share in its benefits."

Consequently, under her supervision the money was used in landscaping and terracing the yard and in having sidewalks laid around the building. Many years later, Thomas Mitchell Jr. begged his wife not to raise begonias because he still remembered the tiresome chore of bringing in his mother's numerous pot plants whenever a frost or freeze threatened. Fannie's decision to use the money for improving the exterior of the building was especially generous because her daughters, who slept in the Sam Houston room, had to move out every time the Governor brought home guests, which was often. In later years after more bedroom space had been added, Fannie looked at it enviously and recalled those times.

In addition to improving the grounds, Fannie left her imprint on Austin as a unique and original hostess. She liked to entertain with musicales, and Maydelle, the youngest daughter, often sang for the guests on these occasions. Among the groups Fannie entertained were the Federated Club women, the Mothers' Congress, The Texas Woman's Press Association, and the American History Club. She also gave a lavish reception for Mr. and Mrs. William Jennings Bryan. For one springtime luncheon she had the dining room filled with flowers over which hovered multi-colored butterflies. One summer she gave a garden party with a table set with a much-talked-about centerpiece — an enormous block of ice that had flowers and fruits frozen inside it.

But Fannie's most spectacular entertainment was the debut she planned for Sammie Belle. It was held at the Eighth Street Hall in Austin. The debutante, accompanied by her sister, Maydelle, made her entrance in a flower-covered airplane as she literally sailed into society over the heads of the astonished guests. When the girls landed, an elegant ball followed. The favors for this affair were also miniature airships.

The New Year's reception on January 1, 1909, was reported by the Austin *Statesman* as having the largest attendance of any ever held at the mansion. Electricity had been put into the building in 1908, and the paper commented on the "beautiful electrical effects." The dining room was decorated with green cedar, gray moss, and red holly. Music was furnished by the orchestra from the Institute of the Blind. The refreshments were served in courses and were "delicious." The paper said that the Governor's wife was exceptionally handsome and stately in a princess gown of white satin striped crepe, embellished with rose point. Her accessories were diamonds. Her daughter Fannie wore an empire style yellow satin crepe with a garniture and duchess and rose point lace plus pearls.

All of this entertaining was expensive, and even more so since the menus were always elaborate and elegant. In addition, the Campbell women wore fine clothes; Fannie much preferred silk to calico and had a taste for costly jewelry. Even in 1907 the $4,000 Governor's salary was inadequate, and the Campbells used their private funds after it was spent.

To save on expenses two prison trusties were used as servants — one, imprisoned as a thief, was assigned yard work so he wouldn't have the opportunity to steal from the house. The other, who did the cooking, was a convicted murderer. The main servant was John Ector, a mulatto man; he drove the carriage and in later years cared for Governor Campbell during his final illness.

Since Campbell openly said that he always consulted Fannie before making any decision, she must have influenced some of the reforms that took place during his administration. Among those were the passage of a pure food law, improvements in the prison system, and creation of the Texas State Library.

In 1911 when Campbell's second term came to an end and Fannie prepared to leave the mansion, the women of Austin, whom she had entertained so often and so well, presented her with a silver tray inscribed:

With the genuine respect

and affection of

The Women of Austin

The Campbells returned to Palestine where Campbell resumed his law practice. Campbell made only one other — unsuccessful — attempt to gain political office when he ran for the United States Senate against ex-Governor Culberson.

In Palestine Fannie was soon caught up again in church and club work and other public affairs. In 1912 she was chairman of the Women's Division of the Woodrow Wilson Campaign Committee of the Seventh Congressional District. And during World War I she was active in Red Cross and other war work.

As the years passed, the children grew up and married; the weddings of the three daughters were solemnized in the First Presbyterian Church, of which the Campbells were members. Thomas Mitchell, Jr., also married, and he and his wife, Erma, lived for a while with the Campbells in their huge, two-storied home near the center of town. Thomas, Jr., was a founder of the Campbell State Bank (which later became the East Texas National Bank).

In the Campbell home in Palestine was a very proper front parlor where Fannie entertained with formality and dignity. The back sitting room was reserved for family and close friends. It was considered quite an accomplishment by the Campbells' acquaintances to be entertained in the back room; many were entertained in the parlor but few ever saw the sitting room. Sometimes Campbell brought home businessmen whose manners Fannie did not approve. It was a family story that when she asked him why he brought home a certain rather uncouth man, he replied that the man might give him a case that would result in a $10,000 fee. This explanation satisfied Fannie, and the man was duly entertained, manners notwithstanding.

Fannie was always ambitious for her husband, and he gave her credit for whatever success he attained as a lawyer, businessman, and statesman. He submitted to her everything he wrote and discussed with her every plan he had. He often remarked that without her encouragement, wise counsel, confidence, love and sympathetic understanding, he would never have achieved success in his various positions. The reluctant sweetheart had become the completely dedicated and devoted wife.

The warm-hearted Campbell fully returned her affection, but he loved to tease her in little ways. He was one month younger than she, and he often told friends she was older without telling how much. She always remained slender, since she was a very light eater (although all of the daughters became heavy in their middle years). But when Campbell became ill and lost his appetite, he would say he wished he could eat like her. He liked to give her nice presents, and on her fifty-fourth birthday gave her a beautiful heavy carved silver tea service.

In 1923 their agreeable life came to an end when Campbell's health became poor. He was discovered to have leukemia and went to John Sealy Hospital in Galveston for treatment. But he rapidly became worse and died there on April 1. Fannie brought his body back to Palestine for burial. She had a fifty-foot obelisk erected beside the grave; on it she had carved only his name and the dates of birth and death.

She continued to live in the big white house with its reminders of her husband's service to the state, such as the Linz Brothers' clock presented to him upon his retirement from office by "Organized Labor of Texas" and the bust of him done from life in 1909 by the sculptor Pompeii Coppini. But her days were not spent sitting around wishing for the past; as always she kept her mind and her hands busy.

In addition to church and club activities, she quilted heirloom quilts and painted fine china. She entertained, played bridge, and took trips to visit relatives and health resorts. And much of her time was spent with her grandchildren, to whom she was devoted. She kept toys on hand for their visits in a small closet in her bedroom, and on her own birthday, St. Patrick's Day, she gave toys to all of them.

Four years after Campbell's death, Fannie's only son, Thomas Mitchell, Jr., died of a heart attack. He was also buried beneath the tall obelisk. When the city of Palestine named Mitchell Campbell Baseball Field in honor of her son, Fannie went with other family members to the dedication. Watching the players warm up for the game, she worried that they would be exhausted before it started.

From the time automobiles became available the Campbells always had a fine car, but Fannie never learned to drive. She sometimes wished she had, especially at times when she felt it would help her keep up with the grandchildren more easily. When Fannie, Jr. and her husband and family moved into the big house to share its responsibilities, Fannie, Sr. had three lively young male grandchildren living with her. In the summers when school was out, she sent them off to camp in Kerrville, probably as much for her sake as for theirs. Another tragedy struck the family when one of these grandsons,

Thomas Mitchell Campbell III, died of polio at the age of sixteen. He was buried beside the other two Thomas Mitchells in the Palestine cemetery.

As long as she lived, Fannie remained the matriarch of her family. As she grew older and had to rely somewhat on others, the members of the family conspired to make her feel that she was still in command of most situations — as she usually was. For some reason, perhaps because she was freest to leave, Fannie's daughter-in-law, Erma Campbell (Thomas Mitchell Jr.'s widow), was her chosen traveling companion. Several times they went to Battle Creek, Michigan, to visit the sanitarium there. Neither of them was ill; they went because it was a fashionable health spa that specialized in baths and health food. It was owned by the cereal tycoon Kellogg, who was a health faddist and a Seventh Day Adventist. Sometimes Erma and some of the other young women would slip into town to eat some "real" food (which meant meat).

Once, while they were on their way to Battle Creek, a train accident detained them in St. Louis for some hours. Mrs. Campbell, Jr. decided to take a bath at the public bathing facilities near the station. The proper Fannie was aghast at the idea, but Erma had her bath anyway and was glad she did, as it took the train another two days to arrive at their destination.

When they went to Chicago, they stayed at the Palmer House. Here Fannie liked to watch people wearing fine clothes and jewelry promenade down the long hall, called Peacock Alley, to the social functions in the famous dining room. She never lost her interest in materials of fine quality — whether it was fine cloth, jewelry, or china.

As she reached her seventies, Fannie suffered from high blood pressure, but she still remained as independent as possible. Perhaps mercifully, she died suddenly of a stroke at her home on November 15, 1934, at the age of seventy-eight. Palestine public schools were dismissed for her funeral. She was buried, as she had planned, beside her devoted husband, beneath the granite shaft she had erected to honor him.

25.

The
Thread
of Gold

Alice Fuller Murrell Colquitt

In 1884, with $175.00 in cash and plenty of nerve, Oscar Branch Colquitt started publishing the Pittsburg, Texas, *Gazette*. For the fiftieth anniversary issue of the *Gazette*, ex-Governor Colquitt wrote a biographical sketch of his life that included a summary of his marriage:

> During the Christmas holidays of 1884-85 I met a modest, unassuming but refined young lady with beautiful golden hair, Miss Alice Murrell, from Louisiana, at the home of her brother-in-law, J. E. Robinson, and on December 9, 1885, we were married. For more than 47 years she has been the thread of gold in my life — always gentle, always thoughtful, always kind, dignified and always considerate of others whether at home or in the Governor's Mansion. And I am happy to say she is still the "crowning glory" of my life.

Alice Fuller Murrell was born to Rebecca and Isaac Murrell on November 19, 1865, at Minden, Louisiana. The Murrells were early colonists in North Carolina. Isaac Murrell's father had moved to Claiborne Parish, Louisiana, in 1818, fifteen years after the United States had bought the Louisiana territory from France. He had become a successful planter and merchant with business interests at Minden and New Orleans. The Murrells reared their eight children in Minden, and

Alice, along with her siblings, attended Minden College, one of the oldest colleges in the South.

Alice Murrell grew up to be an attractive young woman with blonde hair and a lovely pink and white complexion. When she was nineteen, she was invited by one of her married sisters to spend the Christmas holidays in Pittsburg, Texas. It was here that she met the ambitious young newspaper publisher, Oscar Colquitt.

Before the turn of the century, visits were long and leisurely, so there was plenty of time for the young couple to get to know each other well. Oscar told the charming visitor the details of his family background. Seven relatives on his father's side and five on his mother's had taken part in the American Revolution. His mother had been a schoolmate and friend of the mother of Theodore Roosevelt at Wesleyan Female College at Macon, Georgia, the first college in the world to issue graduating diplomas to women.

On the Colquitt side, a great-uncle had been a United States Senator, and an uncle had served as Governor of Georgia. At fifteen, Oscar's father had run away from home to join Texas' fight for independence from Mexico and had gotten as far as Mobile, Alabama, before his father caught up with him and took him home. Oscar was born during the Civil War in December of 1861, while his father was an officer in the Confederate Army.

After the war, when the family lost their plantation and practically everything they owned, Oscar's father revived his dream of living in Texas and moved the family to Daingerfield. Because of the poverty of the family there was little time for attending school, so Oscar educated himself by reading everything he could get his hands on. He worked at whatever jobs he could find. He was a tenant farmer, hod-carrier, railway depot porter, furniture maker, and a printer's devil. Like Jim Hogg, he took advantage of his job in the newspaper office to supplement his education.

When the opportunity came to start the Pittsburg paper, Oscar had taken the chance. And, he told Alice, that is how he happened to be lucky enough to be in the right spot to meet her during her holiday visit to her sister and brother-in-law. Rumor says that he proposed to her before she returned to Louisiana, but that she refused him the first time. However, Oscar Colquitt, although short of stature, was long on persistence. And after more visits and many letters during the year, he changed Alice's mind. Their wedding took place in December of 1885.

The following year when the Colquitts had the chance to buy the Terrell *Star*, they decided to take it. Accordingly, they sold the *Gazette* to Colquitt's brother, W. F. Colquitt. In October of 1886 they moved to Terrell in Kaufman County, where they would live for the next sixteen years. They later bought the Terrell *Times* and consolidated the papers as the *Times-Star*.

Five children — four boys and one girl — were born to the Colquitts during the years they lived in Terrell. They were named Rawlins Murrell, Sidney Burkhalter, Oscar Branch, Jr., Mary Alice, and Walter Fuller. Alice and Oscar Colquitt shared a deep devotion to their home and children. But when it came to politics, Alice could not share her husband's dedication. As a young boy, Colquitt had spent some of his hard-earned money to subscribe to a political weekly, and he had kept up his avid interest in political leaders and events. Now his forceful editorials on issues of the day made him strong friends — and enemies.

In 1890 he strongly supported Hogg and the establishment of a railroad commission, and was active in the gubernatorial campaign. After the election, Hogg appointed him to the board of managers of the North Texas Hospital for the Insane at Terrell.

About this time Colquitt began to study law, and Alice must have realized that her husband was not going to be satisfied much longer with the limitations of his job as the editor and publisher of a small town newspaper. Therefore, it was no surprise when he decided to run for State Senator. He was well-known and popular and was elected without much trouble. Alice stayed at home in Terrell with the children while her husband traveled to Austin for two terms in the Senate. He was friends with both Governors Culberson and Sayers, and both recognized his ability. Culberson appointed him State Revenue Agent, and Sayers asked him to serve as a tax expert on a commission set up to reform the tax laws of Texas.

In 1903 Colquitt was elected to succeed John H. Reagan as state Railroad Commissioner, a position he held until 1910. Her husband's position as Commissioner meant a move to Austin for the family and a more active public life for Alice. In spite of her personal preference for privacy, she was capable of entertaining graciously and of performing the public duties that were required of her. She became known in Austin for her interest in charities and for her good common sense. She resisted efforts to involve her in politics or purely social organizations, but worked untiringly for the causes she undertook to support. Patriotic organizations interested her; she was elected president of the Albert Sidney Johnston Chapter of the United Daughters of the Confederacy and was active in the Daughters of 1812.

In 1906 Colquitt tried for the gubernatorial nomination but was defeated by Thomas Campbell. As Campbell's second term ended, Colquitt decided to try again for the top state office. The Colquitts' oldest son, Rawlins, served ably as his father's campaign manager.

The campaign was a bitter one with prohibition as the main issue. Colquitt championed local option and brought down upon his head the wrath of women's groups, temperance organizations, and preachers. The Colquitts were faithful Methodists, but one Methodist bishop called for Colquitt's banishment from the church because of his stand. The Colquitts refused to leave the church, and no action was taken on the bishop's suggestion. Colquitt was not a polished orator, but he was a colorful and convincing stump speaker who drew large crowds to listen to him. Backed by farmers, laborers, and newspapers, he won the election.

A few months before the campaign ended, the Colquitts suffered a personal tragedy when their youngest son, Walter Fuller, died of typhoid fever. Alice did not have her husband's interest in politics to divert her mind from her grief, so she threw her energies into supporting organizations dedicated to treating and finding causes for children's diseases.

Alice liked white clothing, and for her husband's inauguration she chose a dress of white satin with silver sequins and white shoes. For the Governor's Ball, she wore white lace with pearls, shoes of white satin with beads, and carried a white lace fan.

The new First Lady went about her duties in her usual straightforward way. Her aim was to be hospitable, not showy. Often Boots, her pet Angora cat, rubbed against visitors' knees as they sipped their afternoon tea in the parlor of the Executive Mansion. The refreshments were more simple than they had been in earlier times. At the Tuesday afternoon receptions to which the general public was invited, tea and punch were served. And at the big New Year's receptions, a salad course and tea, coffee, or punch were offered. In spite of the fact that Colquitt was labeled a "wet" because of his anti-prohibition stand, there was never any drinking of alcoholic beverages allowed in the mansion while Alice was mistress there.

A cause in which Alice entered heart and soul was the crusade against tuberculosis. For many years she was president of the state Tuberculosis Society. She worked to establish tuberculosis camps for children in the state and to raise money each year through the sale of Christmas seals for education and research to fight the "great white plague." In 1911 she sold $35,000 worth of Christmas seals; the money was used to build a hospital in Galveston for children suffering from tuberculosis of the joints. The hospital was at first named Walter F. Colquitt for their dead son, but because it had been located on grounds in connection with the medical branch of the University of Texas, the name had to be changed to conform to the deed in the original conveyance of the land to the University. She also worked with the Red Cross to establish hospitals in Austin and Dallas.

Friends of the Colquitts gave them a Victoria and a handsome pair of horses when they moved into the mansion. However, the carriage was seldom used after the Colquitts acquired an automobile. The car was kept in a garage in town, and a man was hired to come to the mansion several afternoons to teach the family how to drive. Oscar and Alice Colquitt became famous as the first Governor and his wife to drive an automobile. Once a dignified English visitor, Sir Christopher Craddock, stayed at the mansion and was quite impressed that Mary could drive; girls in England did not yet drive cars. At times Alice wished that Mary was not such an enthusiastic motorist.

Early in the Colquitts' stay in the mansion, the Texas Legislature finally acknowledged that the time had come when some major refurbishing was needed inside the building, which was over fifty years old and showing its age. Fannie Campbell had used the Legislature's appropriation to improve the exterior of the building. And now, with the help of a decorator, Alice undertook to renovate the interior. A tent was set up outside where the cooking was done while the kitchen was modernized.

Austin citizens knew of the extensive decorating, and they could hardly wait for the New Year's reception in 1912 to see what had been going on inside the building. They were not disappointed. The woodwork had been painted ivory white, furniture had been upholstered in rich mulberry and matching shades, halls were papered in dark green with matching carpets, parlors were in silvery gray with matching carpets and elegant chandeliers. The dining room was in brown and greenish blue with a bronze chandelier, and the library was done in tans and browns.

The Sam Houston room was papered in a rosebud design and the bed was newly hung with pink brocade; the rose-colored carpet and window hangings from the parlors downstairs were thriftily installed here. And an antique chifferobe that Alice had resurrected from a downstairs storeroom had been added.

To add to the comfort and convenience of the inhabitants, gas radiators replaced the baseburner in the hall, and a family dining room was added. Two bedrooms, two baths, and a dressing room were added to the second floor. Plans were made, but not yet completed at the time of the reception, to paint the outside of the mansion white with green blinds so Texans could have their own White House. Alice had a few carefully placed floral arrangements in colors to complement the new furnishings, but as one newspaper noted, it was no longer necessary to hide cracks, peeling wallpaper, and shabby furniture with so much greenery that the interior looked like an overstocked greenhouse. The people were delighted with the improvements their new First Lady had made.

While Colquitt had served as Railroad Commissioner, he had introduced and pushed through to adoption legislation requiring the railroads to build the Galveston causeway, a feat which enhanced his popularity with many south Texans. In May of 1912 the causeway was opened to traffic, and the Colquitts were invited to the ceremonies as honored guests.

Colquitt needed all the popularity he could muster in 1912 as he battled through a stormy campaign for reelection. He made many enemies by opposing Woodrow Wilson's Mexican policy. His opponents made plans to bury "little Oscar" at the primary, but the Governor was not ready to be buried, and the campaign was a memorable one. One of Colquitt's promises was to reform methods of punishment in the Texas prison system. He toured the state brandishing a large bullwhip and asking, "Would you sustain by your ballots this implement of human torture?" And again he ran on an anti-prohibition ticket. When he carried the state by a large majority, his supporters happily proclaimed "little Oscar" as the "little Napoleon" of Texas politics.

As usual Alice remained aloof from the fuss and fury of the

campaign. While it was at white heat, she met the wife of one of Colquitt's bitterest political foes at the glove counter of a leading Austin department store and calmly compared recipes for preserves with her.

Their second term in the mansion was a satisfying one for Alice. Sidney was married shortly before the inauguration, and Mary finished college (which she had been attending in Washington, D.C.) and came back to Texas to live with her parents.

Alice continued her work with the Red Cross and Tuberculosis Association and also her church work. She enjoyed traveling with her husband and used opportunities whenever possible to gather information that would help further the cause of promoting the good health of the people of Texas. In 1913 when they made a trip to Panama, she was impressed by the measures taken there to eliminate such diseases as yellow fever, malaria, typhoid fever, and dysentery. On their return she began a campaign to "Panamaize" Texas, by which she meant the undertaking of similar measures to rid the state of these diseases. She had the facts and figures and at every opportunity stressed the need to take sanitary and educational steps and build more state and county hospitals. Although she usually shunned publicity, she did not mind having her name and position used in the interest of better health for Texans.

At the beginning of World War I, the Colquitts were pro-German, perhaps partly because Oscar's ancestors, the Salzburgers, had come from the valley of the Salza River in Austria. They planned to buy the New York *Sun*, with the financial assistance of the German government, and use it as a German propaganda organ. However, probably fortunately for their future, this plan failed. They didn't try to force their opinions on their children, and Sidney joined the United States Army in 1914. He was stationed in Washington, D.C.

Alice left the mansion with mixed emotions. When she was presented with a diamond pendant by the women of Austin, the gift must have seemed somewhat ironic to her because the

Colquitts were almost penniless, having used their own personal resources to supplement the meager Governor's salary. One of her last acts as First Lady was to plan a turkey dinner with all the trimmings for the incoming Ferguson family.

After they left the mansion, the Colquitts moved to a two-story brick house on Live Oak Street in Dallas, where Alice was to live for the rest of her life except for visits. Her husband made his last attempt for political office in 1916 when he ran for the United States Senate. In the first primary he received a large plurality over six opponents, but in the runoff was defeated by the incumbent, his old friend, Charles A. Culberson.

For the next decade, although he remained active in politics, he devoted most of his time to business, serving as the president of a Dallas oil firm. Alice, who had never enjoyed being in the limelight, found pleasure in their new life together. Mary had married and was living in Philadelphia, but Oscar, Jr. was at home.

Traveling was one of their great pleasures. In addition to visiting their married children in California and Pennsylvania, they made trips to Chicago, New York, and St. Louis. They journeyed to Seattle, Washington, in the summertime, and Alice never forgot the impression made on her by the beauty of that city with all the flowers in bloom. On a trip to Salt Lake City, their train was met by the Sons of the Revolution. Governor Blood of Utah, a Mormon, entertained the Colquitts royally and proudly showed them the sights of the city. At home in Dallas, Alice lived the quiet home-centered life that she loved, occupying her time with household chores and such pastimes as quilt making.

Colquitt kept his interest in politics, and in 1928 bolted the Democratic party to head the "Hoover Democrats" of Texas. As a result, Hoover appointed him a member of the United States Board of Mediation, and in 1935 he was named a field representative of the Reconstruction Finance Corporation. Both of these jobs involved traveling, and as often as she could, Alice accompanied her husband.

In late February of 1940, Colquitt became ill with influenza and was taken to the hospital. Ten days later he suffered a cerebral hemorrhage and died on March 8. Alice accompanied his body back to Austin for burial in Oakwood Cemetery in the old black suit that he had worn for his inauguration as Governor.

The last nine years of her life were quiet and lonely without the husband who had been her constant companion for fifty-five years. Two of her children, Rawlins and Oscar, Jr. (who had lived with her in their Dallas home for twenty-five years), died during this time.

As she aged, her figure became plump and the golden hair that her husband had admired so much turned a dark auburn shade. She wore it long and braided around her head. She suffered poor health during her last years and spent a great deal of time visiting in Mary's home in Merion, a suburb of Philadelphia. She was on an extended visit to Merion when she became ill and died on June 30, 1949, at the age of eighty-three. Her body was flown back to Austin to be buried beside the husband who had given her her best epitaph when he said:

> No man ever had a better wife, no children a more patient, faithful and sympathetic mother. Preferring the seclusion of the domestic circle, she never shrank from public duty — social, religious or official.

26.

"It Was
All Fun"

Miriam Amanda Wallace Ferguson

The band struck up "Put on Your Old Gray Bonnet," and the crowd took up the words with enthusisam as Governor Allan Shivers escorted the white-haired guest of honor to her place at the head table. The setting was the glittering ballroom of Austin's Driskill Hotel, and the honoree was Miriam Amanda Ferguson, who stood for a long moment looking at the smiling faces of the three hundred friends who had gathered to celebrate her eightieth birthday. As she stood before them, characteristically erect and thanking them in her direct, simple way, the guests agreed that, except for her white hair, the years really hadn't changed her very much.

"When the band played, and I saw all you people waiting in here, it reminded me of campaign time. And I thought I was going to a speaking," she declared. The younger guests knew only through hearsay about the public life she referred to. They had been children when she and her husband had made their last campaign fifteen years earlier. But the older guests nodded; many of them had frequently applauded her at "speakings." Of course, she would have dressed much more simply for a "speaking"; instead of the rose mauve gown of lace and taffeta, she would have worn a good dark, practical dress. But she might have worn the same old-fashioned gold lavaliere, a cherished piece of jewelry that her husband had given her early in their marriage.

Probably most of those gathered in the banquet hall realized this would be their last chance to honor the woman who had served Texas as its only woman governor, and they wanted to make a memorable occasion of this lavish dinner party that was the climax of her birthday celebration. The mayor and city council had declared June 13, 1955, "Miriam A. Ferguson Day" in Austin, and both houses of the Texas Legislature had adopted unanimous resolutions honoring her.

Acting as master of ceremonies, Governor Shivers read a telegram of warm greetings from President Dwight Eisenhower. United States Senator Lyndon Johnson, who had made a flying trip from Washington, D.C., to attend the dinner, told the honoree, "Governor, I traveled 1,600 miles to be with you tonight, and I would gladly travel 1,600 more." A beautiful gold bracelet watch engraved simply with the numerals "80" was presented to her on behalf of her friends over the state.

The dinner had cost the guests six dollars a plate, and when it was being planned, Miriam Ferguson had bet a friend that not more than one hundred people would pay that price to celebrate her birthday. For a politician she badly under-estimated the odds, for three times that many enthusiastically responded. That was the way Texans always responded to Miriam and her husband — with enthusiasm, either for or against them. The main speaker for the occasion, Alvin Owsley, reminded the guests, "There was no neutrality in Texas when the Fergusons were the candidates."

Miriam agreed, but on this day of remembering she summed up her turbulent political life for a reporter and concluded, "It was all fun . . . every bit of it!"

There was nothing in Miriam Amanda Wallace's early life as the daughter of a prosperous Bell County farming family to lead anyone to suspect that she would become a dynamic part of Texas history. The Wallaces, who traced their lineage back to the Scottish Clan Campbell of Argyllshire, had come to Texas and settled on the banks of the Little River during the last days of the Republic of Texas. Joseph Lapsley Wallace had married a widow, Eliza Garrison Ferguson, whose first husband had been Wesley Ferguson. The Wallaces worked hard and became well-to-do, chiefly through the raising of cotton and cattle. Miriam Amanda, born on June 13, 1875, was the third of six children born to Joe and Eliza. She had a pleasant, normal childhood on the self-sustaining farm.

The Wallace home was a well-built log house, consisting of five large rooms with a long gallery overlooking the river. As the family grew more prosperous, the logs were covered with painted board siding. The master bedroom had a four-poster bed with a trundle bed underneath, which was pulled out at night for Miriam and her sister Susan to sleep on. The separate kitchen and dining room were connected to the main unit by a covered gallery. In a storehouse next to the kitchen were kept the staple supplies: barrels of flour and sugar, ten-pound cans of coffee, kegs of Scotch mackerel. Beyond the storehouse was the smokehouse and on the other side of that the storm cellar, intended as a refuge in case of tornadoes but also a cool storage place for perishable foods. The servants' quarters were a little distance back of the house, and an orchard and vegetable garden lay to the south. Around all the buildings and lining the walks were flower beds filled with various fragrant blooms. Like her mother, Miriam was to be passionately fond of flowers all of her life.

As she became a toddler, Miriam's special pet and constant companion on the farm was Pat, a big black Shepherd dog with a white ruff around his neck. Her early years were spent in carefree play with her sisters and brothers. Daily prayers were a part of the family's way of life, and the world for little Miriam was warm and secure.

Like so many other Texas pioneers, Joe and Eliza were deeply concerned that their children get a good education. For this reason they decided to move closer to Center Lake School, located seven miles northwest of their farm. They were able to buy a beautiful tract of land on a rolling prairie. Here the Wallaces dug a well and built a frame house in an L-shape. This comfortable home even included the newfangled idea of attaching the kitchen and dining room to the main house.

Joseph, Miriam's youngest brother, showed exceptional talent as he matured. The beautiful fair-skinned, blue-eyed child was the family pet. The most amazing thing about him was his deep religious feeling. He took charge of the family services as soon as he could talk, and had an astonishing ability to memorize long biblical passages that were read to him. In July of 1891 Joseph developed a severe pain in his stomach, which the family doctor diagnosed as cramp colic. Dr. Barton from Salado was sent for and told the family that this was a "new" disease called appendicitis. Although surgeons in the East were removing the appendix, he did not know how to do the operation. Little Joseph died a few days later. The next year Dr. Barton went East to learn to perform an appendectomy.

When the Center Lake School failed to live up to the Wallaces' expectations, a tutor was hired to come to the home to instruct the children. She proved to be a good teacher and remained with the family for two years. By this time Miriam was thirteen, and her parents decided to send her and her two older brothers to Salado College, considered to be one of the best educational centers in Texas. Accordingly, they went to live with their Aunt Betty Smith in Salado. Aunt Betty was a disciplinarian, who considered the Wallaces entirely too indulgent with their "spoiled" children. Life with Aunt Betty was stern and full of punishments, but Miriam made good progress at the school and was especially happy in her art class.

After two years, either Aunt Betty had had enough of the Wallace children, or they had had enough of her discipline. Whatever the reason, Miriam, along with her sister, enrolled in Baylor Female College in Belton. The girls discovered that the regulations at Baylor were also strict; special permission had to be obtained tó leave the campus, and the students wore a blue-gray coat suit style uniform and a square mortarboard cap, popularly known as the "convict" outfit. During summer vacations, Miriam along with her sister, mother, and a "sewing woman" spent much time preparing their wardrobes.

In spite of restrictions, Miriam found those school years pleasant. To relieve the monotony of institutional food, Joe Wallace left a standing order with a Belton grocery to send candy and fruit each week to his daughters. He also frequently brought them goodies from the family kitchen. On holidays and weekends he or one of the girls' brothers often came in the family surrey to take them home.

In the midst of these years a meeting took place that was destined to change Miriam Wallace's life. Her married half-sister, Annie (the daughter of Miriam's mother and her first husband, Wesley Ferguson), gave a party to which she invited Miriam and Jim Ferguson — Annie's cousin. To Miriam, who had never been out of Bell County, Jim Ferguson was a colorful and fascinating young man. She, of course, knew his family, as did everyone in Bell County.

Jim's father, James, was well-known as Parson Ferguson, a circuit-riding Methodist preacher. He had settled his family on a small farm on the banks of Salado Creek, where he supplemented the income from his ministerial duties by serving as a miller to nearby farmers. In James Ferguson could be seen many of the qualities his son inherited. He was dubbed the "fighting parson" because of his readiness to take on all comers with his tongue or his fists. And yet he spent most of his meager income on "poor brother this or that," blissfully ignoring the poverty of his own family. The only thing the Fergusons had in abundance was children. Jim was the sixth (but not the last) of the brood. The day after he was born, Parson Ferguson proudly announced the birth to a Methodist conference meeting in Salado. He said, "We have named him Jim. He weighs thirteen pounds, and some day he will be Governor of Texas."

The parson died when Jim was four, and Fanny Ferguson

struggled to raise her family of seven children. She was willing to make almost any sacrifice to give them the best education available. Jim studied in a log schoolhouse and then enrolled in Salado College at the age of thirteen — a few years before Miriam Wallace attended the school. For four years he studied the classics, history, algebra, and rhetoric. Many years later, Miriam was to point to these years to refute opponents who called him an uneducated school drop-out.

At sixteen Jim left school to travel west. He called this experience his "University of Hard Knocks" and truthfully said it would be easier to tell what he didn't do than what he did. He made his way from Texas to California and back again working as a miner, a bellhop, a vineyard laborer, a roustabout in a barbed-wire factory, a teamster, a lumberjack, a railroad bridge builder, and in various other railroad jobs. He was gone two years.

Jim, consequently, was something of a local celebrity when he and Miriam attended Annie's party. He was an excellent storyteller, and his tales of adventures in the West held audiences spellbound. Miriam, dressed in white lace with her hair styled in dark brown curls around her face, seemed highly attractive and unattainable to Jim. In spite of his travels, he was only a poor boy with no great prospects, and she was the pampered daughter of one of Bell County's wealthiest men.

But Jim Ferguson never gave up easily when he wanted something. Shortly after the party, he wrote "Law by God" on the wall of his room and set out for Belton to borrow some law books to study. In the daytime he farmed and at night he studied law. He joined the Salado Debating Society to improve his speaking ability. In 1897 he was admitted to the bar and opened a law office in Belton. Now that he had a position in life, he began to be a frequent visitor at the Wallace home. Shrewdly, he made friends with Joe and Eliza, who admired the young man's energy and ambitious spirit.

In January of 1898 Joe Wallace left on a trip to Kansas City to sell a large herd of cattle. When he returned home, he distributed gifts to everyone and then went to bed with a "bad cold." He soon grew much worse, and a doctor was called. The diagnosis was meningitis. Within twenty-four hours Joe Wallace was dead.

Miriam's father had been a good businessman; consequently, the family was quite wealthy. Eliza found that she had a large estate, consisting of $50,000 in cash, several thousand acres of rich farm land, a couple of cotton gins, and a sizeable block of stock in a Belton bank. Naturally she needed legal advice in handling all of this property, and naturally Jim Ferguson, her nephew through her first husband, was more than pleased to give it to her, especially since it gave him a good excuse to visit the Wallace home in between his regular Sunday visits.

In spite of this advantage, his courtship proceeded slowly. Miriam had other suitors, and the first time he proposed, she said "no." But Jim Ferguson rarely took "no" as an answer to important questions. He persisted, running for City Attorney of Belton so he would have a more important position to offer her. Finally, Miriam yielded to his persuasions, and on the last day of the nineteenth century at two o'clock in the afternoon, they were married in the parlor of the Wallace home. She was twenty-four; he was twenty-eight.

Ferguson bought a lot on Penelope Street in Belton, and as a wedding gift, Eliza Wallace had a red and white frame house built on it for the newlyweds. "Aunt" Laura and her son, black servants who had been on the Fergusons' farm for years, came to act as cook and houseboy. Laura stayed with Miriam from 1900, running the various Ferguson households with an iron hand until she retired on her savings in 1938 at about eighty years of age.

In November of 1900 a daughter weighing three and one-half pounds was born to Miriam and Jim. The doctor who delivered the baby asked to be allowed to name her. He was a great admirer of a writer named Ouida and always named baby girls — white or black — after her. The Fergusons' first daughter was duly christened Ouida Wallace Ferguson, and grew to despise her first name. Grandmother Ferguson came

to visit her new grandchild and remained as a member of the
family for the rest of her life — except for visits to other
relatives. Three years later the family membership was
completed when a second daughter, Ruby Dorrace, was born
to the Fergusons.

They were prospering in Belton; Ferguson had helped start
the Farmers' State Bank and had been named its president.
But when the opportunity came to open a bank in the larger
town of Temple, he was eager to take it. He helped organize
the Temple State Bank, and for a year commuted by
interurban car daily between the two towns. Miriam didn't
want to leave their comfortable home in Belton and the flower
beds she had spent so much time designing and perfecting.

Even after Ferguson bought two large lots with trees on
North 7th Street in Temple, she was reluctant to move. She
refused to help with the planning of the new house, but Ferguson and the contractor managed to design a large, comfortable
two-storied Victorian house with galleries around both stories.
After the first year in Temple, during which Miriam
discovered that the black, waxy soil of their lots there was
better for growing flowers than the limestone of their Belton
property, she was content. She spent as much time as possible
working in the yard and did not join any of the bridge or social
clubs that occupied the time of many of her contemporaries.

Since she suffered periodically from bouts of asthma and
hay fever, her health was rather delicate, and she saved her
strength for her family and a little work in the Methodist
church. Her frank, often sharp, way of saying what she
thought gained her a reputation of being tactless at times.
When she was invited to join the Colonial Dames, she refused,
saying she had no time to spend on dead ancestors.
Prophetically she added, "I am interested only in making
history."

The Fergusons' marriage bonds strengthened as the years
of their marriage lengthened. Miriam developed a deep and
adamant faith in her husband that was at times an embarrass-
ment to those who heard her declare with complete sincerity

that he was the most brilliant lawyer in Texas and the greatest living businessman. In turn, he would allow no criticism of her and came to depend on her faith and confidence.

During the pre-World War I years in Temple, the Fergusons' lives followed a pattern typical of hundreds of other prosperous middle class families in small Texas towns. They welcomed and enjoyed electricity, telephones, and automobiles. They were fearful of contagious diseases. When Ferguson contracted smallpox, he insisted on having all of the family and servants vaccinated twice. They suffered more with their reactions to the vaccine than he did with the disease. Evenings were usually spent at home where, after school lessons were heard, Miriam did needlework while her husband read the paper.

When live stage performances were brought to the old frame opera house a few blocks from their home, the whole family went. On chilly nights they were glad of the heat from the two huge stoves in the building. One wintry night, after they had attended a show and returned home and settled into their beds, the fire alarm sounded. The opera house was in flames and the wind was whipping the sparks dangerously. The Fergusons' roof was coated with a fireproof paint, but the neighbors were not so fortunate. When the Murphys' house across the street caught fire, Miriam took in the family and prepared beds for them while her husband kept a watch on the flying sparks. The firefighters threw water on the side of the Ferguson home facing the blaze, and the only damage was blistered paint.

This experience left Miriam with a horror of fire. Allied to this was her fear of lightning. During electrical storms, which are fairly frequent in the spring in that part of Texas, she would make the girls get into the Fergusons' big bed. "If one is killed, we'll all die together," she would say. The girls hated those "suicide pacts," but Miriam continued to rout them from their cozy beds during thunderstorms until they were almost grown.

Although their family life was close and happy, there was a distinct partiality on the part of each parent and of each child. From the time they were very small, Dorrace, the docile, predictable child, was Miriam's favorite and Ouida, the adventurous daredevil, was her father's. Ouida often brought Miriam's wrath upon herself by teasing Dorrace, and she worried her mother by her recklessness. At ten she broke her arm playing "pop-the-whip" at school. When Miriam refused to let her have a saddle horse, Ouida brought home a donkey that she had talked a man into letting her keep for his feed. The first thing the donkey did was bite a piece out of the neck of Prince, Miriam's pet carriage horse. That was the end of that experiment.

After they had lived in Temple several years, Miriam, who had suffered from chronic appendicitis for a long time, finally could bear the attacks no longer and agreed to have an operation. She had a deep fear of not surviving and tried to prepare the girls for her death. But medicine had made a great deal of progress in Texas since the tragic death of her young brother Joseph, and she came through the appendectomy with little trouble.

This relatively tranquil life with its minor mishaps and joys might have gone on indefinitely — if Jim Ferguson had been the type of man who could be satisfied with living the placid life of a well-to-do small town banker. Certainly Miriam did not expect or wish for any other kind of life. But she noticed in 1913 that her husband was beginning to have periods of brooding in which he seemed to be far away from his surroundings. When she asked what he was thinking about, he merely came out of his reverie and smiled at her.

Up until this time Ferguson had been involved with politics only as a supporter of other men. (He had helped O. B. Colquitt in his campaign for governor in 1912.) Now he decided that Texans needed a Governor who knew first-hand about their problems — chiefly those dealing with farming, stock raising, and business. When his friends pointed out that he himself met these qualifications, he agreed. So Jim Ferguson entered Texas politics at the top state level. One Sunday morning in 1913, as she was trying on a new hat in preparation for attending church, Ferguson told Miriam that he had decided to run for Governor.

In the campaign that followed, Ferguson put to good use the speaking ability he had acquired. He knew how to appeal to the small farmers and little businessmen. He described his background and convinced them that he was one of them. He would keep the lifelong support of many of those he won over in this campaign.

When Ferguson had been elected, newspapers were eager to tell their readers about the new First Family. The complexity of Miriam Ferguson's personality baffled them (as it always would), and some strange and erroneous stories were printed about her. She was labeled as "domestic," which she was not in the usual sense of the word. She ran their home efficiently, making good use of her servants, but disliked cooking and cleaning and performing other routine household chores. Much of her time was spent doing the things she enjoyed: working in her flower beds, making jams and jellies, doing embroidery and other fancy needlework.

She was called timid and retiring by newspeople; yet she was often scolded by her daughters and close friends for being brutally frank and forthright in expressing her opinions. When her husband, an anti-prohibitionist, was condemned by some ministers in the Methodist church, she promptly became an Episcopalian.

Even her physical description eluded reporters. She was only medium height (five-feet-five) but was generally described as "tall" in the papers, probably because of her ramrod-straight posture.

The division superintendent of the Santa Fe Railroad in Temple offered the Fergusons his private car to convey them in style to their new home in the capital city. They arrived in Austin late Sunday afternoon, January 17, 1915, and made a triumphal entrance into the Driskill Hotel, where a large crowd was waiting to cheer them. The people liked what they

saw: the new Governor made a striking figure in a cutaway
coat; the new First Lady was elegantly gowned and smiling
graciously; Ouida swung her long golden curls, obviously
bubbling with excitement; and Dorrace, a little wistful at
leaving her Temple friends, had a violin tucked under one arm
and her white Spitz dog, Sambo, under the other.

Two days later at noon the Fergusons marched under the
crossed sabers of the Sul Ross Volunteers from Texas A&M to
their places on a platform in front of the Capitol. Then Miriam,
along with a huge crowd of Texans from all over the state,
watched her husband take the oath of office as Governor.

The inaugural ball, held in the House of Representatives,
featured an electric fountain. The chairs, desks, and other
business apparatus of the chamber were camouflaged under
elaborate decorations of balloons, flags, potted ferns and
bunting. Miriam wore a gown of soft, white satin trimmed
with real lace and seed pearls. The grand march was led by
Governor Ferguson and Mrs. Colquitt, followed by
ex-Governor Colquitt with Miriam Ferguson on his arm. The
next day the Fergusons moved into the Governor's Mansion
where the Colquitts had a hot meal waiting for them.

Whatever she might lack in diplomacy, the new First Lady
had a strong sense of duty and was determined to live up to
the social obligations her position demanded. At this time she
had a considerable fortune of her own and hired a social
secretary to help with her duties. She was the first Governor's
wife to do so, and the action was much criticized, even though
Miriam was paying the secretary's salary out of her own
pocket.

The Fergusons' first winter in the capital was unusually
cold, and Miriam suffered a severe attack of influenza which
prevented her from doing much entertaining. Then her
mother died, and again Miriam withdrew from public life.
Rumors began to reach the family that people were saying it
was too bad Mrs. Ferguson was not strong enough to help the
Governor in his new position. "Only the dead stay home
nowadays," sighed Miriam, and took up her round of social

duties.

At-home days were the first and third Tuesdays of each month. Even during the cold winter, narcissus bloomed in the mansion gardens, and Miriam filled the rooms with these fragrant blossoms plus hothouse roses, sweet peas, and tulips. A former First Lady, Orline Sayers, was on hand to help Miriam with her first at-home entertainment.

On Texas Independence Day, March 2, Miriam gave a large reception honoring the Thirty-fourth Legislature. She wore her inaugural gown to greet the six hundred guests. Flowers filled the rooms, and the grand staircase was intertwined with smilax and garlands of East Texas moss. The orchestra from the Texas School for the Blind provided music, and the Driskill Hotel catered the refreshments of chicken salad, sandwiches, cakes, bonbons, and coffee. The punch was non-alcoholic; Miriam was a teetotaler and never allowed any strong drink served in her home. (Her husband's objection to prohibition was based on the principle that it takes the freedom of choice from the individual.)

On Easter Monday, Miriam gave the children of Austin an egg rolling similar to the one held at the White House. Ice cream was served, and they were entertained with music. Miriam hoped the egg-rolling parties would be annual events, but her successors did not continue them, until Mrs. Allan Shivers revived the practice in 1951.

In addition to many state dinners and receptions during her husband's first term, Miriam arranged a number of luncheons and other parties for her daughters. Dorrace was given an elaborate Mother Goose costume party on her birthday. And on her husband's forty-fourth birthday in August, Miriam gave him a surprise party which began with a six-course dinner followed by a smoker for the men.

The First Lady got into trouble inadvertently when she decided to have a series of quilting bees at the mansion for her intimate friends. She thought it would be interesting for them to put together a friendship quilt, with each woman embroidering her name on the square she made. Several who

were not included in the bee were offended. In later years as
the political winds shifted for the Fergusons, some of the bee
members whose names appeared on the quilt became less than
friendly. As Ouida Ferguson remarked, "Politics makes
strange bedcovers."

The Fergusons' first Christmas in the mansion was spent
quietly. Members of the family gathered for a traditional tree
and dinner. A group of 148 friends and appointees of the
Governor presented the Fergusons with a handsome gift — a
silver service and dinner set of more than five hundred pieces,
each piece stamped with the Governor's monogram. A five-
drawer chest of solid mahogany held the set. The customary
New Year's reception was attended by large numbers who
came to see the elaborate decorations and enjoy substantial
refreshments as they wished the First Family well.

For various reasons, Ferguson did a considerable amount of
traveling around the state during his first term. While her
husband was away, Miriam looked after things at the mansion.
The roof leaked, and she had that fixed. The earth was
washing away from the grounds along the 11th Street side, so
she had a retaining wall built. There were never enough
flowers for entertaining to suit her, and the cost of buying
them from florists was high, so she asked for and got an
appropriation from the Legislature to build a small
greenhouse. The building and pagoda connecting it with the
house were built at the southwest corner of the mansion. Her
name and the date were set in the concrete floor at the
entrance of the greenhouse.

In June of 1916 Miriam went with her husband to St. Louis
for the Democratic National Convention. At the convention
Ferguson spoke against woman's suffrage. However, the
suffrage plank carried by a large majority — fortunately for
Miriam eight years later.

During Ferguson's campaign for reelection in 1916, one of
the main issues was the spending habits of the family.
Criticism ranged from the highest level to the lowest.
Ironically, in view of later events, one of the charges against

the Governor was that he authorized large appropriations for higher education. It was rumored that the Fergusons never wore the same clothes twice, but had a chute they dumped them down as they took them off. Some people wrote to Miriam begging her to send them the clothes instead of throwing them down the chute.

In spite of these and other accusations, reasonable and unreasonable, Ferguson won the election, and the family prepared to spend another two years in the mansion. The first few weeks passed fairly smoothly, at least on the surface, but trouble was brewing.

Ferguson had been involved in a quarrel the previous year with officials of the University of Texas over some of its administrative policies. As the quarrel intensified, he angered various factions of the school by demanding abolition of fraternities. He called faculty members "butterfly chasers," among other names, and tried to get rid of certain regents and professors. The University student body staged a dramatic protest march on the grounds of the Capitol, led by the band playing "The Eyes of Texas Are Upon You." Miriam, watching with Ouida and Dorrace from the front porch of the mansion, had a feeling of foreboding. She scolded Ouida for being amused by the display.

The Fergusons spent the first part of the summer of 1917 on the ranch that they had developed in Bosque County. It was a delightful retreat from the heat of Austin, both physically and mentally. Their five-room cottage was painted red and trimmed in white like their first home in Belton that Miriam had hated to leave. The cottage was called "Bonita Vista" because it provided a sweeping view of the valley of the Bosque River. Life there was far from primitive; Miriam liked her comforts, even in a rustic setting. She took her twin-six Packard and her chauffeur along, and there was electricity and a storage box in the barn that held 2,000 pounds of ice.

But Miriam did not have long to enjoy the peaceful retreat. Soon after their arrival, the adventurous Ouida was thrown from a horse and received a brain concussion. She was

delirious for days, and Miriam suffered emotionally and
physically as she anxiously nursed her older daughter to
eventual recovery.

Ferguson made weekly trips back to Austin to attend to
business connected with recruiting Texans to serve in World
War I. He tried to keep from the family the growing reper-
cussions stemming from his having vetoed on June 2 the $1.6
million appropriation for the University of Texas. Other
charges of misconduct were being compiled by his various
foes, and he must have been aware of the imminent disaster
facing him. Finally, he realized that he could remain on the
ranch no longer, and the family moved back to Austin toward
the end of July. The next two months were heartbreaking for
Miriam as she helplessly watched her husband's career
crumbling. The only way she could help him was to keep
assuring him of her absolute faith in him, to remain cheerful,
and to keep the household running as normally as possible.
These things she did.

But events went from bad to worse for Jim Ferguson. On
July 21, he appeared before the Travis County Grand Jury
and several days later was indicted on nine charges. He made
bond of $13,000 and announced his candidacy for a third term
as Governor.

A special session of the Legislature was called; and the
House, after a three-week investigation, prepared twenty-one
articles of impeachment. The Senate considered the charges
for three more weeks and convicted Ferguson on ten of them
— five charged him with misapplication of public funds, three
related to his conduct in regard to the University of Texas,
one concerned his enforcement of banking laws, and one
accused him of contempt for refusing to reveal where he got
$156,000 while in office. Later the Fergusons declared that the
sum was loaned by Texas breweries and was secured by a
mortgage on Miriam's family farm in Bell County, which she
had inherited.

Ferguson resigned the day before the judgment was passed
against him and contended that the decision therefore did not

apply to him. However, the courts ruled otherwise. Lt. Governor William P. Hobby was declared Governor, and the Fergusons packed up their possessions to leave the mansion.

For the sake of her husband, Miriam had maintained a Spartan control over her emotions all during the long weeks of the investigation and trial. Ferguson had insisted that she not attend any of the public sessions, but, of course, she followed intensely every statement made on either side. The heavier the criticism of her husband, and the more snubs she suffered from former friends, the higher she held her head.

In the end it was kindness, not harshness, that shattered the steel barrier she had built around her feelings. Before leaving Austin, she went with Ouida to get a dress from their little seamstress, a Mrs. Davis. The gentle woman spoke kindly of the Governor as she told them goodbye, and Miriam broke down and wept bitterly. Through her tears she said, "It is a terrible thing to be tried and sold down the river by politicians who have their price! But never fear, Jim Ferguson will come back!"

The Fergusons went back to their Temple home which had been rented during their stay in Austin. Naturally they were objects of curiosity, and their lives could never assume the quiet tenor of the years before Ferguson had been elected Governor. Miriam enrolled Dorrace in Temple High School and Ouida in her alma mater, Baylor College at Belton. As she settled her household, she anxiously watched her husband rush into a flurry of activity.

He started a weekly newspaper which he called *The Ferguson Forum*. (Prohibitionists called it the *Ferguson For Rum*.) In it he flayed his enemies with biting wit and homely philosophy. He sued several of the big daily newspapers of Texas for libel because they had accused him of getting the mysterious $156,000 from the German Kaiser, a serious charge since the United States and Germany were at war. He won substantial settlements from three of the papers.

Late in 1917 the family's attention was diverted from politics. Ouida was seventeen and in love. All during the trying months of her adored father's tribulations, George Sampson Nalle had stood by her, encouraging and supporting her. The Sampsons and the Nalles were among Austin's first families, and George's grandmother, Mary Goodwin Hall, had been the first bride at the Governor's Mansion. Although Miriam and Jim Ferguson liked young George, they thought Ouida much too young to marry. She was a true Ferguson, though, and persisted until she won them over.

Miriam and Ouida carefully planned every detail of the wedding which was to be held in Christ Episcopal Church in Temple on February 6, 1918. The church was decorated with tall white candles, Easter lilies, palms, and smilax. Ouida wore a handsome satin gown with a long train, and Miriam wore a dress of white net over silver cloth. When the Fergusons arrived at the little church, they found it overflowing, mostly with uninvited guests who had come to gape. Many of the invited guests were standing on the sidewalk, unable to make their way inside. The center aisle had to be cleared before the bridal party could enter, and the whole thing took on a carnival air. Miriam had more control over the reception, which was held in their beautifully decorated home.

As soon as the wedding was over, Ferguson began campaigning for the Democratic nomination against Hobby. He lost, and the Fergusons' finances were further depleted by the effort. Miriam's inherited fortune was rapidly dwindling, since she continued to use it freely to support all of her husband's political schemes, no matter how impractical.

Now he reacted to his defeat by announcing to the family and the world that the Ferguson motto was "never say 'die'; say 'damn'! " And he proceeded to run as a candidate on the American (Know Nothing) Party ticket in 1919 for the office of President of the United States. Of course, he and everyone else knew it was more a gesture of defiance than a serious bid. Miriam and Dorrace spent many days at "Bonita Vista" while Ferguson traveled around — often on money donated by friends — keeping his name before the public.

When Ouida became pregnant, Miriam, with her Victorian

upbringing, felt that sixteen-year-old Dorrace was too young to be told. She wrote to Ouida, "I have to hide all your letters from Dorrace, but I suppose she will have to find out in time." On Thanksgiving morning in 1919, the Fergusons' first grandchild was born. Miriam had hoped for a girl, but the baby was a boy. At first he was named Ernest, but later when another Ernest was christened in the Nalle family, his name was changed to George S. Nalle, Jr. Miriam soon became a doting grandmother and forgot that she had ever wanted a girl.

Until 1919 Miriam had never known what it meant to be poor. Even in the early days of their marriage, she had her own fortune, and later she had the income from her farm. She loved good clothes and had always bought the most expensive materials for herself and the girls. But one day when she asked for household money, her husband said there was none, and she suddenly realized their condition. From that time on she quit using charge accounts and began to watch the cash and bills.

During the next two years Ferguson continued to make a speech or two each week to keep in touch with the voters. He was dependent on the good will of friendly supporters to get from town to town. Often when he kissed her goodbye, Miriam knew that he did not have enough money for the return trip. But somehow he always got back.

In 1922 Ferguson decided to run for the United States Senate. Miriam objected that she didn't want to live in Washington, D.C., but as always she agreed to go along with what her husband wanted. Ferguson lost the race but gained much political ground. In 1924 there was another gubernatorial race. Hopefully, the Fergusons went to court in a vain attempt to get James E. Ferguson's name put on the Democratic ticket. When the court ruled against allowing his name on the ballot, the Fergusons were prepared — Miriam Amanda Ferguson would file for a place on the ticket.

There was no legal injunction against her being the Governor of Texas. For seven years the Fergusons had lived with a hope now become an obsession — the vindication of Jim Ferguson. There was probably almost nothing that Miriam would have refused to do to gain that goal. The pep and energy she displayed in campaigning amazed even her family. She was forty-nine on June 13, 1924, and had always been considered delicate and comfort-loving, but now she had two causes that stimulated her and gave her extra endurance — vindication of her Jim and annihilation of the Ku Klux Klan; these were the burning issues for which she traveled the length and breadth of the huge state.

During the first part of the campaign, Miriam and her husband traveled together. She spoke first, asking the mothers, sisters, and wives of Texas to help her clear her family's name. She pleaded in the name of her children and her grandson, who sometimes appeared on the platform with her, declaring that she wanted her grandson to be able to say, ". . . as a rebuke to that impeachment that denied my grandfather the right to go to the people, my dear grandmother was elected Governor by the people of Texas — the first woman Governor in the world." After this appeal, she introduced Jim, who lit into his opponents and the Ku Klux Klan, breathing fire and brimstone.

When his enemies proclaimed that Jim Ferguson would be the "real" Governor if his wife was elected, the Fergusons replied that of course she would rely on his experience. They adopted the slogan "two Governors for the price of one." Not only words, but also stones were hurled at the Fergusons. When Ku Klux Klanners rained rocks on the roof of the Ferguson home in Temple, Miriam dismissed their behavior as a "feeble" answer to her attacks on them.

On July 26, primary day, Miriam ran second to the Ku Klux Klan-backed candidate and was in the run-off. The excitement in the Ferguson household was almost unbearable, but they knew they must work just as hard in the race ahead to gain the final victory. Next morning a stream of newspaper reporters descended on the Ferguson home. They all wanted to know what the candidate was "really" like. Miriam, who had planned to make peach preserves that day, resented this concentrated attack on her private life. She was blunt and less than civil to reporters from papers that had said harsh things about her husband. However, if a cub reporter represented the enemy paper, her maternal instinct made her treat him kindly, even though she scolded him for his paper's policies.

This was an opportunity for publicity too good to miss; and with the help of Ouida, who had her father's instinct for doing the right thing politically, Miriam was persuaded to pose in her kitchen peeling peaches. The caption under the resulting picture called her "Ma" Ferguson. Since her initials were M.A. or M.A.W. when her maiden name of Wallace was added, it was almost inevitable that the papers would come up with this nickname. Soon stickers appeared all over the state proclaiming "Me for Ma"; some of them added "And I Ain't Got a Dern Thing Against Pa." But Miriam hated the nickname, and none of her family ever dared use it in her presence.

After the peach-peeling picture, the reporters prevailed upon Miriam to go out to her farm to pose in front of her birthplace. Impatiently, she consented; she would do what she must in the interest of winning the election. Ouida decided her mother should wear a sunbonnet to look like a true farm woman, the helpmate of "Farmer Jim." One of the women on the farm lent Miriam a bonnet. She protested it wasn't clean enough, but after it was turned inside out, she consented to pose in it. The idea of using "Put on Your Old Gray Bonnet" as a campaign song came from this incident and the resulting pictures. Miriam grew heartily sick of the song by election day. She felt she was making a fool of herself by posing with chickens, cows, pigs, and a sunbonnet, but if it would win votes . . . .

During the second phase of the campaign Miriam and her husband went their separate ways to cover more territory. Miriam, who had never made a public speech before she announced for Governor, was now eagerly seeking opportunities to tell the voters of the great wrong done to her husband and of the great menace of the Ku Klux Klan. "I am not seeking glory but only trying to lift a burden that is hard to bear," she said.

Financial support was readily available now. Local Democratic Committees took care of transportation and accommodations, which were the best available for their candidate. There were other problems, however. Miriam's right arm swelled to twice its normal size because of the handshaking. She kept it in warm Epsom salt packs when she was not in public.

The run-off primary day was tense. Voters flocked to the polls to vote for or against the Ku Klux Klan and for or against Fergusonism. When the ballots were counted Miriam Ferguson had won by more than 97,000 votes. The family was jubilant but still cautious. They would remain so until the voters had their final say in November and elected Miriam Governor over her Republican opponent, Dr. George Butte, a professor at the University of Texas. Her triumph in the general election received world-wide attention. European newspapers, including the London *Times*, were intrigued by her victory.

The Fergusons stayed in the Nalles' home in Austin while the entertainments and ceremonies connected with the inauguration were being held. Telegrams and letters of congratulations and flowers of every description filled the house to overflowing. For once in her life Miriam had enough flowers.

Tried by anguish and suffering, the Miriam Amanda Ferguson who marched under the crossed sabers of the Sul Ross Volunteers was not the same person who had passed under a similar formation ten years earlier to become the First Lady of Texas. Physically she had not changed a great deal, although she was somewhat heavier, and her brown hair was just beginning to turn gray. Her erect bearing, strong features and thin-lipped, straight mouth gave her a stern appearance until she smiled her warm, sympathetic smile. She wore a black satin dress and a deep ivory feather boa. The outgoing Governor, courtly Pat Neff, introduced his successor graciously and told her, in his presentation speech, that he was leaving a Bible on the Governor's desk in which he had marked a passage from the Psalms, reading:

Thy word is a lamp unto my feet, and a light unto my path.

This marking of the Bible became a tradition — and sometimes a means of delivering an unkind cut at the incoming Governor.

In her short inaugural address Miriam acknowledged her inexperience in governmental affairs and asked for the good will of the people, promising to seek the "advice and counsel of others." The inaugural ball was held in three locations: the Senate Chamber, the Austin Hotel, and the Driskill Hotel. Miriam was truly the belle of all the balls in a handsome gown of heavily beaded flesh-pink chiffon.

Two days later with Miriam at the wheel, the Fergusons piled into the old twin-six Packard for the move to the mansion. It was a symbol of their triumph for the whole family. Many times since 1917 Miriam had declared that some day she would drive the old car back to the mansion in victory. So she did, even though she owned a brand new car.

That afternoon as Miriam walked around the mansion noting the changes that had been made, she was shocked to discover that her name had been removed from the block of concrete at the threshold of the greenhouse, which had been her proudest addition to the mansion when she was First Lady. She immediately sent for a workman and had her name and the date, 1915, restored to their former place. Two years later when someone tried to persuade Mildred Moody to remove the name once again, Mrs. Moody said, "Not on your life! If I should do such a thing she would be sure to come back in again and restore her name."

Ouida and George Nalle, with their son, moved into the mansion so Ouida could relieve her mother of as many social duties as possible. In addition, entertainments were kept to a minimum.

As Governor, Miriam's first struggle with the Legislature occurred when she cut the state budget by fifteen million dollars, as she had promised to do in her campaign. After a battle, the cut was reduced to thirteen million, still a substantial amount in those days. With great pleasure she signed an anti-mask bill, thus dealing the KKK a death blow. But her pleasure was even greater when she signed on April 4, 1925, an amnesty bill, restoring to James Edward Ferguson the right to hold office in Texas. Vindication was sweet.

Two of her most troublesome problems were the constant stream of applications for appointive positions and the equally constant barrage of pleas from prisoners and their families for pardons, paroles, and stays of executions. She spent hours each week reviewing these requests and agonizing over the merits of each case. When she and Ferguson disagreed over a case, especially when the crime involved was violation of the liquor laws, her decision was final. She was unalterably opposed to the use of alcohol in any form and even scolded Ouida for spiking the dessert with a little sherry at the Nalles' anniversary dinner party.

Nights when there was to be an electrocution in the penitentiary at Huntsville were harrowing for the whole family. Appeals in the form of telegrams, telephone calls, and personal entreaties flowed in. At exactly midnight, just before he threw the switch, the warden called to be sure that she was not going to commute the sentence. Miriam usually hung up the receiver in a burst of tears and lay awake the rest of the night.

By the end of 1925 there was much criticism of Miriam's administration. The question was constantly raised: To what extent was Jim Ferguson running the state government? That question was never answered; even the Ferguson children could not tell. There were accusations that she and Ferguson were selling pardons and possibly road construction contracts. Rumbles of impeachment were heard and demands were made that she call a special session of the Legislature. She refused, and the threats died down.

In her position Miriam found there were many good moments to compensate for the bad. She enjoyed the interesting visitors who came to the mansion. Among them were governors of other states and their wives, and such figures as Mme. Ernestine Schumann-Heink, the opera singer, and Knute Rockne, coach of Notre Dame. But Miriam's favorite celebrity was Will Rogers. She let him call her "Ma" but told him, "See here, you ugly devil, I am going to be in your audience tonight, and don't you razz me as you razz some people." Will Rogers visited the mansion many times, and Miriam always had a big Mexican supper for him. His favorite dish was chili con carne; once he ate five bowls, and when she offered him ambrosia for dessert, he said, "Goodness, no! If I had more room, I would have another bowl of chili."

Another happy occasion was the presentation of a marble bust of Miriam as a tribute from her friends. The work, by Enrico Carracchio, was placed between the bronze figures of President Woodrow Wilson and Governor James Stephen Hogg in the rotunda of the State Capitol.

In 1926 Miriam ran for reelection against her young Attorney General, Dan Moody, and was defeated by a substantial number of votes. Ferguson lost his temper several times during the campaign and made ugly, bitter remarks against Miriam's opponent; the red-headed Moody replied in kind. The New York *Times* and other newspapers kept Ferguson watchers titillated with choice excerpts from speeches in both camps. The Governor kept her dignified distance from the name calling, and in her speech of presentation at Moody's inauguration said:

> I congratulate Mr. Moody upon his election. His election as a 34-year-old governor [*authors' note: Moody was actually 33 at the time*] was about as novel as my election as a woman governor. Time alone will prove whether the people have acted wisely in either instance.

For his guidance she marked the golden rule in the Bible. She did not leave a lunch for the Moodys.

For a few months the Fergusons lived in a rented house while they built a Spanish Colonial home on Windsor Road in Austin. Miriam delighted in the large garden on the grounds of the new home. Undoubtedly she would have been satisfied to stay retired from politics — if Jim Ferguson had been. But he was not. Thinking that the Amnesty Bill passed during his wife's administration gave him the right to hold office in Texas again, he decided to run for Governor in 1930. The Democratic Executive Committee refused to certify him, and the Texas Supreme Court declared the Amnesty Bill unconstitutional. Obviously, there was only one way for the Fergusons to avenge this new insult. Miriam would have to run again.

This time her chief opponent was Ross Sterling, a millionaire oil man from Houston. Again the Fergusons traveled the state from top to bottom and side to side. Miriam's last speech was made from a speaker's platform in front of the Alamo. The audience, which one paper said would have to be measured by the acre, cheered enthusiastically for "Ma." Miriam won the first primary, with Sterling coming in second, but in the run-off, she lost to him by 89,000 votes.

The Fergusons settled down again in their Austin home, making frequent visits to their Bosque County ranch where they were raising livestock. Personal and family affairs occupied Miriam's time. In January of 1931 Ferguson had a nightmare and fell out of bed, breaking his collarbone; as a result, Miriam spent many days nursing him back to good health and good spirits. In June of that year Dorrace was married to Stuart Watt of Austin.

The year 1932 offered another chance at the Governor's race. As soon as her spring flowers had bloomed, Miriam was back in political harness. This time she led in the first primary and also in the second — by not quite 4,000 votes out of almost one million. Governor Sterling's supporters protested the vote and asked for time to investigate the one hundred pro-Ferguson counties in which they claimed the votes cast outnumbered the poll tax receipts.

However, at the Democratic State Convention in Lubbock,

Miriam was declared the Democratic nominee for Governor. If the Fergusons thought that would quiet the Sterling forces, they soon found they were mistaken. Back in Austin, they discovered that a citation had been issued in an effort to get an injunction against letting Miriam's name appear on the ticket at the general election in November. The citation had to be served by midnight of the second day after the Fergusons returned to the capital.

A cloak and dagger drama followed. As the Fergusons hid upstairs in the Nalle home, Ouida turned away an officer who came to the house looking for her father and mother. A few minutes later a friend came to warn them that she had heard the house was to be searched shortly. The family fled down the back stairs in complete darkness. George Nalle backed the car out of the garage; everyone piled in and they headed for the Burnet Road that led to their ranch. There was little traffic, but each time headlights loomed behind them, they feared it was pursuers. Not until they had crossed the county line did they breathe easy. Miriam's election was now assured.

National and international magazines and big daily newspapers puzzled over the Fergusons' popularity. "Ma Ferguson is at it again," commented the New York *Times* and added, "She talks and moves as one who is having a thoroughly good time." A French countess came to interview the governor-elect for *Le Matin*, a leading Paris newspaper. Miriam entertained the countess at home in Austin and was reported to the French people as being *"très charmante."*

Governor Sterling left the capital city before the inauguration and without marking a passage in the Governor's Bible. But Miriam was duly installed anyhow. And the inaugural ball, held at Gregory Gym and two downtown hotels, was a huge success. Miriam had suggested old-time square dancing as a feature, and the guests loved it.

Miriam's second term began as the Great Depression was at its worst. Millions were unemployed, Franklin Delano Roosevelt had just been elected President, and Miriam had the task of setting his reform program in motion in Texas. The

Legislature adopted a constitutional amendment allowing the state to issue twenty million dollars in "bread bonds" for relief of the destitute. Miriam worked night and day until she had signed all of the bonds. The result was a severe cramping in her arm that lasted for months.

Bankers became jittery as rumors spread that there were runs on banks in various northern cities. Fortunately, the peak of the panic was reached on March 2, a state holiday when the banks were closed. This gave Miriam time to have calls sent out over the state ordering that no Texas bank should open its doors on March 3 — thus avoiding a run on the banks. George Nalle, Jr., now thirteen, had been in the mansion on March 1 with his grandparents, and had been told in confidence that the banks were to be closed. He kept the secret so well that his mother, Ouida, was caught with an empty pocketbook when the closing came.

When a bill was introduced into the Legislature to legalize parimutuel betting on horse races in Texas, Miriam threw her support behind it, perhaps because Jim Ferguson loved horse racing. The bill passed, and the family made several exciting trips to the various tracks — Arlington Downs, Epsom Downs, Alamo Downs — when they were opened with great fanfare.

With her husband always at hand to consult on political and state matters, and Ouida and Dorrace ready and willing to handle arrangements for entertainments, Miriam had a great deal of support during her second term. But hers was the final say, and she did not always agree with the advice given her by her family. Her husband admitted that her "hunches" were sometimes better than his judgment, and when they disagreed, both claimed things were done her way.

Again she practiced a liberal pardoning policy and again she received bitter criticism for it. Ferguson enemies referred to the Executive Building as "the House of a Thousand Pardons."

Since she was not running to succeed herself, Miriam's last year was probably the most pleasant one she spent in office. On George Nalle, Jr.'s. fifteenth birthday in November of 1935, Miriam gave a dinner party for him at the mansion. The table was laid with a cloth embroidered by his great-grandmother Sampson, the first bride to be married in that building. The final, formal social entertainment given by the Governor was the traditional New Year's open house on January 1, 1935. It was a relaxed affair with about three hundred callers dropping in to wish the departing First Lady-Governor and her family well.

As she went about the last-minute tasks of her office, Miriam told reporters she was through with politics and looking forward happily to retirement. Knowing the Fergusons, the reporters quoted her with tongue in cheek. Their skepticism was to prove valid, although the Fergusons did manage to remain quiescent for almost five years. During this time Miriam kept up her now quite avid interest in political events.

In August of 1939 the Fergusons became grandparents for the second time as Dorrace gave birth to a boy, James Stuart Watt. There were almost twenty years between the two grandsons — a long time since there had been a baby in the family, and therefore a cause for joy.

Between 1935 and 1940 there had been several "Draft Ma" movements by Ferguson supporters. As the 1940 race approached, letters and pleas for Miriam to run again became more urgent. Ferguson became excited over the possibility of another term in office for "their team." Perhaps to please him, or perhaps because she, too, was infected with political fever, Miriam, in spite of her daughters' strong disapproval, decided to run.

She was sixty-five but still strong and straight. In her platform she promised to support Franklin Roosevelt, economy in government, education, labor, and tenant farmers. Her opponent, W. Lee O'Daniel, declared the Ten Commandments to be his platform. O'Daniel had been a flour salesman, singer of hillbilly music, and an amateur preacher. He was tremendously popular in Texas and had the backing to buy the large amounts of radio time that had become essential for winning campaigns.

Ferguson never managed to adjust his free-swinging style of oratory to radio microphones. And also the Fergusons could afford only a fraction of the time the O'Daniel supporters purchased. Miriam did speak over the radio at seven a.m. two mornings a week. She took one plank from her platform and elaborated on it carefully and thoroughly during each of these sessions. But the Ferguson effort was weak compared to earlier campaigns, and the O'Daniel band wagon rolled across the state. In the first primary he led by a majority of fifty-five percent of all votes cast.

After this defeat, the Fergusons at last retired from office-seeking. Ferguson, partially deaf, troubled by rheumatism, and weighing 230 pounds, was content to spend his time and energy on the business of the ranch. Miriam was quite satisfied to enjoy her grandchildren and her flowers. If her husband's health had been stronger, this would have been a very pleasant time. But in 1942 Ferguson's health began to deteriorate more rapidly. As he became weaker the family searched for medical help by taking him back to his doctors in Temple and to the medical center in Galveston. Christmas of 1942 was brightened by a visit from George Nalle, Jr., who was in training as an aviation cadet in the Air Corps. He also announced his engagement to Anne Byrd Woods.

The next two years were difficult. Ouida took over the management of the Fergusons' financial affairs, and Miriam became nurse to her sick husband. She tried futilely to prepare nourishing food for him as she watched him waste away from 230 pounds to less than 100. On February 28, 1944, Ferguson suffered a stroke. For seven more months while he remained an invalid, Miriam kept watch. Friends and even old political enemies tried to ease her burden with calls, cards, gifts, and other expressions of concern. At the beginning of September, Ferguson's mind became confused, and on September 21, he died.

Texans realized that an era had come to an end; they turned out in large numbers to honor the man who for more than a quarter of a century had seemed to be a part of their daily lives. His wife and daughters, even in their sorrow, recognized that relief from his suffering had come at last. By popular subscription, friends raised money for a monument which was dedicated in the State Cemetery in 1946. A place beside her husband was reserved for Miriam.

Ouida had sold the ranch property and bought 550 acres close to Austin, where the Bosque Creamery was built. This operation provided financial security for Miriam during her later years.

Miriam lived for seventeen years after her husband's death, free for perhaps the first time in her life to spend as much time in her beloved garden as she wished. She felt that a good gardener should try some "new crop" every year. One of her most successful experiments was with ornamental gourds of all shapes. Her favorites were "the ugly ones, the squatty variety."

She also had time to spend with her close friends and with her family. Her special delight was the company of her three great-grandsons, the offspring of George Nalle, Jr., and his wife. Tragedy touched her life again when Ouida died from cancer, at the age of fifty-one, on July 31, 1952.

As Miriam aged, the people of Texas seemed anxious to find ways to pay tribute to her. In 1953, the Texas Senate passed a resolution honoring her "as an example of noble and gentle womanhood, an ideal wife, and a devoted mother." In 1955 three new varieties of flowers were named in her honor — a new amaryllis and a new iris were called "Governor Miriam A. Ferguson," and a new day lily was christened the "Ma Ferguson." This was also the year of the enthusiastic celebration of her eightieth birthday — an event that marked her last formal public appearance. Her remaining years passed peacefully and mellowly. She told a reporter that she felt no bitterness toward former enemies of Fergusonism, adding, "Most of them have seen the error of their ways, anyhow."

Miriam always had an especially warm welcome for the young people from colleges and universities who came to ask about her political experiences — either for material for term papers or as guidelines for themselves as political hopefuls. She also compiled a list of the accomplishments of the Ferguson years of political activity, emphasizing those that provided aid to education, mental health, welfare, and labor.

On November 30, 1960, Miriam suffered a heart attack from which she seemingly recovered. But a little less than two weeks after her eighty-sixth birthday, she suffered a second attack and died June 25, 1961. A simple funeral service was held at her home, and she was buried beside her Jim, while the flag fluttered at half staff over the State Capitol.

On the Fergusons' joint tombstone is carved the inscription:

> Life's race well run
> Life's work well done
> Life's victory won
> Now cometh rest.

27.

"A Lady of Quality"

Willie Chapman Cooper Hobby

When General Alvaro Obregón was inaugurated President of Mexico in 1920, the Governor of Texas and his wife, Mr. and Mrs. W. P. Hobby, attended the ceremony in Mexico City. The occasion was one of great pomp and circumstance and one that called for the most formal dress and manners. The wives of three former ambassadors to Mexico watched as the First Lady of Texas glided with effortless poise through the round of brilliant social and official affairs attending the inauguration. Finally they could stand it no longer and together approached one of the Texas delegation to ask, "At what court was Mrs. Hobby trained?" They obviously found it difficult to believe the answer — that she had never been at any court — for they had not observed anyone, outside of royalty, with such polished manners.

Although it was true that she had not been at court, Willie Cooper Hobby had literally been in training all of her life for her role as First Lady. The daughter of Phoebe and Sam Bronson Cooper, she had been born on June 19, 1877, in Woodville, Texas. She attended the schools there, and then after the family moved to Beaumont, had alternated between that city and Washington, D.C., where her father served fourteen years as a member of the House of Representatives. In Washington, private tutors were hired to instruct her and her two sisters and brother.

Her father became one of the outstanding members of the United States Congress, and along with the rest of the family, Willie became the close friend of statesmen, diplomats, ambassadors, famous men in science and the arts, and Presidents of the United States and their families. In addition to social skills, she developed a deep interest in political matters — particularly those that concerned the feminist movement and suffrage for women.

When it came time to choose a college, Willie decided to attend Kidd-Key in Sherman, Texas, where she would be among many of her childhood acquaintances. The friends she made there, and wherever she lived, remained faithful all of her life. From her mother she had inherited a charisma that drew people to her, and from her father she had acquired diplomacy and a brilliant mind. In time, she became valedictorian of her graduating class, and for the occasion presented a memorable essay she had written entitled, "The Marble Lies in Waiting."

After her mother's death, she ran her father's households and planned dinner parties and other entertainments for his friends. Graceful and pretty, with delicate features, blue eyes and light brown hair, she was popular with her peers of both sexes.

When Bronson Cooper was finally defeated for reelection to Congress, President Taft appointed him to the Board of Appeals of the New York Customs House, and Willie spent part of several years in New York City. Again she quickly won a circle of friends and became a sought-after guest. However, with her energy and love of learning, she was never satisfied with a life that revolved around purely social activities. Studying short story writing at Columbia University, she displayed considerable talent for writing. Some who have written about her think she could have made a name for herself as a writer, if she had ever found enough time to devote to it.

In New York she also became quite active in working for women's rights. She said, "When I realized the big injustice of paying men so much more than women for equal services rendered in the public schools of New York, I became an enthusiastic advocate in aiding women in securing their rights and have since worked hard for suffrage." She became an effective speaker for this cause and later was to influence legislation in its behalf.

During the portion of the year that the family spent in their Beaumont home, Willie took an energetic part in social, civic, and cultural affairs there. On one of these return trips while her father was still in Washington, she met again an old acquaintance with whom she had played as a child. He was William Pettus Hobby, whose father had shared a law partnership with hers many years ago in Woodville.

Now Will Hobby had come to Beaumont to be manager and editor of the Beaumont *Enterprise*. He had stirred the town of about 25,000 into action over the possibility that Beaumont might become a deep-water inland seaport. Willie's father, Congressman Cooper, enthusiastically sponsored the cause in Washington, D.C., and together the two men labored to make it a reality.

Will Hobby and Willie Cooper began to see each other regularly as Hobby and Cooper conferred over plans to carry through the project. The country club, the Elks Club, and the theater were the centers of social life in Beaumont early in the twentieth century. And the popular Willie began to appear frequently at these places with Editor Hobby, one of the town's most eligible bachelors.

When the Coopers moved to New York after Bronson Cooper's appointment to a position there, Hobby found a number of reasons to make trips to that city. Willie was excited when Hobby told her he had been persuaded by his friends to file for Lieutenant Governor of Texas in the 1914 election on the same ticket as James Ferguson, and she was thrilled when he won. They were engaged by this time, although not many people knew it. Having waited so long to marry, they decided to wait a little longer — until the first session of the Legislature ended and Hobby could leave Austin and his official duties.

Willie planned a small wedding at the famous St. Charles Hotel in New Orleans. Her father, sisters, brother and a few close friends of the couple from Beaumont attended the ceremony, which was solemnized on May 15, 1915. When they returned to Beaumont, the Hobbys moved into a house on Broadway near the *Enterprise* office. Friends gave them a round of parties and celebrations.

Predictions were being made that Hobby would be Governor in a few years, and his supporters were pleased that he had married a woman who would be a distinct asset in his political life. Her influence became evident very soon. In 1916 when England passed the first woman's suffrage bill, the *Enterprise* played up the story and came out in strong support of the movement.

When Hobby's first term was up, the Hobbys were pleasantly surprised to discover that he had no opponent in the Democratic primary in his bid for reelection.

In November of the same year, 1916, the Hobbys were honored guests of the big South Texas Fair, and Hobby was the main speaker at its opening. With pride, he welcomed the visitors to Beaumont, which a month before had become "a magnificent fresh-water, land-locked, storm-proof harbor open to the commerce of the world" — thanks largely to his own efforts and those of Willie's father.

The next year, 1917, was a fateful one for the Hobbys. War clouds hung over Texas as they did over all of the United States and much of the world. And the thirty-fifth legislative session in Texas was tense as charges were piled upon charges against Governor Ferguson, accusing him of mismanagement of funds and unwarranted interference in the University of Texas' affairs. A week after the Legislature adjourned in April, the United States declared war on Germany.

Willie Hobby was preparing to move to Houston where her husband had accepted an appointment as director and secretary of the newly formed Federal Land Bank. He clearly intended to retire from politics. But the quarrel between campus and capitol was to change his plans very quickly. In July a call for a special session of the House was issued by the Speaker, so it could consider impeachment proceedings against Governor Ferguson. After twenty-three contentious days, the House adopted twenty-one articles of impeachment, and Will Hobby became acting Governor pending the trial of Ferguson in the Senate.

Instead of moving to Houston, the Hobbys moved into the Driskill Hotel in Austin after Hobby regretfully resigned his position with the Federal Land Bank. The atmosphere in the capital city was hardly a comfortable one for the fill-in Governor and First Lady. Hobby had remained as aloof as possible from the Ferguson affair, and had offered every courtesy to the beleaguered Governor when he was forced to take over the duties of the office. But inevitably the Ferguson supporters became Hobby's opponents.

The new Governor received a great deal more advice than he could use, and much of it was conflicting. He soon realized that he would have to make his own decisions — with the help of his most capable wife. Now he truly began to appreciate her political experience and insight. After her death, an editorial in the Houston *Chronicle* said of her husband's administration, "She had more to do with political and governmental development than was ever recorded." The Hobbys' intimate friends testified to the truth of this statement and to his dependence on her counsel.

When the Senate convicted Ferguson on ten of the twenty-one charges against him, the Hobbys moved into the Executive Mansion. Mindful of the stringent wartime restrictions on spending, the new First Lady asked for only one improvement in the building — steam heat. Friends warned her that her request might lose her husband his chance for reelection. "I'd rather be warm for two years than

freeze for four," she told them. And not only did she get
radiators but also facilities for hot water.

In her new role, many of Willie's activities were influenced
by World War I. She traveled with her husband on endless
rounds of inspection of military training camps, which were
numerous in Texas because of its mild climate. She became a
member at large of the Texas Library War Council, whose
purpose was to furnish books to every United States soldier or
sailor at home or at the front. She also worked actively in the
war effort as a member of the Woman's Division of the State
Council of Defense and the War Camp Community Service.

Many of her hours were spent working with the Red Cross,
rolling bandages and doing other tedious but necessary jobs.
When a Liberty Parade was held, instead of being seated with
the dignitaries in the reviewing stand, she chose to walk with
other Red Cross workers, wearing her blue service veil.

Under her direction, a war garden was planted at the
mansion, and Texas newspaper readers were kept informed of
the progress of the executive onions (which did best), beets,
beans, potatoes and peas. When weeds also began to flourish,
Willie armed herself with a hoe to battle them personally.

In spite of her fondness for entertaining, she felt that any
strictly social entertainment would be out of place in a world
torn by war. Christmas Day of 1918 was spent quietly with
Hobby's mother in Dallas. And the first day of the New Year
passed without the traditional reception at the mansion. When
Miss Margaret Wilson, the President's daughter, visited
Austin, Willie held a simple, informal reception for her.

Willie approved when her husband decided to run for
reelection. She understood his wish to serve a term in which
he felt he had a mandate from the people to carry out his
programs, instead of just being in office by accident.

In the spring of 1918 Hobby submitted and supported a bill
through the Legislature giving Texas women the right to vote
in Democratic primaries. It's not difficult to guess where he
got the idea. Since national woman's suffrage was not yet in
effect, this was a tremendous step toward equality in voting

privileges for the women of the state because the Democratic primary nominees were invariably elected in the general election. The Hobby campaign committee used this action extensively in their literature urging Texans:

> Vote for Hobby and You will vote right and for the man who gave Texas Women the Vote

Hobby's opponent was his old friend, colorful Jim Ferguson, who was running in spite of (or because of) the Texas Senate's decree that he could never again hold public office in Texas.

Newly organized women's groups showed their appreciation of Hobby's attitude toward woman's suffrage by campaigning fervently for him. Among these women was Mrs. I. W. Culp of Killeen, who often left her daughter Oveta and her sisters disgustedly peeling and canning mountains of peaches while she went out to speak for "that Will Hobby — *again!*"

Two ex-Governors, Thomas Campbell and O. B. Colquitt, actively supported Hobby also. Ferguson was a tough and skillful campaigner, and the last weeks before the election Hobby made a number of speeches, winding up his tour in Galveston where Willie joined him. From there they went to Beaumont so they could vote.

The election results were all that they could desire. Hobby won by 461,749 votes to 217,012 for Ferguson. The people had given him victory by the greatest majority ever given a candidate in the primary up to that time.

In the early morning hours of July 30, 1918, the Hobbys returned to Austin via the Southern Pacific Railroad. As the train pulled into the station, Willie peered from their Pullman window to see what all the noise was about. It looked as if half of the city was waiting on the platform, cheering and waving. As she and her husband emerged from the train, a brass band struck up "Hail to the Chief." Dr. R. E. Vinson, the University of Texas president, climbed on a baggage truck to deliver an enthusiastic welcoming speech in which he described Hobby as the leader of a peaceable revolution. A parade of citizens headed by the band escorted the Governor and his wife up Congress Avenue. Early rising passers-by joined in the frequent choruses of "Dixie" rendered by the band. It was a heartwarming welcome home for the Hobbys.

A post-primary survey revealed that most of the women who had exercised their new right to vote had supported Hobby. And also the first woman was elected to public office in Texas; Miss Annie Webb Blanton had been voted in as State Superintendent of Public Instruction. Willie Hobby's role in helping bring about these events was realized by few.

For the next few months as World War I continued, the Hobbys each remained busy with their own particular war work. Just as the end of the war became apparent, a more deadly killer visited Texas and the rest of the world. An epidemic of influenza killed 9,000 Texans at military posts, almost twice the number killed in the war. Early in November the virulent disease, which was no respecter of persons, struck the Texas Governor, and Willie went through an anxious period of nursing and waiting as her husband battled the infection for weeks.

The news of the ending of the war on November 11 cheered the Hobbys, but he continued to suffer from after-effects of the disease until Willie persuaded him to go home to Beaumont for a short vacation and a chance to rest and escape from some of the official pressures.

On January 21, 1919, Willie had the satisfaction of watching her husband sworn in as the elected Governor of the people of Texas. The inaugural ball was delayed until March 4 because Hobby wanted the pressing business of the Legislature to be well under way before social activities in any way slowed it down. Willie planned a large, informal reception at the mansion to precede the ball, which was held at the Driskill Hotel. So successful was the reception that it delayed the arrival of the Hobbys at the ball, and it was eleven o'clock before the grand march began. A brief power failure during the reception failed to dismay the First Lady. She had candles brought, and the party continued merrily by candlelight.

The theme of the ball was a patriotic one with United States flags and American eagles much in evidence. The women's elegant gowns reflected the feeling that austerity could be relaxed now that the war had ended. Willie's dress was an exquisite creation of satin and lace with a long train, and she carried a matching feather fan.

As if to make up for wartime restrictions, a lengthy series of parties and official functions now took place under Willie's direction. Thousands of guests visited the mansion during her tenure as mistress there; they included a record number of prominent and distinguished citizens of the United States and foreign countries. Like Orline Sayers, Willie had a flair for pleasing all manner of guests; her concern and skill enabled her to make people from all levels of society feel welcome and wanted.

In addition to planning these elaborate affairs, Willie gave equal time to making arrangements for groups like the farm boys and girls she entertained at a big reception that received statewide recognition in newspapers.

A quieter event was the wedding Willie arranged in the mansion for her maid, Savannah Jackson, and a Capitol porter. The Negro preacher, impressed by the surroundings, announced at the conclusion of the ceremony, "And now, in the presence of the Governor of Texas and God Almighty, I pronounce you man and wife."

Willie was also freer now to make long trips with her husband. On one trip which the Hobbys made to New York with the Ross Sterlings, Willie and Maud Sterling enjoyed a shopping expedition. Discovering a silver sale being held by an Episcopal church, each of them found a bowl she "had" to have. Willie's choice was a sterling silver Tiffany footed flower bowl of ornate design. Willie and Maud talked the Episcopal women into allowing them to make a deposit on the bowls; then they returned to their hotel and talked their husbands into giving them the balance of the amount due. During the Sterling administration, Hobby had Willie's bowl engraved, "In memory of my beloved wife, Willie Cooper Hobby, whose presence graced the Governor's Mansion. 1917 to 1921. W. P. Hobby.", and presented it to the mansion.

In February of 1920, the Hobbys went to Houston to help welcome General John J. Pershing to Texas. A reception, formal banquet, and a visit to Rice Institute were the main events that they attended.

At the International Carnival held in El Paso in 1920, Willie shared the honors showered on her husband as they were entertained at receptions, banquets, teas, and dances. Five governors and General Obregón, the President-elect of Mexico, were among the distinguished guests at the celebration. Later in the year the Hobbys traveled to Mexico City to take part in Obregon's inaugural festivities. They enjoyed a ten-day visit there as Obregon's "personal and special guests of honor."

When President-elect Warren G. Harding visited Texas in November of 1920, the Hobbys traveled to Port Isabel to greet him officially. With the President-elect and Mrs. Harding was Mrs. Evalyn Walsh McLean, whose dazzling Hope Diamond was the major topic of interest at the social gatherings held for the group.

In the midst of her busy schedule, Willie made time for her personal friends. When one of them became ill and was hospitalized, Willie decided she could give her better attention than she was receiving, so she took the woman to the mansion and looked after her personally until she was able to return home.

Hobby did not run for reelection in 1920. As his term drew to a close, he said he was glad he had been Governor and glad he was through being Governor. Now he looked forward to returning to the newspaper business. His administration had been remarkably harmonious, and he could point with pride to several accomplishments in the field of education: the compulsory school law had been put into effect, free school textbooks had been authorized by a constitutional amendment, aid for rural schools had been increased, and teachers' salaries had been raised. Also among his achievements (thanks to the influence of his wife) was his success in persuading Texas legislators to ratify the nineteenth amendment to the Constitution of the United States, providing for woman's suffrage, despite the fact that the voters of Texas had rejected a woman's suffrage amendment to the state constitution.

The Hobbys' last official act was to attend the inaugural ceremony for the incoming Governor, Pat Neff. Like her husband, Willie looked forward to their new life, and felt that the time spent in the Governor's Mansion was a beginning — not an end. She told a reporter that the experience ". . . had prepared me to live a big and full life."

After a busy year in Beaumont, during which both the Hobbys worked hard for a number of worthy causes, they decided to move to Houston "to look around." They were still in their early forties, and the fast-growing city on the banks of Buffalo Bayou seemed to offer many opportunities for a man of Will Hobby's abilities.

Hobby's hoped-for opportunity soon came in a pleasing way when his friend Ross Sterling bought the Houston *Post* and combined it with the *Dispatch*. Sterling asked Hobby to become president of the combined papers, and the Hobbys knew they had found their permanent home.

They bought a house on Montrose Boulevard, which was then a fashionable part of the city. Willie loved decorating and selecting furnishings and appointments for their homes, but she hated the menial side of housekeeping. Fortunately, the Hobbys could always afford servants to do the chores she disliked.

In Houston she became an active member of a number of civic groups such as the Houston League of Women Voters, literary clubs such as the Current Literature Club, and patriotic associations such as the John McKnitt Alexander Chapter of the Daughters of the American Revolution. She worked actively in the First Methodist Church, being particularly interested in the "Blue Bird Circle" that raised money to care for sick and helpless children in the city's charitable hospitals.

She told a friend: "I am hungry for more time to read the

things that are worth reading; to understand spiritual values.
I have made up my mind that from this time on I shall MAKE
time to read each day something that feeds my soul. God has
been good to me. I want to be worthy of these blessings; I
want to share them with others; I want to be a help to those
who need assistance."

As always, the Hobbys were deeply interested in and
involved in politics. Willie entertained many political friends.
When financier Jesse Jones managed to arrange for Houston
to be the site of the Democratic National Convention in June
of 1928, the Hobbys, along with many other Houston citizens,
went into a flurry of activity. Willie put in many hours and
weeks of hard work in helping with the preparations. These
efforts were followed by active campaigning for the
Democratic nominees. She traveled with her husband inside
Texas and out — making at least one trip to New York.

Willie was fifty-one now and seemed to be in excellent
health and spirits. Friends commented they had never seen
her looking so well and marveled at her "unceasing activity."
Because of her apparent well-being, the shock was great when
on January 15, 1929, she died in her sleep after a stroke.

The news of her unexpected death stunned her friends. In
person, through calls, telegrams, letters and floral offerings
they tried to express their affection for Willie. Her casket was
buried under mounds of flowers, which also filled the rooms of
the house and lined both sides of the walk. Scholarships and
contributions to many charities were given in her name. Both
the Texas Senate and House adjourned out of respect, after
passing resolutions of sympathy and condolence to her
husband. Governor Dan Moody ordered the state flag flown at
half-mast.

Willie's husband lived thirty-five years longer. He married
again — Oveta Culp, the young girl who had gotten stuck with
canning the peaches while her mother campaigned for "that
man, Will Hobby." Like the first Mrs. Hobby, Oveta Culp
Hobby proved to be an extremely capable woman, also
knowledgeable about the law and politics. She became a

national figure in her own right as head of the first women's military organization in the nation's history, the Women's Auxiliary Army Corps, during World War II. She also served as Secretary of the Department of Health, Education and Welfare. She and Hobby had two children: a son, William Pettus, Jr., and a daughter, Jessica Oveta. As her husband's health failed, Oveta ably took over the management of the Houston *Post* and its broadcast affiliates.

Will Hobby felt he was a man blessed by fortune to have married two such extraordinary women. For the benefit of Willie's friends, he published the many telegrams, letters, and poems of condolence and tribute that he received when she died. In a preface to them he said:

> Like everything else in our sweet partnership so were our friends, mine were hers and hers were mine . . . These expressions are put in printed form so I may pass them on to those I believe will read and understand . . . As precious to me as their words are I feel they knew the story of her worth and virtues only in part while it was given to me to know it all.

Myrtle Mainer Neff

A psychologist searching for examples of the extrovert and introvert might choose Myrtle and Pat Neff as his models. "Outgoing," "genial," "aggressive" are the adjectives that occur again and again in descriptions of Pat Neff, while "retiring," "modest," "unassuming" are the key words used to describe Myrtle Neff. The archetype of the southern gentlewoman, Myrtle was content to live mostly in her husband's shadow. He made all the decisions, big and little, in their marriage; however, this was a way of life which suited them both, and they seem to have had a happy existence together.

The Mainers had been among the early settlers of Lovelady, Texas, where Nicholas Mainer became a successful merchant. His wife, Ella, gave birth to Myrtle on August 18, 1873. Her childhood was spent in the comfortable family home with her seven brothers and sisters. Then her parents sent her to Waco to attend the high school department operated at that time by Baylor University. After completing the high school courses, she went on to attend the University, majoring in music.

Quiet and retiring, Myrtle usually sat on the back row in her classes. From her position in the rear of her Texas history class, she noticed a tall black-haired young man seated at the front. He always seemed to know the answers to the professor's questions, and he obviously had a gift of gab. In fact, she discovered, he was one of the University's outstanding orators, Pat Neff from McGregor, Texas.

Social life between the sexes was under strict control at Baylor. On rare occasions, such as George Washington's birthday, receptions were held at which the young men of the school were invited to meet the young ladies. These "soirees," as they were called, were held in the chapel under stern surveillance with no one permitted to go outside once the event was under way. The young men and women were formally introduced, and then couples were allowed to talk together for three minutes. At the end of that time, everyone had to change to another partner. But a persistent male could return to the same female a number of times during the evening.

Pat Neff found himself returning again and again for three minutes worth of talk with an attractive young lady who had a slender figure, shining brown hair, blue eyes, and an intriguing smile. If Myrtle Mainer was a little shy, that only added to her appeal for him. And Myrtle found herself eagerly waiting for the next snatch of conversation with her goodlooking admirer. He was easy to talk to, for he was more than willing to do most of the talking!

In spite of the limited opportunities for fraternizing at the school, the friendship between Pat and Myrtle deepened as the months passed. Then in Myrtle's junior year her father died, and she had to return home without taking her degree. Under her mother's guidance, she became an expert housekeeper, and found that she enjoyed practicing homemaking skills.

There were visits and exchanges of letters with Pat Neff, and Myrtle came to look forward to these more and more. Over the years, he finished Baylor, taught school, completed his law degree at the University of Texas, and was elected to the Legislature.

Finally, on May 31, 1899, the couple were married at her family home in Lovelady. Between their meeting at the "soiree" and at the improvised wedding altar, eight years had passed. The pastor of the Lovelady Baptist Church officiated. A reporter for the local paper enthused:

> This was the most pleasant occasion ever witnessed by the people of this city. The decorations were simply grand. The happy couple left on the south bound midnight train for Galveston.

After a short honeymoon, the newlyweds settled at first in Waco, but soon moved to Austin when Neff was elected Speaker of the Texas House of Representatives. Myrtle was the first woman to set up housekeeping in the Speaker's apartment in the Capitol Building, where all of the Speakers' families have lived since that time. For her husband's sake, Myrtle entertained frequently and soon gained a reputation as an adept and gracious hostess.

When the Neffs returned to Waco after his term as Speaker was finished, their lives fell into a pattern. Aggressive and outgoing, Pat Neff was an enthusiastic joiner. He busied himself with the affairs of numerous activities and institutions in Waco, such as the Masons, in which he became grand master, and the Knights of Pythias, in which he became grand chancellor. He also took a keen interest in politics and headed the Democratic Party organization in Waco. He was president of the Conference for Education of Texas for a number of years. And for six years he served as prosecuting attorney for McLennan County.

In contrast, Myrtle much preferred to spend her time at home. The one organization in which she joined her husband wholeheartedly was the First Baptist Church. Both attended faithfully and worked actively in this church all of their lives. Myrtle taught Sunday school, visited the sick members, and took flowers from her own gardens to hospitals, in addition to doing almost anything else that was asked of her by the church.

Although she enjoyed most being with members of the family or a few close friends, she planned numerous dinner parties and other entertainments for her husband's business friends and associates.

After their two children — Pat, Jr. and Hallie Maud — were born, she was quite content to devote her time to her children, house and garden. But Pat Neff had other ideas. Like his friend, James Ferguson, who had been born in the same year (1871), Neff was not satisfied to be a successful and important person within a limited area. And, like Ferguson, he decided to try for the highest office in the state without asking anyone's advice or being asked by anyone to run. Myrtle wasn't eager to leave their Waco home, but she was willing to agree with whatever her husband wanted to do.

Neff's opponent in the gubernatorial race was the brilliant orator, Joseph Weldon Bailey, and Neff's strategy was not to compete with him as a speaker but to personally meet as many voters as possible. As a result, he put on a far-ranging campaign that took him to counties that had never seen a candidate for Governor. He drove 6,000 miles, spoke 850 times, and stopped to shake hands wherever he found warm bodies.

He found the life of a candidate so exciting that he called the campaign "a big, bright day." Myrtle didn't share his enthusiasm for traveling long and hard, meeting one group of strangers after another. She occasionally went with him on the shorter trips, but usually preferred to stay at home taking care of the house and children.

In his speeches, Neff told his audiences that he had never tasted liquor, tobacco, coffee, or tea. His only campaign pledge, to "make Texas a better place in which to live," apparently satisfied Texans, who voted him into office by a large majority of the votes cast.

The traditional reception was held after Neff's inauguration on January 18, 1921, but the traditional ball was not. Since the Neffs did not approve of dancing, Myrtle helped plan a huge banquet to be held at the country club. A high-ranking representative of the President of Mexico and all of the governors of the Mexican states bordering on the Rio Grande and their families attended. The Mexican women were exquisitely dressed and bejeweled, and the affair was a brilliant success.

As Myrtle afterward said, "I came to the mansion reluctantly, because I have never been in any sense of the word a society woman, having felt that my time and the strength which has been given me rather sparingly belonged to my home and my family." But she also felt that when the people of Texas called her husband to service, "the call included me," and she was determined to serve well.

Accordingly, she set aside every Tuesday to be "at home at the mansion" to the public, and she also planned and carried out with great care and attention all of the traditional formal entertainments that went with her role.

Meticulous as always in her housekeeping, she made several practical additions to the mansion. Two big cedar-lined closets were added to the upstairs, as were a sun parlor and a rear sleeping porch. Also under her direction, new hangings and a cover were added to the canopied Sam Houston bed, and the state dining room was redecorated. The mansion was kept in spotless order and the rooms were filled with floral decorations that Myrtle usually arranged personally, selecting the flowers from the mansion greenhouse.

The most agreeable kind of entertainments for Myrtle were those she planned for her young son and daughter, but she never shirked the effort required in staging state affairs. And she never failed to dress impressively for her public appearances — to please her husband and to fulfill her concept of her role. In October of 1921 the Dallas *Morning News* described the gown she wore to a reception honoring her presence at the State Fair. It was of silver cloth embroidered with black sequins and had a green girdle from which hung a garland of scarlet poppies.

Myrtle made many friends in Austin for herself and for her husband by her gentle, unassuming manner and by her democratic treatment of the numerous guests she entertained at the mansion. She agreed to her husband's desire for a second term without objection, even though she hated the long hours he worked and felt that he was at times "almost a stranger to us."

Neff was reelected with little trouble and continued his project of making Texas "a better place in which to live" by championing a state parks system, stressing the development of educational institutions and industries, and instituting advance planning for the 1936 Texas Centennial.

During the four years that they spent in the Governor's Mansion, the Neffs were, as always, faithful in their attendance at weekly church services. Myrtle had one self-assigned duty (and pleasure) during the entire time they lived in Austin. This was to furnish and arrange the flowers for the services each Sunday in the First Baptist Church. When there was time, she also joined in other work for the church.

After four years in the mansion, Myrtle felt some regrets upon leaving, but she was happy at the thought that her husband would be able to spend more time with the family. She proved, however, to be overly optimistic in this hope.

The Neffs had scarcely settled into a large home on Austin Avenue in Waco when President Coolidge appointed Neff to the National Railway Mediation Board. The children were in college, and Myrtle did not want to be separated from her husband, so she went with him to Washington, D.C., where they spent several months.

In 1928 Neff was appointed to the chairmanship of the Texas Railroad Commission by Governor Dan Moody. This job entailed frequent trips to Austin, about one hundred miles from Waco, and Myrtle sometimes went along to visit her friends there.

During these years Pat, Jr. obtained a law degree and went to Houston to practice. Hallie Maud graduated from college and married Frank Wilcox, a lawyer, of Waco.

In 1932 Neff was asked to accept the position of president of Baylor University, and Myrtle again was called upon to fill a role that involved a great deal of entertaining and formal social life. In her position as first lady of the university, she did everything she could to support her husband. Aside from entertaining various school groups and visiting dignitaries, her main activities were in connection with the Woman's Missionary Union of the First Baptist Church and the Baylor Round Table, an organization of Baylor women teachers and faculty wives.

As usual, even her informal social life was directed by her husband. When he influenced the famous Keys quadruplets from Hollis, Oklahoma, to attend Baylor, Myrtle extended warm hospitality to them, as she did to other groups of students. But when Neff took the quads on an extensive trip to Canada to see the Dionne quintuplets, and through the East to advertise the Texas Centennial, Myrtle did not go because she did not feel up to making the trip.

Her strength, which had never been great, diminished as she grew older; consequently, she became less active as the years went on. As she aged she took pleasure in her grandson, Pat Neff, III, in raising flowers, in visiting the sick, and in keeping up with her church work. She was loved by her small circle of friends and generous to a fault. When Hallie Maud took her mother some treat, such as half a turkey she had cooked, she would often find later that Myrtle had given it to someone she felt would enjoy it.

Pat Neff retired from the presidency of Baylor in 1947. For the next five years Myrtle at last had the quiet, private life with him that she had always wanted. Neither of them was in good health, but her husband's death in 1952 was a great blow to Myrtle. She never really recovered from it. Before a year had passed she died — on July 19, 1953, just a month before her eightieth birthday. Funeral services were held in the chapel of the First Baptist Church.

Myrtle was buried in Oakwood Cemetery in Waco beside her husband. Appropriately, a single monument was erected over both graves. Many words of praise were written about Myrtle Mainer Neff, but perhaps the best summary of her life was written by a reporter for *The Baylor Line*, who called her "a lady of modest grace."

Mildred Paxton Moody

In the fall of 1974 a doctor completed examining his patient, a seventy-seven-year-old woman, who had fallen down a long flight of stairs. Along with assorted bumps and bruises, he found that she had head and backlash injuries and a broken nose. He carefully explained the operating procedure necessary to restore the nose cosmetically to its normal appearance.

"Never mind all that, doctor," she told him. "Just treat me like they do football players — straighten it around and send me back in the game!"

Mildred Paxton Moody knew what she was talking about, as she had been an avid football fan for many years. Her chief concern about her injuries was that they would keep her from riding her bicycle or swimming in the icy waters of Barton Springs, a pastime she has enjoyed for forty years, and one that she used to share with her friends until they deserted her for the more comfortable water of heated pools.

Life began for Mildred Paxton in Abilene, Texas, where she was born April 20, 1897, to George and Mathilde Warren Paxton. The Warrens had moved from Alabama to be among the first ranchers in the Abilene area. The Paxtons had come from Kentucky, where they had bred fine horses. At the time of Mildred's birth, George Paxton was president of and held controlling interest in Citizens National Bank of Abilene. In this West Texas town in a great, old semi-colonial house with big shade trees, she had a "wonderfully happy" childhood within the limits of a strict Baptist upbringing. The church was next door to their home, and her mother was a devout member and leader in the Woman's Christian Temperance Union. One of her early memories is of riding in a W.C.T.U. parade, wearing a white dress with a blue sash and loudly singing "Vote, vote, VOTE for prohibition." Her father owned one of the first cars in Abilene, which delighted the adventurous Mildred.

From the age of thirteen through twenty she attended Simmons College, graduating with a B.A. degree in 1917. At Simmons she established the first newspaper — the *Simmons Brand* — displaying a talent for writing that she would put to good use later. From Abilene Mildred went to Austin to work on her master's in English at the University of Texas. At a friend's wedding she met an earnest, red-haired law student from Taylor, Texas. There was a mutual attraction between Mildred Paxton and Daniel Moody. But to the fun-loving Mildred, with her newly acquired freedom from puritanical restraints, Dan Moody seemed to represent the kind of strait-laced thinking she was trying to escape. And, anyway, life was much too exciting for the little girl from Abilene to think of settling down at the moment.

She was working on the University of Texas student newspaper, which was a weekly publication at that time. A highlight of the year for the paper was a special coed edition when for one week a female was allowed to occupy the sacred editorial chair. In the spring of 1918, Mildred won that privilege. She discovered that her stint as editor happened to coincide with an important event in the Governor's Mansion. The First Lady, Willie Hobby, was giving a reception for

Margaret Wilson, the President's daughter, who was appearing in Austin on a nationwide concert tour for the benefit of the American Expeditionary Forces.

Crashing the reception, the enthusiastic young reporter got her first glimpse of the historic building. She was greatly impressed by the mansion and the gracious Willie Hobby, who arranged for her to have an interview with Margaret Wilson. Nine years later Mildred was to receive a quite different impression of the mansion when she entered by the back door and saw it bare, stripped down to the state-owned furniture and lacking the softening effect of numerous floral arrangements.

As soon as she received her M.A. from the University, Mildred looked around for a way to join the effort her country was making in World War I. The Defense Department, in association with the Red Cross, had a plan for relieving the acute shortage of nurses. College-educated young women were given three months of intensive course work at Vassar and then were sent to one of several large general hospitals for their practical training. Mildred completed the academic work at Vassar and was doing nursing at Philadelphia General Hospital when the war ended in November of 1918.

Hoping to combine traveling, writing, and work that would enable her to support herself, Mildred decided to get an R.N. degree; but her father disapproved of her plan. Although he had not objected strongly to her working as a nurse during the national emergency, he didn't consider nursing a "suitable" career for his daughter. However, he agreed to finance any further education she wanted so long as the course of study was one he felt proper and so long as she did well in school.

Mildred returned to Abilene to live while she considered what she wanted to do. She took a job at Simmons teaching a class popularly known as the "flunkee course in English" for veterans of World War I. The problems involved in teaching college English to young men with slight fundamental knowledge of the subject, she summed up in one word — "grim." When she complained to the president of the college that it was a hopeless task, he told her, "Oh, well, they're nearly all preacher boys who will be in little country churches. It doesn't really matter greatly that they become proficient in English. Just make allowances." She learned to do this, but she didn't learn to enjoy it.

Aware of her writing ability, the owner of the local newspaper, the Abilene *Reporter*, asked her to develop a society section for the paper. Since Mildred responded with horror to the idea of reporting endless teas and social gatherings, the editor challenged her to *make* it interesting. She found a number of ways to do so for her readers, but still found the routine of covering social events dull.

When her experiences made her realize that she needed more training to secure more interesting jobs, Mildred decided to accept her father's offer to finance her further education. Consequently, she went to Columbia University to study in the Pulitzer School of Journalism and acquired a third degree — Bachelor of Literature.

Again she returned to teach at Simmons College in Abilene. But this time the course was journalism, and she loved it. She also worked again for the local paper but in areas other than the society page. For a time she served as publicity director for the Chamber of Commerce and wrote glowing accounts of "fabulous West Texas."

During the years of moving about among various schools and jobs, Mildred had kept in touch with old friends from her University of Texas days, often visiting the Alpha Phi house where she had lived as a charter member of the UT chapter of that organization. Among these friends was Dan Moody, who had taken a law degree and then completed officers' training school at Camp Taylor, Kentucky, where he was commissioned a second lieutenant in the infantry.

He had been elected County Attorney of Williamson County, and in 1922 was appointed District Attorney of Williamson and Travis Counties by Governor Neff. In this position he soon made a name for himself as a vigorous prosecutor of the Ku Klux Klan.

On one of her visits to Austin, Dan took Mildred for a moonlight ride in his old Model-T Ford. He remarked that he wanted to show her "the finest residence site in Texas" and stopped in front of the Governor's Mansion, which appeared dignified and mellow in the soft romantic light. Mildred looked at the young District Attorney and thought, "Is that the direction your ambitions run? Why, you good old country boy, you will never make that!" Much later, she told Dan what she had thought that night, and he took pleasure in reminding her of the incident as they stood together in reception lines greeting their guests in the mansion.

He was becoming more serious, but she still had no intentions of marrying him. There were many differences between them. He was too prudish for her taste. He was a strict prohibitionist (as were her parents). And he was poor. She reminded him that she drove a big, brown Cadillac (her father's) while he drove an ancient "flivver." He replied that someday he would be able to afford a Cadillac, too.

In 1924 Dan Moody ran for Attorney General and was elected on the same ticket as Miriam Ferguson. Both he and Miriam had based their campaigns largely on an anti-Klan stand, and for a short time he and the Fergusons were friends. But when Moody began to prosecute against corruption in the form of kickbacks on highway contracts and other alleged administrative abuses, the friendship quickly changed to enmity.

During his term as Attorney General, Moody gained many supporters, and they urged him to run for Governor in 1926. The decision was difficult for him. A gubernatorial campaign in Texas was usually rough. Against the fighting Fergusons it was bound to be even more so. He was just on the point of persuading Mildred that he might, after all, be the husband for her. He finally left the decision up to her: if she would marry him, he would not run for Governor if she did not want him to.

Mildred thought it over and decided to accept the man and his political ambitions. She set the wedding date for her birthday, April 20, one month after Moody announced his candidacy for Governor.

Dan Moody was a favorite with Austin society, and together
he and Mildred had hundreds of friends over the state. The job
of deciding whom to send invitations seemed hopeless. The
forthright bride-to-be solved it by announcing that no formal
invitations to the wedding would be issued, but friends of her
fiance and herself would be welcome. As a result, hundreds of
friends and well-wishers came by every form of locomotion,
including the still-rare airplane. Telegrams and gifts poured
into the Paxton home. Among the presents was a new car
from the bride's father.

An overflow crowd filled the First Baptist Church where
the vows were read by an uncle of the bride, the Reverend Mr.
Lee R. Scarborough of Fort Worth. A musical program
preceded the ceremony, and Easter lilies and palms and tall
candles in branching candelabra made a romantic background
for the evening service. Mildred wore a gown of palest pink
crepe Romaine, and the bridal party was dressed in a rosy
color scheme, ranging in tone from pink seashell tint to flame
colors.

After a reception at the Paxton home, Mildred and Dan
Moody left for a brief honeymoon. By May 1 they had taken up
quarters in the Stephen F. Austin Hotel in Austin. From this
base they went on the campaign trail together. The "honeymoon campaign," as the papers termed it, did nothing to hurt
Moody's chances. The attractive young couple won the hearts
and votes of many Texans by their charm and sincerity.

In the first primary Moody received only a few thousand
votes less than the combined vote for four opponents, and in
the run-off, he received the largest vote that had been cast for
any candidate for Governor of Texas up to that time. Much to
her chagrin, one Texan who did not get to vote for Dan Moody
was Mildred Moody. She had paid her poll tax in Abilene, but
was told that she couldn't vote there since she had changed
her residence; and in Austin she was informed that she
couldn't vote because she had not lived there the required six
months.

After the election returns were in, the Moodys, with some friends, took a three-day vacation on a ranch near Kerrville and went deer hunting. The Moodys each bagged a buck, but Mildred's had eleven points while her husband's only had ten, a comparison the Governor-elect was not allowed to forget.

A short time later when her husband had to travel to Washington, D.C., on business connected with the office of Attorney General, Mildred went with him. She had been saving her clothes money for several months to buy an inaugural gown. Entering a nice shop, she asked to see suitable dresses.

"I'm Mrs. Dan Moody, and we're going to have an inauguration," she confided.

"Oh, yes," responded the clerk, "your father is Governor of Texas."

The young-looking First Lady-to-be answered with dignity, "No, that's my husband, and he's not now, but he's going to be."

She bought a pretty chiffon dress decorated with sequins in a typical style of the twenties — with a long waistline and short skirt. When the D.A.R. set up its exhibit of inaugural gowns of the First Ladies of Texas for the Texas Centennial, they asked to display the dress. She told them she wasn't ready to give it up because she still enjoyed wearing it occasionally; however, as a substitute she sent a long dress she had worn at mansion entertainments. The long dress was high-necked in front, sleeveless, and open almost to the waistline in the back, with sequined flowers at the bottom of the opening. When a picture of the dress on the model was printed, Mildred was amazed to see that as First Lady she had worn "the original plunging neckline" — the dress had been put on the model backwards! Later she gave the D.A.R. her short, ruffled, silver-sequined inaugural gown.

The Moody inaugural was held on a temporary platform built on the steps of the Capitol, the first ceremony to be held out of doors. The Cowboy Band from Simmons College played. A tremendous crowd came from all over the state to see the youngest Governor (at thirty-three) sworn in. A reception was held in the Senate chamber, followed by balls in two hotels.

Dan Moody was determined that no tinge of suspicion concerning expenditures and state property would mar his administration. He insisted that they stay in their hotel another week after the inauguration so everything in the mansion could be inventoried before they moved in. Mildred's family and many of her friends had come from Abilene for the ceremonies, and they wanted to see the mansion. She knew they couldn't stay in Austin for another week, so she planned a breakfast at the Governor's house for them.

They entered the mansion by the back door, and the new mistress was dismayed at the sight. Without personal belongings of the Hobbys or the Neffs and bouquets of flowers to cover the shabbiness of the furnishings, it was a dreary place. Brown oatmeal paper hung loosely from the walls, and the whole atmosphere seemed gloomy.

Toward the end of January, the Moodys and their big white Collie, Tex, a wedding present, finally moved into the mansion. And Mildred for the first time in her life began housekeeping. A very able helper was George, a black man who had worked at the mansion after Governor Hobby had given him a stay of execution from the electric chair. Later Governor Miriam Ferguson had given him a full pardon, and he could have gone elsewhere to work, but he asked Mildred to keep him on. She reluctantly agreed although she was a little afraid of him at first because of his history. However, she soon came to rely on him and was glad to have someone around who knew something about the house.

Also helpful were the former First Ladies, Willie Hobby, Orline Sayers, and Fannie Campbell, who came to call and gave useful advice on managing the mansion household. But no one could tell Mildred how to stretch the Governor's salary of $4,000 a year to cover expenses and entertainments expected of her. The possibility of making ends meet and maintaining a gracious image on the gubernatorial wage of

$76.92 a week would take something of a miracle. But Mildred managed it with only a few traumatic experiences, such as the one connected with having the walls repapered.

When the Moody administration began, the State Board of Control told the First Lady they could only allow her $500 to redecorate. Mildred felt the most immediate need was new wallpaper; however, she was appalled at the idea of picking it out herself. She let a friend talk her into hiring an interior decorator who spent the whole sum on the dining room paper. Actually, the paper, which contained panoramic scenes of nineteenth century America, was probably a bargain. It came from a French factory, and was hand-blocked from the same plates of the antique paper that Jackie Kennedy later chose for the diplomatic reception room at the White House at a cost of $12,000. Nevertheless, Mildred had to call on her father for help in getting enough money to finish papering the other rooms.

The papers she selected for them were copies of original designs used in early American homes. The choice for the reception rooms was a cream-color paper with gold figures and touches of wisteria. During one of her "at homes," Mildred noticed a sweet-faced little lady with white hair softly weeping in a corner. Asking the reason for her tears, Mildred found the woman had been overcome by memories that the wallpaper had stirred, because it was exactly like the paper in the parlor of her girlhood home in Tennessee. The tears were tears of joy, and Mildred felt the paper had been a happy choice.

Some of the drawbacks to housekeeping in the mansion were ancient plumbing, moth-eaten carpets, tattered drapes, and rats in the basement. Rodents were so large and numerous that the Governor practiced his marksmanship by shooting them. The draperies, which were in shreds, were replaced by damask wall hangings from which the tattered edges were cut, and Mildred learned to place the furniture judiciously to cover the holes in the carpets. The miserable plumbing they simply endured.

The warm and friendly Moodys were extremely popular,

and Mildred found herself entertaining hundreds of guests on the traditional "at home" days. Abundant friendliness made up for the slight refreshments, and flowers from the mansion greenhouse instead of florists' arrangements furnished the decorations.

Dan Moody would not allow his wife to take money from her father for food, but he didn't object to her accepting money for clothes. Mildred surreptitiously and thankfully funneled most of the "clothes" money into the food budget, which was always in a state of crisis. While the depression was in full force, tours of the mansion replaced the "at home" open houses.

Another inconvenience connected with entertaining groups of any size was that there was never enough silver or dishes. What silver there was had a tendency to disappear in the pockets of souvenir hunters. Therefore, Mildred found it practical to rent cheap silverware, which was not a temptation.

Almost immediately after her husband's election, Mildred had been surprised to learn that babies all over the state were being named for her. At first she sent silver spoons to each little namesake; as they became more numerous, she sent autographed pictures; and finally, although she appreciated the honor, she had to "keep quiet."

Unable to afford a secretary, she tried with increasing lack of success to handle the large volume of mail that poured into the mansion addressed to her. Many letters contained requests which probably seemed simple to the writer. After all, what was one autographed recipe or one handkerchief for a church bazaar? But when the requests were multiplied by the dozens every week, they became impossible to respond to.

The opportunity to travel with her husband was one of the most interesting aspects of her position to Mildred. In February of 1927, the Moodys were part of a joint celebration of George Washington's birthday by Texas and Mexico. A train, furnished by the citizens of Laredo, took them, along with members of the House and Senate, to San Antonio where they stopped for dinner and the theater before going on to

Laredo. Here they joined the two Laredos on each side of the
border in the twenty-eighth annual celebration of the
anniversary. A speech by Moody and a two-mile-long parade
led by the University of Texas band were highlights of the
event.

On April 1 they returned to Mexico — this time to inspect
the new Laredo-Monterrey highway. More than 100 cars were
in the caravan that wended its way from San Antonio to
Monterrey, where a banquet honoring the Moodys and the
highest officials in Mexico had been arranged.

On the Moodys' first wedding anniversary, April 20, 1927,
which was also Mildred's birthday, the Baptist church gave
the Governor and First Lady a pounding. Pounds of sugar,
lard, flour, pecans, peanuts as well as hams, honey, ribbon
cane syrup, canned fruit, and other assorted groceries were
gratefully received. For a time the mansion grocery budget
was balanced.

In the summer of 1927 Mildred had an encounter that made
an indelible impression on her. A few months earlier, Charles
Lindbergh had thrilled the world with his daring solo flight
across the Atlantic. Now he was on a last cross-country flight
in the *Spirit of St. Louis* before it was placed in the
Smithsonian Institution. The Governor had been invited to
head the official greeters in Fort Worth, which was to be the
aviator's first stop in Texas. But the planning committee had
arranged all-male festivities, failing completely to include the
First Lady in its plans.

Somewhat miffed, Mildred decided to visit her parents in
Abilene, about 150 miles west of Fort Worth. She had just
reached her hometown when news came that Lindbergh
considered Abilene a better refueling spot than Fort Worth
and would make his first stop in Texas there. Frantic plans
were made by the city fathers to honor the hero. Mildred was
asked to ride in a car with Lindbergh in the parade and to
make the "presentation" speech from the bandstand on the
courthouse square.

When the modest Lindbergh caught a glimpse of the

fantastic purple velvet-draped "throne" improvised for him in an open car, he protested. The chair was hastily ripped out, and the blonde aviator and Texas' First Lady took seats in the car on either side of the gaping hole where it had been. Mildred would never forget a minute of that ride; she was impressed by the genuine feeling of the cheering crowds for the tall, quiet man in the car with her.

When they arrived at the bandstand, she made her brief introduction, and then the crowd swarmed around Lindbergh, shaking his hand and begging for autographs until he was almost smothered. Seeing the trapped expression on his face, Mildred felt it was her duty to rescue him from her enthusiastic hometowners. Her father's big Lincoln was parked in the square. Grasping Lindbergh firmly by the arm, she said, "Come on, I'll get you out of this." Ducking through the crowd, they ran for the car, making their getaway before most of the surprised bystanders realized what was happening.

Lindbergh was relieved to escape the fuss. At the airport he thanked her simply and quickly took off in his waiting plane. She watched until the *Spirit* became a speck against the blue sky.

True to her journalistic instincts, Mildred wrote a lively account of the encounter for the papers. She included some anecdotes of the event that amused her. One old man, when asked if he had seen Lindbergh, reported, "I shore did, seen him and his Ma, too." And as Mildred got ready to introduce the boyish-looking hero, one little boy told his neighbor, "Shut up, Mrs. Coolidge is getting ready to speak." Along with the laughs, though, she had lasting memories of what she described as "a moment spent with true greatness."

There were other highlights of 1927 for Mildred. She was elected sponsor of the Franklin-Webster Club, which was composed of capital correspondents and newspaper men in the 40th Legislature. At her suggestion, the Governor was elected "wood and water toter" of the club. In November of 1927, she led the Armistice Day parade. And in December she received a surprise Christmas gift from about 150 Austin women — a valuable oil painting.

At their first New Year's reception the Moodys received thousands of guests. The year 1928 was a campaign year for Moody as he sought his second term. But for Mildred it was a much quieter year than the preceding one, because she was expecting their first child. She was pleased when her husband was reelected with little difficulty. He had earned the nickname "Honest Dan" during his administration, and no other candidate was a serious threat to him.

During their first year in the mansion, Mildred's younger sister, Helen, had lived with them while she attended the University of Texas. Now, in the fall of 1928, Mildred helped plan the wedding of Helen and Weaver Moore of Houston; they were married in the mansion on October 2, 1928.

The traditional New Year's open house had to be omitted on January 1, 1929, because of Mildred's advanced pregnancy. There was much excitement and publicity over the impending birth of the second mansion baby. Endowed with a strong sense of history, Mildred Paxton Moody wanted her first child to be born in the same room and the same bed in which Margaret Houston had given birth to her eighth and last child. When complications forced her to be taken to the hospital for a Caesarean birth, she shed tears of frustration. However, the birth of a healthy son soon changed her mood, and her normal lively sense of humor was restored so that she could laugh at the story of the little Austin schoolboy who hurried home to tell his parents that he had heard the Moodys had an "Assyrian" baby.

After his arrival on January 6, 1929, Dan Moody III was joyfully welcomed by the citizens of Texas. Hundreds of telegrams and gifts poured in, including a $25.00 savings account in a bank and a Gorham sterling silver bowl, dish, and cup with animal designs from the ladies of the 41st Legislature. Mildred sent pictures of the baby with thank-you notes to the well-wishers.

Lacking Margaret Houston's personal servants, Mildred

soon discovered the inconvenient arrangement of the mansion for a new mother. The only kitchen at that time was downstairs. Once a group of tourists caught the First Lady barefoot, warming the baby's bottle. A constant problem was the continual flow of tourists, many of whom came at other than visiting hours with pleas that they were just "passing through" and this would be their only chance to see the mansion. In the heat of summer with a teething baby, Mildred would sometimes be driven to distraction. But then her good nature and her love of people and history would restore her good humor, and she would often conduct the tours personally.

In the summer of 1929 in an impressive ceremony, Mildred joined the Austin Girl Scouts. At a regional conference, she was invested as a tenderfoot, and Scouting in Texas received a big boost.

When the Calvin Coolidges visited Texas after his second term as President, the Moodys got up early and traveled to San Antonio to have breakfast with them. Then the ex-President and his wife and the Moodys traveled to Austin together by train for a short visit.

During her last year as mistress of the mansion, Mildred planned an attractive flower garden on the north side of the house. It was surrounded by a ligustrum hedge, a cactus rockery in each of the four corners, stone seats, a trellised arbor, and a gazing globe, which reflected the mansion. Roses and other flowers added color and beauty. In this pleasant setting Mildred gave several large outdoor parties.

Another improvement made to the mansion toward the end of the Moodys' stay was iron-railed cement front steps. In these steps were imbedded the footprints of young Dan Moody. The little boy had spent a happy two years in this home with Tex as his constant companion and playmate. He continued to be the favorite of Texans, who were eager for any tidbit of news of his latest doings and sayings.

In spite of the urging of friends to run for a third term, Moody decided to retire to private practice at the end of his second administration. He could be proud of the beginning of a system of fine highways and the reorganization of the penitentiary system. Mildred could share with him credit for a reputation for unquestioned honesty connected with all the expenditures made during his terms.

With a strong feeling of nostalgia, Mildred and Dan Moody left the mansion, which had been their first and only home since their marriage. Shortly afterward, two-year-old Dan-Dan, as he called himself, kept asking to go home. To ease the transition, Mildred took Dan, Jr. to Abilene to visit his grandparents for several weeks while Moody stayed at the Stephen F. Austin Hotel to prepare to resume private practice.

The Moodys bought a home on Woodlawn in a hilly section of Austin with room for a small boy and a large dog to roam and play. Although there were still many social and civic activities that demanded her time, Mildred found many opportunities to be with Dan — reading to him, walking with him, and enjoying each stage of his development. Three years after they left the mansion a daughter, Nancy Paxton, was born and the Moody family foursome was complete.

Since Mildred had the strong writer's urge to make experiences permanent by putting them into words, she wrote a delightful article called "Housekeeping in the Governor's Mansion." It was published in the March 5, 1931, issue of the Dallas *Morning News*. In it she described the trials and tribulations of trying to keep house and entertain in a goldfish bowl on a shoestring salary in a manner commensurate with the dignity and ceremony expected of Texas' First Family. She also traced with touches of humor her own reactions, from the time she was a novice First Lady, somewhat intimidated by the watchful gaze of the portrait of the dignified Mrs. Richard Coke.

At the end of the article, she shared with readers her deep concern for the condition and care of the mansion and suggested that a board of mansion regents be established to oversee the maintenance of the historic old building. Following her suggestion, Governor Ross Sterling created such a board and named her chairman. The board has been responsible for much that has been done to collect and preserve items of great historical value in connection with the building, and for suggesting and overseeing necessary maintenance and decorating that has greatly enhanced the appearance and usefulness of the mansion.

Other projects that Mildred was involved in during these years included Junior League activities such as free baby clinics and helping victims of cerebral palsy; working with the Settlement Club and its home for children from broken families; and various civic drives like the United Fund.

During World War II she helped manage the Nurses' Aide work of the official Red Cross organization of Austin. She also donned her uniform and worked as an aide in all three of the Austin hospitals when extra help was needed.

Mildred and her husband took great pride in the fact that both Dan, Jr. and Nancy were scholastically at the head of their big law classes at the University of Texas.

After World War II Mildred's brother, who served with the Flying Tigers, became disabled and the Moodys helped educate his four children. These children were like a second family after Dan and Nancy married and left home.

Moody was highly successful in his law practice and made a national name for himself. President Franklin Roosevelt called on him to prosecute federal income tax evaders, and he secured a number of convictions. Although he remained quite actively interested in politics, only once more did he actually run for office. This was during World War II when he ran for United States Senator in a race that included two other former Governors — James V. Allred and W. Lee O'Daniel, who was the winner.

In May of 1961, Moody gave up his law practice when his health began to fail. He was in increasingly poor health until his death in May of 1966. He was buried with honors in the State Cemetery. Mildred had a monument erected listing his terms of service to the state and ending with a quotation from *Hamlet:*

This above all — to thine own self be true
And it must follow, as the night the day,
Thou canst not then be false to any man.

Since her husband's death Mildred has continued to be a popular member of Austin society and is a frequent guest at social events in the mansion. In addition to swimming and bicycle riding, she enjoys walking and playing golf. A voracious reader of new magazines, history, biography, and mysteries, she also keeps up with the current best sellers. She has retained an avid interest in politics and world events, occasionally writing for publication her own strong views on these subjects. Two grandchildren, a girl and a boy, have helped brighten her life.

Of the future she says, "Death holds no fear at all for me. I feel that there is a life after death, the form of which I do not know. God, I believe to be a spirit, and I do not know the nature of that — perhaps the Holy Spirit. This belief is a great comfort to me."

In describing the former First Lady, people who know her well use such terms as "vigorous" and "sparkling," and several sum her up simply as "a great gal." Yet she is a figure out of history, the oldest living First Lady, a link to the past — but one who lives very much in the present, with gusto and grace. Mildred Paxton Moody remains a free spirit and the liberated woman she has always been.

"A Quiet Somebody"

Maud Abbie Gage Sterling

Shortly after lunch on a sunny spring day in 1930, a servant hurried along the Sterling Mansion pier on Galveston Bay near the town of La Porte. When he came to the end of the pier, he handed a telegram to one of the three women he found fishing there. Maud Sterling adjusted her spectacles, read the message and — suppressing a sigh — laid down her hook and line. Bidding her companions a hasty good-bye, she hurried across the terraced lawn to the palatial house. There she changed from fishing clothes into a well-made cotton dress, brushed back wisps of dark hair that the bayshore breeze had separated from her simple hairdo, and stepped into the car that the chauffeur had brought to the front door. In a few hours she arrived in Waco, just in time to appear on the platform with her husband, who was making a major speech that night in his campaign for Governor.

This was neither the first nor the last time that Maud would forsake her favorite pastime to answer a summons to help in her husband's race for the state's highest office. However, there were times when other things took priority over appearing with him. Connected with their bayside estate, the

Sterlings had a farm of more than 100 acres. Once, when her husband had sent a message inviting Maud to attend a political rally with him, she telephoned to tell him it was buttermaking day at the farm and she thought she'd better stay home to see that the milk was handled properly.

Maud Abbie Gage Sterling was born near Hamilton, Illinois, on November 21, 1875, to Milla Brewer and Frederick Higbee Gage. Two years later the family moved to a farm in central Kansas, where Maud led the healthy, busy childhood of a farmer's daughter. Wiry and agile all of her life, she early developed a love of outdoor sports. In the country school she attended, she helped to organize a girls' baseball team, on which she was a star player.

Since very few occupations were open to respectable young women before the turn of the century, Maud and her parents decided that she should become a teacher. Accordingly, she attended the Normal School in Salina, Kansas, for two years and earned a teacher's certificate. Before she could put the certificate to use, her mother became ill. Laying aside plans to teach, Maud took over the job of running the Kansas farm home. It was hard work, but she learned to do it well. In the process she learned to be self-reliant and developed an impatience with inefficiency and waste of any kind.

After a few years, Maud persuaded her parents to move to the Gulf Coast of Texas, in the hope that her mother's health would improve in this environment. The Gages settled on a farm near Anahuac, where Maud energetically and efficiently managed the farm household.

She also found time for other activities in the community. Coming from a Puritan background, her parents had instilled in their daughter a deep religious faith. In the spring of 1898 she took a leading part in the organization of a Sunday school at Anahuac and served as one of the teachers in the school.

The main store in Anahuac at this time was owned by Mary Jane and Benjamin Franklin Sterling. The Sterlings' son, Ross, who clerked in the store, was so attracted to the small but vital Maud Gage that he made it a point to wait on her himself whenever she shopped. Maud was impressed by the size (265 pounds) and tremendous strength of the eager clerk, who could carry a 200-pound bag of feed under each arm. Too, she agreed wholeheartedly with his philosophy for getting ahead in life, which he told her he had worked out while hoeing on his family farm. It was to "take three or four licks while the other men took two."

Soon Ross Sterling was inviting Maud to picnics, basket suppers, husking bees, and community sings. Before long they were engaged, and on October 10, 1898, they were married in a simple ceremony. Sterling later said that marrying Maud Gage was the "most momentous step" of his career.

There were no funds for a honeymoon. Between them the couple had sixty-five dollars, which belonged to Maud. They spent it for furnishings for the modest home they rented in Anahuac.

Here they began fifty years of a happy marriage, during which their fortunes would swing from one extreme to the other. Probably one of the reasons for their compatibility was the great respect they had for each other; another was that both were devout Christians. Sterling enjoyed his wife's keen sense of humor and admired her intellect. He had only a few years of public schooling himself, and often turned to her for advice.

Maud and Ross Sterling were not destined to remain poor long. Ross was a born businessman and soon found clerking in his father's store boring. Recognizing his son's restlessness, the elder Sterling turned management of the store over to Ross, but even that responsibility was not enough to satisfy the young man. He established a second store, which was successful, and looked around for other opportunities. He took a contract to serve as postmaster, and Maud served as assistant postmaster.

She became less active in their business affairs when their children began to arrive. The oldest, Mary Maudine, died in infancy, but five other children — two boys and three girls — survived. They were Walter Gage, Ross, Jr., Mildred, Ruth, and Norma. For twenty-five years, from the time the first child began school until the last child graduated from high school, Maud was an active member of the Parent-Teacher Association. At one time, in the midst of the children's schooling, she belonged to four different PTA's at the same time.

As Sterling began to broaden his business interests, the family moved to various homes in the Gulf Coast area — from Anahuac to Galveston to Sour Lake and finally to Houston in 1905. Here, their lawn on Rossmoyne Boulevard enclosed a miniature football field, a tennis court, and croquet grounds. Every afternoon found from ten to twenty-five children there — running, shouting, knocking balls around with mallets and rackets. At their insistence, Maud sometimes joined in the games. Whenever a new youngster who fancied himself as a runner moved into the neighborhood, it was the children's delight to match him in a race against Maud, who invariably won. Walter was sixteen before he could beat his mother in a one-block sprint.

The family belonged to the South End Christian Church and contributed heavily to its support. At one time or another, Maud worked in nearly every department of the church.

In 1910 Sterling bought two oil wells which he developed into the Humble Oil and Refining Company. When this venture made the Sterlings wealthy, they remained the same friendly, outgoing, down-to-earth people they had always been. Being able to afford servants meant for Maud more time to enjoy her children and the sports she loved, especially fishing, as well as time for needlework and gardening.

Her relationships with those who worked for her reveal her ability to win friends at all levels of society. She had the same happy, singing cook until the cook died. A doctor reported that he had been called to attend a woman who did washing for a living. As he left he asked her if she needed anything. She replied, "No, suh. I used to wash for Miz Sterling when her chilluns was babies, and whenever I let her know I'se sick, she allus takes keer of me."

During World War I Maud plunged into Red Cross work; she was a graduate of the first class of instructors and logged 3,000 hours of work. Her older daughters, Mildred and Ruth, each earned 1,000 hours.

When Walter attended the University of Texas, he was assistant manager and manager of the football teams, and Maud became an avid and knowledgeable fan. She had never lost her interest in baseball. Whenever Sterling had to make a business trip to New York during baseball season, she went along to attend the major league games. Once, at a social gathering on the eve of a Rice-A&M baseball game, a Rice Institute junior started to explain the game to Maud. When he found that she knew more than he did about the year's conference records, he asked her to go to the game with him. She went.

In 1924 the Sterlings suffered a terrible blow in the death of their son, Ross, Jr. He had been an active member of the Y.M.C.A., and both of the bereaved parents became workers and supporters of this organization for the rest of their lives. For six years Maud was a member of the Board of Directors. In memory of their son, the Sterlings gave a large tract of wooded land on Galveston Bay for the establishment of a boys' camp.

Sterling sold his valuable Humble interests in 1925 and became involved in developing real estate in and around Houston. He also purchased the Houston *Dispatch* and the Houston *Post*, which he combined as the Houston *Post-Dispatch*. In addition, he established Houston's first commercial radio broadcasting station, acquired controlling interest in a bank, and erected office buildings. Everything he touched seemed to turn to gold, and the Sterlings became multimillionaires.

The children were sent to excellent schools, and Walter was taken in as a business partner by his father. Mildred married Wyatt Hedrick of Fort Worth, and Ruth married Winn Wheeler of Houston.

Near La Porte the Sterlings built their large estate and

luxurious home, "Miramar," fronting on Galveston Bay. It was richly furnished with fireplaces, and a large, well-used library of fine books. The grand piano was covered with pictures of the children and two grandchildren, and the dining chairs had needlepoint cushions made by Maud. The terraced gardens led down to their own private pier where Maud could fish to her heart's content.

The ranch-farm of 100 acres was stocked with cows, horses, and chickens. Maud supervised production of the household food, including butter, eggs, vegetables, and meat, and the plantings of trees and flowers around the house. Her busy daily routine suited her, and she told a reporter, "I don't know what I would do if I couldn't stay busy, if I couldn't feel that every day was being made to count for something."

The Sterlings did take time to make some trips — to Mexico, to the eastern and western sections of the United States, and on cruises to the West Indies. They talked of going to Europe or the Orient, but as Maud said, by dinner time they were always back home again. They really had no desire to go that far from their pleasant surroundings.

Ross Sterling's reputation as a successful businessman with an ability to get things done made him well-known throughout the state. In 1927, Governor Moody appointed him chairman of the Texas Highway Commission. He was so effective at this job that in 1930 Moody and other high-ranking officials backed Sterling to run for Governor against eleven other candidates, including, as usual, Miriam Ferguson. In the first primary, Mrs. Ferguson led the ticket, and Sterling ran second. A bitter, hard-fought contest preceded the second primary in which Sterling was nominated by a margin of about 89,000 votes.

A rumor was spread that Maud did not want Sterling to be elected. When asked if it were true, she answered with a straight face, "Why, of course not. Don't you know that the Governor is always given the best box in the stadium for all the football games?" Whatever truth there might have been in the rumor, Maud never revealed publicly her reluctance to leave the pleasures of Miramar for the exacting duties attached to the role of First Lady of the state. She told reporters modestly that she was "a quiet somebody" who preferred informality to formality, and added that she "hoped" to make friends in Austin. She did not add that she was already acquainted with and had entertained nearly every prominent family in the state at Miramar. After Sterling's election in November, Mildred Moody, the incumbent First Lady, formally "introduced" Maud Sterling to Austin society at a large reception.

During Sterling's term of office the Great Depression affected every level of government and society. The traditional reception and ball were held after his inauguration on January 20, 1931, but the decorations and refreshments were not elaborate. The fact that most formal social affairs were omitted or severely curtailed did not dismay Maud. She was "at home" almost any day or time to mansion visitors and liked to answer the door herself instead of letting the servants do it.

The Sterlings' youngest daughter, Norma, who had just returned from a year at Miss Semple's School in New York, moved into the mansion with them. Walter, Mildred, Ruth and their families were frequent visitors. With some of them as her companions, Maud sometimes managed to slip away for an occasional fishing trip by getting up before daylight.

Maud took a great interest in the planting and cultivation of the shrubs and flowers on the mansion grounds. State income had fallen off sharply, and there were no funds for any sizeable renovations during Maud's tenure as mistress. But, practicing one of her hobbies, she managed to leave a valuable memento — a beautiful needlepoint cover for one of the footstools.

Probably to her surprise, Maud made an impression in the area of fashion. The clothes she chose for most occasions were made of cotton — a fabric not considered elegant enough by many society women of that time. But Maud, who liked the feel of cotton, had dresses and suits made from it. The idea of cotton clothing caught on, and since her time as First Lady, it has remained highly regarded as a fabric suitable for almost any kind of clothing.

The depression caused one crisis after another in the state's economic affairs in 1931, and Sterling was forced to take a number of unpopular measures. Many voters became discontented and felt that a change in leadership might improve their situation. Walter Sterling managed his father's campaign in 1932; again Sterling's chief opponent was Miriam Ferguson.

Realizing that depression fear and lack of understanding of her husband's accomplishments in office threatened his chances for reelection, Maud went on the campaign trail for him. She traveled extensively throughout the state, making speeches and winning friends and votes for Sterling. Former Governor Moody and other prominent Texans also campaigned diligently for Sterling, but in the second primary Miriam Ferguson beat him by the small margin of 3,798 votes out of a total of almost a million.

Supporters of Sterling questioned the count and tried to prevent Mrs. Ferguson's name from appearing on the general election ballot in November, but they did not succeed.

The Sterlings lost not only the election, but also personal fortune. The cause was a combination of the depression and Sterling's inability to look after his own business interests while he was minding the state's affairs. Gone were their vast real estate holdings, their bank, their ranch, and their newspaper, plus almost all of their cash.

Probably because of hard times, the Sterlings' daughter, Norma, was married quietly with little publicity and no fanfare. Her engagement to Cleo C. Miller of Corsicana was announced on December 11. No parties were given for her, and on December 18 she was privately married before an improvised altar in a downstairs mansion parlor.

Christmas of 1932 was brightened for Maud by a gift presented to her by the women of Austin. It was a silver tray inscribed with her name and a legend stating that it was given in appreciation of her "dauntless courage, clear thinking, mental and spiritual sincerity, generous hospitality, and her unfailing charity of word, thought, and deed."

Bitterly disappointed over his defeat, Sterling broke tradition by not attending the inauguration of Miriam Ferguson. Gossip spread that Maud's servants "refused" to serve the conventional hot lunch for the incoming Governor and her family. Maud heatedly denied the rumor and stated firmly that her servants never refused to do anything she asked of them and that a hot meal would be left for the Fergusons.

Ross and Maud Sterling were both fifty-seven when they moved back to Miramar, which was the only property salvaged from the wreck of their personal fortunes. Sterling told reporters, "When I became Governor, I was well-to-do, and now I return to the ranks of the poor from which I sprang."

He had, however, no intention of staying in those ranks. Deciding to try to recoup his fortune in the area where he had originally started them, he began laying the groundwork for another oil company. Since he lacked the necessary money to pay the state charter fee, Maud gave him her last $100 Liberty Bond. The Sterling Oil and Refining Company was successful, and eventually Sterling became the head of other major businesses, including the American Maid Flour Company, The Ross Sterling Investment Company, and the Houston National Bank. The Sterlings were back in the ranks of the well-to-do.

During the twelve years between their departure from the mansion in 1933 and the year 1945, the Sterlings lived at Miramar, where Maud continued to pursue her hobbies of fishing, needlework, sports, gardening and enjoying her grandchildren.

In 1945 the Sterlings gave Miramar to the Houston Optimist Club to be used as a home for underprivileged boys. They moved to Houston, settling in a comfortable home on West Lane. Their activities included working with the Y.M.C.A., donating to various organizations, including several large sums to Texas Christian University, and active memberships in the Lakeside Country Club and Trinity Episcopal Church. Their favorite way to pass a quiet evening at home was to play dominoes together or with old friends.

In September of 1948 the Sterlings took a trip to Fort Worth, where they planned to combine business and a visit to Mildred and her family. Soon after their arrival, Sterling suffered a stroke and was taken to a Fort Worth hospital. There he lay paralyzed for six months while Maud constantly watched over him and comforted him. On March 25, 1949, he suffered a cerebral hemorrhage and died.

Maud brought his body back to Houston, where their longtime friend, Bishop Clinton S. Quinn, asked if he could officiate at the funeral service in Christ Episcopal Church. Burial was in the family plot in Glenwood Cemetery in Houston. Because Sterling had been one of the founders of the Shrine Crippled Children's Hospital, Maud requested that instead of flowers, donations be sent to the fund for crippled children maintained by the Arabic Temple of the Shrine.

After her husband's death, Maud continued to live in Houston where she was an active member of Trinity Episcopal Church and of the Alexander Love Chapter of the Daughters of the American Revolution. Her eight grandchildren presented her with a total of fourteen great-grandchildren. Her health remained good until she was well into her eighties.

In the early spring of 1963, she became ill and was taken to Hermann Hospital. (Sterling had served on the board of directors of the hospital for a number of years.) She remained hospitalized until her death on March 7; then Maud was buried beside her husband in Glenwood Cemetery. The "quiet somebody" had gone to a deserved rest after a busy life spent in fulfilling her desire to "make every day count for something."

Joe Betsy Miller Allred

In a modest frame house in Wichita Falls lives a gentle piano teacher who takes delight in sharing with her friends prize roses from her well-kept flower beds. The house belongs to her ninety-three-year-old mother, with whom she has lived for fifteen years. The two women begin each morning with daily devotionals, reading from the Bible and two devotional books; then each starts a busy routine. The energetic mother cooks, washes, irons, and sews, while the daughter cleans the house and takes care of the yard, in addition to giving piano lessons to twenty-six pupils throughout the week.

As she goes about her busy round of duties, the daughter's thoughts sometimes turn back forty years to the days she spent as First Lady of Texas. For Joe Betsy Miller Allred those days are a vivid memory, and returning to live in Wichita Falls has brought her life full circle from the days of her childhood.

Born in Altus, Oklahoma, on October 15, 1905, the daughter of Daisie Kimberlin and Claude Miller, she was named Josephine Elizabeth, after her two grandmothers. But the name was quickly and permanently shortened to Joe Betsy.

She was the only girl in the family — a middle child between an older and a younger brother — and Joe Betsy's early childhood was normal, except for her ardent interest in music.

Her mother played the piano, and on his trips to New York (in connection with his ladies' ready-to-wear business) her father would often bring back the sheet music for numbers from Broadway hits. Joe Betsy was fascinated by the songs and eagerly tried to play them herself. Recognizing his daughter's talent, Mr. Miller bought her a Steinway grand when she was five. When she was nine, she began studying music formally, and it has remained a lifelong passion.

In 1916 Joe Betsy's father decided to move his business to Wichita Falls, Texas. She attended Wichita Falls High School, and was president of the Girls' Club for two years. Her parents sent her to Chicago to study at the Glenn Dillard Gunn School of Music and to New York City to study with Arthur Friedheim during one summer. After these inspiring experiences, Joe Betsy decided to enroll in Southern Methodist University to work toward a degree that would allow her to use her musical talent in a practical way.

While she had been in the north, an energetic young lawyer with a brand new degree joined the law firm of Martin and Oneal in Wichita Falls. He was Jimmie Allred from Bowie, Texas, one of nine children of Renne and Mary Allred. Early in life he had learned to work at such jobs as soda pop bottler, shoeshine boy, and newsboy. He had attended Rice Institute on a scholarship and had served in the United States Navy during World War I. Now he was launching his career as a lawyer in Wichita Falls, just as Joe Betsy was preparing to go off to college in Dallas. Jimmie Allred was good at meeting challenges, though, and distance only added spice to his courtship. As often as they could, he and Joe Betsy attended shows like "Blossom Time" or went to dances.

He had many excuses to travel to Dallas as his career began to accelerate spectacularly. While he was still under twenty-five, Allred became Assistant District Attorney; then Governor Pat Neff appointed him District Attorney of the

Thirtieth Judicial District of Texas. In this office he earned a reputation as a strong opponent of the resurgent Ku Klux Klan.

When he ran unsuccessfully for Attorney General of Texas in 1926, some frivolous questions were raised as to his qualifications. He was accused of being a West Texan, too young for state office, and a bachelor. He replied that his birth occurred in West Texas because his mother was there at the time, he was growing older, and he was working toward ending his bachelorhood.

Allred successfully removed the third count against him on June 20, 1927, by marrying Joe Betsy, who only three weeks earlier had graduated from Southern Methodist University with a major in teaching public school music. The bride loved plants and flowers, and the Miller living room was turned into a flower garden for the occasion. Baskets of daisies and banks of smilax filled the room; the vows were solemnized under an arch of smilax, centered with a wedding bell of shasta daisies and pink roses. Joe Betsy's gown was of white duchess satin trimmed with lace and seed pearls, and she carried white rosebuds and lilies of the valley. The Reverend Mr. Leslie Miller, pastor of Grace Methodist Church of Wichita Falls, read the vows. After a reception, the couple left for a three-week honeymoon in California.

During the first year of their marriage, Joe Betsy got some teaching experience by doing substitute work in the public schools of Wichita Falls. The next year their first son, James V., Jr., was born two days before Christmas.

Allred decided to make a second try for Attorney General in 1930. This time he was successful, and Joe Betsy packed the household for the move to Austin. An exciting thirty years would pass before she would return to live in her hometown.

In the capital the family settled in a modest white painted house on West 32nd Street. The outside was planted with shrubs and flowers; and inside, Joe Betsy's grand piano dominated the living room. Two days before Thanksgiving of 1933 a second son, William David, arrived to join the family.

The serenity of their home life contrasted with the tumult of Allred's two terms as Attorney General, during which he filed numerous antitrust suits and waged a vigorous war against crime. Joe Betsy was proud when her dynamic husband was given the title "Outstanding Young Man in America" by the National Jaycees in 1934.

In that year, with her blessing, he also announced his candidacy for Governor, and after a close primary race against Tom Hunter, a Wichita Falls oil man, won the general election easily. January 15, 1935, dawned as a typical mid-Texas foggy winter morning. But before the inaugural ceremonies began on the Capitol steps at noon, a brisk breeze had swept away the mist and the sun shone brightly on the crowd of 10,000 persons who watched every move of their new First Family. The watchers applauded enthusiastically when the newly installed Governor departed from his formal address to introduce his pretty wife and handsome sons. The family made a harmonious picture. Joe Betsy wore a blue boucle suit that had been knitted by two of her cousins in Wichita Falls; on it was pinned a white gardenia corsage. Her hat was an off-the-face navy blue taffeta, and she carried navy blue accessories. Five-year-old Jimmie, Jr. was dressed in navy blue, fourteen-month-old David in baby blue, and the Governor wore a bright blue tie with his gray wool suit.

The ceremony ended at one o'clock, and the Allreds returned to the mansion for lunch, but they found the cupboard was bare. Outgoing Governor Miriam Ferguson had not left the semi-traditional hot meal for the incoming Governor's family, so an aide hastily arranged a dinner for the Allred family at a downtown hotel.

Mrs. Ferguson did follow another custom, which was to leave a Bible open at a marked verse on the Governor's desk. The passage she had marked was from Jeremiah:

And the proud shall stumble and fall and none shall raise him up; and I will kindle a fire in his cities, and it shall devour all round about him.

Another verse from Ecclesiastes was marked in pencil. It

read:

> Woe to Thee, O Lord, when thy king is a child thy princes eat in the morning.

The inaugural ball was held in four ballrooms in order to accommodate the largest crowd ever to attend the traditional celebration in Austin. When the gown that Joe Betsy had ordered for the occasion failed to arrive on time, she calmly went to a downtown store and selected another one of peach blow silk maline over taffeta. The old-fashioned dress was most becoming to the demure twenty-nine-year-old First Lady. She carried an arm bouquet of roses whose salmon and rose tones shaded into the pastel tint of her dress.

Both of the Allreds had a strong appreciation of the historical associations of the aging Executive Mansion, and they moved into it with mixed feelings of awe and inspiration. The second youngest Governor ever to be elected remarked:

> It is not hard to conjure up the vision of the great Jim Hogg treading his massive way up and down the room before the open fireplace. Through the haze of cigar smoke, the shadowy figure of the immortal Houston can be visioned . . . .

And the new First Lady told a reporter, "If I had my choice between being the first Governor's wife to live in a new mansion and the last to live in this old house, I'd certainly choose to be right where I am."

The mansion soon seemed like home to the family, especially after Jimmie Junior's tricycle and his Russian wolf hound, Ranger, were moved in, and Joe Betsy's grand piano was installed in her bedroom. She found herself lucky enough to have a splendid cook, Clarence Chance, from the penitentiary in Huntsville, to which he had been sentenced for murder. Before his conviction, he had been chef of a Dallas Country Club. The houseboy, likewise a trusty, kept the eleven rooms of the mansion clean and also served the meals in the family dining room three times a day. In addition, there was a yardman to take care of the greenhouse and grounds. David's and Jimmie's nurse was Margaret Manz, and the Texas Ranger guide assigned to the mansion helped her keep up with two active little boys.

Spurred by her deep interest in history, Joe Betsy searched long and hard to discover any original furnishings that might have been relegated to the basements or attics by other mistresses of the mansion. But she had little success, which is not surprising when one remembers that from the very first, little money had ever been allocated for buying durable furniture for the house. She did uncover in the basement of the Capitol a handsome early Victorian walnut sideboard with carved fish and duck on the doors, which she had placed in the service hall of the mansion. In the servants' quarters she found a large, round mirror with an ornate oak frame which she had restored and hung over the fireplace in the Governor's bedroom. The old "haunted" room she turned into her study, calling it the "studio photograph gallery" because in it she assembled photographs of her husband that connected him with significant events and people of his time. In this room she dictated letters to her secretary, who also helped her plan the decorations and refreshments for the numerous official social functions and other entertainments. The secretary and Joe Betsy worked together to keep the rooms of the mansion filled with the fresh flowers that the First Lady loved.

Local organizations were permitted to entertain in the Governor's Mansion. Church circles, sorority groups, the University Women's Club, the Daughters of the American Revolution, the United Daughters of the Confederacy, the Girl Scouts, the University of Texas football team and their dates — all enjoyed the hospitality of the house. The Austin Symphony Society was organized in the mansion.

Dinners and receptions for members of the Legislature were frequent during the Allreds' tenure. Too, many Governors and their wives from other states were entertained. The night that Governor and Mrs. Paul McNutt of Indiana came to dinner, a girl had been hired to come from the Stephen F. Austin Hotel to help serve. After she slipped and spilled a bowl of rice and a bowl of gravy all over the buffet, she ran out the back door and Joe Betsy never saw her again.

The chef opened some canned corn to fill in for the spilled food, and the meal was a success.

Vice President and Mrs. John Nance Garner were overnight guests, as were the Honorable Albert Sydney Burleson (United States Postmaster) and Houston financier Jesse Jones and his wife. When Will Rogers traveled to Austin to appear at Gregory Gymnasium, he came to the mansion for dinner. He brought the children a little dog in a shoe box; it was promptly named Will Rogers. The humorist kept the dinner guests laughing and paid a great deal of attention to David and Jimmie, Jr., which pleased their parents immensely.

Joe Betsy planned two weddings while she was First Lady. The first was for her husband's sister, Hazel Allred, who married William Bayard Stokes, Jr., of Gladewater in March of 1935. The ceremony was held before an improvised altar covered with palms and smilax and set in the drawing room. In front of it were calla lilies and Talisman roses; white tapers in seven-branched candelabra lighted the room. Before the wedding, a solo was sung by a family friend, accompanied by Mrs. Gordon Wilcox, whose mother had been a mansion bride herself when she was married during the tenure of her parents, the Irelands. A young nephew of the bride served as ringbearer, wearing the same satin suit and carrying the same ring-pillow used in the wedding of the Governor and Joe Betsy.

Joe Betsy played the wedding march, as she did for the second wedding that occurred during her occupancy of the mansion. In the second, her cousin, Helen Ince (one of the two relatives who helped knit her inaugural suit), married Jimmie Blundell. Future Governor John Connally served as best man on this occasion.

Another event of importance to the new First Lady occurred in March of 1935 when her mother, Mrs. Claude Miller, was honored as the most distinguished mother-in-law in Texas. The celebration was in Amarillo, and the Allreds flew to it. Newspapers pictured the couple standing by a Bowen Air Lines' new Vultee plane which they proudly announced cut the time from Austin to Fort Worth down to "about an hour."

In spite of all her official duties, Joe Betsy found time for activities and hobbies that were important to her. The family were members of Central Christian Church, where she taught a girls' Bible class, and she saw to it that they never missed attending weekly services when they were in Austin, except for illness.

She also managed, with her husband's encouragement, to practice daily on the piano, and she tried her hand at composing. One of her achievements was to set to music a poem, "Farewell to My Country," which Davy Crockett wrote as a young man. The words and music capture the poignancy of the young man's feelings on leaving his mountain home in Tennessee to travel westward seeking adventure.

Another hobby led to rather disagreeable consequences. Joe Betsy was in the habit of riding horseback at Camp Mabry for outdoor exercise, and she continued this practice after she became First Lady. One day her horse ran under a tree and she was knocked to the ground. In addition to being bruised and shaken, she suffered an injury to her sacroiliac from which she has never fully recovered.

An insight into the personality that won friends wherever she traveled is given by an incident that happened shortly after her injury. Instead of excusing herself, she responded graciously to an impromptu request by the toastmaster at a Knights of Columbus banquet in Taylor, and played the piano for four hundred delighted guests.

The Allreds' first Christmas in the mansion was a hectic one — twenty-five relatives and in-laws, including the parents of both, were invited to a big, old-fashioned mid-day dinner. A huge, lighted tree was set up in the library, and the socks and stockings of Jimmie, Jr., David, and numerous young cousins were hung by the fireplace. It had been four years since there were small children living in the Governor's Mansion, and the public delighted in any news or pictures of the enchanting young Allreds. Many newspapers carried stories about their first Christmas there.

Texas celebrated its Centennial in 1936, and the Allreds provided enthusiastic leadership for the birthday celebration. The attractive couple took pleasure in traveling far and wide to acquaint the world with the greatness of their state, and crowds everywhere responded to their appearances with equal pleasure. Joe Betsy's only worry was in leaving the children while they were at an impressionable age, but she tried to make up for their absences by planning as many quiet family evenings "at home" as possible. Of course, there was much extra entertaining to be done in connection with the Centennial.

Besides the Centennial trips, there were other important trips to make. Allred was a strong backer of Franklin D. Roosevelt, so when Vice President and Mrs. John Nance Garner gave a banquet and reception honoring the President and Mrs. Roosevelt in Washington, D.C., the Allreds flew to the nation's capital. All members of Congress and their wives were present. Wearing a red velvet evening gown, Joe Betsy sat between Henry Wallace and Senator Hugh McNary and had a "marvelous" evening.

On another occasion, the Allreds were guests of the Roosevelts at a dinner at the White House, and Joe Betsy sat beside Chief Justice Harlan Stone of the Supreme Court. Artichokes, a vegetable known to few Texans in those days, were served. Being at a loss as to how to approach the strange food, Joe Betsy carefully watched how the President ate his before she attempted to tackle hers.

In the early spring of 1937 Joe Betsy took time out from her busy schedule to give birth to the Allreds' third son. He was born on March 17, 1937, in the Sam Houston bed, and was appropriately named Sam Houston Allred. A few days later she was entertaining Mrs. Franklin Roosevelt as a guest at the mansion.

By August Joe Betsy was again traveling with her husband on another good will tour — this time on a fifteen-day visit to Mexico. Jimmie, Jr. and Joe Betsy's mother were among those accompanying the Allreds. The vice president of the Missouri-Pacific Railraod loaned them his private car for the trip through Texas, and their traveling in Mexico was done in the luxurious private car of the Mexican presidential train. They spent about a week at the Embassy in Mexico City. (Joe Betsy noted that it was where Anne Morrow and Charles Lindbergh courted.) President and Mrs. Cárdenas entertained them royally, and each city where they stopped provided banquets, orchestras, opera performances, and other elaborate celebrations. Joe Betsy was showered with flowers at each stop, and numerous gifts were presented to the visiting Texans by various groups. A large round flower-patterned silver tray on display in the mansion is a memento of this trip.

Another memorable trip was made by the Allreds when they accompanied President and Mrs. Roosevelt on a four-day train campaign tour across the state. The Roosevelts had a private coach on the rear of the train, and the Allreds had an elegant stateroom. At each city they were elaborately entertained.

The former First Lady takes pride in recalling some of the lasting contributions her energetic husband made to the people of Texas. Among his accomplishments were urging through the Legislature constitutional amendments to authorize old age pensions, teachers' retirement, and workmen's compensation for state employees and others; setting up a Board of Pardons and Paroles; instituting prison reforms; combining the Texas Rangers and the Highway Patrol; putting an end to parimutuel betting in the state. He named the first woman member, Judge Sarah T. Hughes of Dallas, to the Texas judiciary. And he encouraged and counseled other rising young men just entering politics, such as Lyndon B. Johnson and Ralph Yarborough. Also during his administration salaries of state officials were raised, including a long overdue hike in the Governor's salary from $4,000 to $12,000.

As Allred's second term drew to a close, Roosevelt

appointed him a Federal Judge in the district that included Houston. Friends of the Allreds gave them an appreciation dinner before they left Austin. Joe Betsy made several trips between Austin and Houston to supervise the moving of their personal belongings (of which the largest was her piano), to attend the inaugural ceremonies for W. Lee O'Daniel, and to welcome the new first family to the mansion. Joe Betsy arranged to have a delicious hot lunch waiting for them.

For the next eleven years the Allreds lived in the Houston area. At first they occupied a large, colonial home on Emerson. Then they built their own brick home on a three-acre tract in suburban Bellaire. Here they had chickens, two horses, a truck garden, and many fruit trees. Joe Betsy had 150 rose bushes and beautiful perennial plants of every description. Allred's father, whom they all called "Granddad," lived with them and was the gardener. They were all proud when one year they received the award for having the prettiest yard in Bellaire.

The three boys loved Houston and the warm, congenial family life they enjoyed there. Each was assigned chores to do: Jimmie, Jr. fed the chickens; he and David took turns mowing the lawn, and Sam Houston helped de-weed flower beds. Joe Betsy was den mother for the Scout troops of each of them. Sam Houston showed musical talent and studied piano; he practiced every day — like his mother. The family became active members of the First Christian Church where Allred taught the Men's Bible Class and served as an elder.

When Allred was assigned to be Federal Judge for the Corpus Christi, Brownsville, and Laredo district, in 1949, the Allreds had to sell their beloved home in Bellaire. Again in Corpus Christi they were active in the First Christian Church, where Allred taught the Young Couples Bible Class, and Joe Betsy served wherever she was needed.

While they were in Corpus Christi, Jimmie, Jr. became a cargo pilot for an airline in South America. He married Barbara Mathis of Dallas, and on July 3, 1956, the Allreds became the grandparents of Lisa Fa.

In 1959, Joe Betsy suffered two tragedies. In January her father died; and on September 24, 1959, during a court session at Laredo, her husband suffered a heart attack and died. Joe Betsy brought his body back to Wichita Falls, where he is buried in Riverside Cemetery.

At this time David was working on his master's degree in journalism at Columbia University in New York City, and Sam Houston was completing his senior year at Southern Methodist University. Joe Betsy remained another year in Corpus Christi, and then sold the house and moved to Wichita Falls to live with her mother, Mrs. Claude Miller, who owned her own home on a three-acre tract.

Joe Betsy obtained a position as a teacher in the City View Elementary School, next door to her mother's home, and continued to teach there for eleven years — until she reached the retirement age of sixty-five. She taught fifth grade at first, but later was made teacher of all music classes in the school of over 900 students. As a bit of serendipity for her students, she made Texas history come alive by describing life in the Governor's Mansion. For a year after her retirement, she worked as a substitute teacher in the school. She was made a life member of the Parent-Teacher Association and is a member of the Retired Teachers Association.

In 1961 David married Patricia Moyer and settled in Wichita Falls, where he was a reporter for the Wichita Falls *Daily Times*. Since then he has been a Representative in the State Legislature for four terms. His marriage resulted in three more grandchildren for Joe Betsy — Becky, now fourteen, Stephen, twelve, and Jimmie, six.

In April of 1965 Joe Betsy lost her oldest son when Jimmie, Jr., was killed in a plane crash in Paraguay.

Sam Houston married Mary Sue Ogg and lives in Corpus Christi, where he works for a television station and continues his interest in music by giving occasional concerts, at which he plays and sings.

Now, as always, Joe Betsy takes an active part in the work of her church, which is Faith Village Church of Christ, where she teaches in the Primary Department. She belongs to the Musicians Club and to the Daughters of the American Revolution, and is an honorary member of the Century Club, a literary group.

Much of her time is spent in keeping in close touch with the members of her family. Two of her mother's sisters spend quite a bit of time in Wichita Falls, and Joe Betsy and her mother spend a part of every summer in Wenatchee, Washington, at the home of Joe Betsy's brother in the heart of a forty-acre apple orchard. When they are in Wichita Falls, David's family comes over every Sunday for dinner, for which Mrs. Miller makes and bakes delicious rolls.

Music, flowers, religion, family, and friends continue to fill and enrich Joe Betsy's life, as they always have. When she served the state as its First Lady, one hundred years had passed since the indomitable Hannah Burnet had followed her husband and the peripatetic government of the newly formed Republic of Texas from tent to shanty to shack by horseback and wagon. But, although Joe Betsy Allred traveled by train and plane and lived in an elegant "mansion," the two women had many similar qualities. Each filled her role with dignity and credit; each had the self-discipline and poise to meet every situation that confronted her; and each had a deep religious faith that guided her actions and showed in her loving kindness toward her fellow men.

32.

First Ladies

from 1939 to 1975

There have been eight First Ladies since Texas completed the first one hundred years. Until enough time has passed to gain a deeper perspective on their lives and contributions, they rank as contemporary rather than historic. Their turn will come after the second one hundred years. But to omit them from a survey of First Ladies would be an injustice, for each in her own way has served the people of Texas and left her mark upon the state. This final chapter, therefore, contains a brief summary of the lives and accomplishments of these most recent mistresses of the Governor's Mansion of Texas.

MERLE ESTELLE BUTCHER O'DANIEL
(Mrs. Wilbert Lee O'Daniel)

When W. Lee O'Daniel decided to quit selling flour in order to try to sell himself to the citizens of Texas as their choice for Governor, he had an able campaign manager. His wife, Merle Butcher O'Daniel, set up her typewriter on the dining table of their home in Fort Worth and prepared to put her business school training to good use. Before the campaign was over, their home headquarters had become so filled with desks, records, radio equipment, typewriters, filing cabinets, boxes of papers of every description, and mementos from supporters that the O'Daniels literally were forced out of it. They could either eat standing up in the kitchen or go out to nearby cafes.

The campaign was very much a family affair with Merle's mother serving as her first assistant. The O'Daniel children — Pat, Mike, and Molly — joined their father as members of his famous Lightcrust Doughboys Band, which drew crowds of 10,000 and 20,000 as it roamed across the state playing songs that O'Daniel composed, and making "Pass the biscuits, Pappy" a household slogan. O'Daniel's platform, the Ten Commandments and the Golden Rule, pleased a majority of the voters, who enthusiastically swept him into office.

January 17, 1939, was a holiday for school children all over Texas, of whom nearly 10,000 had a part in the day's activities. A spectacular five-hour inauguration was held in the University of Texas Memorial Stadium. A central control booth with batteries of telephones and an elaborate communications network to various points in, under, and around the stadium helped to keep the events running smoothly. They included, besides the inaugural ceremony itself, the presentation of forty high school and college bands, a pageant entitled "The American Way of Life" in which 200 young people took part, and mass singing.

In line with O'Daniel's strong stand urging Texans to use products made in their own state, the family was dressed in materials made by textile students at Texas Technological University in Lubbock. Merle's suit was gray wool with a powder blue pin stripe, her wrap a silver gray fox scarf, and her black straw hat had three blue pom poms on it that matched her blue eyes. At forty-one, she was tall and slender with wavy hair just beginning to turn gray.

That evening there was street dancing in addition to the three receptions — one at Gregory Gymnasium and two at downtown hotels. For the evening affairs O'Daniel continued his "plain citizen" role by wearing a dark suit instead of formal clothes, but Merle wore a pink lace and marquisette gown purchased in Dallas. The climax of the day's celebrations was a gigantic fireworks exhibition that turned the night into day.

The O'Daniels brought into the Executive Mansion a few cherished items such as the Edison phonograph that had been her husband's first Christmas gift to Merle, the grandfather clock that had been his gift on their second Christmas together, and the small organ used on his radio programs. They also moved in their twelve-year-old canary and Merle's pet goldfish, while out on the lawn they tethered a huge mountain goat, a gift from an admirer.

The three young O'Daniels were enrolled in the University of Texas, and the stately old mansion often rocked with the noise of their parties and music. Along with the hillbilly band and other members of the family, Merle participated in the Sunday morning broadcasts from a front room of the Governor's Mansion that were a regular feature of the O'Daniel administrations.

The first night entertainment that Merle arranged was a reception for legislators and their wives. Open houses or "teas" were held every Wednesday from three to five, and the women of Austin and the surrounding areas flocked to meet the new First Lady. School children were given a special invitation to visit the mansion on weekdays and Saturdays.

Merle used her business know-how in running the mansion, setting up a budget and shopping systematically. She had the kitchen modernized and renovated so that it was more efficient. Outside, she had some unused buildings behind the house torn down and replaced with a rose garden.

The O'Daniels belonged to the Central Christian Church in Austin, but on many Sundays they continued a custom begun while living in Fort Worth. During the Sunday broadcast, O'Daniel would announce to his listeners which church in which small town the O'Daniel family would visit that morning. Then the whole family would drive to the chosen small town in the Austin vicinity and attend services — along with an overflowing crowd. After the minister had recovered from the shock of having the Governor and his family and probably the largest crowd ever in his church, he would issue a warm welcome and praise the O'Daniels for remaining members of the "common folk."

Another custom the O'Daniels followed while they were in residence was to take into the mansion each Christmas two orphans — from the Corsicana Home and the Waco Home.

In spite of problems with the Legislature (which made it

impossible for him to get passed social security measures which he had promised) O'Daniel was reelected to a second term by a large majority. Again the inauguration ceremonies were memorable. Twenty thousand persons were served barbecue on the front lawn of the mansion. Employees from thirteen state departments were called upon to serve 19,000 pounds of barbecue, including beef, sheep, and a buffalo shot by the Governor himself; 1,000 pounds of potato salad; 1,300 pounds of onions; 1,300 pickles; 3,500 loaves of bread; 32,000 cups of coffee; and 25,000 grapefruit. Lemonade made from 6,000 lemons and 1,000 pounds of sugar was also available. After they had eaten, the guests danced in the roped-off street in front of the mansion. Merle and Molly served as hostesses, and when it was over Merle wearily looked out over the lawn that was a shambles of crumpled paper cups, soggy paper plates, and assorted bits of food.

Shortly after O'Daniel's second inauguration, Texans were shocked by the sudden death of their beloved United States Senator, Morris Sheppard. O'Daniel appointed the Houston's aged son, Andrew Jackson Houston, to the office until a special election could be held on June 28, 1941. And with the help of his band and his family he began to campaign for the office himself.

While they were in the midst of the campaign, Molly, a nineteen-year-old junior at the University of Texas, announced her engagement to Jack D. Wrather, Jr. of Tyler, Texas. Molly and Jack had met at the University, and Jack was now in the oil business with his father. So, along with her regular duties as First Lady and her campaigning chores, Merle began to plan an O'Daniel-size wedding for the only daughter of the household. When O'Daniel defeated Lyndon Johnson to win the special election, Molly's wedding date was set for July 31 — just four days before her father was scheduled to take his Senate seat.

In contrast to the quiet, private marriage of Norma Sterling that had passed almost unnoticed by the news media, Molly O'Daniel's wedding was reported in minute detail to an eager public. A series of pre-nuptial parties was concluded with a rehearsal dinner given by the O'Daniels at the Austin Country Club. Platforms, canopies and elaborate decorations which included yards and yards of white satin ribbon, huge bouquets of flowers and ferns, tall silver candelabra, and dozens of white candles were set up. Gifts poured into the mansion in such profusion that keeping track of them became almost impossible. On his weekly radio talk, the Governor invited all Texans to the wedding, and about 25,000 did come.

Loudspeakers broadcast the wedding ceremony to the crowd gathered on the lawn. In addition to the 150-pound four-tiered cake served to friends and guests inside the mansion, 1,000 pounds of wedding cake were fed to the throng congregated outside the building to catch a glimpse of the bride and groom and other members of the First Family. The bride wore the traditional white satin gown and carried orchids, and Merle wore a marquisette dress of heavenly blue. All in all, the farewell performance of the O'Daniels at the mansion was as dramatic as their entrance had been.

When World War II began, Merle became involved in defense work in Washington, D.C. She is credited with organizing the Senate wives as an auxiliary to the American Red Cross. But when her husband entered his fourth campaign for public office in 1942, running against former Governors Moody and Allred for his Senate seat, Merle dropped everything else to help him. She rented a big, roomy onetime mansion in Fort Worth to serve as campaign headquarters.

The campaign was bitter. The O'Daniels felt that the press and radio had been unfair in their reporting and editorializing. "The newspapers and radio drew our blood," Merle said. On election night O'Daniel's campaign headquarters exuded a mood of grim satisfaction as it became apparent that they had won.

From this time on, the O'Daniel style became more subdued. For his six-year term they lived in Washington, D.C. When he decided not to seek reelection, the O'Daniels returned to Fort Worth in 1949 to live quietly while he served as president of the W. Lee O'Daniel Insurance Company. He later made a couple of unsuccessful attempts to win back his Senate seat.

After O'Daniel's death, Merle moved to Dallas, where she was an active member of the Christian Church and of the Eastern Star. Over the years she acquired seven grandchildren and eight great-grandchildren. At the time of her death in 1972 at seventy-four, she was living in the Dallas Convalescent Center.

MRS. BLANCH FAY WRIGHT STEVENSON
(Mrs. Coke Robert Stevenson)

MRS. EDITH WILL SCOTT STEVENSON
(Mrs. Coke Robert Stevenson, Jr.)

When Governor W. Lee O'Daniel resigned to become a United States Senator, Lt. Governor Coke Stevenson moved up to become the state's chief executive. He was sworn into office on August 8, 1941, in a ceremony held in the House of Representatives Chamber. After the dignitaries had gathered on the platform, hospital attendants wheeled in a stretcher bearing the new First Lady, exquisitely dressed in black crepe with an orchid corsage on the shoulder, wearing a small hat with a jaunty bluebird perched on it. There was hardly a dry eye in the chamber as she was lifted into a velvet draped wheelchair, which was placed beside her husband. Smiling and waving, she acknowledged the applause of the audience, which rose to cheer the courage of "Miss Fay."

Everyone in the room knew that at best Fay Stevenson had only a few months to live before her tormented body yielded to cancer. Stevenson had urged that there be no formal ceremony; he wanted to take the oath of office in his wife's hospital room, but Fay quickly vetoed that idea. She wanted her husband to have the public honors that went with the office — and as she had always been, she would be beside him.

Popular, outgoing Fay Wright Stevenson had a will as strong as the rocks in her native Hill Country of Texas. Her father was a physician and rancher in Junction, and Fay had attended public schools there and in Kerrville. After graduating from high school at sixteen, she married Coke Stevenson, a hard-working young bank cashier, who had been born in a log cabin. To forestall any parental objections to their marrying, Fay and Coke arranged for the minister to read the ceremony on Christmas Eve of 1912 in the vestibule of the First Methodist Church in Junction, while their families, unaware of the couple's intentions, attended a Christmas tree celebration inside the church.

The newlyweds solved their housing problem by buying two old houses, wrecking them, and using the timber to build a home of their own. They did the work themselves, hammering and sawing away after Coke came home from the bank in the evening. In December of 1913 their only child, Coke, Jr., was born, and their lives took on a new dimension. Both were active in community affairs and in the Methodist church. Fay was deeply interested in Eastern Star work, and over the years she served in many offices of that organization, including some of the highest state positions.

Stevenson studied law and eventually became a successful lawyer and County Judge. In all of his campaigns Fay was his active partner. She was a good public speaker, and when it came to the legwork, she would take one side of the street while he took the other, shaking hands and distributing cards.

They acquired a ranch on the banks of the South Llano River, seventeen miles from Junction. When the frame house on it burned down, Fay drew plans for a big rock house to replace it. Again, they did much of the work themselves. Fay designed stair rails, window adornments, and balcony rails in wrought iron. At her direction, artists combined Texas cowhorns carved in the shape of birds with copper bowls and iron framework to form unique light fixtures. For her husband's many gavels, pipes, and other trophies, she designed an ingenious wrought-iron case that swung back on its hinges, leaving a doorway between the kitchen and high-ceilinged living room. She collected rocks and built tables, seats, and bird baths from them, often mixing the cement herself.

The years while Coke, Jr. was growing up were happy, active ones for the family, who enjoyed horseback riding, fishing, and hunting together. When Stevenson was elected to the House of Representatives and then Speaker, they left their beloved ranch home to live in the Speaker's apartments in the Capitol. A happy event during this time was the marriage of Coke, Jr. to Edith Will Scott; in Scottie the Stevensons acquired the daughter they had never had.

Gregarious Fay made scores of friends for her husband and was credited with winning many votes for him when he ran for Lieutenant Governor on the ticket with W. Lee O'Daniel. Even after she became a victim of cancer and had to spend much time in bed, she continued to welcome cheerfully the many callers who came to see her husband on business. When forced to give up the vigorous sports she loved, she kept busy at hobbies of painting and needlework.

By the time she became First Lady, she was so feeble that the Green Room downstairs in the mansion was converted into her bedroom and a hospital bed installed. The adjoining half bath between the State Dining Room and the Green Room, and the back elevator were also added at this time for her convenience. Stevenson's trips were planned so that he could return home to her each evening. As she became progressively worse, her physician-brother, Dr. Carlton Wright of Dallas, came to take care of her. In November of 1941, a long series of blood transfusions was begun, during which her husband and son gave blood in a futile effort to build up her resistance.

Fay was aware, as were all of her family and friends, that Christmas of 1941 would be her last one. But in spite of this knowledge and of her pain, she refused to let it be gloomy. When the Longhorn band and singers from the University of Texas serenaded the family with carols from the mansion lawn, she had the carolers called in. After they had gathered around her bed, she asked them to sing again "Silent Night." When they finished, she told them, "You've made this the happiest Christmas of my life."

Death released Fay Stevenson from her suffering on Saturday, January 3, 1942. The next day a funeral cortege, escorted by state highway patrolmen, traveled for four hours from Austin to Junction, where simple services were held in the Methodist church that had been built on the same site as the one in which she had been married twenty-nine years earlier. The highest honors and tributes were paid her by the state and by the thousands of friends she had made as her husband's chief assistant. She was one of the very few women whose portraits have been hung in the Senate chamber in the Capitol Building.

After Fay's death, Coke, Jr.'s wife, Scottie, became acting First Lady for her father-in-law; along with her two daughters, Scottie Gayle and Linda, she moved into the mansion. Coke, Jr., a rancher and attorney like his father, joined the army to serve in World War II.

Scottie was efficient in her role, although, because of Fay's death and wartime restrictions, social life was restrained and many traditional entertainments were omitted. She found the neighborhood around the mansion an isolated one for her small daughters. Since there were no other children living in the downtown area, one of her daily problems became the transporting of playmates. The children themselves missed the freedom of their ranch home.

But Scottie had an optimistic nature, a large capacity for enjoying life, and a determination to do a good job. She acted as her own secretary for the voluminous mail that poured into the mansion addressed to her in her capacity as First Lady. She also supervised the redecoration of part of the mansion during her tenure.

Her first party was in the fall of 1942 — a buffet dinner for sixty-five members of the University of Texas football team and their coaches. The centerpiece she designed for the table was a replica of a football field on a board nine feet by four feet on which real grass was growing in real dirt. All through dinner Scottie wondered why the rolls never got to the table; later she discovered the boys were intercepting them at the door to the butler's pantry. At dessert time the players went into the pantry to cut the pies themselves because the serving girl was cutting the pieces too daintily for them!

A more sedate entertainment was the dinner party she arranged for Lord and Lady Halifax of England when they visited Austin. Scottie also was generous in opening the mansion to ladies' clubs and church groups for meetings.

Today Scottie looks back on her years as First Lady as "quite an experience." She learned not to expect too much of people and says that there is something fine about everybody. "If you do your part," she says, "it is easy to get along with all people." Since leaving the mansion, her career has been in being a wife, a mother to her two daughters, and a grandmother to two "fine grandsons."

Coke Stevenson won two full terms as Governor after he moved up to fill O'Daniel's place in 1941. During his administrations, the attention and interests of Texans were largely devoted to World War II; no other state had such a wide range of military activity, and Texas industry and farming broke all production records. In a bitterly contested election in 1948, Stevenson was defeated by Lyndon Johnson for a United States Senate seat. He returned to ranching, and in 1954 married Mrs. Marguerite King Heap, a widow whose first husband was killed in World War II.

MABEL BUCHANAN JESTER MORRISS
(Mrs. Beauford Halbert Jester)

In Texarkana "on the Texas side" lives a former First Lady whose memories of the Governor's Mansion are overcast with sadness, for her husband was the only Governor to die in office. After attending Ward Belmont School in Nashville, Tennessee, and Finch College for Women in New York, Mabel Buchanan married Beauford Jester on June 15, 1921, in her hometown of Texarkana, Arkansas.

Jester was a rising young lawyer with oil interests in Corsicana and a love for playing baseball. He had left Harvard Law School to serve as a captain in World War I, and had been a charter member of the American Legion and a member of the Veterans of Foreign Wars and other veterans' organizations.

After their three children — Barbara, Joan, and Beauford, Jr. — were born, Mabel considered her family and her home to be her career. Unlike her husband, she was not a "joiner" and belonged to only a few clubs, but she did enjoy gardening. Calm and reserved, she took her husband's political progress in stride. After serving on the Railroad Commission for several years, he ran for Governor and was elected in 1946.

Shortly before Jester's election, their oldest daughter, Barbara, married Howard Burris, an army officer, and moved with him to Mitchel Field, Long Island. So only the two younger children moved into the mansion with their parents.

Mabel's staff consisted of a social secretary, a cook, a housemaid, and a laundress. Whenever possible, she liked to do the family's shopping and marketing, but found that the constant round of social duties expected of a First Lady often made this impossible. On rare evenings when state business did not make demands on their time, the family liked to seclude themselves in the Gold Room, where the Governor would play the piano for a while, and they would catch up on their reading. On their twenty-sixth wedding anniversary, Beauford gave Mabel a gold charm bracelet, which she cherished.

Although Mabel found the lack of family life one of the biggest drawbacks to living in the mansion, she did enjoy the interesting people it gave her an opportunity to meet. Among the most memorable ones were Randolph Churchill, journalist son of Winston Churchill, who visited the Jesters while making a lecture tour of the United States, and General Jonathan M. Wainwright, the hero of Bataan in World War II.

The chief improvement made in the mansion during Mabel's time as First Lady was the conversion of the west sleeping porches into a comfortable suite of rooms — a bedroom, sitting room, bath, and a cedar storage closet. She also updated some of the kitchen equipment and added a small kitchen and dinette to the family quarters upstairs to afford them more convenience and privacy.

Jester won the approval of most Texas citizens by his handling of the disaster at Texas City in 1949, when more than four hundred persons were killed and three thousand injured in the explosion of a ship carrying chemicals. The Governor took personal charge of the rescue operations. Other concerns that frequently took him away from home were his battles for states' rights and Texas' tidelands. He made so many trips to Washington, D.C., in behalf of these interests that he became known as the "flyingest" Governor in Texas' history.

In 1948 when he was reelected for a second term, Mabel prepared for another two years of official life, which meant sharing her husband and herself with the people of the state.

During the next six months, she saw even less of him than usual as the Legislature met for the longest regular session in Texas history. When it finally adjourned in July, she helped arrange a party at the lake for her husband's staff on the evening of July 10, 1949. The next day she saw him off on a train trip to Galveston; he was tired but was looking forward to doing some fishing after he had a physical checkup in the coastal city. When a Pullman porter went to the Governor's berth to rouse him the next morning at 7:30, he discovered that the Governor was dead. Sometime during the night he had apparently died of a heart attack.

His body was flown back to the capital in a C-47 escorted by fighter planes that flew fast and low three times over the Capitol before landing at the airfield. Stunned, but composed, Mabel made arrangements for her husband's funeral. After lying in state in the Senate chamber, his body was flown to Corsicana for burial.

Mabel moved back to Texarkana and later married Joshua R. Morriss. She and her second husband have enjoyed traveling, and she makes trips to Washington, D.C., to visit Barbara and to Houston to visit Joan and her family. Beauford, Jr. died some years ago.

Still not a "joiner," Mabel enjoys her garden club and being an active member of the Wadley Hospital Auxiliary. Her advice to incoming First Ladies is to "be prepared to give of your time to state affairs."

MARIALICE SHARY SHIVERS
(Mrs. Allan Shivers)

The first night that Marialice Shivers spent in the Governor's Mansion was something of a nightmare. Her husband was in Mexico, and her mother had come to stay with her. "The funeral home next door had its neon lights going; traffic was buzzing by on all streets and none of us got any sleep," she recalled. Mrs. Shivers found it ". . . like sleeping on a bench in a park," compared to the peacefulness of Sharyland, the twenty-four-room family home in the heart of the citrus orchards of the Rio Grande Valley between Mission and McAllen.

Marialice's father, John H. Shary, was a pioneer and an important developer of the citrus industry in the Valley, where Marialice had spent a happy childhood. Here she acquired a love of rural life; from her grandmother she learned

the art of quilting and today treasures several of her grandmother's quilts. She obtained a B.A. degree in 1932 from Our
Lady of the Lake College in San Antonio, where she studied
voice and history.

In 1935, on a visit to Port Arthur, Marialice was introduced
to lawyer Allan Shivers, who at twenty-seven had become one
of the youngest men ever elected to the Texas Senate. Two
years later on Shivers' birthday (October 5, 1937), he and
Marialice were married at Sharyland. The Shiverses' first son,
John Shary, was born on June 1, 1940.

When the United States entered World War II, Shivers
resigned from the Legislature and enlisted in the army. For
the next four years, Marialice followed the war news intently
as her husband served with distinction in North Africa, Italy,
France, and Germany. He had acquired five battle stars and
the Bronze Star when he was discharged from the army in
1945.

Two important events happened for the Shiverses in 1946 —
a second son, Allan, Jr., was born, and Shivers was elected
Lieutenant Governor. The next year a daughter, Marialice
Sue, joined the family, and in 1948 Shivers was elected to his
second term as Lieutenant Governor. While he was serving
this term, the state was shocked by the unexpected death of
Governor Beauford Jester, and Marialice found herself in the
role of First Lady of Texas.

For the next seven years, while her husband served Jester's
unexpired term plus three more elected ones, Marialice filled
that role with charm and efficiency. She left behind an
impressive list of improvements in the aging mansion (which
reached its one hundredth year during the Shiverses' tenure).
The structure was in bad condition; when it rained Marialice
would hurry to the kitchen for pans to catch the water that
dripped through the leaky ceiling into the upstairs rooms. One
day just after a group of school children had been through the
state dining room, she found the mantle hanging several
inches from the wall and was horrified to realize it could have
fallen on a child. Another day a carpenter fell through the roof

onto the desk of Marialice's secretary in the upstairs hall. The secretary, a confirmed spinster, joked that she had finally caught a man.

Under Marialice's supervision foundations were braced; old flooring was replaced; exposed pipes and wiring were recessed; an air-conditioning and new heating system was installed. The building was finally covered with a completely new steel roof, and other improvements in lighting and fencing were made. Working with an interior decorator from Houston, Marialice had the family living room upstairs and all of the downstairs rooms, except the hallway, redecorated. In keeping with the new decor, she had the historic portraits in the mansion reframed and rehung. She was pleased to be able to add to the collection three extremely valuable paintings by Sir Joshua Reynolds, Carle Van Loo, and Thomas Gainsborough, which were presented to the state by Mr. and Mrs. W. L. Moody III of San Antonio. To complete the transformation of the building, Marialice made use of her own handsome accessories, including vases, paintings, and silver.

The Shivers children also contributed to the appearance of the mansion while it was their home. An active Boy Scout, John Shary always had the paraphernalia for some of his various projects scattered about. In his room he raised fish, and on the second story gallery he had a large cage in which he kept parakeets and lovebirds. His leathercraft materials and weather-watching instruments were also in evidence. A visitor to the mansion reported that Bud and Cissie, the two younger children, had enough toys to open up a small store, and added that "everyone who met the family" must have sent Cissie a doll. After Brian McGee was born (in San Antonio on August 15, 1952), one of the bedrooms was converted into a nursery.

The staff attached to the mansion included nine persons, which added to the six members of the family meant that forty-five meals a day had to be served, in addition to arranging for the constant round of formal and informal entertainments. For family-only meals, Marialice often planned the cornbread, turnip greens, and black-eyed peas that the East Texas-bred Governor liked. And on Thursday nights, a Mexican dinner prepared by a Mexican man who had been with the family for thirty years was standard fare.

Marialice entertained small groups such as the Senate Ladies Club with luncheons and larger groups with receptions, for which a typical menu was assorted sandwiches, coconut balls, nuts, mints, and frozen fruit punch. Among the notable guests she entertained were General and Mrs. Douglas MacArthur and their son. In 1951 she reinstated the tradition of having an egg rolling for the children of legislators on the mansion lawn on Easter Monday.

During the years her husband served as Governor, Marialice gave generously of her time to arranging for and appearing at benefits, meetings, dinners, receptions, and other events that helped Shivers carry out certain programs. As a result, during his administrations he was able to bring about improvements in the educational, hospital, and prison systems of the state.

In 1957 the Shiverses' long tenure in the mansion came to an end. They bought the stately Pease Mansion, Woodlawn, that had been built by the same architect who had designed the Governor's Mansion. This impressive but ancient building also needed extensive renovation, and under Marialice's direction became a beautiful, gracious, and comfortable home.

Since leaving the mansion, Marialice has devoted considerable time to church and civic work. She served as director of the Home of Holy Infancy and is a member of the Settlement Club, Junior Helping Hand, McAllen Junior Service League, Pi Beta Phi Sorority, Austin Symphony League, Board of Directors of Laguna Gloria, and St. Mary's Cathedral. She enjoys doing needlepoint and antiquing.

In the 1960's the Shiverses purchased and restored an 1885 two-story house in Woodville, the former Governor's hometown. It has been named the Allan Shivers Library and Museum. Shivers' family memorabilia are on display in the museum, and the building serves as the Tyler County Public

Library, containing a rare books room. A few years ago, Our Lady of the Lake College at San Antonio named Marialice Shary Shivers the recipient of its first Outstanding Alumna Award. In conferring the award the college summed up her accomplishments:

> Community service, professional achievement, church-related activities, family dedication and unusual and special accomplishments.

JEAN HOUSTON
BALDWIN DANIEL

(Mrs. Marion
Price Daniel)

Most appropriately, Jean Houston Baldwin Daniel was the
First Lady in residence in the Governor's Mansion during the
years 1959 to 1961 — exactly one hundred years after
Margaret Houston had occupied the stately house. Born in the
city of Houston to Franklin and Jean Houston Baldwin, Jean
Daniel is the great-great-granddaughter of Sam and Margaret
Houston. Her great-grandmother was the Houstons' oldest
daughter, Nancy Elizabeth.

In addition to her heritage, Jean Houston Baldwin seemed
fated for her role in history; twenty-five years before she
became First Lady, her brother, Thomas, told her prophetically, "Jean, you should marry a Governor or somebody like
that. You are so pretty you should be somewhere on display."
For a brief time she resisted her destiny. When Price Daniel
was campaigning for her hand, she told her family emphatic-
ally, "I won't marry a politician!" Daniel, however, did not give
up; he had been in politics long enough to know that many a
mind has been changed by gentle persuasion before the final

vote is taken.

At the time she met Price Daniel, Jean was doing temporary work for a Houston law firm. Her chosen career was teaching, and after attending Rice Institute for two years, she had transferred to the University of Texas, where for a time she slept in a linen closet while she waited for some girl to drop out of school so she could have a room in the Scottish Rite Dormitory. She was a Bluebonnet Belle nominee, president of Kappa Kappa Gamma — and received her B.A. degree in English, cum laude, in 1937.

She returned to the University to earn a permanent teacher's certificate and substituted as a teacher of English in Houston junior high schools before taking the summer secretarial job. That is how she happened to meet a clever young lawyer from Liberty, Price Daniel, who had beaten her employer in a lawsuit and had come to the office to talk about terms for settling the case.

Not only did he talk her into marrying him (on June 28, 1940), he also persuaded her to spend their honeymoon on a vote-seeking tour in his campaign for reelection to the Texas House of Representatives. Her aversion to politics soon evaporated, and her charm won many votes for her husband. In June of the next year Price, Jr. was born. The events of this first year of their marriage more or less set a pattern that their lives would follow for the next ten years — campaigns alternating with the arrival of their children as Daniel moved up the political ladder to become Speaker of the House, Attorney General, and United States Senator.

At the end of his term as Speaker, Daniel enlisted in the army to serve in World War II. A daughter, Jean, had been born in September of 1942, and much to the consternation of both sets of grandparents, Jean decided to take the two small children and follow her husband. She felt that separation was a greater hardship than any she would have to endure as an army wife. Tenaciously, she stuck with her husband, spending four months in Amarillo, four months in Baton Rouge, Louisiana, a few weeks at Ann Arbor, Michigan, and finally arriving in Lexington, Virginia, in time to give birth to their third child, Houston, who was born in Rockbridge County where his great-great-great-grandfather, Sam Houston, had been born. Six weeks later, Daniel was sent overseas, and Jean stayed in Lexington with the three children.

Upon his discharge from the army, they returned to Texas to plunge into a hard-fought race for Attorney General. True to form, their fourth child, John, was born in April of 1948, shortly after Daniel won the election. They bought a pleasant home in Austin on a large corner lot, with plenty of room for the children to play. They delighted in being able at last to unpack Daniel's library of more than five hundred books on Texas history. Busy as she was with the children, Jean found time to follow her husband's cases with interest. When he was selected to attend the 44th Conference of the International Law Association at Copenhagen, Denmark, because of his work on the tidelands issue, she went along to hear him deliver a paper.

In 1952, the Daniels were campaigning again — this time for the United States Senate seat vacated by Tom Connally. And again they won. For the next few years Jean transplanted her four children from schools in Texas to schools in Washington, D.C., when Congress convened in January. Her social life in the nation's capital consisted chiefly of attendance at Texas State Society affairs once a month; serving as corresponding secretary of the Ladies of the Senate; rolling bandages for the Red Cross; and entertaining Texas friends. Price, Jr. had a paper route, and on some snowy, icy mornings, she was up before dawn, driving him on his rounds. On fair weather days, she saw him off at dawn on his bicycle.

After the Daniels acquired a small ranch, Holly Ridge, near Liberty, their chief delight was to relax there on vacations, wearing blue jeans, fishing, hunting, and riding horseback. Jean especially enjoyed being the camp cook for outdoor breakfasts and picnics.

In 1956, Daniel entered the gubernatorial race and won, with considerable help from his family. Slender and youthful, with dark brown hair, blue eyes, fair skin, and a charming smile, the new First Lady intrigued Texans. She set herself a goal of trying to keep life as normal as possible for the children and as serene as possible for her busy husband. She decided that insofar as possible, state entertaining would be done at breakfast and noon, for two reasons: she didn't want to serve liquor — no one expected it at these times — and the evenings would be free for the family to be together.

Saturdays and Sundays were the children's special days. On Saturdays they could invite their friends to the mansion for hamburgers; and on Sundays in the morning they went to church — the children and Jean to the First Methodist Church **across the street, and Governor Daniel to the First** Baptist Church. On Sunday afternoons the family got together for "Family Talks" in which they discussed what had happened to each of them during the week.

The children shared their parents' love of books and reading and considered one of the advantages of living in the mansion the fact that it was only a few blocks from the public library.

Soon after the Daniels moved into the mansion, Jean gave a coffee. She was greeting guests in the Blue Room when she heard a crash and screams from the hall. Rushing to the scene, she found that a large chunk of plaster had fallen from the ceiling, narrowly missing the Governor and a group of women guests. After making sure that no one was hurt, Jean had the Texas Rangers rope off the area and the party continued.

When work was begun on replacing the plaster, it was found that the staircase was sagging badly and that the foundation underlying the central part of the building needed reinforcement. Jean went to the archives to study records on the mansion and made sure that the entrance hall and stairwell retained their original appearance in the redecorating.

This project was only the beginning of Jean's contributions to preserving and restoring historic features of the house. She began intensive research to identify the pieces of furniture and accessories which were in the state rooms of the mansion and to locate other pieces once there. She wrote volumes of letters and made public appeals for help in the form of old photographs or clippings describing gifts made to the mansion or giving clues as to where various items had come from. The result of her research is a comprehensive 104-page inventory of the mansion furnishings, listing the location, description, value, and historical information about each item.

Her other major undertaking during her six years as First Lady came to be known as "Jean's Project." When she discovered that Marialice Shivers had collected the five mementos that remained in the building from earlier Governor's terms and placed them in a breakfront in the Blue Room, Jean decided that there should be a memento from *every* Governor's time.

Systematically she began to contact the living former occupants and to trace descendants of those who had been the residents of the mansion. Year after year she pursued the idea until finally in December of 1962 the project was completed. She identified and placed each heirloom or memento in a handsome case presented to the mansion on permanent loan from the University of Texas.

At an open house given in honor of those who assisted her in assembling the collection, Jean expressed the hope that "these reminders of the people who helped make Texas history might inspire present and future generations." In addition to the Daniels' contribution of an antique silver almond dish and a large silver tray to the collection, Jean gave her cherished rock crystal dresser pieces with silver tops. They had belonged to Margaret Houston.

Versatile Jean enjoyed the "kaleidoscopic" view of history that her role as First Lady gave her and found the most interesting part of being the Governor's wife was the chance to meet a broad selection of people. As overnight guests she entertained two men who became United States Presidents, John F. Kennedy and Lyndon B. Johnson. And in addition to holding receptions for many United States Senators and Governors of other states, she arranged dinners for President Adolfo Lopez Mateos of Mexico and Chancellor Konrad

Adenauer of Germany.

Jean takes great pride in her husband's state building program and especially of the State Archives and Library Building. Before its existence, priceless records such as the Texas Declaration of Independence and Travis' letter from the Alamo had been stored in non-fireproof quonset huts on Highway Department storage grounds.

Since retiring from the duties of First Lady, Jean Daniel has continued to lead a busy life while her husband has served as Director of the Office of Emergency Preparedness under President Lyndon Johnson and as an Associate Justice of the Texas Supreme Court. She is active in the United Methodist Church, the Thankful Hubbard Chapter of the D.A.R., the W. B. Travis Chapter of the D.R.T., and the Austin Junior League.

Two sons, Houston and Price, Jr. (who served as Speaker of the House of the 63rd Legislature and was president of the 1974 State Constitutional Convention) are lawyers. Daughter Jean is the wife of a minister (the Reverend Mr. David Murph) in the Christian Church, and John is a rancher in Liberty. The Daniels have acquired three grandchildren: Marilyn and Daniel, children of Jean and her husband, and Tom, Price, Jr.'s. son. Tom is a descendant of three Texas Governors and their wives — Sam Houston and Margaret and Price Daniel and Jean on his father's side and Thomas Campbell and Fanny on the side of his mother (who was Diane Wommack, great-granddaughter of the Campbells).

In 1969 a beautifully illustrated book which Jean and Daniel had compiled, entitled *Executive Mansions and Capitols of America*, was published.

Out of her deep love of the past and her intimate knowledge of contemporary events that will soon become history, comes Jean Houston Daniel's advice to future First Ladies:

". . . keep in mind the privilege of serving Texas as one of a long line of First Ladies. The days may seem endless in the living, but soon the role ends and it becomes a memory of a rare adventure experienced by only a few . . ."

IDANELL BRILL CONNALLY
(Mrs. John B. Connally)

The years she spent at the University of Texas were fruitful ones for Idanell Brill, resulting in many honors, a degree, and marriage to the president of the Student Association. Pretty and vivacious, Nellie, as she was called by her friends, was elected a Bluebonnet Belle, Queen of the Texas Relays, and Sweetheart of the University. She was a member of Delta Delta Delta sorority and the Curtain Club.

It was while both were acting in a play that she met John

Connally, a very big man on the campus, literally and figuratively. On December 21, 1940, they were married in the First Methodist Church of Austin, the city where Nellie had been born to Mr. and Mrs. Arno Brill. John Connally, from Floresville, had come to the University to study law, and after their marriage they settled in Austin. When World War II broke out the next year, Connally joined the Navy; while he was on duty in the Atlantic and Pacific, Nellie took a job on the sales staff of an Austin radio station.

In 1947 John III was born and two years later the Connallys moved to Washington, D.C., so Connally could serve as an assistant to Senator Lyndon Johnson. From there they moved to Fort Worth, where Connally practiced law. Two more children, a daughter, Sharon, and a son, Mark, were born in 1950 and 1953.

The Connallys acquired a ranch of some 1,200 acres near Floresville and built a rambling two-story house on it, furnishing it with antiques that Nellie picked up through her hobby of attending auctions. They called their ranch home "Picosa" and delighted in relaxing there.

When Connally accepted the position of Secretary of the Navy in 1960, Nellie packed up her family to move back to Washington. However, the nation's capital never really seemed like home to her, and she was pleased when Connally resigned his post to run for Governor of Texas in 1962. "Our roots are in Texas," she said. "This is where we want to be." She campaigned as actively as her husband and undoubtedly won many votes for him in his successful race.

After enrolling the children, who were then sixteen, thirteen, and ten, in Austin public schools, she set about with enthusiasm planning her domestic and official duties as mistress of the Executive Mansion. She had a staff of six for whom she wrote out daily detailed instructions. Her secretary, Mrs. Frances Morton, described her as ". . . a perfectionist — in the nicest way, not the way that bothers you," and added that Nellie's keen sense of humor made her pleasant to work with.

She refused to join clubs and organizations that she could not contribute to and worked very hard in those she belonged to, such as the Settlement Club, a service organization that maintains an Austin home for dependent and neglected children. On February 22, 1963, she represented the Governor at the annual Washington's birthday celebration at Laredo, and she toured the state's tuberculosis hospitals as part of a fund-raising campaign. Later that year she accompanied the Governor to the National Governors' Conference in Miami and the Southern Governors' Conference in White Sulphur Springs, West Virginia.

When President and Mrs. John Kennedy came to Texas in November on a political tour, Nellie and Connally visited San Antonio, Houston, and Fort Worth with them. Dallas was the next stop. On November 22, 1963, the Connallys were riding in the presidential limousine on jump seats in front of the Kennedys when the fatal shots were fired that killed the President and seriously wounded John Connally. For Nellie it was ". . . unbelievable . . ." But probably thanks to her instinctive action, her husband's life was saved. After he was hit, she pulled him down across her lap and leaned over him. By a "kind of miracle" his right arm fell over the large wound in his chest, covering it and preventing air from entering the cavity. For two and a half hours Nellie sat in the corridor at Parkland Hospital, not knowing whether her husband would live. Although the hall was crowded with people, she says "I was never so alone."

After that nightmarish day, Connally improved slowly but steadily. Nellie remained with him until he could leave the hospital, while her parents stayed with the children in Austin. On the day after the tragedy, she made a tearful television speech from the hospital to thank the thousands of people who had sent messages and to ask those who were sending flowers to the wounded governor to contribute instead to the fund for the family of Officer Tippit— the Dallas police officer who was killed by the suspected assassin. She told her listeners, "Our grief is all the greater because of his sacrifice."

Connally returned to the mansion with his shattered right wrist in a cast. Nellie was his nurse, guardian, protector, and constant companion. She did whatever he needed her to do, from carrying out state duties to tying his shoelaces for him. He was under many restrictions from his doctors, and as he became stronger, Nellie found the task of keeping him housebound somewhat like trying to keep a tiger in a cage. Toward the end of his convalescence, she announced, "Having him **here all the time was nice, but now it's nice to know he's going** back to his office!"

As time passed, the emotional and physical trauma of that November day faded, and life assumed a more normal aspect for Nellie. Connally was elected Governor twice more, and she gave her time and support to many worthwhile projects. From 1965 through 1968 she served as honorary state chairman of the Texas Mental Health Association for its fund-raising campaigns and was the honorary chairman of the Galaxy Ball, a statewide benefit for the organization. She considered mental health "the most complex, most critical health program in our state." She was also chairman of the Texas Division of the 1965 Cancer Crusade.

In addition to the conventional teas and receptions for various groups, Nellie arranged a unique tea in the spring of 1965 to honor all of the living wives of ex-Governors of the state. She wore a white silk sleeveless sheath with hand-painted spring flowers to welcome the five hundred guests who came to pay their respects to the former First Ladies.

During 1968, Nellie spent a great deal of time in San Antonio at the Hemisfair, where she served as hostess.

Nellie undertook two major projects in connection with improving the mansion. She discovered that there were few pieces of silver belonging to the house when she prepared for her first big dinner party, so she launched a program to enlarge the mansion's silver service to take care of sixty persons. Among the contributors was Heloise Cruse, a syndicated newspaper columnist famous for her household hints, who presented Nellie with a 145-piece set of gold-plated solid bronze flatware from Thailand. Through other gifts, Nellie acquired a lovely collection of silver for the mansion.

Nellie's most extensive project (and one that lasted throughout the six years she served as First Lady) was landscaping and illuminating the mansion grounds. She traveled over the state in behalf of the program to raise the needed private funds, enlisting the assistance of various civic groups, including Texas Garden Clubs, Inc. With the aid of Joe Lambert of Lambert Associates of Dallas, she decided upon plans to beautify the grounds and to make parts of them useful as entertainment areas. Under her supervision, white brick walls and a rustic iron fence were constructed to enclose the mansion block. Gardens, terraces, patios, walks, a Greek colonnade, fountains and reflecting pools with soft illuminating effects transformed the grounds.

In the spring of 1968 the beautiful grounds were the setting for the wedding of Sharon Connally to Robert C. Ammann III of Austin. The couple repeated their vows under the classic Greek colonnade in the formal garden with Dr. Robert Tate, Jr., pastor of the First United Methodist Church in Austin, officiating.

Since Connally's decision not to run for a fourth term, Nellie has moved her household between Washington, D.C. (while her husband served as Secretary of the Treasury); and Houston, where he is a member of a law firm; and Picosa, where they look after their ranching interests. At the Picosa Nellie has planned entertainments for Presidents, Ambassadors, Governors, First Ladies, and royalty. She has traveled extensively with her husband on a number of presidential missions and has met with wives of foreign dignitaries in over thirty countries.

The Connallys' children have all attended their parents' alma mater, the University of Texas. John III and his wife, Tracy Smith, live in Houston, where he is an attorney. Sharon and her husband, Robert, have presented the Connallys with two granddaughters.

Nellie continues to work actively with service organizations.

Both she and her husband have been awarded one of the University of Texas' highest awards — the Distinguished Alumni Award. Her hobbies are hunting, painting, and collecting antiques, paintings, and other art objects. She enjoys attending the theater and has referred to herself as a frustrated actress. She is especially interested in historical preservation projects and likes to visit beautifully landscaped gardens as well as cathedrals and museums.

While continuing to be always with her husband, wherever his various positions have led him, Nellie Connally has managed to lead a remarkable full and satisfactory life, making lasting and worthwhile contributions to society.

IMA SMITH SMITH
(Mrs. Preston Smith)

As was his custom, the professor of a government class at Texas Technological University in Lubbock arranged his students in alphabetical order. And that is how in 1933 Ima Smith officially met Preston Smith. She was aware that he had been watching her as she walked home every day past the service station he managed. She wasn't interested, though, because she was already engaged. Soon Preston persuaded her to go on a few dates, and his sense of humor almost overwhelmed her. He was a continual cut-up, and she thought "that man will never be serious." However, she realized that he was very serious about his education.

In spite of his father's objections, he had hitchhiked to Lubbock from his home in Lamesa and taken the job at the service station and also one in a tire store. Later he leased a house to rent out to students, since at that time Tech didn't have dormitories. Ima's landlady told her she would do well to marry such a hard-working young man because he would always be a good provider.

Ima and Preston discovered that they had more in common in their backgrounds than their surnames. Both had come from small towns and both were members of large farming families. There were thirteen Smith brothers and sisters in

Preston's family and ten in Ima's. She was born in Jacksboro, and had moved with her family to Ralls at the age of eleven, while he had grown up in Lamesa.

Ima studied elementary education and homemaking at Tech, where she belonged to Zeta Tau Alpha sorority. Without taking her degree, she left to teach in Ralls — the first grade one year and the second grade another year. She continued to see Preston, who eventually persuaded her to break her previous engagement and become engaged to him. He received a degree in business administration from Tech, and on June 20, 1935, the two Smiths were married in Ralls.

They settled in Lubbock, and Ima found that her study of home economics came in handy, since her food budget was $1.00 a day. Out of that sum she managed to feed the two of them nourishing meals and saved enough to buy their first radio!

In 1936 they built the first of their theaters in Lubbock. Their theaters later became part of a corporation with headquarters in Oklahoma City. The Smiths had free passes, and Ima became fond of the movies, feeling that they were one place "where you can get away from the world."

The newlyweds became charter members of St. John's Methodist Church in Lubbock, which was organized in one of their theaters. They also belonged to a group of young marrieds who learned to play bridge together, and then organized a club which remained intact for over thirty years. When the bridge group reached its twenty-fifth anniversary, the entire club went to Austin to celebrate the occasion with the Smiths.

In December of 1940, a son, Preston Michael (Mickey), was born, and in February of 1945, a daughter, Jan Lauren. In the early 1940's Smith decided to enter politics. Devoted to her home and friends in Lubbock, Ima was not enthusiastic about the idea. She never really liked politics, but for almost the next quarter-century, she supported her husband loyally as he progressed through six years as a member of the Texas House of Representatives to six years as a member of the Texas

Senate to six years as Lieutenant Governor and four years as Governor.

The Smiths kept their home in Lubbock and commuted to Austin for his terms of office — twelve hours by bus during World War II, seven by car, or two by jet in later years. Despite the difficulties involved, both Mickey and Jan were graduated from Lubbock High School and Texas Tech.

In spite of her dislike for campaigning and politicking, Ima attended endless receptions and banquets during her husband's public life, and she always took pains to be gracious and to make a good appearance. Her hair, prematurely gray, contrasted with her dark eyes, and her clothes were usually classic in style in her favorite colors of blue, red, or pink.

While her husband was busy with his duties as Lieutenant Governor, Ima pursued her hobbies of needlepoint, listening to jazz and reading fiction. Since the children were married and the state supplied a cook and servants to take care of the three-bedroom apartment in the Capitol, she sometimes found that time passed slowly. When her husband could get away, they spent weekends at the lake home they acquired near Austin.

After Ima became First Lady, there was no time for boredom. She was caught up in the constant round of planning and attending entertainments that went with the role. She enjoyed more the entertainments at which she was the hostess rather than the honored guest. Hard work didn't bother her, and she was "so particular" she liked to do things herself.

In addition to planning the official receptions, buffets, and parties, which averaged one per week, she worked with special projects such as the March of Dimes and did volunteer work for mental health. Some of the best hours were on Sunday evenings when the Smiths retreated to the privacy of their family quarters and prepared ham and egg suppers for themselves.

The years that the Smiths occupied the Executive Mansion were nervous ones for the men assigned by the Department of

Public Safety to guard the First Family. It was a time of
violent protest, and more than the usual number of crank calls
and threatening letters came to the mansion. Once, when the
Smiths were out of town, a bomb was thrown into the gardens.
Red swastikas and insulting slogans appeared on the white
walls around the building. Gates were installed in the front
wall and fire extinguishers were placed in strategic locations.
The security guards stood watch on the top gallery with guns
at the ready position after particularly violent threats were
received. Ima was instructed what to do if a bomb were
thrown; at times, she admitted, "it was pretty frightening."

When her husband told her he would try for a third term,
she begged him not to run. Not only the constant threats on
his life, but also the effects of the strain of the office on him
worried her. He had changed from the young man she felt
would "never be serious" to one who was "too serious." But he
chose to run, and after his defeat, she told a reporter he was
more relaxed because "he doesn't have to carry the world
anymore." Her husband's greatest accomplishment, she
believes, was the establishment of a system of state technical
schools.

Before the Smiths moved out of the mansion, Ima planned
one last big family Christmas with both children and their
families there. She hoped the three grandchildren would be
able to remember being in the historic home and having a
Christmas tree there.

Going home to Lubbock was pleasant, as always, and Ima
took up her role of homemaker with feelings of relief. It was
nice to have her husband charcoaling steaks for neighborhood
parties in the backyard again. She resumed her social and civic
life, which included membership in the Women's Organization
of the Lubbock Chamber of Commerce, and life memberships
in the Women's Council of West Texas Museum and the
Methodist Hospital Auxiliary. Texas Tech awarded her its
Distinguished Alumnae Award.

Mickey became a parks administrator and Jan a teacher;
and Ima enjoyed her role of grandmother to her granddaugh-

ter and twin grandsons. After years in the glare of public life, it was good to be just a private family named Smith.

But there would always be memories. While she was First Lady, Ima prepared a colorfully illustrated pamphlet on the Governor's Mansion, describing the state rooms and their furnishings. In this booklet she wrote, "I can't help but feel a kinship to all the people who ever lived here. Though we live here in different times, we share many of the same burdens, sorrows, and joys . . . ."

BETTY JANE SLAUGHTER BRISCOE
(Mrs. Dolph Briscoe)

A Texas State Senator once called Janey Briscoe "a very astute political woman," and he was undoubtedly right, for she has worked hard at acquiring knowledge of the government of her state. She is also her husband's greatest booster and asset in his campaigns. During the 1972 campaign for Governor, she told an interviewer, "I'm always amused when people say how quiet he [Dolph] is. It took a great deal of courage to try to change the sex life of a fly!" She was referring to Briscoe's leadership in efforts to wipe out the screwworm, a longtime scourge of Texas livestock and wildlife, by producing sterile flies that lay the eggs which cause screwworm.

Moving to Austin to become First Lady was like coming home to Janey, who grew up in the capital. At the University of Texas her raven-haired good looks won her Bluebonnet Belle honors and the attention of upper classman Dolph Briscoe. The attraction was mutual, and they married in December of 1942, right after Briscoe's graduation and just before he went into the army — to serve in the China-Burma-Indian theater for two and a half years. While he was away, Janey lived with her parents, Mr. and Mrs. Sam Slaughter of Austin, and completed work at the University to earn her B.A. in education. She also studied history and government, because these subjects interested her.

When Briscoe returned, they moved to the ranch that they still call "home," situated on the Frio River, about twenty-one miles from Uvalde. Although it's filled with antiques and every modern convenience now, at that time the house had no gas or electricity, and Janey cooked on a coal oil stove. Janey's experience with this unpredictable appliance was one of the reasons Briscoe supported the rural electrification bill when he was in the Legislature.

In 1948 when Briscoe ran for a seat in the Texas House of Representatives, Janey divided the campaigning chores with him. She went from door-to-door while he handled the businessmen. He won the seat and kept it for eight years without opposition, but when his father died, the Briscoes returned to South Texas to take care of their ranching interests, which now included a second large ranch, Caterina, and the raising of purchased Santa Gertrudis cattle, and sheep and goats for mutton, mohair, and lamb.

After their three children — Little Janey, Dolph III (Chip), and Cele — were born, Janey became involved in their activities and found that commuting between the ranch and Uvalde where they attended school was increasingly complicated. The Briscoes solved the problem by buying a third home in Uvalde, a comfortable frame house, so the children could come home for a hot lunch and take part in such extracurricular activities as cheerleading, ball games, music lessons, and band.

Besides serving as president of the PTA, Janey taught Sunday school in the Reagan Wells Baptist Church, was a charter member of a D.A.R. chapter, and headed the ladies' auxiliary to the Texas Sheep and Goat Raisers Association. She helped launch the Miss Wool contest through that organization.

The Briscoes became noted for their hospitality, which varied as the children grew up from barbecues for two hundred or more at their Caterina Ranch, parties for Cele's high school classmates or Chip and Little Janey's friends from the University of Texas, to small intimate dinners for close friends at the Uvalde home — with Janey doing the cooking.

In her spare time, Janey took courses in Spanish and art for her own pleasure as well as in government and history to complete her work on an M.A. degree; her thesis was on Richard Coke, Governor of Texas in the 1870's. She received her M.A. from the University of Texas at the same time Little Janey received her B.A.

Janey refers, with justification, to Briscoe's campaigns by using the pronouns, "we," "our," and "us." When they lost their first campaign for Governor in 1968, Janey felt it was because she could not devote enough time to it, since the children were still so young. The 1972 race was a different story. In a year-long effort, a typical two-day trip included flying into Dallas on the Briscoe plane, a Lockheed Lodestar called the Janey B., on Monday morning, attending a luncheon at the Dallas Woman's Club, spending the afternoon at a hotel with Dolph, visiting with individual callers, and attending a dinner honoring her husband in the evening.

The next day started with a campaign breakfast, followed by visits to Texas Instruments and Southern Methodist University, an orientation coffee for workers, a meeting at the Dallas Club with Young Men for Dolph, and a City Club reception in the afternoon before flying home to Uvalde to be with their youngest daughter Cele, a junior in high school. This rugged schedule paid off, and the Briscoes defeated Preston Smith, the incumbent who had defeated them in their unsuccessful bid for the state's highest office two years earlier.

One of Janey's early projects as First Lady was to redecorate the Governor's office in the Capitol Building. Using oriental rugs, a rocking chair, and Victorian furniture brought from their home in Uvalde, she changed its official atmosphere into a warmer, more comfortable one. Little Janey worked as a receptionist for her father until her impending wedding took precedence over everything else.

Some 1,700 guests, including a large portion of the Uvalde population, attended the wedding of Janey Briscoe to Edward Vaughan of Hillsboro on December 29, 1973. The bride, the seventh governor's daughter to be wed at the mansion, wore a traditional gown of silk satin and French lace, and her mother wore a long velvet gown in her favorite color of deep red burgundy. At a few minutes past seven the bridal party walked down the ancient mansion's red-carpeted stairway, which was intertwined with white satin and bouquets of white roses. The vows were solemnized in a setting that reminded the guests of the Garden of Eden. The grounds were covered and warmed by white tents; fragrant and colorful Victorian bouquets — of azaleas, roses, carnations, daffodils, iris, spider mums, and daisies — were arranged in tiers along the sides of the tents. Chandeliers containing hundreds of candles lighted the scene. A chamber music group provided music for the ceremony that was held in the Grecian garden in an altar setting framed by wide arcs and bowers of greenery.

The Briscoes won reelection in 1974 without much trouble, and because of a change in the Texas Constitution were the first to have a four-year instead of a two-year term. Janey continues to be politically-oriented, spending a great deal of time in her husband's office and in the galleries of the Capitol, auditing sessions of the Legislature.

Janey Briscoe was awarded the honorary Doctor of Humanities degree by Mary Hardin-Baylor College, Belton, May 15, 1976. She is the first First Lady to be given this recognition.

Warm and personable, Janey impresses those who come to know her well as gracious and sincere in her actions. That she is interested in and knowledgeable about politics, she frankly concedes. She belongs, after all, to a time when women's roles are being reevaluated at every level. That she has moved away from the traditional and conventional role of a political wife is symptomatic of the times and is highlighted by the fact that she has moved out of the confines of the mansion into the Capitol. Janey Briscoe may well be the prototype of a new breed of First Lady to emerge from our changing society. Only time can tell.

Acknowledgements

The authors are deeply appreciative of the encouragement and help received from many friends and relatives. We are especially indebted to H. C. Farrell, Marsha Talley, and Weldon Cannon for their invaluable help and the many hours they have given to our project.

We sincerely appreciate the assistance of the staffs of the following libraries and are grateful for their permission to use the material in these collections:

Austin-Travis County Collection, Austin Public Library.
   (Pease family papers)
Barker History Center, Austin, Texas.
   (personal papers of Presidents and Governors of Texas)
Rosenberg Library, Galveston, Texas.
   (personal papers of Presidents and Governors of Texas)
Texas Collection, Baylor University, Waco, Texas.
   (personal papers of Governors of Texas)
Texas State Library, Austin, Texas.
   (personal papers of Governors and First Ladies of Texas)
Our very special thanks go to Mrs. Dolph Briscoe and to her secretary, Ms. Maria Gonzalez, for their kind assistance.

We are grateful to Nati Doughty for aid in translating and composing correspondence in German.

We also wish to express our sincere appreciation to the following people who gave us help and information:

Mrs. James V. Allred, Wichita Falls, Texas.
Ms. Mary Keys Anderson, Dallas, Texas.
Ms. Judith Ann Benner, San Antonio, Texas.
Ms. Marion M. Branon, Librarian, Texas Room, Houston Public Library, Houston, Texas.
Ms. Rose Anne Brasher, Temple Junior College.
Mrs. Thomas Mitchell Campbell, Jr., Austin, Texas.
William Bruner Campbell, Austin, Texas.
Ms. Trudy Champion, Consultant, Houston Public Library, Houston, Texas.
Mrs. David A. Cheavens, Waco, Texas.
Miss Elizabeth Clark, College Station, Texas.
Mrs. Neville Clark, San Antonio, Texas.
Mrs. John Connally, Houston, Texas.

Mrs. Price Daniel, Sr., Austin, Texas.

Ms. Mary Kaye Donahue, Local History Librarian, La Retama Public Library, Corpus Christi, Texas.

Dr. Jean Duncan, Huntsville, Texas.

Marc Eisen, Head of Reference Department, Free Public Library of East Orange, East Orange, New Jersey.

Mrs. Walter Espy, San Antonio, Texas.

Mrs. Edward A. Everitt, Houston, Texas.

Mrs. George B. Graves, Waco, Texas.

Paul Haire, Temple Junior College.

Mrs. Barbara Haskins, Librarian, The Joint Free Public Library, Morristown, New Jersey.

Rev. Edmund Heinsohn, University United Methodist Church, Austin, Texas.

Miss Ima Hogg, Houston, Texas.

Dr. Chester Kielman, Director, Barker Texas History Library, Austin, Texas.

Mrs. Doris Keller, Temple, Texas.

Ms. Ruth E. Kelly, Librarian, Archives, Rosenberg Library, Galveston, Texas.

Ms. Marie Lentz, Hartberg, Austria.

Mrs. Claude Maer, Fort Worth, Texas.

Mrs. Paul Mason, College Station, Texas.

Mrs. Ralph C. Miller, Houston, Texas.

Mrs. W. S. Millington, Bastrop, Texas.

Mr. and Mrs. Bill Ming, Texas Collection, Baylor.

Mrs. Dan Moody, Austin, Texas.

Mrs. Mabel Buchanan Jester Morris, Texarkana, Texas.

Ms. Mary L. Muir, Philadelphia, Pennsylvania.

Miss Marion Day Mullins, Fort Worth, Texas.

Mrs. J. M. Murphy, Temple, Texas.

George S. Nalle, Sr., Austin, Texas.

Howard O. Pollan, Smith County Historical Society and Survey Committee, Tyler, Texas.

Mrs. Thomas G. Sayers, Austin, Texas.

Mrs. Allan Shivers, Austin, Texas.

Mrs. L. O. Shudde, Austin, Texas.

Mrs. Preston Smith, Lubbock, Texas.

Mrs. Coke Stevenson, Jr., Austin, Texas.

Mrs. Callie Hayhurst Wagner, Pasadena, Texas.

Miss Lucille Wasson, Independence, Texas.

Mrs. Frank Wilcox, Waco, Texas.

Drew Wommack, Palestine, Texas.

Larry J. Wygant, Archivist, Rosenberg Library, Galveston, Texas.

Mrs. Saida Yoder, Librarian, Weatherford Public Library, Weatherford, Texas.

In addition, we would like to thank the many unnamed archivists and reference and consultant librarians in numerous libraries in Texas and in other states who have patiently aided our long search.

Bibliography

GENERAL BIBLIOGRAPHY

Adair, A. Garland and Ellen B. Coates. *Texas, Its History*. Dallas: The John Winston Co., 1954 .

Bolton, Paul. *Governors of Texas*. San Angelo, Texas: *The San Angelo Standard-Times*, 1947 .

Brooks, Elizabeth. *Prominent Women of Texas*. New York: J. S. Redfield, 1855. 2 volumes.

Historic Costumes and Furnishings. DAR, Texas. Temple, Texas: American Printing Co., 1940 .

Hogan, William R. *The Texas Republic: A Social and Economic History*. Norman: University of Oklahoma Press, 1946 .

Jackson, Pearl Cashell. *Texas Governors' Wives*. (Austin: Steck Vaughn Co., 1915.)

Moore, Walter B. *Governors of Texas*. (Dallas: *The Dallas Morning News*, n.d.)

Richardson, Rupert Norval, *et al. Texas: The Lone Star State*. New Jersey: Prentice-Hall, Inc., 1970 .

Texas Almanac (1974-1975). Dallas: A. H. Belo Corporation .

Webb, Walter Prescott, *et al*, eds. *The Handbook of Texas*. Austin: Texas State Historical Association, 1952 . 2 volumes.

Wooten, Dudley G., ed. *A Comprehensive History of Texas, 1685 to 1899*. Dallas: William G. Scarff, 1898. 2 volumes.

Yoakum, Henderson. *A History of Texas*. New York: J. S. Redfield, 1855. 2 volumes.

SELECTED BIBLIOGRAPHY FOR HANNAH ESTE BURNET

Christian, A. K. "Mirabeau Buonaparte Lamar." *Southwestern Historical Quarterly*, XXIII (1919-20).

Clarke, Mary Whatley. *David G. Burnet*. Austin: The Pemberton Press, 1969.

Clopper, Edward N. *An American Family*. Standard Printing and Publishing Co., 1950 .

Fields, Dorothy Louise. "David Gouverneur Burnet." *Southwestern Historical Quarterly*, XLIX (1945-46).

Stephenson, Mrs. Charles. "Burnet." *The Dallas Morning News*, December 4, 1927.

Texas Almanac 1857-1873. Compiled by James M. Day. Waco, Texas: Texian Press, 1967 .

Unpublished Material

Burnet Bible. Barker Texas History Center, Austin, Texas.
Burnet Papers. Barker Texas History Center, Austin, Texas.
Burnet Papers. Rosenberg Library, Galveston, Texas.
Hannah Burnet notebook. Rosenberg Library, Galveston, Texas.

SELECTED BIBLIOGRAPHY FOR MARGARET LEA HOUSTON

"All's Fair in Politics." *Texas Parade*. (December, 1971).

Boney, F. N., ed. "The Raven Tamed." *Southwestern Historical Quarterly*, LXVII (1964). pp. 90-92.

Crane, William Carey. *Life and Select Literary Remains of Sam Houston of Texas*. Philadelphia: Lippincott and Co., 1884 .

Fifty Years of Achievement: History of the Daughters of the Republic of Texas. Dallas: Banks, Uphsaw and Co., 1942.

Flanagan, Sue. *Sam Houston's Texas*. Austin: University of Texas Press, 1965 .

Friend, Llerena Beaufort. *Sam Houston: The Great Designer*. Austin: University of Texas Press, 1956 .

Gambrell, Herbert. *Anson Jones*. Garden City: Doubleday and Co., 1948 .

Guild, Josephus C. *Old Times in Tennessee*. Nashville: Tavel, Eastman, and Howell, 1878 .

Houston, Margaret Lea. "Collected Poems by Margaret Lea Houston." *The Sam Houston Memorial Museum Quarterly*. (Spring, 1970).

Houston, Sam. *Autobiography of Sam Houston*. Donald Day and Harry Ullon, eds. Norman: University of Oklahoma Press, 1954.

Hunt, Lenoir, ed. *My Master by Jeff Hamilton*. Dallas: Manford Van Nort and Co., 1940.

James, Marquis. *The Raven: A Biography of Sam Houston*. Indianapolis: Bobbs-Merrill Co., 1929 .

Laune, Seigniora Russell. "General Sam Houston." *Sturm's Oklahoma Magazine*. (March, 1911) pp. 3-6.

Lockhart, John. *Sixty Years on the Brazos*. Privately printed (1930).

Porterfield, Bill. "Sam Houston, Warts and All." *Texas Monthly*. (July, 1973) pp. 63-67.

Seale, William. *Sam Houston's Wife: A Biography of Margaret Lea Houston*. Norman: University of Oklahoma Press, 1970 .

Shuffler, R. Henderson. *The Houstons at Independence*. Waco: The Texian Press, 1965 .

Turner, Martha Anne. *Sam Houston and His Twelve Women*. Austin: Pemberton Press, 1966.

Van Demark, Harry. "Sam Houston's First Marriage." *Bunker's Monthly*. (April, 1928) pp. 530-537.

Warren, Robert Penn. "Sam Houston and the Battle of San Jacinto." (San Jacinto Museum of History, 1959).

White, Olive Branch. "Margaret Lea Houston: Wife of General Sam Houston." *Naylor's Epic-Century Magazine*, III. (1936) pp. 30-42.

Williams, Amelia W. and Eugene C. Barker, eds. *The Writings of Sam Houston*. 8 vols. Austin: University of Texas Press, 1938.

Newspapers

Artesia, Waco. July 15, 1900 .

Austin Statesman, May 18, 1964 .
Birmingham News Magazine, n.d.
Galveston News, May 2, 1878 .
                 April 3, 1892 .
                 May 29, 1892 .
                 October 11, 1896 .
The Houston Post, September 11, 1900 .
                 November 25, 1957 .
New Orleans Republican, September 14, 1871 .
Temple Texas Times, June 7, 1901 .

Unpublished Material

Letters: Mrs. Margaret D. Everitt, Houston, Texas, to Mrs. H. C. Farrell, Jr. (1973-1974).
Rosenberg Library, Galveston:
     Sam Houston Manuscripts.
     Papers pertaining to Sam Houston.
Sam Houston Memorial Museum, Huntsville:
     Personal belongings of Sam and Margaret Houston.
     Letters and poems of Sam and Margaret Houston.
San Jacinto Museum of History:
     Personal papers and belongings of Sam and Margaret Houston.
Texas State Library, Austin:
     Houston Unpublished Correspondence.
Travis County Public Library, Austin:
     Sam Houston Papers.
Barker Texas History Center, Austin:
     Ashbel Smith Manuscripts.
     Henderson Yoakum Diary.
     Houston Unpublished Correspondence.

SELECTED BIBLIOGRAPHY FOR TABITHA JORDAN LAMAR

"Biographical Sketch of General Mirabeau B. Lamar." *Texas Almanac.* (1857).
"Editor's Notes." *Texana.* VII, No. 3. (1969).
Graham, Philip. *The Life and Poems of Mirabeau B. Lamar.* Chapel Hill: The University of North Carolina Press, 1938.
"Mirabeau Buonaparte Lamar." Pamphlet #3. Department of Publicity for Texas Centennial Celebrations, Dallas, Texas.
The Papers of Mirabeau Buonaparte Lamar. 6 vols. Texas State Library, 1920-1927.
Siegel, Stanley. *Big Men Walked Here.* Austin: Pemberton Press, 1971.

Newspapers

Austin American-Statesman:
  Brewer, Anita. "Mighty Man Was Lamar." October 18, 1956.
  "Lamar Was a Man of Versatile Talents." September 28, 1963.
  Mitchell, Mary H. "The Pioneers of Austin." n.d.
Austin Dispatch
  "Mirabeau Buonaparte Lamar." n.d.
Dallas Morning News:
  Gambrell, Herbert P. "Lamar Timed His Texas Debut." April 11, 1942.

Unpublished Material

Lamar letters. San Jacinto Museum of History Association. San Jacinto
Monument. Deer Park, Texas.

SELECTED BIBLIOGRAPHY FOR MARY McCRORY JONES

Alderman, Elora Buck. "Odd Fellow Work Gave Anson Jones His First
  Start on Diplomatic Career." *IOOF News.* (n.d.)
"Barrington." *The Texas Public Employee.* (August, 1970) 10-12.
Butcher, Ruth. "Dr. Anson Jones." *Biographical Encyclopedia of Texas.*
  New York: New York Publishing Co., 1880.
*Fifty Years of Achievement: History of the Daughters of the Republic
  of Texas.* Dallas: Banks, Upshaw and Co., 1942.
Gambrell, Herbert. *Anson Jones.* Garden City: Doubleday and Co., 1948.
Hogan, William R. "Mr. Jones of B." Book Review. *Southwest Review.*
  XXXIII (1948).
Jones, Anson. *Memoranda and Official Correspondence Relating to the
  Republic of Texas, Its History and Annexation. Including a Brief
  Autobiography of the Author.* Chicago: The Rio Grande Press, Inc.

Newspapers

Austin American-Statesman:
  Hale, Leon. "Barrington, Anson Jones' Family Home, Is Restored."
  "This Day in Texas." September 2, 1962, October 20, 1962, December
  9, 1962.
Dallas Times Herald:
  "Last Chief Executive." May 11, 1960.
Houston Daily Post:
  Address by Mrs. Anson Jones, May 9, 1898.
  1904, 1906, 1907.
Houston Chronicle:
  Redding, Stan. "Fate of Widow McCrory." March 13, 1960.

Unpublished Material

Personal papers and letters of Anson and Mary Jones. Barker Texas History Center, Austin.

Proceedings of the Thirteenth Annual Meeting of the Daughters of the Republic of Texas. Houston, 1904.

Resolutions Adopted by Daughters of the Republic of Texas on the Death of Mrs. Anson Jones, President. January 2, 1908.

Seventeenth Annual Meeting of the Daughters of the Republic of Texas. Houston, 1908.

SELECTED BIBLIOGRAPHY FOR FRANCES COX HENDERSON

Cox, John Lyman. *Some Family Sketches*. Philadelphia: privately printed, 1952.

Crocket, G. L. *Two Centuries in East Texas*. Dallas: The Southwest Press, First Printing, 1932, Reproduction, 1962.

Henderson, Frances Cox. *Dunderviksborg, and Other Tales: Forming an Epitome of Modern European Literature*. Philadelphia: J. B. Lippincott and Co., 1881.

Pickrell, Annie Doom. "Mrs. J. Pinckney Henderson, Born Frances Cox." *Pioneer Women in Texas*. Austin: The E. L. Steck Co., 1929.

Winchester, Robert Glenn. *James Pinckney Henderson: Texas' First Governor*. San Antonio: The Naylor Company, 1971.

Newspapers

Dallas Morning News:
  Hughes, Mrs. Vannie H. "Wife of First Texas Governor, Mrs. J. Pinckney Henderson, Was Woman of Unusual Ability." January 14, 1940.
  Tolbert, Frank X. "Buried Under Pulpit." n.d.
East Orange Gazette:
  "Mrs. Frances C. Henderson." Obituary. January 28, 1897.
San Antonio Express:
  "The Life Story of Frances Cox." November 3, 1912.

Unpublished Material

Henderson, Frances Cox. Diary, 1860-63. Barker Texas History Center, Austin.

Henderson, Mrs. F. C. *Ms. Sketch of Christ Church, San Augustine.*

Lamar, Mirabeau Buonaparte. Papers. The Texas State Library, Austin. Charles Adams Gulick, Jr. and Katherine Elliott, eds., 1920.

Letter: Marie Lentz, Reitenau, Austria, to authors. (December 5, 1973).

Letter: Mary L. Muir, Philadelphia, Pennsylvania, to authors. (January 20, 1974).

SELECTED BIBLIOGRAPHY FOR
MARTHA EVANS GINDRAT WOOD

German, S. H. "Governor George Thomas Wood." *Southwestern Historical Quarterly*, XX (1917) 260-268.
Vincent, Louella Styles. "Governor George Thomas Wood." *Southwestern Historical Quarterly*, XX (1917) 269-276.

Newspapers

Austin American-Statesman:
"Wood County Named in Honor Texas' 2nd Governor." July 27, 1950.
Houston Post:
"George T. Wood." September 23, 1958.

Unpublished Material

Buller, Talmadge Levell. "The Life and Times of George T. Wood." M. A. Thesis, University of Houston. (August, 1952).
Dixon, Jesse L. "George Tyler Wood: Unpublished history of a noted man, who was second governor of Texas." (n.d.).

SELECTED BIBLIOGRAPHY FOR LUCADIA NILES PEASE

Hart, Katherine, ed. *Pease Porridge Hot*. Austin: Encino Press, 1967.
Hart, Katherine and Elizabeth Kemp, eds. *Lucadia Pease & the Governor; Letters: 1850-1857*. Austin: Encino Press, 1974.

Newspapers

Austin American-Statesman:
Brewer, Anita. " 'A Levee . . . at the Mansion.' " April 16, 1961.
Brewer, Anita. "Attractive 'First Lady' Wanted to Tame the Young, Wild Texas." n.d.
"Early Families in Mansion Suffered Many Hardships." August 12, 1956.
"Elisha M. Pease." August 28, 1883.
Hart, Katherine. "Great Debt Owed to Gov., Mrs. Pease." December 6, 1969.
Hart, Katherine. "New Year's Day Was a Time for Calling." December 26, 1970.
Matlock, Cora B. "Mrs. Hamilton Reports: Life Here: As Lucadia Pease Lived It." n.d.
"Mrs. L. C. Pease Died Yesterday." January 29, 1905.
"Twas 100 Years Ago This Autumn Work Was Started on the Mansion." September 23, 1955.

Dallas Morning News:
  Hall, Jay. "War Dogs Step of Man Seeking Life of Peace." April 11, 1942.
  Keever, Jack. "History Stalks Corridors." February 16, 1964.
Houston Chronicle Magazine:
  Poff, Claudia. "A House for a Governor." n.d.
San Antonio Express:
  "Governor's Wife Who Selected Mansion's Site." n.d.
Texas State Gazette:
  "Governor's Mansion Point of Interest." August 30, 1856.

Unpublished Material

Pease family letters in R. Niles Graham-Pease Papers. The Austin-Travis County Collection of the Austin Public Library.
Personal Diaries. Lucadia Pease. The Austin-Travis County Collection of the Austin Public Library.

SELECTED BIBLIOGRAPHY FOR
MARTHA CAROLINE ADAMS RUNNELS

Jennings, Nancy Moores Watts, ed. *Texarkana Pioneer Family Histories.* Texarkana: Texarkana Pioneer Association, n.d.

Newspapers

Houston Post:
  "Hardin Richard Runnels." September 29, 1958.
Texarkana Daily News:
  "Texarkanians' Ancestor Served as First Lady When Texas Was Young." April 2, 1962.

Unpublished Material

Letters and biographical material: Mrs. Walter Espy, San Antonio, to Mrs. H. C. Farrell. (1974).

SELECTED BIBLIOGRAPHY FOR
MARTHA MELISSA EVANS CLARK

Newspapers

Houston Post:
  Mathis, Jim. "Edward Clark." n.d.
San Antonio Express:
  "Martha Evans Clark." December 1, 1912.

Unpublished Material

Cannon, C. Letter to Mr. J. E. Clark. April 17, 1910.
Clark, Edward. Diary. Barker Texas History Center, Austin.
Garrison, J. L. Typescript, biographical sketch of Edward Clark.
Letter: Mrs. O. H. Clark, Marshall, Texas, to Mary D. Farrell. (July 15, 1974).

SELECTED BIBLIOGRAPHY FOR ADELE BARON LUBBOCK

"In Way of Progress." Heritage Society of Austin. (November, 1956).
Lubbock, Francis R. *Six Decades in Texas: The Memoirs of Francis R. Lubbock, Confederate Governor of Texas.* C. W. Raines, ed. Austin: B. C. Jones & Co., 1900.
"Lubbock and Reagan." *The Bohemian.* (1904).
Roper, William. "The Lubbock Brothers." *Texas Parade.* n.d.
Waller, John L. *Colossal Hamilton of Texas: A Biography of Andrew Jackson Hamilton.* S. D. Myres, ed. The University of Texas at El Paso: Texas Western Press, 1968.

Newspapers

Austin American-Statesman:
Hart, Katherine. "Wives Were Relatively Unknown." April 21, 1973.

Unpublished Material

Francis R. Lubbock papers and letters. Barker Texas History Center, Austin.

SELECTED BIBLIOGRAPHY FOR SUE ELLEN TAYLOR MURRAH

Newspapers

Austin American:
Brewer, Anita. "Unhappy Marriage Left Mansion with Memories." August, 1954.
Houston Post:
Mathis, Jim. "Pendleton Murrah." n.d.
San Antonio Express:
Grimes, Roy. "A Gallery of Texas Governors." 1952.

Unpublished Material

Bryson, Tandy A. Letter to Miss Mattie Austin Hatcher, Archivist, University of Texas. (October 5, 1931).
Mitchell, Vivian A. Letter to librarian, Barker Texas History Center, Austin. (January 30, 1963).

SELECTED BIBLIOGRAPHY FOR
MARY JANE BOWEN HAMILTON

Hamilton, Andrew Jackson. *Biographical Encyclopedia of Texas.* New York: Southern Publishing Co., 1880.
Pickrell, Annie Doom. *Pioneer Women in Texas.* Austin: The E. L. Steck Co., 1929.
Waller, John L. *Colossal Hamilton of Texas: A Biography of Andrew Jackson Hamilton.* S. D. Myres, ed. The University of Texas at El Paso: Texas Western Press, 1968.

Newspapers

Austin American-Statesman:
   "Mrs. Mary Hamilton Mills, Pioneer Citizen of Austin, Succumbs." October 5, 1932.
   "Staunch He Stood in His View of Right." November 24, 1968.
   "Wife of Provisional Governor of Texas Dies in This City." April 26, 1916.
Houston Post:
   "Andrew Jackson Hamilton." n.d.

Unpublished Material

Chiles, Ann. "Andrew Jackson Hamilton." Biographical Sketch. n.d.
Hamilton letters. Barker Texas History Center, Austin.
Pease letters. The Austin-Travis County Collection of the Austin Public Library.

SELECTED BIBLIOGRAPHY FOR
ANNIE RATTAN THROCKMORTON

Elliott, Claude. *Leathercoat: The Life History of a Texas Patriot.* San Antonio: Standard Printing Co., 1938.
Nixon, Pat Ireland. *The Medical Story of Early Texas: 1528-1853.* San Antonio: Mollie Bennett Lupe Memorial Fund, 1946.
"Texas' Masonic Governors." *The Texas Freemason.* (April, 1964).

Newspapers

McKinney Democrat:
   Obituary of Mrs. Ann Throckmorton. October 31, 1895.

Unpublished Material

Throckmorton letters. Barker Texas History Center, Austin.
Interview: Mary D. Farrell with Mrs. Callie Hayhurst Wagner, Pasadena, Texas. (September 22, 1974).

SELECTED BIBLIOGRAPHY FOR
ANN ELIZABETH BRITTON DAVIS

Newspapers

Austin American-Statesman:
  Bishop, Curt. "This Day in Texas." December 1, 1962.
  "First Ladies Not Always Ladylike." January 31, 1957.
  "He is Dead." February 8, 1883.
Daily State Journal:
  "Mrs. Gov. Davis' Letter — Her Trial and Suffering During the War."
    September 29, 1871.
Dallas Morning News:
  Wasson, Alonzo. "E. J. Davis Rules Texas During Bitter Period."
    April 11, 1942.
Galveston Weekly Free Man's Press:
  "E. J. Davis." July 25, 1868.
Washington Evening Star:
  "Mrs. Davis-Smith Dies." May 6, 1925.

Unpublished Material

Certificate of Death. Anna E. Davis-Smith. District of Columbia. May 7,
  1925.
Schwien, Annie Moore. "When Corpus Christi Was Young." Typescript.
  Corpus Christi Public Library. n.d.
Letters: Mrs. E. J. Davis to J. DeShields. DRT Library, San Antonio.
Family records in possession of Mrs. Sarah Creson, Galveston.

SELECTED BIBLIOGRAPHY FOR MARY EVANS HORNE COKE

Duncan, Merle Mears. "The Death of Senator Coke." *The Southwestern
  Historical Quarterly.* LXIII (January, 1960).
Fett, B. J. "Early Life of Richard Coke." *Texana.* X No. 4 (1972) 310-317.
"University Medals." *Ranger.* (November 21, 1899).
Scrapbook of news articles on the Coke family. Barker Texas History
  Center, Austin.

Newspapers

Austin American-Statesman:
  "Eight Marriages — Simple to Spectacular — Held in Historic
    Governor's Mansion." August 12, 1956.
  "Gambling Strikes at Decency Roots." May 20, 1950.

Unpublished Material

Letter: Richard Coke to Major E. Surfit. (May 31, 1864). Barker Texas
  History Center, Austin.
Richard Coke Scrapbook — Barker Texas History Center, Austin.

SELECTED BIBLIOGRAPHY FOR JANIE ROBERTS HUBBARD

Hubbard, Richard B. *The United States in the Far East: or Modern Japan and the Orient.* Richmond, Va.: B. F. Johnson Publishing Co., 1899.

Newspapers

Austin American-Statesman:
"Eight Marriages — Simple to Spectacular — Held in Historic Governor's Mansion." August 12, 1956.
Dallas Morning News:
French, J. S. "Texans Observed Japan's Eagerness Half Century Ago." April 11, 1942.
Pass, Fred. "East Texas Notebook." April 14, 1964.
Houston Post:
"Richard Bennett Hubbard." September 25, 1958.

Unpublished Material

Hubbard Family Bible. Mrs. Ralph C. Miller, Houston, Texas.
Duncan, Jean Sutherlin. *Richard Bennett Hubbard: Texas Politician and Diplomat.* Dissertation. Texas A&M University. August, 1972.
Letters:
Mrs. Ralph C. Miller, Houston, Texas, to Mary D. Farrell, 1974.
Mrs. Edward A. Everitt, Houston, Texas, to Mary D. Farrell, 1974.
Interview: Mary D. Farrell with Dr. Jean Duncan, Huntsville, Texas. December 28, 1974.
Interview: Mary D. Farrell with Mrs. Ralph Miller, Houston, Texas, December 28, 1974.

SELECTED BIBLIOGRAPHY FOR
FRANCES WICKLIFFE EDWARDS ROBERTS

Newspapers

Austin American-Statesman:
Bishop, Curtis. "This Day in Texas." July 3, 1953. August 11, 1953.
Brewer, Anita. "Governor's Mansion was Homey Place Under the Hand of Mrs. Oran Roberts." August 11, 1954.
Dallas Morning News:
Switzer, David. "O. M. Roberts Pioneer with Great Faith." April 11, 1942.
Houston Chronicle:
"In Memory of O. M. Roberts Glamorous Era is Etched." December 31, 1931.
Waco Tribune-Herald:
"Texas Mansion Improves with Age." February 26, 1961.

Unpublished Material

Scrapbook Collection — Speeches, News items, Autobiographical sketch. Barker Texas History Center, Austin.
Letter: Howard O. Pollan, Smith County Historical Society and Survey Committee, to Mary Farrell. October 21, 1974.

SELECTED BIBLIOGRAPHY FOR ANNE MARIA PENN IRELAND

Weinert, Mrs. Willie Mae. *An Authentic History of Guadalupe County.* n.d.

Newspapers

Austin American-Statesman:
    "Eight Marriages — Simple to Spectacular — Held in Historic Governor's Mansion." August 12, 1956.
    "Governor's Mansion Point of Interest." February 7, 1883.
    Smith, Annette. "Mansion Has Varied Through Years . . ." August 12, 1956.
    Articles: March 16, 1896, March 18, 1896.
Dallas Morning News:
    Menn, Alfred E. "Texas Governor Wanted a Son." October 15, 1953.

SELECTED BIBLIOGRAPHY FOR
ELIZABETH DOROTHY TINSLEY ROSS

Anthony, Mrs. Augusta Houghton. "Lawrence Sullivan Ross: Soldier and Statesman: *The Texas Magazine.* (September, 1912).
Bennett, Jerry. "Famous A&M President Founded Aggie Traditions." *The Battalion.* (May 15, 1953).
Conger, Roger N. et al. *Rangers of Texas.* Waco: Texian Press, 1969.
De Shields, James T. *Cynthia Ann Parker.* San Antonio: The Naylor Co., 1934.
Gougler, Doyle. "Sul Ross." *The Cattleman.* (August, 1963).
"L. S. Ross." Biography. *Texas Aggie.* (May, 1967).
Perry, George Sessions. *The Story of A&M.* New York: McGraw-Hill Book Co., Inc., 1951.
"Sully's Death Was Mourned Here 54 Years Ago Today." *The Battalion.* (July 16, 1952).

Newspapers

Austin American-Statesman:
    "Early Families in Mansion Suffered Many Hardships." August 12, 1956.
    "Governor's Mansion from Pease to Daniel Center of Social Whirl." 90th Birthday Edition, August 26, 1961.

"Governor's Mansion Point of Interest." August 30, 1890.

Smith, Annette. "Mansion Has Varied Through Years from Dull to Gay, Staid to Informal." August 12, 1956.

Dallas Morning News:

Tolbert, Frank X. "Sully Saved A&M From 'Lunatic Role.' " October 26, 1965.

Turner, Thomas. "Cynthia Ann Kin Gather in Texas." July 4, 1953.

Houston Chronicle:

Shuffler, R. Henderson. "The Man Who Tamed the Aggies." *Texas Magazine*, May 23, 1965.

Houston Post:

Gardner, William H. "Lawrence Sullivan Ross." October 14, 1958.

Peattie, Donald C. "The Ballad of Cynthia Ann." October 25, 1959.

Waco Tribune-Herald:

Ainsworth, E. M. "Nephew of Lawrence Sullivan Ross, Indian Fighter, Confederate Veteran, Governor, Says Accidental Poisoning Caused Death." February 17, 1929.

Caulfield, Tom. "Sul Ross Letters Tell Sidelights on War Between States." July 10, 1960.

"Inaugural Ball of Sul Ross." Centennial Issue, October 30, 1949.

Plunkett, Virginia. "Miss Clarke Honored Guest at A&M Sul Ross Reunion." May 7, 1957.

Plunkett, Virginia. "Texas Mansion Improves with Age." February 26, 1961.

"Remains of Mrs. Ross Laid to Rest Today." June 9, 1905.

"Sul Ross." February 26, 1961.

"Sul Ross' Career Full of Thrills From Time He Was Born in a Frontier Cabin." October 30, 1949.

"Tinsley Farm Now Is Paved." Centennial Issue, October 30, 1949.

Unpublished Material

"Board of Directors A&M College of Texas." *The Olio*. A&M annual, 1895.

Clark, Bessie. Typescript. Texas A&M archives.

Clark, E. R. "Ya-A-H-H-oo: Warwhoop of the Comanches." Barker Texas History Center, Austin.

Mayfield, Jr., Henry D. Address to Lawrence Sullivan Ross Chapter of the Daughters of the Confederacy. October 21, 1960.

"The Ross Volunteers." *The Olio*. A&M annual, 1895.

Ross letters and papers. Barker Texas History Center, Austin.

Ross letters. Texas Collection, Baylor University, Waco, Texas.

Letter: Judith Ann Benner, San Antonio, to Mary D. Farrell. (November 26, 1974).

Interview: Elizabeth Silverthorne with Mrs. Paul M. Mason, College Station. (January 8, 1975).

Interview: Elizabeth Silverthorne with Miss Elizabeth Clarke, College Station. (January 8, 1975).

Interview: Elizabeth Silverthorne with Mrs. Neville Clarke, San Antonio. (January 8, 1975).

SELECTED BIBLIOGRAPHY FOR SARAH ANN STINSON HOGG

Cotner, Robert C. *James Stephen Hogg: A Biography*. Austin: University of Texas Press, 1959.

James, D'Arcy. "The Hogg Family." *Texas Parks and Wildlife*. XXXII, No. 8. (August, 1974) 2-10.

Sproul, Kathleen, ed. *James Stephen Hogg*. Pamphlet. Houston: Premier Printing Co., 1958.

Newspapers

Austin American-Statesman:

Barlow, Jim. "Hogg Wealth Enriches Causes." January 10, 1971.

Brewer, Anita. "Sarah Hogg Gave Dignified Elegance to Life of Political Hero in Mansion." August 25, 1954.

Finley, Texie B. "In Memory of Mrs. Hogg." October 29, 1895.

Dallas Morning News:

Keever, Jack. "Texas Executive Mansion: History Stalks Corridors." February 16, 1964 .

Houston Chronicle:

Garewood, Ellen. "Miss Hogg Reminisces Back to 1891-1895." October 13, 1957 .

Houston Post:

"UT Cites Miss Hogg for Cultural Contributions." n.d.

Unpublished Material

Bailey, George M. Typescript. Barker Texas History Center, Austin.

Biographical Files. Historical Association. Barker Texas History Center, Austin.

Hogg, Ima. "Life in the Governor's Mansion, 1891-1895." Typescript. Barker Texas History Center, Austin.

Letters and biographical typescript of Sarah Hogg. Miss Ima Hogg to Mary D. Farrell. (October 23, 1974, December 28, 1974).

SELECTED BIBLIOGRAPHY FOR SALLIE HARRISON CULBERSON

Madden, James William. *Charles Allen Culberson*. Austin: Gammel's Book Store, 1929.

Research Data, Fort Worth and Tarrant County, Texas. Texas Writers' Project, Fort Worth Public Library Unit, 1941, II, 477.

Newspapers

Austin Daily Statesman:

"New Year's Reception at Mansion." January 2, 1898.

Fort Worth Record-Telegram:

"Mrs. Charles A. Culberson." April 20, 21, 24, 1926.

Unpublished Material

Cannon, Weldon. Sketch of Harrison Family Burial Plot, Oakwood Cemetery, Fort Worth. (November 30, 1974).
Letter: Charles A. Culberson to George L. Beatty, Washington, D.C. (June 15, 1922).

SELECTED BIBLIOGRAPHY FOR ORLINE WALTON SAYERS

Bowers, Beth. "Texas DAR Museum." *DAR Magazine.* (n.d.)
Jones, Margaret Belle. *A Compilation of Material Relating to the History of the Town of Bastrop.* Bastrop, Texas: June 8, 1936.
Moore, Bill. *Bastrop County 1691-1900.* Bastrop County Historical Society. San Angelo: Educator Books, Inc., 1973.
Slayden, Ellen Maury. *Washington Wife: Journal of Ellen Maury Slayden, from 1897-1919.* Terrell D. Webb, 1962.

Newspapers

Austin American-Statesman:
  "Compliment to Mrs. Sayers." 1915.
  "Mrs. Joe Sayers, Dolly Madison of Mansion, Dies in Hospital." December 26, 1943.
  "Memento of Sayers Presented." May 14, 1959.
  "Mrs. Sayers to be Buried in Bastrop Plot." December 28, 1943.
Bastrop Advertiser:
  "Plans Made to Memorialize Gov. & Mrs. Joseph D. Sayers." April 6, 1967.
  Waugh, Lillian. "Civil War Leader Marker Installed." July 9, 1964.
Gossip:
  "Ex-Governor Joseph D. Sayers at Home." Austin, December 31, 1921.
  "Ex-Governor Joseph D. Sayers & Mrs. Sayers." January, 1925.

Unpublished Material

Sayers Bible. Methodist Episcopal Church, South. Bastrop, Texas.
Scrapbook, pictures and clippings. Mrs. Thomas G. Sayers, Austin.
Letters to Mary D. Farrell, 1974-1975:
  Mrs. W. S. Millington, Bastrop, Texas.
  Mrs. Thomas G. Sayers, Austin, Texas.
  Ralph S. Sayers, Houston, Texas.
Interview: Mary D. Farrell with Mrs. L. O. Shudde, Austin, Texas. (October 19, 1974).

SELECTED BIBLIOGRAPHY FOR
SARAH BEONA MENG LANHAM

Holland, G. A. *History of Parker County and the Double Log Cabin.* Weatherford, Texas: The Herald Publishing Co., 1937.

Moreland, Sinclair. *The Texas Women's Hall of Fame*. Austin: Biographical Press, 1917.

Newspapers
Houston Post:
  "Samuel W. T. Lanham." October 20, 1958.
Weatherford Democrat:
  "Governor Lanham is Dead; Long Public Career Ended." July 31, 1908.

Unpublished Material

Lanham, Martha Anderson. "The Life of Governor Samuel Willis Tucker Lanham." Thesis, Baylor University, Waco, Texas, 1930.
Martin, Ruby Lee. "The Administration of Governor S. W. T. Lanham, 1903-1907." Thesis, University of Texas, 1937.
Letter: Fritz G. Lanham to Miss Frances Harvey. (Washington, D.C., March 5, 1928) Barker Texas History Center, Austin.
Interview: Mrs. Claude Maer, Fort Worth, Texas. Typescript. (March 27, 1934).

SELECTED BIBLIOGRAPHY FOR FANNIE IRENE BRUNER CAMPBELL

Hohes, Mrs. Pauline. *Centennial History of Anderson County*. San Antonio: The Naylor Co., 1936.

Newspapers
Austin Statesman:
  "Governor and Mrs. Campbell Entertain at Mansion." January 2, 1909.

Unpublished Material
Cambell-Bruner family correspondence. William Bruner Campbell, Austin, Texas.
Wommack, Fannie Campbell. "Fannie Bruner Campbell; Wife of Thomas Mitchell Campbell; First Lady of Texas, 1907-1911." Typescript. Palestine, Texas, January, 1940.
Interview: Mary D. Farrell with William Bruner Campbell and Mrs. Thomas Mitchell Campbell, Jr., Austin, Texas. (November 29, 1974).
Interview: Mary D. Farrell and Elizabeth Silverthorne with Drew Wommack, Palestine, Texas. (December 3, 1974).

SELECTED BIBLIOGRAPHY FOR ALICE FULLER MURRELL COLQUITT

Moreland, Sinclair. *The Texas Women's Hall of Fame*. Austin: Biographical Press, 1917.

Newspapers

Austin American-Statesman:
"Colquitt Services Slated Tuesday." July 4, 1949.
"Mrs. Colquitt's Service to State Noted in Rites." July 6, 1949.
"Reception at Mansion Last Night." January 2, 1913.
Stephenson, Mrs. Charles. "Austin Social Notes." January 1, 1912.
Austin Times Herald:
"Would Panamaize Texas." October 27, 1913.
Dallas Morning News:
"Colquitt's Burial Set at Austin." March 9, 1940.
"Mrs. Colquitt, Ex-Governor's Wife, Dies." July 1, 1949.
Pittsburg Gazette:
"Colquitt, O. B. Biographical Sketch." February 13, 1934.

Unpublished Material

Colquitt papers. Barker Texas History Center, Austin.
Merritt, Billie. "A First Lady of Texas." Typescript of interview with Mrs. O. B. Colquitt. (January 24, 1941).
Texas Historical Marker at Alexander Hospital, N. Francis St. at W. Nash, Terrell, Kaufman County, Texas.

SELECTED BIBLIOGRAPHY FOR MIRIAM AMANDA WALLACE FERGUSON

"Can Ma Ferguson Finish Her Comeback?" *The Literary Digest*, CIL. (June 13, 1956).
Moreland, Sinclair. *The Texas Women's Hall of Fame.* Austin: Biographical Press, 1917.
DeShields, James T. *The Fergusons: "Jim and Ma" Stormy Petrels in Texas Politics.* Dallas: Clyde C. Cockrell Pub. Co., 1932.
Gallagher, Robert S. "Me for Ma — and I ain't got a dern thing against Pa." *American Heritage.* (October, 1966).
Jones, Billy M. "Miriam Amanda Ferguson." *Women of Texas.* Waco: The Texian Press, 1972.
Nalle, Ouida Ferguson. *The Fergusons of Texas.* San Antonio: Naylor Publishing Co., 1946.
West, Felton. "The Case Against 'Pa' Ferguson." *The Texas Star.* (December 26, 1971).
Whitman, Willson. "Can a Wife Be Governor?" *Colliers.* (September 5, 1925).

Newspapers

Austin American-Statesman:
"Austin Set for 'Ma's' Birthday." June 13, 1955.
Barnes, Lorraine. " 'Ma' Will Take Spotlight Again." June 13, 1955.

Beshell, Jean. "Mistresses of Texas Governor's Mansion Repeat 'How-Do-You-Do's' for 91 Years." January 14, 1945.

Brewer, Anita. "Mrs. Ferguson No Candidate." June 13, 1956.

Clark, Mabel. "Ma Ferguson Retired Only from Politics." June 13, 1952.

Cook, Molly Connor. "Texas First Ladies Whom I Have Known." January 13, 1931.

Fenner, Nell. "Past Hostesses Tell About Mansion Life." June 3, 1956.

"Mrs. Ferguson's Arm Swells From Shaking Hands with 1000." July 20, 1924.

"First Lady's First At Home." 1915.

Fitzgerald, Hugh Nugent. "Governors I Have Known: Miriam A. Ferguson." December 11, 1927.

"Friends Present Silver Service to the Governor." October 2, 1915.

"George S. Nalle and Miss Ouida Ferguson United in Marriage." February 6, 1918.

"Governor — Gardener." April 24, 1955.

"Honored on Mother's Day." May 10, 1953.

"Inaugural Ball Tuesday Outstanding Event." January 15, 1933.

"Jim Receives Callers When Wife Shows Strain of Office." December 1, 1925.

" 'Ma' at 80, Has Another 'Campaign'." June 13, 1955.

"Ma Swings Into Square Dance at Inaugural Ball." January 18, 1933.

"Ma's Statue is Unveiled." November 20, 1926.

"Reception for Legislators." March 2, 1915.

Wrightman, Mary. "To Mrs. Ferguson: A Happy Birthday!" June 13, 1960.

Dallas Morning News:

"Ferguson's Amazing Political Life." April 11, 1942.

Goodwin, Mark L. "Eastern Newspapers Look With Favor Upon 'First Woman Governor' in United States." August 26, 1924.

Hornaday, Walter C. "Governor Miriam Ferguson: Sometimes She Said No." March 5, 1966.

"Last Rites Held for Ex-Governor." June 27, 1961.

" 'Ma' Ferguson Fascinated Nation During Her Tenure." June 27, 1961.

Gossip:

"Master Ernest Nalle and His Parents." Austin, January, 1924.

Houston Post:

Gardner, William H. "Miriam Amanda Ferguson." October 28, 1958.

"Letter from Governor to Thirty-Ninth Legislature." January 21, 1925.

London Times:

"Governor of Texas: A Woman of Character." March 31, 1925.

New York Times:

Adams, Mildred. "Again the Fergusons Rouse the Texans." October 23, 1932.

White, Owen P. " 'Ma' Ferguson to Test Her Record at Polls." July 18, 1926.

White, Owen P. "Two Governors Rule in Texas." April 5, 1925.

Temple Daily Telegram:
  Hood, LeWard. "Ferguson Saga Began 100 Years Ago Today Along Salado Creek." August 31, 1971.

Ferguson news clippings. Barker Texas History Center, Austin.

Unpublished Material

Interview: Mary D. Farrell and Elizabeth Silverthorne with Mrs. J. M. Murphy and Mrs. Doris Keller, Temple, Texas. (March 15, 1974).

Interview: Mary D. Farrell with George S. Nalle, Sr., Austin, Texas. (November 16, 1974).

Telephone Interviews: Mary D. Farrell with George S. Nalle, Sr. (1975 - 1976).

SELECTED BIBLIOGRAPHY FOR WILLIE CHAPMAN COOPER HOBBY

Moreland, Sinclair. *Texas Women's Hall of Fame.* Austin: Biographical Press, 1917.

Patterson, Norma. "Mrs. William Pettus Hobby." Austin: Texas State Library, Reference Division, n.d.

Newspapers

Austin American-Statesman:
  "The First Lady of Texas." n.d.
  "Governor Names 180 Texans Upon Library Council." 1917.
  "Music, Flags, and Crowds Honor Chief Executive and First Lady." March 4, 1919.
  "Scholarship Honors Ex-Governor's Wife." April 12, 1929.
  Scott, Mrs. Fred. "Women Worth While." 1918.

Houston Chronicle:
  "Hobby Husband-Wife Team Rates High Here." October 12, 1951.

Houston Post-Dispatch:
  "Hobby Burial to be Tuesday." January 15, 1929.
  "Mrs. W. P. Hobby is Laid to Rest." January 15, 1929.

Houston Press:
  "Brilliant Career of Mrs. Hobby Recalled." January 15, 1929.

Unpublished Material

"Tributes in Memory of Willie Cooper Hobby." Texas State Historical Collection, Barker Texas History Center, Austin.

Interview: Mary D. Farrell with Mrs. Thomas Mitchell Campbell, Jr., Austin, Texas. (November 29, 1974).

SELECTED BIBLIOGRAPHY FOR MYRTLE MAINER NEFF

"Mrs. Pat M. Neff Dies on July 19." *The Baylor Line*. (August, 1953).

Newspapers

Austin American-Statesman:
  Cook, Molly Connor. "Texas First Ladies Whom I Have Known."
    January 18, 1931.
  "Mrs. Neff's Rites Set Today." July 20, 1953.
  "Peeler Recalls Inaugural Receptions Given in Past." January 16,
    1935.
Dallas Morning News:
  "Neff." October 13, 1921.
Galveston Daily News:
  "Neff-Mainer." June 2, 1899.
Gossip:
  "Mrs. Pat M. Neff 'First Lady of Texas' Soon to Leave the Mansion."
    Austin, January 12, 1925.

Unpublished Material

Pat Neff Collection. Baylor University, Waco, Texas:
  Personal papers
  Biography
  Scrapbook
Hubbell, Mackleyn Ward. "The Life of Pat Neff." Thesis. University
  of Houston, 1953.
Shirley, Mrs. Newton A. "Mrs. Pat M. Neff." Typescript. Texas Collec-
  tion, Baylor University, Waco.
Letters:
  Mrs. George B. Graves, Waco, Texas, to Mary D. Farrell. (January
    17, 1975).
  Mrs. David A. Cheavens, Waco, Texas, to Mary D. Farrell. (January
    27, 1975).
  Mary Keys Anderson, Dallas, Texas, to Mary D. Farrell. (March 25,
    1975).
Interview: Mary D. Farrell with Mrs. Frank Wilcox, Waco, Texas.
  (January 15, 1974).

SELECTED BIBLIOGRAPHY FOR MILDRED PAXTON MOODY

Whitman, Willson. "The Dollar Stretchers." *Colliers*. (November, 1927).

Newspapers

Austin American-Statesman:
  Brewer, Anita. "Mrs. Moody Learned Housekeeping as Bride in
  Governor's Mansion." August 18, 1954.

Cook, Molly Connor. "Texas First Ladies Whom I Have Known."
January 18, 1931.
"Mrs. Dan Bests Governor-Elect at Hunting by Single Deer Point."
1926.
MacNabb, Betty. "A Texas Bargain." October 31, 1961.
Moody, Mildred Paxton. "Hero Lindbergh Refused Abilene Tour on a
Throne." May 19, 1957.
"Moodys Open Mansion for Official Reception." 1927.
"Moody, Solons Leave for Laredo." 1927.
"Moody to Visit Mexico." 1927.
Roe, Ethel. "1928 Mansion Wallpaper." May 3, 1962.
"Somewhere in Texas Dan and His Bride are Honeymooning Today."
April 21, 1926.
Dallas Morning News:
Moody, Mildred Paxton. "Housekeeping in the Governor's Mansion."
March 5, 1931.
Moore, Walter B. "Governor's Mansion is Dangerous Disgrace."
July 1, 1966.
Gossip:
"New Garden at the Governor's Mansion Planned by Mrs. Dan
Moody." Austin, April 28, 1931.
Houston Chronicle:
"History of Governor's Mansion." November 26, 1960.
Temple Daily Telegram:
"Former Governor Moody Dies at Age 72." May 23, 1966.

Moody news clippings. Barker Texas History Center, Austin.

Unpublished Material

Letters: Mildred Paxton Moody, Austin, Texas, to Mary D. Farrell.
(1974-1975).
Interview: Mary D. Farrell with Mildred Paxton Moody, Austin, Texas.
(October 26, 1974).

SELECTED BIBLIOGRAPHY FOR
MAUD ABBIE GAGE STERLING

"R. S. Sterling of Harris County." Campaign Pamphlet. (1930).
"Sterling, Ross Shaw." *Encyclopedia of Biography.* New York: The
American Historical Co., 1955.
West, Ruth. "The New First Lady." *Houston Gargoyle.* (August 31,
1930).

Newspapers

Austin American-Statesman:
Blodgett, Dorothy. "Past Inaugurations Recalled as Next One Draws
Nearer." January 9, 1961.

Cook, Molly Connor. "Texas First Ladies Whom I Have Known."
    January 18, 1931.
Gossip:
"The New First Lady of Texas: Mrs. Ross S. Sterling." Austin, n.d.
Houston Chronicle:
"Mrs. Sterling, Governor's Widow, Dies." March 8, 1962.
Houston Post:
"Maud Gage Sterling." March 9, 1963.
Waco Tribune-Herald:
Plunkett, Virginia. "Texas Mansion Improves with Age." February
    26, 1961.

Unpublished Material

Mills. Mr. Warner Everett. "The Public Career of a Texas Conserva-
    tive." Dissertation. The Johns Hopkins University, Baltimore,
    Maryland, 1956.

SELECTED BIBLIOGRAPHY FOR JOE BETSY MILLER ALLRED

Newspapers

Austin American-Statesman:
"Allreds Try Out New Swift Ship." March 6, 1935.
Barnes, Lorraine. "Santa Scores Hit in Early Call at Allreds." Decem-
    ber 22, 1935.
Cook, Molly Connor. "Mrs. Allred is Demure in Gown Cut Old-Fashion-
    ed." January 16, 1935.
"Cupboard Was Bare When Allreds Got There So They Dined Else-
    where." March 16, 1935.
"Hazel Allred is Married at Mansion." March 2, 1935.
Bastrop Advertiser:
"James Allred Takes Governor's Oath in Austin at Noon Tuesday."
    January 17, 1935.
Dallas Morning News:
"Allred Family Starts Moving From Mansion." January 13, 1939.
"Allreds Greeted by Mexican Cowgirls." August 8, 1937.
"Allred Party Guests of Mexican Government." August 1, 1937.
"Appreciation Dinner is Given for Allreds." January 7, 1939.
Crozier, Harry Benge. "Proud Shall Fall, Governor Marks in Bible
    of State." January 15, 1935.
Houston Chronicle:
Rider, Lecta. "Mrs. Allred is Glad That Texas Will Not Build New
    Executive Mansion While She's First Lady." December 3, 1936.
Houston Post:
"Mrs. James V. Allred Gave Up Career In Music to Become Wife and
    Mother." May 20, 1934.

Wichita Falls Times:
   "Miss Joe Betsy Miller and James V. Allred Are Married." June 21,
   1927.

Allred news clippings. Barker Texas History Center, Austin.

Unpublished Material

"Governor James V. Allred." Texas Historical Association Vertical
   Files. Typescript. n.d.
Autobiographical sketch prepared for authors by Joe Betsy Allred.
   (November, 1974).
Letters: Joe Betsy Allred to Mary D. Farrell. (1974-1975).

SELECTED BIBLIOGRAPHY FOR FINAL CHAPTER

MRS. W. LEE O'DANIEL

"Austin Wedding Ready at Mansion." *Fort Worth Star Telegram*. July
   31, 1941.
Bolton, Dolly. "Blue Eyes and Sky Match First Lady." *Austin American-
   Statesman*. January, 1939.
Douglas, C. L. and Francis Miller. *The Life Story of W. Lee O'Daniel.*
   Regional Press, Inc.: 1938.
Keeney, Elizabeth. "Molly O'Daniel, Jack Wrather Wed in Double Ring
   Rites At Mansion." *Austin Tribune*. August 1, 1941.
"Little Things that Happened at the Big Inaugural Ceremony." *Dallas
   Morning News*. January 18, 1939.
"Mansion's Teas Open to All, O'Daniel Insists." *Dallas Morning News*.
   March 13, 1939.
"Molly O'Daniel to Marry Tyler Oil Man Soon." *Dallas Morning News*.
   June 17, 1941.
"Normalcy Returning to O'Daniel Home." *Dallas Morning News*. Febru-
   ary 16, 1939.
"O'Daniel Family Likes Returns, But is Bitter . . ." *Dallas Morning News*.
   July 26, 1942.
"Mrs. O'Daniel Gives Mansion Homey Touch." *Dallas Morning News*.
   January 29, 1939.
"Mrs. O'Daniel Has Made Governor's Mansion Look Like Family Home."
   Fort Worth Star Telegram. January 28, 1939.
O'Daniel, Molly. "Molly O'Daniel's Own Story of Thrills in Campaign."
   Dallas Morning News. August 21, 1939.
O'Daniel, Molly. "Molly O's Pen Pals." *Dallas Morning News*. March 19,
   1938, January 3, 27, 1939, March 1, 1939, June 28, 1939.
"O'Daniel — Super Salesman." Official Souvenir Program, Inauguration
   of Governor W. Lee O'Daniel. January, 1939.
"Quiet, Reserved Mrs. O'Daniel Exerts Big Force Behind Husband's
   Career." *Austin American-Statesman*. 1956.

"Mrs. W. Lee O'Daniel Funeral Rites Pending." *Dallas Times-Herald*. July 17, 1972.

"Mrs. W. Lee O'Daniel Says, 'Our Cup is Full to Overflowing.' " *Longview News*. July 25, 1938.

"Mrs. W. Lee O'Daniel, Widow of Senator, Dies." *Dallas Morning News*. July 18, 1972.

MRS. COKE R. STEVENSON, SR.

"All Texas Mourns Beloved First Lady." *Frontier Times*. January, 1942.

Brooks, Raymond. "Mrs. Coke Stevenson Dies After Long Illness." *Austin American-Statesman*. January 4, 1942.

"First Lady." *Austin American*. August 4, 1941.

"Lieutenant Governor Coke Stevenson and Mrs. Stevenson — At Home in the Texas Capitol." *Gossip*. March 6, 1941.

Mooney, Booth. *Mister Texas: The Story of Coke Stevenson*. Dallas: Texas Printing House, Inc., 1947.

"Wife of Governor Dies; Rites Today at Junction." *Dallas Morning News*. January 4, 1942.

Unpublished Material

Daniel, Jean Houston Baldwin. *The Governor's Mansion of Texas*. Speech delivered before The Open Forum, Austin, Texas. (March 8, 1960).

Biographical sketch compiled for authors by Mrs. Edith Will Scott Stevenson on Mrs. Blanch Fay Wright Stevenson, 1975.

Autobiographical sketch compiled for authors by Mrs. Edith Will Scott Stevenson, 1975.

MRS. BEAUFORD H. JESTER

Cheavens, Dave. "Shivers is New Governor: Sudden Death of Jester." *Temple Daily Telegram*. July 12, 1949.

"First Lady of Texas." *San Antonio Express Magazine*. October 19, 1947.

Grimes, Roy. "A Gallery of Texas Governors." *San Antonio Express*. 1952.

"Mansion to Museum Solution; Mrs. Joshua R. Morriss." *Dallas Morning News*. 1965.

Unpublished Material

Daniel, Jean Houston Baldwin. *The Governor's Mansion of Texas*. Speech delivered before The Open Forum, Austin, Texas. (March 8, 1960).

Autobiographical sketch compiled for authors by Mrs. Mabel Buchanan Jester Morriss, 1975.

"Birthsite of Beauford H. Jester." Official Texas Historical Marker, Corsicana, Texas.

MRS. ALLAN SHIVERS

Duckworth, Allen. "This is Home Life in State Mansion." *Dallas Morning News*. March 1, 1953.

"Easter Hunt on the Mansion Lawn." *Austin American-Statesman*. April 2, 1969.

Fenner, Nell. "Past Hostesses Tell About Mansion Life." *Austin American-Statesman*. June 3, 1956.

Grimes, Roy. "A Gallery of Texas Governors." *San Antonio Express*. 1952.

"Mansion to Museum Solution; Former First Lady of Texas Recalls Leaky Roof." *Dallas Morning News*. 1965.

Pitts, Avis. "At Home with Texas' First Lady." *Progressive Farmer*. June, 1953.

"Mrs. Shivers Receives Award." *Austin American*. 1963.

Unpublished Material

Daniel, Jean Houston Baldwin. *The Governor's Mansion of Texas*. Speech delivered before The Open Forum, Austin, Texas. (March 8, 1960).

News Release on Allan Shivers Library and Museum. Texas State Historical Survey Committee, Austin, Texas. n.d.

Autobiographical sketch compiled for authors by Mrs. Allan Shivers, 1975.

MRS. PRICE DANIEL, SR.

Brewer, Anita. "First Lady." *The Alcalde*. (October, 1958).

Brogan, Maryrice. "Mrs. Price Daniel Turns Sleuth to Write Exciting History of Governor's Mansion." *Houston Chronicle*. January 27, 1960.

Daniel, Jean Houston and Price Daniel. *Executive Mansions and Capitols of America*. Waukesha, Wisconsin: Country Beautiful, 1969.

"Descendant of Sam Houston, Jean Daniel Mothers Five, Including Attorney General." *Austin American-Statesman*. October 8, 1950.

Hobby, Bill. "Mrs. Daniel's Research to Show in Restored Mansion." *Houston Post*. 1960.

Keever, Jack. "History Stalks Corridors." *Dallas Morning News*. February 16, 1964.

Keever, Jack. "109 Years of Mansion Life." *Austin American-Statesman*. February 16, 1964.

McAdams, Ina May Ogletree. "Mrs. Marion Price Daniel." *A Biographical History*. Austin: McAdams Publishers, Inc., 1962.

"Mansion to Museum Solution: Mrs. Daniel Holds to Old Idea." *Dallas Morning News*. 1965.

"Meet Mrs. Daniel — Quiet, Efficient Coordinator of Busy Household." *Austin American-Statesman*. June 10, 1956.

"Mrs. Price Daniel." *Austin American-Statesman*. January 6, 1963.

Sutherland, Carol. "First Family Adapts to Mansion." *Austin American-Statesman*. March 17, 1957.

Wheelock, Ernestine. "Mrs. Price Daniel, Jr." *Austin American-Statesman*. April 4, 1971.

Unpublished Material

Daniel, Jean Houston Baldwin. *The Governor's Mansion of Texas*. Speech delivered before The Open Forum, Austin, Texas. (March 8, 1960).

Daniel, Mrs. Price, ed. *Furnishings of Historic Interest in the Governor's Mansion*. December, 1962.

Autobiographical sketch compiled for authors by Mrs. Price Daniel, Sr., 1975.

MRS. JOHN CONNALLY

Anderson, David. "No 2 Days the Same for Texas' First Lady, Mrs. Connally." *Galveston Daily News*. December 8, 1963.

Barnes, Lorraine. "Exclusive: Nelly Connally's Story." *Austin American-Statesman*. December, 1963.

Dreyer, Martin. "Meet Nellie — Texas' No. 1 Ranch Woman." *Houston Chronicle*, Texas Magazine. March 7, 1965.

"Formal Garden Wedding United Miss Connally, Robert Ammann." *Temple Daily Telegram*. March 24, 1968.

"Former UT Sweetheart Returns." *Austin American-Statesman*. October 8, 1972.

Galvin, Lois Hale. "Gift for Beautification." *Austin American-Statesman*. March 1, 1967.

"Honorary Chairman of Galaxy Ball." *Austin American-Statesman*. July 2, 1967.

"Mansion to Museum Solution; Mrs. Connally for New Home." *Dallas Morning News*. 1965.

Patrick, Carolyn. "First Ladies of Past Honored at Mansion." *Dallas Morning News*. May 6, 1965.

Pett, Saul, et al. *The Torch is Passed*. Associated Press. 1963.

Wheelock, Ernestine. "Here's Heloise." *Austin American-Statesman*. April 30, 1967.

Unpublished Material

Biographical Data on Mrs. John Connally. Texas Governors' Wives. Reference Division. Texas State Library.

Biographical typescript. Prepared for authors by Mrs. Cynthia Steininger, Secretary to John B. Connally.

MRS. PRESTON SMITH

"Lots of Smiths Coming to Inaugural Festival." *Austin American-Statesman.* January 19, 1969.
"Quiet Life Choice of Ima Smith." *Austin American-Statesman.* January 19, 1969.
Shipp, Dixie. "Texas First Lady Bids Farewell." *Austin American-Statesman.* January, 1973.
Smith, Mrs. Preston. *The Governor's Mansion.* 1970.
Stewart, Lloyd. "Texas Second Lady." *Fort Worth Star Telegram.* June 9, 1967.

Unpublished Material

Autobiographical sketch prepared for authors by Mrs. Preston Smith, 1975.

MRS. DOLPH BRISCOE

Bengtson, Carolyn. "Janey Briscoe Marries in Outdoor Ceremony." *Austin American-Statesman.* December 30, 1973.
Brinkerhoff, Mary. "Janey Answers 'Calling.' " *Dallas Morning News.* March 19, 1972.
Fish, Dottie. "Mrs. Dolph Briscoe . . ." *Austin American-Statesman.*
Holmquist, Kay. "Wife's Touch Warms Governor's Mansion." *Fort Worth Star Telegram.* March 4, 1973.
Koock, Mary Faulk. "Uvalde Hostess Moves Gracefully Between Town and Ranch Life." *The Texas Star.* (May 7, 1972).
Lenz, Mary. "Miss Briscoe Wed in Austin." *Dallas Morning News.* December 30, 1973.
"Texas: Boss Lady." *Newsweek.* (January 27, 1975).

Unpublished Material

Interviews with mansion personnel and others associated with Governor and Mrs. Briscoe.
Letters: Mrs. Dolph Briscoe to authors. (1975-1976).

Index

ABOUT THE AUTHORS

MARY D. FARRELL is an instructor of American history at Temple Junior College, Temple, Texas. She holds the Bachelor of Arts degree from North Texas State University and Master of Arts from the University of Northern Colorado. She is a member of the Texas State Historical Association and of the Texas Junior College Teachers Association.

ELIZABETH SILVERTHORNE is Director of the Division of Communications and Modern Languages at Temple Junior College, Temple, Texas. She earned her Bachelor of Arts degree at Texas Women's University and Master of Arts at North Texas State University. Her other published works include *The Ghost of Padre Island* (Abingdon Press, 1975) which was a Weekly Reader Book Club Selection in 1977) I, Heracles (Abingdon Press, 1978); as well as short stories, articles, and poetry in various periodicals.

Harris County Public Library
Houston, Texas